D0151975

HUMAN REASONING

Human Reasoning
The Psychology of Deduction

Jonathan St. B. T. Evans

University of Plymouth, UK

Stephen E. Newstead

University of Plymouth, UK

Ruth M. J. Byrne

Trinity College, University of Dublin, Ireland

LAWRENCE ERLBAUM ASSOCIATES, PUBLISHERS
Hove (UK) Hillsdale (USA)

Lawrence Erlbaum Associates Ltd., Publishers
27 Palmeira Mansions
Church Road
Hove
East Sussex, BN3 2FA
UK

British Library Cataloguing in Publication Data
Evans, Jonathan St. B. T.
Human Reasoning: Psychology of Deduction
I. Title
153.4
ISBN 0-86377-313-3 (Hbk)
ISBN 0-86377-314-1 (Pbk)

Typeset by J&L Composition Ltd, Filey, North Yorkshire
Printed and bound in the United Kingdom by BPCC Wheatons Ltd., Exeter

Contents

Foreword and Acknowledgements

This book provides a review of a research field—psychological studies of deductive reasoning—in which the three authors are active participants. Since the last major review of work on this topic in 1982 (J.St.B.T. Evans, *The Psychology of Deductive Reasoning*, Routledge), the field has expanded rapidly and changed almost beyond recognition. Several major new theories have been developed from scratch to assume dominant positions in the literature, and hundreds of new experiments have been conducted and reported in the journals.

Sometime during 1990, or thereabouts, it dawned upon Jonathan Evans that not only was a new textbook desperately needed, but that there was precious little chance of anyone else deciding to write it. A brief feasibility study was sufficient to convince him that the task had grown too large to contemplate for an individual author—or at least for this one. Steve Newstead and Ruth Byrne joined the enterprise, with some ground rules agreed at the outset. First, we decided that the work would be self-contained and eclectic in its coverage. We would cover all the main fields of study of deductive reasoning, include reference so far as possible to every study published in the past 10 years and a good deal of the earlier ones as well. Second, we decided that the book would be theoretically neutral—providing the arguments for and against each main theory in the area, but advocating none. Third, we would strive to make the book as accessible as possible to readers of various backgrounds.

Whether or not we have achieved these objectives is for the reader to judge: we certainly tried. Of the four major theoretical approaches in the area, both the heuristic and mental model accounts are represented in the research of the authors. However, we cannot claim the direct participation of an inference rule or schema theorist to guarantee our theoretical balance. We have nevertheless tried to be fair to all, and if one theory has more coverage than another it is simply because it has inspired a larger number of papers for us to review and discuss. The result, we very much hope, is a book which anyone can use for an introduction to what we believe is a fascinating and important field of study.

The main mechanism by which we tried to ensure neutrality as well as breadth of coverage was by mutual critical readings of each other's drafts and redrafts: a task conducted without inhibition and, at times, with excessive zeal. This process took some two punishing years to complete and not the least of our achievements is that we remained friends at the end of it all.

There are, of course, many people who have influenced us directly and indirectly in the writing of this book, including our various collaborators and students. A special mention should be made of Peter Wason who established the recent history of psychological interest in research on reasoning with his innovative work in the 1960s and 1970s, and whose enormous influence on the field as we find it today will quickly become evident to readers of this volume. He also supervised the doctoral research of Jonathan Evans.

Several psychologists assisted us directly by providing additional critical readings of sections of this book. In particular we would like to thank Phil Johnson-Laird, Leo Baker, Richard Griggs, Simon Handley and Ken Gilhooly. We also acknowledge the facilities and support provided by the Department of Psychology at the University of Plymouth, the Computer Science Department of University College Dublin and the Psychology Department of Trinity College Dublin.

Finally, we must acknowledge the patience and tolerance of our long-suffering families: Jane, Frances, Joseph, Robin and Hugh Evans as well as Jane, Beth and Amy Newstead. Special thanks go to Mark Keane for his encouragement, help and infinite patience as well as to Alicia Byrne Keane for her great sense of timing, allowing the book manuscript to be delivered just a few days before she was. We also thank Mary and Paul Byrne, Alicia "Molly" Tracey, Linda, Noel, Paul and Laura Deighan, and Cathy, Tony, Lisa, Steven and Jenny Fitzgerald.

We dedicate this book to our families.

1 Introduction

Reasoning is fundamental to human intelligence. Inferences are the means by which we can make use of our vast stores of knowledge and apply them to particular situations. Most reasoning, however, takes place automatically and efficiently and we take it for granted, in just the same way that we are largely unaware of the immensely complex processes by which the brain constructs our instant perceptions of the world around us. As an example, consider the following scenario.

You are invited to a friend's house and he makes some introductions. "This is my father", he says, "and my sister Mary". Mary smiles and says, "Father is fanatical about cricket, don't let him bore you." It may not be immediately apparent that in following this discourse you needed to make an inference, namely that Mary's father is the same person that was introduced to you as your friend's father. You know as a general rule that if two people are siblings and the parent of one of them is a particular individual, then that individual is also the parent of the other. Somehow we must have applied this knowledge to infer who Mary's father is. Such an inference would normally be made unconsciously and indeed without awareness that reasoning had occurred at all.

Consider how feeble our intelligence would be if we could not make inferences of this kind. In the above case, we would need to be told separately about each specific family relationship. We would not be able to learn and apply general principles or generalise our experience from one situation to another. Knowledge would have to be entirely specific to be useable. Without extensive reasoning, we also would not be able to understand most of the utterances which are commonly made in natural language. Suppose, for example, someone says to you: "Take my car. The keys are on the sideboard." This comment is immediately comprehensible, but when you look at its literal content you find two apparently unconnected statements. The inferences you draw—again unconsciously in all probability—are that (a) the keys are the keys to the car and (b) that the speaker expects you to fetch them. You are only able to do this because of certain implicit rules of cooperation that speakers and listeners engage in (Grice, 1975). In particular, listeners assume that speakers will be relevant (Sperber & Wilson, 1986). Hence, the keys are assumed to belong to the car as they would otherwise be irrelevant to the context created by the first sentence. Similarly, the only way in which you can make the speaker's reference to the location of the keys relevant is by assuming that she wishes you to collect them. Why would she tell you where the keys were if she was going to collect them herself?

Inferences are not, of course, confined to the understanding of utterances. Everyday problem solving of all kinds involves reasoning. If your car fails to start one morning, then you try to figure out the reason why so that you may be able to cure it. If you have little knowledge of cars, you may reason in a rather primitive fashion; for example, to infer that the battery was flat the last time it failed to start, then that is probably the problem this time. A more knowledgeable driver might notice that the engine is turning over but not firing, so the battery cannot be responsible (another inference). The mechanic you call out would use a more sophisticated level of reasoning again, for example by carrying out tests to distinguish between ignition and fuel faults.

What each of these examples illustrates is that we make inferences in order to bring our knowledge to bear on particular situations and make use of them. In general, the better our knowledge, then the more accurate these inferences are likely to be, although knowledge can sometimes interfere with reasoning as we will see later in this book. We have not, however, so far indicated what kind of inferences we are talking about. The focus of this book, as the title suggests, is specifically on deductive inference. Classically, this is contrasted with inductive inference, though the distinction is not as helpful as one might expect. A deductive inference is one which draws out a conclusion which is latent but implicit in the information given. New information cannot be added in a deductive inference. In contrast, an inductive inference is one which adds information and is therefore not a logically necessary conclusion. For example, when we make an inference from a generalisation to a particular case—"All swans are white, therefore *this* swan is white"—we are reasoning deductively. The reverse process—empirical generalisation—is a typical case of induction. Thus we may reason "All the swans I have ever seen are white, therefore all swans are white." Such generalisations are not logically sound, but are an important and pervasive feature of our thinking about the world.

Deductive inferences are those whose conclusions necessarily follow from their premises or assumptions. The normative theory for how such inferences should be made is the study of formal logic, a subdiscipline of philosophy to which we shall return later. Of the inferences discussed so far, the one with the clearest claim to be a deductive inference is the first. Given the knowledge of parent–sibling relationships, the conclusion you drew was inevitably true. Assuming, that is, that the language used was precise, and no stepfathers or half-sisters were involved.

The second example—the case of the car keys—might appear to be a classical case of *pragmatic inference*, a type of inductive inference which is plausible given the context rather than logically necessary. Whether such pragmatic inferences are inductive or deductive is a matter of debate. Clearly, they go beyond the information given and so appear to be inductive. Some authors, however, prefer to describe such reasoning as involving first an elaboration of the context by use of prior knowledge and assumptions, followed by a process of deductive reasoning on the expanded representation of the problem (e.g. Henle, 1962; Sperber & Wilson, 1986).

Some inferences are, however, clearly probabilistic in nature, such as the argument that the car won't start because the battery is flat. Even the owner of this inference had little confidence in it. Inferences whose conclusions are drawn with a certain degree of probability or confidence are often referred to as *statistical inferences*. Everyday statistical inferences occur frequently and form the subject of some very interesting psychological work (see Kahneman, Slovic & Tversky, 1982) which has many natural connections with the study of deductive reasoning (see Evans, 1989). A review work on statistical inference is, however, beyond the scope of the present volume.

A further distinction between explicit and implicit reasoning is also needed to define the range of psychological research to be discussed in this book. As pointed out above, many of the inferences we make in understanding language and thinking about the world are implicit, i.e. we do not know that we are engaged in reasoning when we are doing it, and may involve unconscious introduction of prior knowledge and belief. Explicit reasoning also occurs in everyday life, as for example when we try to understand rules and regulations and apply them to our own circumstances. Working out whether we qualify for a home improvement grant or a tax rebate, or whether our child can choose the combination of school subjects that he or she wishes, are all examples of explicit deductive reasoning. The information required is all laid out openly and does not rest upon hidden assumptions or extra knowledge that we bring to bear. Our reasoning can be checked by others and can be objectively demonstrated to be sound or unsound.

To write a book on implicit inference would be almost the same as writing one on the whole of cognition. Our humble enterprise is therefore to be limited not only to deductive reasoning but to explicit reasoning tasks. That is to say, we will focus on experimentation in which laboratory subjects are explicitly asked to engage in reasoning, for example by being given the premises of an argument and asked to decide what necessarily follows from it. The problems will all have solutions which are verifiable in some kind of standard logic (see below) and will not, in principle, depend upon individual knowledge and belief. In practice, as we shall see, the prior beliefs of the subjects nevertheless exert a major influence on the inferences that they make.

This restriction is a necessary one in order to delimit a literature of sufficiently limited size and clear focus to permit an in-depth review and discussion. However, the restriction we place is on the kinds of task that experimental subjects are engaged in and not on the cognitive processes which they bring to bear. There are many theories about what people do when confronted with logical reasoning problems and it is by no means apparent, as we shall see, that explicit reasoning tasks are solved by an explicit process of reasoning or on the basis of only the information presented. However, let us elaborate more upon the field of research with which we are concerned, including its history and its current concerns.

THE COGNITIVE PSYCHOLOGY OF DEDUCTIVE REASONING

Historical Background

When the history of psychological thought is taken back by more than 150 years or so, it merges with the parent discipline of philosophy. In one sense, then, one can see the psychology of deductive reasoning as being as old as the study of logic, which originated in the writings of Aristotle. However, with the separation of psychology and philosophy, logic has come to be viewed by most as a normative theory of deductive reasoning, i.e. a theory of how valid conclusions can be drawn, whereas psychological study focuses upon such issues as how do people actually reason and what causes them to make mistakes.

The first study of deductive reasoning problems in psychology was made by early researchers of intelligence testing such as Binet. However, the earliest "cognitive" studies concerned with the understanding of mental processes involved in deduction were probably those of Wilkins (1928) and Woodworth and Sells (1935). The methodology introduced by these authors was essentially that which the field retains to the present day. Subjects are taken into the laboratory and given the premises of an argument which can be analysed by some form of standard logic. They are then asked to demonstrate their understanding of logical validity by one of the following methods: (a) decide whether a conclusion presented does or does not necessarily follow from the premises or (b) decide which of a list of alternative conclusions follows from the premises. A third method, developed later and least often used, is one in which no conclusion is presented for evaluation, but the subjects are asked instead to write down any conclusions which they believe will follow. It is a common, though not invariant practice for researchers then to describe the decisions of the subjects as right or wrong relative to a normative, logical analysis.

The early papers referred to above presented subjects with classical syllogisms consisting of two premises and a conclusion, such as:

Some books on reasoning are written by psychologists
No philosophers are psychologists
Therefore,
Some books on reasoning are not written by philosophers

This particular syllogism is valid, i.e. its conclusion follows from its premises, but deciding this has nothing to do with one's knowledge about philosophers and psychologists. In fact, any syllogism of the form:

Some C are B
No A are B
Therefore,
Some C are not A

is valid, no matter what A, B and C might stand for. Logical validity can be viewed here as a function of the syntactic structure of the sentences only.

The very first papers on reasoning actually reported the two major findings in the area that have taxed theorists to the present day, namely (a) that people make many logical errors on such tasks (e.g. the frequent acceptance of invalid syllogisms reported by Woodworth and Sells, 1935) and (b) that their responses depend very much on the content used to construct the problem, despite its logical irrelevance (Wilkins, 1928). The task that they employed, syllogistic reasoning, has also remained popular and is one of the most intensively researched in the field (see Chapters 7 and 8).

Comparatively little further work was conducted on the psychology of deductive reasoning—at least in adult subjects—until the 1960s, when an intensive set of studies was conducted by Peter Wason, together with students and colleagues. This lead to the first survey of the area in book form by Wason and Johnson-Laird (1972). During this period, Wason invented two tasks, one in the area of inductive reasoning, known as the 2-4-6 problem (Wason, 1960), and one known as the four card problem or more commonly as the "selection task" (Wason, 1966). Both of these are still in use by current researchers, and indeed the Wason selection task is probably the single most commonly used paradigm in the whole field.

In the 2-4-6 task, subjects are told that the experimenter has in mind a rule concerning a group of three whole numbers, or triples. An example which conforms to the rule is "2 4 6". The subjects are asked to discover the rule by generating examples of their own. In each case, the experimenter will tell them whether or not their own triple conforms to the rule. The example given is deliberately biased, since the rule is actually "any ascending sequence". What happens on this task is that subjects form a particular hypothesis such as "ascending with equal intervals" and test triples such as 6 8 10, 1 2 3, 20 30 40, etc., and are told in all cases that their triples conform. The majority of subjects, even of high intelligence, become convinced that their hypothesis must be right because they never think of testing negative cases such as 1 2 4, which would immediately allow them to eliminate their hypothesis. This is a good task to try out on a friend—it rarely fails to baffle.

This simple task has lead to a major debate about "confirmation bias" in reasoning and is the focus of continuing interest. As a problem in inductive reasoning, research on the 2-4-6 problem is not reviewed in this book, but the interested reader is referred to recent discussions by Klayman and Ha (1987) and Evans (1989, ch. 3). Wason's selection task problem, which involves the logic of conditionals, has inspired so much recent research that a whole chapter of this volume has been dedicated to reviewing the work concerned (Chapter 4).

Partly because of the popularity of Wason and Johnson-Laird's (1972) volume, the field grew substantially in the following decade and by the time of the next book-length review by Evans (1982) there were hundreds of papers specifically concerned with deductive reasoning tasks to be considered. At this time, however, the field had remained comparatively isolated from mainstream research in cognitive psychology that had emerged with a clear identity during the 1970s. For example, most reasoning researchers did not work in other areas of cognitive psychology, a number employed different kinds of theoretical concepts and there was little cross-reference between work on reasoning and other aspects of cognition. Evans' (1982) review ended with the hope that integration of reasoning research into mainstream research on cognition would occur. While we believe that this has happened in the past decade, the nature of cognitive psychology itself has changed during the 1980s with the emergence of the meta-discipline of cognitive science.

Cognitive science is an interdisciplinary attempt to understand the nature of intelligence and is founded on the notion that intelligence has a nature which is not restricted by the system, be it biological or physical, in which it resides. Building upon the already close links between cognitive psychology and artificial intelligence, cognitive science has also come to encompass linguistics, logic, philosophy of mind and the neurosciences. For this reason, there is now some reconnection between the philosophy and psychology of reasoning. The major connection of relevance here, however, is with the study of artificial intelligence. If reasoning is central to intelligence, as we have argued, then smart machines must be able to draw inferences. The other side of the coin is that psychologists in the area have become increasingly interested in computational models of their theories, some of which are instantiated as working computer programs.

The reader will doubtless have noted that we have restricted the scope of the current work by the modifier "human" in choosing our title. It would serve no useful purpose for us to survey here the state of play in machine reasoning as such, in the context of a work concerned with the natural science of deduction. We will, however, deal with computational models which have a direct role in the development of the psychology theory of reasoning, and particular coverage of this approach is given in Chapters 5 and 8. In the following sections, we identify first the main theoretical issues with which the field is currently concerned and next the major theoretical approaches which address these issues.

Phenomena and Issues in the Psychology of Reasoning

Theories of reasoning reflect attempts to explain the available data. Hundreds of papers have been published reporting studies of deductive reasoning, many of which will be described and discussed in the chapters which follow. We will, however, illustrate here the broad categories of finding which are addressed by theorists in the area. The traditional interest has been in logical accuracy. How often do subjects provide the inferences dictated by logic? When they go wrong, do they make random errors and are they systematically biased by features of the task?

Many papers emphasise the extent of errors and biases observed. We believe that this is because psychologists find the conditions which produce error to be informative about underlying cognitive processes. In fact, all of the main types of reasoning task described in this book are associated with high rates of logical errors. That is not to say that subjects perform randomly, for correct answers are almost always observed more often than by chance alone, and the errors which occur often reflect systematic *biases*. For some authors, the term "bias" has pejorative connotations, suggesting irrationality. We use the term in this book purely descriptively, to refer to behaviour which is systematically related to a logically irrelevant feature of the task. It is a matter of theoretical debate to decide how such biases arise, and whether they result from a rational attempt to reason or form other causes or indeed whether the logical system used is an appropriate criterion for judging error. We take this point up below and also in Chapter 9 where we discuss the relationship between reasoning research and the concept of human rationality.

To illustrate what we mean by a bias, take the case of the inference Modus Tollens, which is one of several possible inferences that are associated with conditional sentences (see Chapter 2). Given two statements such as:

If a shape is a triangle then it is red
This shape is blue

it follows logically that this shape is *not* a triangle. Why? Because if it was a triangle, then it would have to be red. Student subjects make this inference more often than not, but quite often err in saying that no conclusion follows. For example, Evans (1977a) found that 75% of subjects would make a Modus Tollens inference with this kind of problem. Hence, we need to explain why subjects usually are able to make the inference, but also why they quite often fail to do so. The problem is complicated by biasing factors. For example, suppose the premises of the above argument are slightly modified as follows:

If a shape is not a triangle then it is red
This shape is blue

The difference is the negative in the first premise. A Modus Tollens inference can still be made, but now it leads to the conclusion that this shape *is* a triangle (because if it were not, then it would have to be red). This change of wording has, however, a dramatic effect on responding. Evans (1977a) reported that only 12% of his subjects made the Modus Tollens inference with problems of this kind. Because the presence of the negative in the rule affects inferences but not the logic of the Modus Tollens principle, we can describe it as a biasing factor (see Chapter 2 for detailed discussion of the effect). Obviously, understanding deductive reasoning is not simply a matter of deciding whether people can make a certain inference or not. Most people probably do understand the idea of Modus Tollens reasoning, but they frequently fail to apply it, and are more likely to do so in some situations than others.

This example involves so-called "abstract" reasoning problems which have little connection with prior knowledge that people associate from real-world reasoning. Where reasoning problems do evoke associated knowledge—so-called "thematic" problems—things get more complicated again. While instructions in reasoning tasks normally ask subjects to ignore their prior knowledge and reason only on the basis of the information given, they are patently unable to do so. Consider another conditional inference:

If a shape is a triangle then it is red
This shape is a circle

Logically, we can infer nothing about the colour of this shape. If we decide that it is not red, then we are committing a fallacy known as denial of the antecedent. With affirmative abstract statements of the above kind, subjects are again strongly affected by the presence of negatives in the conditional statement, but this effect disappears when thematic content is introduced. Instead, the inference rate depends critically on the context. For example, Ellis (1991, experiment 5), who embedded problems in short scenarios, reports that when causal statements are used such as:

If the truck is heavier than the legal limit, then the alarm bell will ring

then almost all subjects will deny the antecedent by inferring that a truck under the limit will not ring the bell. However, when arbitrary universal claims are made such as:

If the student is doing Economics, then he is a socialist

the fallacy is only committed about 50% of the time. Clearly, then, pragmatic factors (i.e. those involving prior knowledge) have a profound effect on the way in which we reason. Actually, we can distinguish between effects of problem *content* (i.e. what terms the premises of the argument contain) from effects of the *context* (e.g. a preceding scenario in which the problems are embedded). We will see that problem content and context can interact with one another in determining the role of prior knowledge. For example, Byrne (1989b) has shown that presenting the same premises in different contexts can have marked effects on the inferences drawn (see Chapter 3), and that the use of scenarios can play a vital role in determining responses to the Wason selection task (Chapter 4). We will also see examples in this book of cases in which pragmatic factors improve logical accuracy and cases where they are detrimental.

Evans (1991a) recently proposed that research is (often implicitly) driven by the pursuit of three separate but interrelated issues, which he calls the *competence question*, the *bias question* and the *content question* (see Table 1.1). These three questions in turn reflect the three basic findings to have emerged from the hundreds of experimental studies of deductive reasoning that have now been conducted, namely that (a) subjects are mostly able to solve logical problems with well above chance

TABLE 1.1
Three Questions Motivating Research on Reasoning

Competence question	By what mechanism can subjects reason the solution to logical problems?
Bias question	What factors cause systematic errors and biases in reasoning and what do such biases tell us about the nature of reasoning purposes?
Content question	What features of problem content and context affect the ability of subjects to reason the solution to logical problems and what does this tell us about the nature of reasoning processes?

frequency, (b) that many systematic errors and biases nevertheless occur and (c) that responses are highly dependent upon the content of the problems and the context in which they appear.

The distinction between competence and bias might at first sight seem a little strange. You might think that in a task where people can get things right or wrong, you need only explain one thing, i.e. the error rate. What Evans argued, however, is that we need to explain both why people get it right to an extent and why they make the mistakes that they do. The analysis offered by Evans (1991a) shows that some authors have been primarily oriented to one side rather than the other of the right/wrong coin. For example Rips (1989, p. 109), who is an author of one of the main theories of deductive competence (see next section), has commented: "Explaining errors is usually easy since . . . there are multiple ways in which they can occur. Correct performance is what taxes a theory, since it suggests more elaborate and interesting processes." In contrast, Evans (1989) devoted a whole book to the explanation of errors and biases in reasoning without being willing to commit himself on the question of how competence is achieved, stating: "I have not previously, nor will I here, commit myself to a definite view on the mechanism by which analytical reasoning is achieved . . . At present—for me at least—there is no singular solution to the problem of reasoning competence" (p. 15). Both of these arguably extreme positions have attracted criticism; for example, Rips has been attacked for his apparent lack of interest in explaining errors of reasoning by Evans (1990a), while Evans in turn has been reprimanded for his lack of attention to competence by Oakhill (1991). Perhaps the most notable attempt to explain both competence and errors within a single framework is that of the mental models theory (Johnson-Laird & Byrne, 1991) discussed in the next section.

The frequent reports of bias and error in reasoning have caused controversy on another level which we will refer to as the rationality debate. This argument goes beyond the cognitive psychological level of who is best explaining what and introduces a philosophical dimension. The philosopher L. Jonathan Cohen (1981) startled the psychologists studying bias in both deductive and statistical reasoning by arguing that such experiments could never demonstrate human irrationality. Cohen argued by analogy with Chomskian linguistics that observed performance should not be confused with underlying competence, that experimental tasks were artificial and unrepresentative, that subjects might reason by alternative logics to those of the standard text books and so on.

Some of us were surprised by Cohen's attack because we had not thought that we were in the business of demonstrating irrationality in the first place. However, there have been a number of similar concerns raised subsequently by psychologists engaged in decision and reasoning research, expressed at the psychological level of concern with external validity. The suggestion is that psychologists in this area may extrapolate too freely from the results of laboratory experiments to real-world decision making. For example, Christensen-Szalanski and Beach (1984) have claimed that bias researchers are themselves biased in citing papers reporting poor reasoning more frequently than those which discover good reasoning.

Funder (1987) and Lopes (1991), commenting respectively on bias research in the fields of social judgement and decision making, have each put forward a similar argument. They say that the purpose of studying error and bias in the laboratory is properly to discover the nature of the underlying processes (by analogy to the study of forgetting, visual illusions, etc.), but that researchers have instead tended to focus on the erroneous performance itself and infer that real-world reasoning and judgement is substantially defective. Lopes complains about the somewhat extravagant "rhetoric of irrationality" of which she cites a number of examples.

The implications of reasoning research for the rationality debate is of interest, and is addressed by several papers in a volume edited by Manktelow and Over (1993). We will return to this issue in our final discussion (Chapter 9), but it will not influence our main review of the field. Our concern here is with the explanations of the behaviour of experimental subjects that have been offered, rather than with assessments of the rationality of such behaviour. The review that we have undertaken of the experimental literature on deductive reasoning will reveal a weighty catalogue of systematic errors and biases. Our treatment of this literature, however, will not involve judgements of rationality, but instead will be concerned with examining the implications that such findings have for the nature of underlying reasoning processes, and the ability that contemporary theories of human reasoning have to explain the phenomena concerned.

The other issue that will feature strongly throughout this review is that of the role of problem content and context. As already explained, in a deductive reasoning task, by definition the logical solution to the problems will be independent of both content and context. Every influence of problem content is therefore an extra-logical effect and one which reveals the sensitivity of human reasoning to *pragmatic* factors, i.e. influences arising from prior knowledge. (Some psychologists use the term "semantic" to describe any factors relating to the meaning of problem content, but we will use the term "pragmatic" for these broader factors, and use the term "semantic" in its narrower sense of describing meaning in language.) Our treatment of content effects will, however, again reveal a concern for what it tells us about the nature of human reasoning processes rather than with its implications for rationality. If the intrusion of pragmatic influences leads a subject to make an "error" relative to the task instructions, this should not necessarily be taken as evidence of irrationality. It may be that effective everyday reasoning methods are being carried over into the laboratory task.

The distinction between the competence, bias and content questions is a useful one for readers to bear in mind during the specific review of reasoning literature and the various theoretical arguments that arise. We will return specifically to the issue of the extent to which we have satisfactory answers to each of these questions in the final chapter of this book.

Contemporary Theories of Reasoning

As noted earlier, one of the major advances since Evans' (1982) previous review of this field has been the development of systematic theories of reasoning. Of the four main contemporary approaches summarised in Table 1.2, only that of formal inference rules had been articulated to any clear extent by the beginning of the 1980s and this theory—based upon a long-standing idea in philosophy and psychology—has been subject to much enhancement and development since.

The detailed implementation of these types of theory will be discussed at appropriate stages throughout the book and their overall performance assessed in the final chapter. At this stage, we wish only to introduce to readers the basic concepts of each of these main approaches. The first, which we will describe as *formal rule theory*, is often known as "mental logic" following Johnson-Laird (1983). While formal rule theorists do presume that there is a "logic in the mind", the problem with the latter term is that there are logics based on principles other than inference rules. In particular, the mental models theory described below is closely related to model-theoretic logics and also proposes inherent deductive competence. Thus mental models theory can also be construed as a form of mental logic (see Rips, 1986). For this reason, we will generally refer to this approach as formal rule theory rather than as mental logic.

TABLE 1.2
Four Main Theoretical Approaches in Reasoning Research

Formal rules	Subjects reason by constructing proofs using an internal set of abstract, general purpose reasoning rules
Mental models	Subjects reason by constructing models to represent states of the world in which the premises are true and then constructing conclusions by generating a parsimonious description of their models
Domain-sensitive rules or schemas	Reasoning in real-world domains is achieved with the aid of domain-specific rules or context-sensitive schemas which are retrieved and applied. Schemas include rules for reasoning in particular pragmatic contexts
Heuristics and biases	This approach attributes biases to the operation of non-logical heuristics which are separate from the processes responsible for competent reasoning. These heuristics are often used to explain systematic errors or "biases" in reasoning tasks

The basic assumption of formal rule theory is that there is an inherent mental logic comprised of a set of abstract inference rules or schemas which are applied in a general purposes manner for reasoning in all contexts. This approach has a long history, for as stated earlier, the purpose of logic for many philosophers was the description of human reasoning. Thus the logic is abstract and general purpose and all real-world problems must be translated into some type of abstract code in order for reasoning to occur.

The assumption of logicality in human reasoning is not quite the same thing as the theory of mental logic. Looking at papers on reasoning more than 20 years or so old, and perhaps more recently in the developmental literature, one sees a strong presumption of logicality in that authors felt obliged only to explain errors of reasoning, defined as departures from logical prescription. The assumption that logicality did not need explaining perhaps presupposed the existence of an internal logic but did not provide any kind of explanatory mechanisms for deductive competence. Perhaps the strongest and most influential explicit assertion of logicality was that of Henle (1962), who claimed that human reasoning was invariably logical and that apparent errors were due to misrepresentation of problem information.

While the validity of arguments in formal logic can be established by a method known as "truth table analysis" (described in the next section), philosophers and psychologists in search of a mental logic have proposed that people adopt what are termed "natural logics" for deductive reasoning. A natural logic is comprised of a limited set of abstract rules of reasoning which can be applied in combination to deduce conclusions from premises. There have been a number of different proposals about the precise number and nature of rules or inference schemata that are required to account for natural inference (Braine, 1978; Braine & O'Brien, 1991; Johnson-Laird, 1975; Osherson, 1975; Rips, 1983). There have been various attempts to demonstrate empirically that people reason by application of formal rules (e.g. Braine, Reiser & Rumain, 1984; Rips, 1983; 1989) and increasing recognition of the need not only to specify the rules of reasoning but the mechanisms by which such rules are applied (Braine & O'Brien, 1991; Rips, 1983).

For example, all the formal rule theorists assert that a rule of reasoning that people possess is Modus Ponens, i.e. $p \supset q$, p entails q. So given the problem:

If the letter is an A then the number is a 3
The letter is an A

subjects would be able to apply the rule directly and give the conclusion "The number is a 3". On the other hand, they are not assumed to have a rule for Modus Tollens, so that given:

If the letter is an A then the number is a 3
The number is not a 3

subjects could not discover the valid inference "The letter is not an A" by direct application of a rule. Instead, they might use the Modus Ponens (MP) rule in conjunction with other rules (see Table 1.5). Hence they would assume that the letter is an A, derive the conclusion that the number is a 3 (by MP), derive the contradiction "3 and not 3" by a rule of And Introduction (p, q entails p and q), and finally infer that the letter is not A by the rule of Reductio Ad Absurdum (any assumption that leads to a contradiction is false). The more complex reasoning process required for Modus Tollens can be used to explain why this inference is less often made by subjects in reasoning experiments (see Chapter 2).

Formal rule theories stand—or fall—on the assumption that all reasoning is achieved by one set of abstract and general purpose reasoning rules. Critics of the theory (e.g. Evans, 1991a; Johnson-Laird & Byrne, 1991) have noted that it is not well suited in its nature to the explanation of either biases or content effects, although as we shall see later in the book explanations of such effects have been attempted by mental logic theorists. For example, it might be argued that content effects occur during the translation of domain content into the underlying abstract representations to which the rules of inference are applied.

The mental models theory also has old roots in model-theoretic approaches to logic, but was first articulated as a modern psychological theory of reasoning by Johnson-Laird (e.g. 1983). The theory proposes that reasoning is semantic rather than syntactic in nature, and depends not upon inference rules but upon systematic procedures for constructing and evaluating mental models. Reasoning follows three main stages:

1. Subjects formulate a mental model to represent a possible state of the world consistent with the information supplied by the premises.
2. Subjects formulate a putative conclusion by generating a description of the model that is semantically informative (not a repetition of a premise or a statement less informative than a premise).
3. The putative conclusion may be tested by trying to construct alternative models in which the premises of the argument are true but the conclusion is false. If no such counterexample is found, then the conclusion is inferred to be valid.

As an example, we show how the mental models theory accounts for the greater difficulty of Modus Tollens than Modus Ponens. Consider the Modus Ponens problem presented above:

If the letter is an A then the number is a 3
The letter is an A

According to the mental models theory of conditional reasoning (Johnson-Laird & Byrne, 1991), the first sentence would initially be represented as

[A] 3
. . .

where different models are represented on different lines and the square brackets mean that A's are exhaustively represented with respect to 3's. That is, A's cannot occur in any other model unless 3's occur in that model also. The notation ". . ." means that there may be other models compatible with the premise which are not explicitly represented at this stage. Hence, given the additional information "A", it follows immediately—since A is exhaustively represented in the explicit model—that there must be a 3. On the other hand, when the Modus Tollens problem is presented (i.e. the second premise reads "The number is not a 3"), then no inference follows immediately, as the case ¬3 (not-3) is not explicitly represented. To draw the inference, according to Johnson-Laird and Byrne, the representation would need to be fleshed out to include extra models:

[A] 3
¬A [¬3]
¬A [3]

Subjects must then realise that the premise "the number is not a 3" rules out the first and last of these models, and hence that the conclusion "the letter is not A" necessarily follows as it is true in the only model possible. Since not all subjects will succeed in doing this, Modus Tollens will be made less frequently. Both the formal rule and mental models accounts of conditional reasoning are presented in detail in Chapter 3.

Although the mental models theory does not presume rules of inference, it does suppose *implicit* understanding of some logical principles by human reasoners. First, they must appreciate that a conclusion is only valid if it must be true given that the premises are true. Second, the construction of models implies identification of the truth conditions of a propositional or quantified assertion, so that models are correctly formulated such that the premises are true rather than false. The mental models theory does, however, permit people to represent problem information in the form of concrete tokens rather than abstract symbols and is more readily applicable to the explanations of biases and content effects than the mental logic theory. For example, subjects may fail to find counterexamples due to limitations in working memory capacity or be influenced by content because prior knowledge adds information to the models they construct. A recent and detailed presentation of the mental models theory together with empirical evidence is presented by Johnson-Laird and Byrne (1991).

The next main type of theory proposes that reasoning is achieved by domain-sensitive rules, or by schemas which are elicited by the context and contain rules which can be applied for reasoning in a particular domain. The theory of pragmatic reasoning schemas (Cheng & Holyoak, 1985) is the best known theory of this type, is specifically concerned with the explanation of content effects in reasoning and has been mostly restricted to the explanation of findings on the Wason selection task (see Chapter 3). In essence, it is proposed that we learn to reason in certain contexts and formulate schemas (or schemata as some prefer) to abstract our knowledge. For example, we may have a permission schema which can be applied to rules of the general form:

If an action is to be taken then a precondition must be met

If a conditional statement is used in context which can be interpreted as involving permission, then the relevant schema is retrieved, together with embedded reasoning rules which are applied. Conditionals used in a different context may evoke a different schema with different rules and hence lead to logically inconsistent inferences. As an example, the theory might predict that Modus Tollens reasoning—relatively difficult with abstract material as illustrated above—could be facilitated if the schema aroused includes a specific rule corresponding to this inference. The permission schema is actually assumed to include a rule of the form:

If a precondition is not met then the action may not be taken

Like formal rules, pragmatic reasoning schemas are abstract. Unlike formal rules, however, they are not all-purpose but limited to a particular domain of application. Suppose that a subject is given the following problem:

> If a person is drinking alcohol in a bar then they must be over 18 years of age
> Jim is 16 years of age

If a permission schema is evoked, then the associated rule described above will facilitate Modus Tollens reasoning, since its variables of "action" and "precondition" will be instantiated in this context as:

> If a person is under 18 years of age then they may not drink alcohol in a bar

Subjects would thus be expected to draw the inference "Jim may not drink alcohol in a bar" with greater ease than they would solve the abstract problem about letters and numbers given earlier for which no pragmatic schema will be available.

The strength of the schema theory is hence in its explanation of the effects of content on reasoning and its weakness—as various authors have noted—is its lack of applicability to reasoning on abstract or artificial problems where subjects still show above chance competence on most tasks. However, this consideration cannot be used to rule out the schema theory, because it is quite possible that people have a general purpose method of reasoning based upon mental models or some other mechanism that they use for unfamiliar problems, but still tend to abstract and use schemas in domains where they have relevant experience.

Finally, we consider the "heuristics and biases" approach, which is more often associated with research on statistical judgement and inference and in particular the work of Daniel Kahneman and Amos Tversky (see Kahneman et al., 1982). Pollard (1982) explored the application of the *availability heuristic*, devised to explain certain kinds of probability judgement (Tversky & Kahneman, 1983) to the explanation of inductive and deductive reasoning experiments. The original theory proposed that people judge probabilities of events by the ease with which examples of the event occurring could be brought to mind. In many situations, as Tversky and Kahneman demonstrated, this leads to systematic bias in probability judgements. Pollard extended the idea to the psychology of reasoning by arguing that the availability of problem features which are salient in the presentation, or associated information which is retrieved from memory, will influence the response to reasoning tasks, often inducing biases.

Evans (1984a; 1989) argued that reasoning does occur at what he calls an analytic stage, but is preceded by a heuristic stage in which preconscious selection occurs. The key concept here is that of *relevance* rather than availability. That is, subjects are assumed to focus on information which appears relevant due to a variety of linguistic and pragmatic factors. Biases occur because logical relevant features of the task are not selected or irrelevant features are selected during the heuristic stage. Subjects reason about those features which are perceived as relevant. Determinants of relevance—and hence in some cases bias—include linguistic suppositions, pragmatic associations and salience of features in the task presentation. Since, as noted earlier, Evans does not specify the mechanism for deductive competence in the analytic stage, the approach is not necessarily incompatible with other theories. For example, that which is relevant could be equated with that which is explicitly represented in a mental model, an idea to which we will return later in the book.

We illustrate the heuristics and biases approach again with the case of Modus Tollens. As stated earlier (see also Chapter 2), the inference is made far less often when the antecedent of the conditional is negative, as in the following pair of premises:

If the letter is not an A, then the number is a 3
The number is not a 3

In this case, Modus Tollens leads to the conclusion that the letter is an A (because if it was not, the number would be a 3), but most subjects fail to draw the inference. Pollard and Evans (1980) propose a caution heuristic to explain a general preference for negative conclusions. They point out that a statement such as "The letter is not an A" is only false in the case of one letter, whereas the statement "The letter is an A" is only true for one letter. Detailed accounts of heuristic explanations of reasoning phenomena will be given in Chapters 2 and 4.

FORMAL LOGIC AND REASONING TASKS

It is necessary at this stage to talk some more about the nature of logic. We are well aware that to introduce formal logic too early or too enthusiastically into the proceedings would be to risk the alienation of readers with a psychological background. In truth, most of the reasoning tasks employed by psychologists have involved relatively simple logical principles and structures and no more than a rudimentary understanding of formal logic is required to follow the arguments involved. However, we must endeavour to ensure that the reader untrained in logic has some adequate basis for understanding the nature of the tasks employed, and some of the psychological theory which is closely connected with logical systems. Readers familiar with formal logic may skip this section without loss of continuity.

Propositional Logic

Standard logic is normally described within the framework of the propositional and predicate calculi in logic textbooks (e.g. Lemmon, 1965). Brief consideration of the elements of each will suffice for our current purposes. A proposition is an atomic concept, a simple assertion which cannot be broken down into components and which is either true or false. For example, the sentence "The boy who was laughing took the grateful dog for a walk" contains several underlying propositions: the boy was laughing, the dog was grateful, the boy took the dog for a walk. Negation has a special function in logic, namely that of reversing truth value. Hence, "The boy did not take the dog for a walk" would be analysed as a negation of the proposition that the boy took the dog for a walk. If this proposition is true, then the negated assertion is false and vice versa.

In propositional logic, it is possible to analyse arguments by two separate methods based on truth table analysis and on rules of inference. In truth table analysis, we have to consider the possibility that each component proposition is true or false in systematic permutation. For example, given a rule such as:

If the switch is turned, then the light is on

there are four logically possible situations to consider:

Switch on, light on (TT)
Switch on, light off (TF)
Switch off, light on (FT)
Switch off, light off (FF)

The abbreviations refer to the truth value of each component proposition. For example, TF means that the first proposition is true and the second false. The logic of the rule can be understood in terms of its prescription for the truth of each of these cases. We might, for example, believe that the rule could apply to any situation except TF. This would give a truth table rating of TFTT for the four cases. On the other hand, we might believe that it also excludes the case FT, i.e. a truth table evaluation of TFFT is correct. The difference is that in the first case we believe only that the state of the switch implies the state of the light. In the second case, we believe that the light will only be on if the switch is down, so the implication goes both ways. In logic these two relations are known as *material implication* and *material equivalence*.

The logic of certain propositional connectives, represented in natural language by such words as *if, and* and *or*, can be expressed via truth tables as shown in Table 1.3. For example, the connective $\supset$ for material implication is often said to be represented in natural language by conditional

TABLE 1.3
Truth Tables for Differing Propositional Connectives

Connective	*Logical Form*	*Linguistic Form*	*pq*	*Truth of Rule*
Material implication	$p \supset q$	If p then q	TT	T
		or	TF	F
		p only if q	FT	T
			FF	T
Material equivalence	$p \leftrightarrow q$	If and only if	TT	T
		p then q	TF	F
			FT	F
			FF	T
Conjunction	$p \wedge q$	p and q	TT	T
			TF	F
			FT	F
			FF	F
Inclusive disjunction	$p \vee q$	p or q	TT	T
		(or both)	TF	T
			FT	T
			FF	F
Exclusive disjunction	p/q	p or q	TT	F
		(but not both)	TF	T
			FT	T
			FF	F

statements of the form *if p then q* or *p only if q*, although there are great difficulties with this as we shall see in Chapter 2. As illustrated above, a material implication is considered to be false when the antecedent (*p*) is true and the consequent (*q*) is false, and is otherwise true. For example, the assertion "If the animal is a dog, then it has four legs" could only be disproved by finding a dog with a number of legs other than four.

The other connectives shown in Table 1.3 are for material equivalence (also known as a biconditional), which is falsified if either the antecedent is true and the consequent is false or vice versa: for conjunction which is only true if both components are true, for inclusive disjunction where the connected statement is true if either component proposition is true, and for exclusive disjunction where one component must be true but not both.

Truth table analysis can be used to demonstrate the validity of logical arguments without the use of any rules of inference. To appreciate how this is done, we need a formal statement of the principle of logical necessity as follows: *A valid argument is one in which a false conclusion can never follow from assumptions which are all true*. Consider the following argument:

If an animal is a fish then it is not warm-blooded $p \supset \neg q$
If an animal is a mammal then it is warm-blooded $r \supset q$
Therefore,
If an animal is a fish then it is not a mammal $p \supset \neg r$

The validity of this argument is fairly easy to perceive because of the content in which we have chosen to phrase it. From the standpoint of logic, however, we cannot use our real-world knowledge that mammals and fish are exclusive categories but must prove that the conclusion follows on the basis of the information presented alone. A proof using truth table analysis is shown in Table 1.4. The first step is to analyse the statements into their three constituent propositions and to represent these symbolically by the letters *p*, *q*, and *r*. We now consider all eight possible situations in which the premises could apply by systematically permuting the truth values of each of our propositions.

In truth table analysis, we draw up a separate line in the truth table for each possible state of the world. With three propositions, as in this case, there are eight possible states—and hence lines in the table—corresponding to the possibility of each proposition being true or false in different combinations. For each of the eight states, we have to decide the truth of

TABLE 1.4
Truth Table Analysis of an Example Argument

Argument
If an animal is a fish then it is not warm-blooded
If an animal is a mammal then it is warm-blooded
Therefore,
If an animal is a fish then it is not a mammal

Propositional analysis
p = an animal is a fish
q = an animal is warm-blooded
r = an animal is a mammal

Truth table analysis

pqr	If p then not q	If r then q	If p then not r
TTT	F	T	F
TTF	F	T	T
TFT	T	F	F
TFF	T	T	T
FTT	T	T	T
FTF	T	T	T
FFT	T	F	T
FFF	T	T	T

each premise in our argument and also its conclusion. Hence, there is a column for each of these. Consider how the first line is constructed in the table. This is for the case where all three propositions *p, q*, and *r* are assumed to be true.

Our first task is to decide whether or not the first premise is true or false. This has the general form *if p then not q*. In logic we assume that *if . . . then* represents a material implication, so this will be true except in the case TF where it is false. Since *p* and *q* are both true, we have the case TF. Hence we enter the value F for the first premise.

The second premise is the conditional *if q then r* and is in this case TT, since both *q* and *r* are true in this line of the table. Hence, the premise as a whole is true (T). The conclusion is also a conditional of the form *if p then not t*. Since for this line in the table both *p* and *r* are true, we have the case TF, which again makes the conditional implication false. The same process is repeated for the other seven lines in the table. In each case, we use our knowledge of the truth conditions of the connective *if* to work out the truth value of both the premises and the conclusion.

Once the table is written out in full, we now apply the following test for validity: If there exists at least one case where the premises are all true and the conclusion false, then the argument is invalid, otherwise it is valid. Inspection of the table shows several lines in which both premises are true, but in each case the conclusion is also true. Thus the argument is logically valid. Note that in some cases a true conclusion follows from a false premise, but this does not matter. The function of logic, as it were, is to guarantee that conclusions are true *provided* that the premises are true.

It is extremely unlikely that anyone untrained in logic would assess the argument by the method just explained and in fact no authors in the psychology of reasoning suggest this as a plausible mechanism for natural inference. However, the mental models theory of deduction does assume that subjects reason by considering possible world states and implies that they can use their knowledge of truth conditions to elaborate some of the cases arising in a truth table analysis. It also assumes that subjects understand the principle of necessity, i.e. that the argument is only valid if there is no possible world in which the premises are true and the conclusion false. The process proposed by Johnson-Laird and Byrne (1991) for propositional reasoning imposes considerably less of a cognitive load than truth table analysis, since subjects are assumed (a) to represent only those cases in which the premises of the argument are true and (b) often to leave some of these implicit unless a reason is found to flesh them out.

A possible means of modelling the problem we have been considering is by Euler circles as shown in Fig. 1.1. Euler circles are used to represent set memberships and the relations between sets. Instead of eight lines of a truth table, the problem can effectively be represented in the single

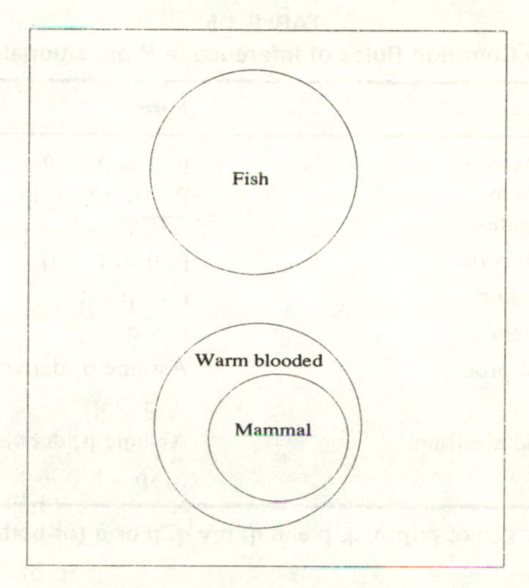

FIG. 1.1. Euler circle representation of an example reasoning problem.

diagram shown in Fig. 1.1. By premise 1, the set of fish cannot overlap with the set of warm-blooded creatures which is therefore drawn separately. Since all mammals are warm-blooded, from premise 2 the set of mammals must be entirely contained within the set of warm-blooded animals and is drawn appropriately. Inspection of the diagram now reveals the truth of the conclusion, since no animal which is a fish can also be a mammal. Strictly speaking, other diagrams can be drawn to represent other possibilities compatible with the premises, e.g. the sets of mammals and warm-blooded animals might be identical, but none of these variations could falsify the conclusion.

The alternative method of proof taught to logic students is that based upon inference rules, which can themselves be derived from a truth table analysis. A set of commonly used inference rules in the propositional calculus are shown in Table 1.5 and an inferential proof of the same argument is shown in Table 1.6. By comparison with the truth table analysis, the argument appears quite straightforward and is based upon a method known as conditional proof (CP). The CP rule states that if by assuming p you can deduce q, then it follows that the implication $p \supset q$ must be true. Moreover, you can now expunge the assumption of p. In other words, you need only show that *if* p is true then q follows.

The argument proceeds as follows. Assume that the animal is a fish. This matches the antecedent of the first premise, so we can deduce by Modus Ponens that the animal is not warm-blooded. Since it is not warm-blooded, we can infer by Modus Tollens that it is not a mammal, using the second

TABLE 1.5
Some Common Rules of Inference in Propositional Logic

Rule	*Form*
Modus Ponens	$p \supset q, p \therefore q$
Modus Tollens	$p \supset q, -p \therefore -p$
Double negation	$\neg\neg p \therefore p$
And introduction	$p, q \therefore p \wedge q$
Or introduction	$p \therefore p \vee q$
And elimination	$p \wedge q \therefore p$
Conditional proof	Assume p, derive q $\therefore p \supset q$
Reductio ad absurum	Assume p, derive $q \wedge \neg q$ $\therefore -p$

Symbols: $\neg p$, not p; $p \wedge q$, p and q; $p \vee q$, p or q (or both); $p \supset q$, p implies q.

TABLE 1.6
Inferential Proof of an Example Argument

Argument	
If an animal is a fish then it is not warm-blooded	1
If an animal is a mammal then it is warm-blooded	2
Therefore,	
If an animal is a fish then it is not a mammal	3
Proof	
Assume the animal is a fish	4, Assumption
Hence, the animal is not warm-blooded	5, Modus Ponens (1, 4)
Hence, the animal is not a mammal	6, Modus Tollens (2, 5)
Hence, if the animal is a fish then it is not a mammal	Conditional proof (4, 6, eliminating assumption)

premise. Hence, by conditional proof, if the animal is a fish then it is not a mammal.

Formal rule theory, discussed earlier, assumes that human deductive reasoning proceeds by constructing mental proofs similar to this, although Modus Tollens is not normally assumed to be a primary inference rule.

Quantifiers, Relations and Predicate Logic

Propositional logic is sufficient for analysis of the kinds of conditional and disjunctive reasoning problems which we shall review in Chapters 2–5. However, in later chapters, we shall look also at deductive reasoning problems based upon relational and quantified reasoning. Some relational reasoning problems lack a formal logical calculus of their own, although their validity can be formally demonstrated (see below). A good example is transitive inference, which concerns objects that are placed upon a single scalar dimension. For example, if John is taller than Mike and Mike is taller than Paul, then John must be taller than Paul. People's ability to reason about transitive relations and other types of relational inference are considered in Chapter 6.

Quantifiers denote relations between sets rather than propositions and include such terms as all, some, many and few. We have already met quantifiers in the example of an Aristotelian syllogism discussed earlier. In Aristotle's system, all arguments were expressed in a very restricted form with just two premises and a conclusion relating just three terms. The validity of each such syllogism can then be established, for example, by reference to Euler circle diagrams. A large number of modern psychological studies have, in fact, consisted of presenting experimental subjects with these classical syllogism sets and testing their ability to judge the validity of conclusions. The experimentation and associated theoretical explanations in this tradition are discussed in detail in Chapters 7 and 8.

It is evident that problems in quantified logic need not be confined to the syllogistic form and a more powerful form of logic is needed to deal with both quantifiers in general and with propositions containing internal relations. Consider the transitive inference:

Mary is taller than Joan
Sue is shorter than Joan
Therefore,
Mary is taller than Sue

The validity of this argument can be readily seen intuitively and knowledge of the formal means of proof is not required to follow the discussion of psychological work on relational reasoning discussed in Chapter 6. However, for completeness, we provide the interested reader with an example of how predicate logic works by proving the above argument. To do this, we can introduce the relational terms T and S to represent taller and shorter, so symbolising the argument as:

1. (mTj)
2. (sSj)
   Therefore,
   (mTs)

In order to prove our argument, we have to formalise our assumptions about the transitivity of taller/shorter as follows:

3. $(\forall x)(\forall y)(\forall z)$ (xTy & yTz ⊃ xTz)
4. $(\forall x)(\forall y)$ (xSy ⊃ yTx)

Here ∀ is the universal quantifier and means "for all x", etc. So in English the above statements read:

3. For all x, all y and all z, if x is taller than y and y is taller than z, then x is taller than z
4. For all x and all y, if x is shorter than y, then y is taller than x

Reasoning in the predicate calculus proceeds by eliminating quantifiers, reasoning with the resulting propositions and then reintroducing the quantifiers if necessary. In this case, our particular people can be instantiated into the universal rules, so that rule 4 can be rewritten as:

5. (sSj) ⊃ (jTs)

And rule 3 can be rewritten as:

6. (mTj & jTs) ⊃ (mTs)

The formal proof of the conclusion by propositional logic is now straightforward:

7.	(jTs)	Modus Ponens (from assumptions 2, 5)
8.	(mTj & jTs)	And Introduction (1, 7)
9.	(mTs)	Modus Ponens (8, 6)

Since we are reasoning only about specific individuals, we do not need to reintroduce quantifiers. Suppose, however, the first premise had read:

Some children are taller than Joan

This would be represented in the predicate calculus by:

$(\exists c)$(cTj)

using the existential quantifier ∃ and read as

There exists at least one child such that the child is taller than Joan

Predicate logic would have allowed us to eliminate this quantifier as long as it were reintroduced at the end. Hence, the argument would be exactly as above with a (specific) child substituted for the name "Mary", but the final conclusion would have been:

Some children are taller than Sue

The rules would not, however, have allowed a second substitution for the same existential quantifier in another premise. Hence, the premises:

Mary is taller than some children
Sue is shorter than some children

would not permit the conclusion "Mary is taller than Sue" for the very good reason that the "some children" referred to in each premise might be different children.

As with propositional logic, the predicate calculus provides a means for formal proof of arguments and is not in itself intended as a psychological theory of reasoning.

FORM OF THE BOOK

We have now explained the objectives of research on deductive reasoning and the major theoretical approaches and issues. We have also introduced sufficient principles of logic for the time being, but further specifics will be presented where they are relevant to the tasks under review.

The following chapters are organised in order to attain our objective of eclectic and balanced coverage of both experimental findings and theoretical explanations. Chapters 2–5 are all concerned with reasoning that can be discussed within a framework of propositional logic in which quantifiers and relations are not introduced. In Chapter 2, we discuss studies of conditional reasoning which involve asking people to make various inferences from conditional statements, or which involve them in constructing or evaluating truth tables. In Chapter 3, we present in some detail the two major theories of deductive competence in conditional reasoning—based upon formal rules and mental models—and assess their ability to account for psychological findings on conditional reasoning in general, including biases and content effects.

Chapter 4 is devoted to the Wason selection task, which involves the logic of conditionals but is also a hypothesis testing task. This is the single most investigated problem in the recent history of work on the psychology of reasoning and hence easily justifies a chapter of its own. Since the theory of reasoning by pragmatic reasoning schemas has mostly been investigated using selection task experiments, detailed presentation and evaluation of this theory is included in this chapter along with other pragmatic approaches such as social contract theory. Our review of research on propositional reasoning is completed by a survey of the interesting, though much less intensively researched topic of disjunctive reasoning in Chapter 5. Here we consider a number of parallels with research on conditional reasoning of the type reviewed in Chapter 2.

In Chapter 6, we look at relational reasoning, most of which is concerned with transitive inference both in explicit reasoning tasks and in text comprehension and recall. We consider rival theories based upon linguistic and spatial representations and examine a variety of sources of evidence which bear on different issues in this theoretical debate, such as whether or not premises are integrated into a single mental model. This chapter also includes coverage of studies which asked subjects to draw inferences from statements concerning the spatial relationships of objects, and ends with a consideration of individual differences in reasoning strategies.

Chapters 7 and 8 are concerned with reasoning with syllogisms and other types of quantified statements. Chapter 7 focuses on theories of syllogistic reasoning and discusses a range of experimental evidence which has been presented in order to distinguish one account from another. Chapter 8 includes discussion of the belief bias effect in syllogistic reasoning as well as discussion of alternative reasoning tasks, including the use of problems with multiple quantifiers.

In Chapter 9, we attempt an overview and synthesis of the material contained in the main review chapters of the book. First, we concentrate on the phenomena, summarising the evidence for deductive competence, the nature of errors in reasoning and the influence of prior knowledge. Next, we summarise the current state of theory in the psychology of deduction and the prospects for its development and integration. Finally, we discuss the role of reasoning research in the context of the current debate about human rationality.

2 Conditional Reasoning

If is a two-letter word that has fascinated philosophers for centuries and has stimulated equal interest in the more recently developed disciplines of linguistics and cognitive psychology. The conditional construction *if . . . then . . .* seems to epitomise the very essence of reasoning. The use of the conditional *if* requires the listener to make suppositions, to entertain hypotheses or to consider once or future possible worlds. If some particular condition was, is, could be or might one day be met, then some particular consequence is deemed to follow.

It is perhaps unsurprising then that the study of conditional reasoning with statements of the form *if p then q* (and to a lesser extent *p only if q*) has formed a major part of the cognitive psychology of deductive reasoning which requires three full chapters of the current volume for adequate treatment. Much of the study of conditional reasoning has utilised a single paradigm known as the Wason selection task. Research into this task is fully covered in Chapter 4. Here we consider the nature of conditional reasoning and review experimental studies which use methods other than the selection task. In Chapter 3, we will review a major theoretical debate concerning the nature of human propositional reasoning: this contrasts inference rule and mental models theory.

As already indicated, the topic of conditional reasoning is of equal interest in logic and linguistics (see Traugott, ter Meulen, Reilly & Ferguson, 1986). While our primary interest here is in experimental psychological studies of conditional reasoning, it is necessary for us to consider first some background on the logical and linguistic nature of *if*.

CONDITIONALS IN LOGIC AND LANGUAGE

Let us first consider the treatment of conditional statements in standard propositional logic. Logicians are wont to distinguish *if*, meaning *if p then q*, from *iff*, read as *if and only if p then q*, and sometimes referred to as a biconditional. These two relations are then represented logically by truth tables for material implication ($p \supset q$) and material equivalence ($p \leftrightarrow q$), respectively (see Table 2.1). The standard logic of the propositional calculus, introduced in Chapter 1, is a "two value logic", since it assumes that all propositions are either true or false. Thus, *if p then q* is false in the case where *p* is true and *q* is false (i.e. TF) and otherwise true, whereas *iff p then q* (i.e. *if and only if p then q*) is false in this case and also in the case where *p* is false and *q* is true (FT).

Consider the example

If the ignition key is turned then the engine runs

If we interpret this sentence as a material implication, then the statement can be falsified only by observing the situation where the key is turned and the engine is not running. However, if we interpret the statement as an equivalence, we assume that the engine running also implies that the key is turned. In this case, the statement would also be falsified by the situation where the engine is running and the key is not turned.

TABLE 2.1
Four Possible Truth Tables for a Conditional Statement, *if p then q*

pq	*Material Implication*	*Material Equivalence*	*Defective Implication*	*Defective Equivalence*
TT	T	T	T	T
TF	F	F	F	F
FT	T	F	I	F
FF	T	T	I	I

T = True, F = False, I = Indeterminate or Irrelevant.

TABLE 2.2
Four Conditional Inferences

Inference	*Abbreviation*	*First Premise*	*Second Premise*	*Conclusion*
Modus Ponens	MP	If p then q	p	q
Denial of the Antecedent	DA	If p then q	not-p	not-q
Affirmation of the Consequent	AC	If p then q	q	p
Modus Tollens	MT	If p then q	not-q	not-p

Another way of looking at the logic of the above example is to consider the inferences that we might or might not be prepared to make, according to our knowledge of the state of either the ignition key or the engine. There are four classical inferences associated with conditionals, of which two—Modus Ponens (MP) and Modus Tollens (MT)—were met in Chapter 1. The other two, known as Denial of the Antecedent (DA) and Affirmation of the Consequent (AC), are shown in Table 2.2 in a general form. In the case of the above statement, these would read:

MP The key is turned, therefore the engine is running
DA The key is not turned, therefore the engine is not running
AC The engine is running, therefore the key is turned
MT The engine is not running, therefore the key is not turned

Using truth table analysis, we can demonstrate formally that a rule of material implication will support the MP and MT inferences, but not the DA and AC inferences which are, for this reason, often referred to as fallacious inferences. We do this by identifying the false case in the truth table which must not occur if we assume the statement is true. This is the case TF, i.e. a turned key together with an engine that is not running. Hence, if we assume that the key is turned, the engine must be running (MP), and if the engine is not running the key cannot have been turned (MT). Neither DA nor AC follow from this truth table, however. If the key is not turned, then the rule can still hold whether or not the engine runs (FT and FF). Similarly, if the engine is running, the rule holds true whether or not the key is turned (TT and FT).

Under a truth table for material equivalence, however, all four inferences would be valid. This is because the AC and DA inferences are effectively MP and MT for the converse conditional, *if q then p*, which is assumed to hold in addition to *if p then q*. In terms of the truth table, the rule is now incompatible with the situation in which the key is not turned and the engine is running (FT). Hence, if it is not turned, the engine must not be running (DA) and, if the engine is running, the key must be turned (AC). Of course, in natural language we rarely use the form *if and only if*, so it is arguable that a biconditional or equivalence reading may be implicitly made by the listener and account for any tendency for people to draw the classically fallacious DA and AC inferences. We return to this point below.

Implication and equivalence relationships can be understood further by reference to the notion of *necessary* and *sufficient* conditions. If *p* implies *q*, then this means that *p* is a sufficient condition for *q*, i.e. *q must* occur if *p* does. It also means that *q* is a necessary condition for *p*, i.e. *p cannot* occur unless *q* does. When an equivalence or biconditional relationship holds, it means that *p* is both a sufficient and a necessary condition for *q* (and vice versa).

The treatment of conditionals via material implication and equivalence in standard propositional logic is neither linguistically nor psychologically adequate for many reasons. One difficulty arises from the proposal that conditionals with false antecedents (i.e. in the cases FT and FF) are true. This works for the purposes of truth table analysis, but is psychologically implausible and leads to anomalies. Who, for example, would consider (in the year 1993) the statement

> If Mrs Thatcher is Prime Minister then Britain will leave the European Community

to be true in virtue of the knowledge that the antecedent is false? One would be more likely to regard it as meaningless. A more subtle problem arises with the evaluation of natural conditionals such as:

> If the animal is a bird then it can fly

where most people would happily agree that the statement is verified by the case of a bird, such as a sparrow, that flies, and falsified by discovery of one such as an ostrich that cannot. What, however, of animals that are not birds? As Wason (1966) has suggested, the statement seems to be irrelevant in such cases rather than true. Thus Wason suggests that a psychologically plausible truth table for a conditional is that of "defective" implication (Table 2.1). Conditionals which are read as equivalences will, of course, appear relevant in the case FT, since this is a falsifier, but may still be seen as *irrelevant* if neither the antecedent nor consequent is true. This case might be termed "defective equivalence". For example, with a biconditional reading of our first example, you might think the rule is confirmed by observation of the key being turned and the engine running (TT), falsified when either the key is turned and the engine is not running (TF) or vice versa (FT), but irrelevant rather than true when both switch and light are off. Wason's proposal can be read as an argument that people use a three-value logic for conditionals. The statement may be true or false, or it may simply not apply in the current circumstances.

Conditionals are used in many ways in natural language, common examples of which are shown in Table 2.3. The usage which appears to have most in common with the logician's notion of material implication is that of the *contingent universal*, such as:

> If the molecule is water then it contains oxygen

which states the universal occurrence of a *q* with a *p*, without temporal or causal connotations. This type of conditional is also known as a definitional. Of course, we can still argue for a defective implication truth table, i.e. that the statement is irrelevant to non-water molecules. In the above case, anyone with elementary (!) knowledge of chemistry would take this to be an implication rather than an equivalence, since there are many other molecules that also include the oxygen atom. The following contingent universal might, however, be read as an equivalence:

If the element is hydrogen then it has the atomic number 1

by implicit knowledge of the fact that elements have unique atomic numbers.

Most other uses of conditionals in natural language, such as the examples shown in Table 2.3, are ones in which the antecedent and consequent refer to events which have a temporal sequence and often a causal connection as well. Thus we frequently use a conditional to express the notion that if one event occurs, then another will occur as a consequence. For example:

If water is heated above 100 degrees Celsius then it will boil

While the above example can be stated as an abstract scientific principle, many temporal/causal statements occur in the context of conversations. From a linguistic point of view, it is useful to distinguish further these as promises, threats, advice, warnings and so on, since the implications will depend upon the common assumptions of the participants (Grice, 1975; Sperber & Wilson, 1986). It has been argued by Geis and Zwicky (1971) and others that many such contexts carry with them *invited* inferences, such as Denial of the Antecedent, which are not logically implied but which are appropriate in context. For example, consider a conditional promise from a parent to a child such as:

If you pass your examinations then I will buy you a bicycle

While logically the speaker could intend to buy the child a bicycle in any event, the presumption must be that if the examinations are not passed then the bicycle will not be bought. If this (DA) inference were not intended, then the speaker would have violated the principle of *relevance*

TABLE 2.3
Examples of Conditional Statements

Contingent universal	If the animal is a fish then it is cold-blooded
Temporal/causal	If the glass is dropped then it will break
Advice	If you work hard then you will do well in life
Promise	If you clear up your toys then I will give you an ice cream
Threat	If you do that again I'll hit you
Warning	If you break the speed limit here the police will catch you
Counterfactual	If I had made some putts I would have won easily
Non-truth functional	If you want a good book to read there is one on the table

(Sperber & Wilson, 1986). Why attach a condition to your promise if fulfilment of the condition is not necessary?

Two other types of conditional are worth a brief mention, although little psychological work has been done with them. One is the counterfactual statement which invites listeners to reason about a once, but no longer possible, world. For example:

> If the Argentinians had not invaded the Falkland Islands then Margaret Thatcher would have lost the next general election

The other is a non-truth functional conditional such as:

> If you want a cup of tea there is one in the pot

In the above case you could not reasonably interpret the desire for a cup of tea to imply the presence of one in the pot. However, like other conditionals the statement is one where the consequent assertion will be relevant only if the antecedent is true. The speaker is hypothesising that you may be thirsty and providing information—and implicit hospitality—that will be relevant to you if this hypothesis is correct.

The point that we are trying to convey, prior to a review of the psychological research on conditional reasoning, is that the use of *if* in natural language is a good deal more complex than the treatment of *if* as material implication in textbook logic. Where the propositional calculus allows two truth values, people may have three—seeing the conditional statement as sometimes irrelevant to the case under consideration. Also, where logic prescribes that certain inferences are always valid and others fallacious, the implications that a speaker may convey to a listener with a conditional statement may vary according to context, the rules of conversational exchange and the tacit assumptions that are shared in the dialogue. For these reasons, we do not follow the practice of describing reasoning data as yielding right and wrong answers, as though formal logic were an undisputed authority of good and bad reasoning. If we want to understand how and why people draw the inferences we do, then we must be aware of the ways in which they might use and understand conditional statements in everyday life.

STUDIES OF CONDITIONAL INFERENCES

Psychological research on conditional reasoning has been conducted largely within three main paradigms. First, a number of studies have examined the frequency with which people accept each of the four basic conditional inferences shown in Table 2.2. We will describe these as conditional inference tasks, although these problems are sometimes also known as conditional syllogisms. Here, the method involves giving people a conditional statement together with a premise and asking them either to evaluate a conclusion, to choose from a list of possible conclusions or simply to draw any conclusion they wish. The second main paradigm involves the study of people's understanding of the logic of conditionals via the construction or evaluation of truth tables. In the construction task, they are asked to produce cases which make the statement true or false; in the evaluation task, they are given a conditional together with examples of each possible truth table case and asked to judge the truth of the rule. The third paradigm involves a task invented by Wason (1966) and generally known as the selection task. The selection task and its many psychological studies are the subject of discussion in Chapter 4.

We will review research using the first two paradigms in the current chapter, and focus initially on studies using abstract or arbitrary problem content. By this we mean materials which do not directly invoke prior knowledge or belief by the use of content and context. In this section, we consider studies which have presented experimental subjects with the opportunity to make the inferences MP, DA, AC and MT shown in Table 2.2, using abstract or arbitrary problem content. As well as discussing the basic inference patterns in adults, we also look briefly at conditional reasoning in children. Finally, we consider the effect of linguistic variations of the conditional rule form by the introduction of negative components and by the use of the alternative *p only if q* phrasing of the conditional.

Basic Inference Patterns and Their Interpretation

Do adult subjects have the competence to make the Modus Ponens and Modus Tollens inferences, and do they fall prey to the fallacies of Affirming the Consequent and Denying the Antecedent? A significant number of studies have addressed these questions head on by presenting subjects with examples of these arguments and asking them whether they are valid. Typically, authors have then scored their subjects by the number of logical errors made. For reasons indicated above, we will avoid this practice and instead present the basic frequencies with which all kinds of inference are made or endorsed.

The results from a relevant set of studies are summarised in Table 2.4. The studies have been selected (and some selectively reported) such that they have broad similarities in procedure. Specifically, adults subjects are used (typically college students) and the task presentation is broadly similar. The subjects are normally given the premises and the conclusions and asked whether it follows, or else given a list of conclusions including the normal one and "nothing follows" to choose from. All these studies involve either so-called "abstract" problem materials or ones which are

TABLE 2.4
Frequency (%) of Endorsement of Conditional Inferences for Affirmative *if p then q* Rules by Adult Subjects in Various Studies

Study	*n*	*MP*	*DA*	*AC*	*MT*
Taplin (1971)	56	92	52	57	63
Evans (1977a)	16	100	69	75	75
Wildman and Fletcher (1977)[a]	39	95	51	36	62
Marcus and Rips (1979)					
Experiment 1 – 3 choice	18	100	21	23	57
Experiment 1 – 2 choice	36	99	31	29	62
Experiment 2	24	98	21	33	52
Kern, Mirels and Hinshaw (1983)					
Abstract material	72	89	28	27	41
Concrete material	72	100	17	28	69
Rumain et al (1983)[a]					
Experiment 1	24	98	48	54	81
Experiment 2	24	100	73	65	63
Markovits (1988)	76	100	52	42	59

[a]Adult control group data from developmental studies.

concrete but arbitrary, so that prior beliefs and pragmatic associations are not likely to be cued. Such rules might be:

If the letter is an A then the number is a 3

or

If Mary is in Paris then Julia is in London

but not

If the switch is turned then the light is on

In this last example, reasoning is likely to be influenced by *pragmatic* factors, meaning associated knowledge or prior belief. We are likely to hold *a priori* theories about the connection between switches and lights, whereas we could have no such preconceptions about the locations of unknown people like Mary and Julia.

As we can see, there are considerable variations between studies. Modus Ponens is made almost universally but drops as low as 89% in one of the experiments. Modus Tollens is clearly the more difficult inference, being made less often than Modus Ponens in all studies reported and with rates varying from 41 to 81%. Of particular theoretical interest are the relative rates of the two fallacies, DA and AC, which might be expected to occur with equal frequency if they reflect subjects adopting an equivalence interpretation of the rule. In fact, the overall inference rates are fairly similar, with AC occurring more often in six of the experiments listed and DA more often in five. The absolute rates of these inferences are, however, highly variable across studies, ranging from 23 to 75% for DA and from 41 to 81% for MT. One possible explanation for the large variability between studies is the use of arbitrary problem content for which people do not have established, stable tendencies to make these inferences. Hence, the precise presentation of the task may be crucial.

The importance of apparently small procedural changes is illustrated in the study of Taplin and Staudenmayer (1973), who got quite different results according to whether subjects were asked to rate conclusions as either "true or false" or also given intermediate "sometimes true/false" choices. This methodological issue was taken up in a recent paper by Dugan and Revlin (1990), who argued that the relatively high rate of endorsement of the indeterminate problems (DA and AC) might be due to the use of the response option "sometimes true" for rating conclusions in many studies, and that the existentially neutral "could be true" was a more accurate response choice. They found that subjects were more likely to choose "could be true" than "sometimes true", and when given both options gave considerably more indeterminate conclusions to DA and AC problems than when given only the "sometimes true" option. While other findings by Dugan and Revlin complicated the interpretation, their study graphically illustrates the influence that procedural variation can have on responding.

The variability between studies obviously limits the conclusions that we can draw from Table 2.4. However, it is clear—and unsurprising—that Modus Ponens is made almost universally, whereas the equally valid Modus Tollens is much less often endorsed. We should perhaps not be too surprised that the overall level of the so-called fallacies of DA and AC varies a lot between studies, since procedural variation could easily affect the perception of the statements as implications or equivalences. The overall finding of roughly equal frequency seems safe enough, since inspection of the table reveals that although differences occur either way within individual studies, the margins are rarely large.

A number of authors have assumed that responses to the four conditional syllogisms would reveal a tendency in their subjects to conditional (implication) or biconditional (equivalence) readings of *if*, and thus have presented their data in terms of the frequency of two patterns: endorsement of Modus Ponens and Modus Tollens only, or endorsement of all four inferences (Marcus & Rips, 1979; Rips & Marcus, 1977; Staudenmayer, 1975; Staudenmayer & Bourne, 1978; Taplin, 1971; Taplin & Staudenmayer, 1973). However, typically only around 50% of subjects produce an inference pattern that is *truth-functional*, i.e. consistently in line with either an implication or equivalence truth table. The reason for this is immediately apparent when we examine the overall frequencies of the four inferences in Table 2.4. If reasoning were truth-functional, then all subjects should endorse the MP and MT inferences, while a smaller but equal number (those interpreting the rule as a biconditional) should endorse all four inferences. The glaring exception to this pattern is the Modus Tollens inference, which is drawn only around 60% of the time across the various studies.

We can construct a modified version of the hypothesis of truth-functional reasoning which distinguishes between subjects' *competence* in reasoning, which is their ideal behaviour given their understanding of logic, and their *performance*, which is influenced by cognitive constraints such as working memory limitations. According to this view, subjects are truth-functional in principle, but the less immediate Modus Tollens inference is not always made due to performance factors. As illustrated in Chapter 1, most reasoning theories can account for Modus Tollens being more difficult than Modus Ponens. However, this revised hypothesis does *not* fit the data shown in Table 1.4 either. On this view, the AC rate would indicate the true frequency of biconditional readings, since Affirmation of the Consequent is Modus Ponens for the converse rule *if q then p* and MP is universally made. Since Denial of the Antecedent is then a Modus Tollens for the converse rule, it should occur at a rate about 60% of the AC rate instead of at an equal rate.

All the studies considered so far tested for single conditional inferences in isolation, and inference rule theorists (e.g. Braine, 1978; Rips, 1983) normally assume that when sequences of inferences are required, then these are simply achieved by combining individual inferences. However, the one study which actually investigated sequences of conditional inferences showed that inference rates in sequences are not predictable from the simple inference rates in isolation. Byrne (1989a) compared a sequence such as:

If she works hard then she will leave work early
If she leaves work early then she will eat out
She worked hard

with the combination of two separate simple inferences:

If she works hard then she will leave work early
She worked hard

and

If she leaves work early then she will eat out
She left work early

Byrne found that subjects spontaneously produced more inferences from the transitive sequence than from the separated premises, as predicted, since the sequence can be represented in a unified mental representation, such as a mental model. She also compared arguments based on transitive and atransitive sequences, using a variety of combinations of the MP, DA, AC and MT inferences, and found that the atransitive sequences, which cannot be integrated into a single model, lead to the same amount or fewer inferences than the separated premises. Byrne (1989a) proposed that these findings present problems for a theory of reasoning based on the application of inference rules, and we will consider this claim in the next chapter.

The main findings reviewed in this section suggest that the frequency of endorsement of conditional inferences in adult subjects cannot be accounted for in terms of the implication/equivalence ambiguity even when allowance is made for performance factors. We will return to this issue later in the chapter. The findings of Byrne (1989a) on reasoning with conditional sequences give ground for further caution in the interpretation of conditional inference rates studied in isolation. Her findings suggest that when conditionals are used in natural discourse, the inferences drawn will be more than the sum of the parts, and may reflect the mental representations that subjects construct of the text as a whole.

Development Studies of Conditional Inferences

The focus of this book is on deductive reasoning in adult subjects, and we do not intend to provide any depth of coverage of studies of children's reasoning. For example, a large number of such studies have been conducted within the paradigms of the Geneva School derived from the work of Jean Piaget, which are in an entirely different tradition from the research on adult reasoning. However, a small number of studies have administered the conditional inference paradigm to children, often with adult control groups included. Since these studies shed some light on the issue addressed in the above section—namely people's basic competence in conditional reasoning—a brief review is in order here.

The data for a set of studies testing conditional inferences in children are shown in Table 2.5. Although the base rate levels vary between studies—presumably due to procedural variations—some general developmental trends are apparent. MP is not universally endorsed by very young children, although the frequency rises quickly towards the near 100% observed with adults. Both DA and AC inferences are endorsed with high frequency in young children with a dropping developmental trend towards the adult rate.

The rate of Modus Tollens is particularly interesting, with apparently contradictory results between studies and differing opinions in the literature. Some researchers (e.g. Kodroff & Roberge, 1975) report improved MT reasoning in older children and claim that this is a usual finding,

TABLE 2.5
Frequency (%) of Endorsement of Conditional Inferences for Affirmative *if p then q* Rules by Child and Adult Subjects in Various Studies

Study	*Age (years)*	*n*	*MP*	*DA*	*AC*	*MT*	*Comments*
Roberge (1970)	9	57	64	83	81	52	
	11	57	62	83	81	47	
	13	57	89	95	88	76	
	15	57	90	78	66	69	
Kodroff and Roberge (1975)	6	12	74	—	—	51	Verbal mode
	7	12	74	—	—	57	of presentation
	8	12	80	—	—	75	
Wildman and Fletcher (1977)	13	45	87	82	84	75	
	15	116	89	72	78	60	
	17	81	92	53	65	59	
	Adult	81	95	51	36	62	
Rumain et al. (1983)							
Experiment 1	10	44	100	81	99	96	Simple premises
	Adult	24	98	48	54	81	
Experiment 2	7	34	96	57	68	52	
	10	20	100	80	82	70	Single premises
	Adult	24	100	73	65	63	

whereas others (e.g. Wildman & Fletcher, 1977) claim that a paradoxical *decline* in MT is the usual result. The effect may well depend to an extent on the age of the children studied, since the relationship may be curvilinear, with MT endorsement increasing up to the age of around 10–12 years and then declining again, as suggested for example by the data of Rumain, Connell and Braine (1983, experiment 2).

One explanation of the high DA and AC rates in young children which is commonly offered is that they are interpreting the rule as a biconditional or equivalence. However, as with adult subjects, this explanation does not rest too comfortably with the rate of MT inferences, especially in view of the "paradoxical" finding in many studies that MT rates are higher in certain age groups than in adult subjects. A more likely possibility which can also explain the MT finding is that young children interpret the conditional statement *If p then q* as an existential conjunction *There is a p and a q*. As Rumain et al. (1983) put it, "Most children and some adults do well on Modus Tollens problems . . . because they accept the invited inference: they reason that *p* and *q* 'go together' and that *not p* and *not q* go together."

There is some evidence from other tasks that children do not understand the conditional nature of *if*. For example, Paris (1973) asked children to rate the four truth table cases TT, TF, FT and FF as true or false, and found that on conditionals young children tended to rate TT as true and all other cases as false. This is the truth table pattern for the conjunctive rule *p and q*. Further evidence comes from a paradigm presented by Kuhn (1977) and developed by O'Brien et al. (1989). In O'Brien and co-workers' version, children are shown four boxes containing a toy cat and a banana, a toy dog and an orange, a toy dog and an apple, and a toy horse and an apple. The boxes are closed, shuffled and one chosen at random. The subjects then have to rate the truth of a set of conditional statements. The error discovered by Kuhn occurs with a sentence of the type "If there is an apple in the box then there is a horse", which was correctly rated as "false" by only 5% of 7-year-olds and 15% of 10-year-olds, compared with 75% of adults in their experiment 1. The statement would appear true if the children are reading it as the existential, "There is a box which contains an apple and a horse". As a conditional, it should of course be regarded as false, owing to the presence of a box with an apple but a dog instead of a horse (the TF case).

Most authors in the developmental literature are influenced by the Piagetian theory that competence for abstract logical reasoning develops during adolescence (Inhelder & Piaget, 1958) and are thus broadly in the mental logic or inference rules camp (see Chapter 1). For example, in a series of papers, O'Brien and Overton (1980; 1982; Overton, Byrne & O'Brien, 1985) have argued that logical training will only be effective in older children who have the capacity for abstract thought. They used a contradiction training paradigm based upon the paper of Wason (1964). Subjects are invited to make a DA inference and are then shown a counter-example to the fallacy. O'Brien et al. looked at the effects of such contradiction training not only on the conditional inference task itself, but on subsequently presented conditional reasoning tasks such as truth table evaluation and the Wason selection task. O'Brien et al. found that performance on both the inference and the transfer tasks was facilitated by contradiction training for adult subjects and the oldest (grade 12) children, but not for children in various groups between the ages of around 8–14 years.

O'Brien and co-workers' findings are more informative about the growth of logical competence than are the basic inference rate data themselves (Table 2.5), whose interpretation is problematical. However, the fact that older children and adults can benefit from contradiction training provides no evidence in itself that the competence is based upon a mental logic of the kind envisaged by Piaget. If we suppose that the older reasoners have developed, for example, the ability to reason by manipulation of mental models, then the provision of contradictory examples would provide a prompt to look more carefully for counterexample models—an intrinsic part of the theory—which in turn would benefit performance on all the logical tasks employed.

These developmental studies confirm some of the conclusions drawn from our review of conditional reasoning in adults. Thus Modus Ponens is very easy from about the age of 12 onwards, and consistently easier than Modus Tollens. The tendency to endorse the classically fallacious DA and AC inferences is also present, and indeed more marked in children than adults. The main developmental finding appears to be that young children have difficulty grasping the conditional nature of *if p then q* and tend to read it as a conjunction.

Reasoning with Negated Conditionals

All the studies considered so far have used affirmative conditionals of the form *if p then q*. It is possible to produce three other conditionals by negating either the antecedent or consequent component or both. These negated conditionals occur quite naturally in everyday language as the following examples show:

If the engine is OK then the warning light will not come on — *If p then not q*
If it doesn't rain then we will go out for a picnic — *If not p then q*
If you don't hurry then you won't get there in time — *If not p then not q*

The usual four conditional inferences can be constructed for each of these rules by altering the negations within the premises and conclusion (Table 2.6). For example, we might reason that if the warning light comes on then the engine is not OK (MT), or that if we hurry then we will get there in time (DA) and so on.

It turns out that the inferences that human subjects make are substantially affected by the presence of negative components. This was first discovered by Roberge (1971; 1974), although his analysis and presentation of the data did not illustrate clearly the trends which emerge in later

TABLE 2.6
Conditional Inference for Rules with Negated Components

Rule	*MP*		*DA*		*AC*		*MT*	
	Given	*Conclude*	*Given*	*Conclude*	*Given*	*Conclude*	*Given*	*Conclude*
If p then q	p	q	not-p	not-q	q	p	not-q	not-p
If p then not q	p	not-q	not-p	q	not-q	p	q	not-p
If not p then q	not-p	q	p	not-q	q	not-p	not-q	p
If not p then not q	not-p	not-q	p	q	not-q	not-p	q	p

studies (Evans, 1972; 1977a; Pollard & Evans, 1980; Wildman & Fletcher, 1977). For example, Evans (1977a) gave subjects problems with the appropriate conclusions as shown in Table 2.6, using a problem format such as the following:

Given: (1) If the letter is not G then the number is 9
(2) The number is not 9
Conclusion: The letter is G

The example shown is Modus Tollens for the rule *if not p then q*. Subjects were required to indicate whether or not the conclusion necessarily followed from the premises. One finding was that subjects made more MT inferences on rules with affirmative antecedents than negative ones. More generally, with the exception of Modus Ponens—which is almost always endorsed—all inferences are made more often on rules where the conclusion stated is negative rather than affirmative (see Table 2.7, Fig. 2.1). This tendency was labelled as *negative conclusion bias* by Pollard and Evans (1980).

This is the first of a number of "biases" that have been identified in the deductive reasoning literature, so we should clarify what we mean by the

TABLE 2.7
Frequency (%) of Conditional Inferences on Negated Rules in Several Studies (Adult Subjects)

Rule	*n*	*MP*	*DA*	*AC*	*MT*
If p then q					
Evans (1977a)	16	100	69[a]	75	75[a]
Wildman and Fletcher (1977)	81	95	51[a]	36	62[a]
Pollard and Evans (1980, exp. 1)	40	—	54[a]	66	59[a]
If p then not q					
Evans (1977a)	16	100[a]	12	31	56[a]
Wildman and Fletcher (1977)	81	97[a]	21	41	69[a]
Pollard and Evans (1980, exp. 1)	40	—	30	37	72[a]
If not p then q					
Evans (1977a)	16	100	50[a]	81[a]	12
Wildman and Fletcher (1977)	81	90	54[a]	69[a]	23
Pollard and Evans (1980, exp. 1)	40	—	47[a]	72[a]	34
If not p then not q					
Evans (1977a)	16	100[a]	19	81[a]	25
Wildman and Fletcher (1977)	81	95[a]	36	49[a]	33
Pollard and Evans (1980, exp. 1)	40	—	37	64[a]	44

[a]Argument has a negated conclusion.

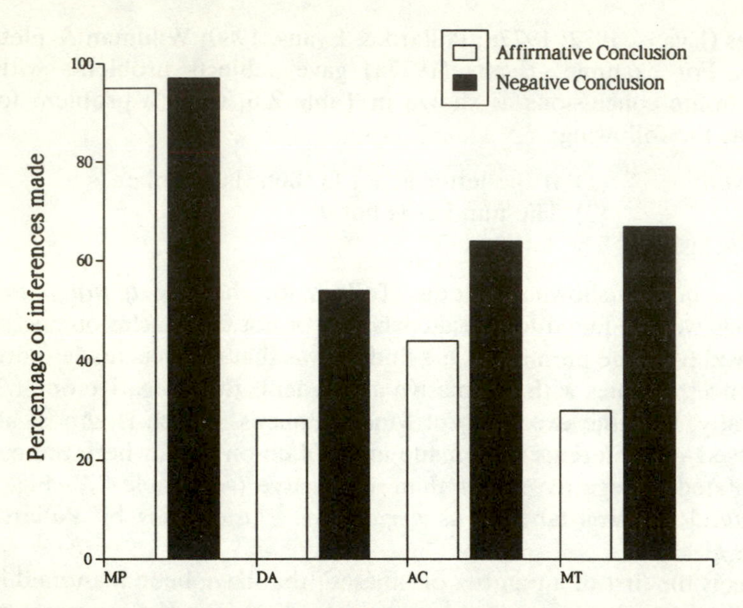

FIG. 2.1 Graphical illustration of negative conclusion bias. Based on weighted averages of data shown in Table 2.7.

term. A bias is a systematic error, relative to the normative model provided by formal logic. Thus accepting more negative than affirmative conclusions, regardless of the logic, is an example of responding which is systematically related to a logically irrelevant feature of the task. However, our use of the term is descriptive and does not beg theoretical issues. It does not, for example, presume that subjects are failing to reason or are reasoning badly. It is simply a phenomenon for reasoning theorists to explain.

The obvious explanation for negative conclusion bias, however, is that it is a response bias. Pollard and Evans (1980), for example, proposed the use of a caution heuristic. They noted that while a statement such as "The letter is a G" is true for only one letter and false for 25, the negative statement "The letter is not a G" can be falsified in only one way but verified in many ways. Hence, perhaps when in doubt, subjects prefer to make a weaker, less falsifiable conclusion. The idea of a caution heuristic originates with the interpretation of syllogistic reasoning data provided by Sells (1936).

Before moving on, we note circumstances in which the negative conclusion bias is *not* observed. First, there is a curious finding concerning negative conclusion bias that is reported by Evans and Brooks (1981). Under a standard control condition, they replicated the bias for DA, AC and MT inferences. However, when subjects were asked to perform concurrent articulation with a working memory load (following the method of Baddeley & Hitch, 1974), the bias disappeared, even though the overall rate of making each inference was unchanged. The effects of competing tasks on reasoning are, however, very unclear (see Brooks, 1984).

Of more general importance is some sporadic evidence that negative conclusion bias disappears when reasoning with semantically rich material, in contrast with the abstract problem materials used in the studies considered here. Fillenbaum (1975), for example, studied Denial of the Antecedent inferences with conditional threats and promises such as "If you mow the lawn then I will pay you five dollars." The introduction of negative components into either component of the conditional had no effect on inference rates. In the study of conditional sequences by Byrne (1989a), discussed earlier, negated components were also used in order to create intransitive sequences. Although Byrne does analyse the data for negative conclusion bias (which is any case controlled across the comparisons she makes), inspection of her tables provides little evidence of its presence. Again, however, her materials were thematic; in this case of the causal–temporal kind.

It appears that the introduction of pragmatics may override a simple syntactic bias found with abstract materials. Comparable evidence has been found for a separate effect called "matching bias" discussed later in this chapter and in Chapter 4.

If and *only if*

Surprising though it may seem, the statement *p only if q* is another way of expressing the relation "*p* implies *q*" and is thus logically equivalent to *if p then q*. Both forms share the same truth table in propositional logic whereby they are false only if we have the case *p* and *not-q*. For example, consider these two assertions:

If the animal is a fish then it has gills
The animal is a fish only if it has gills

In either case, the statement can only be falsified by observation of a fish without gills. Both statements also support the same two valid inferences:

The animal is a fish, therefore it has gills (MP)
The animal does not have gills, therefore it is not a fish (MT)

There are clear linguistic differences between the two forms which we will come to shortly. Evans (1977a) tested conditional inferences for *only if* as well as *if then* statements, again permuting the presence of negative components. Negative conclusion bias was demonstrated on *if then* rules but there was no evidence for the bias on the *only if* rules. This may, however, have been due to a lack of statistical power, as Roberge (1978) demonstrated the effect for both *only if* and *if then* rules in a replication study.

Evans (1977a) also found significant differences in the rate of the four inferences made on the *if then* and *only if* forms using abstract materials. Specifically, subjects drew more Modus Ponens inferences with the *if then* form and more Affirmation of the Consequent and Modus Tollens inferences with the *only if* form. The AC difference may reflect some tendency to convert *p only if q* into *if q then p*, but the other trends are more interesting. Evans hypothesised that the two forms might be used in natural language to express the different aspects of implication. Specifically, he argued that *if then* emphasises the sufficiency of the antecedent (hence facilitating Modus Ponens), whereas *only if* emphasises the necessity of the consequent (hence facilitating Modus Tollens). For example, consider the logically equivalent statements given above.

The *if then* form appears to invite the Modus Ponens inference, since knowing that the animal is a fish is a sufficient condition for inferring that it has gills, whereas the *only if* form draws attention to the necessity of possessing gills if something is to be a fish, i.e. it cannot be a fish if it does *not* have gills (Modus Tollens). It may, however, be the case that the *if then* form encourages forward (antecedent to consequent) rather than backward inferences. Evans and Beck (1981), using a rather unusual procedure to manipulate temporal orders (discussed below), found that both MP and DA were made significantly more often on *if then* than *only if* rules, whereas AC and MT were made significantly more often when the rule was in the *only if* form. Roberge (1978), who looked only at AC and MT inferences, provides a further replication in that these occurred more frequently for *only if* rules. The data from these three studies are summarised in Table 2.8.

Johnson-Laird and Byrne (1991) present a mental models theory of conditional reasoning which is discussed in detail in Chapter 3. Their account includes discussion of reasoning with *only if* rules and an explanation of why fewer Modus Ponens and more Modus Tollens inferences occur than with *if then* rules. Essentially, they propose that subjects' initial

TABLE 2.8
Comparative Frequency of Conditional Inferences on *if then* and *only if* Rules

Study	*Rule*	*MP*	*DA*	*AC*	*MT*
Evans (1977a)[a]	IT	100	38	67	42
	OI	76	38	84	59
Evans and Beck (1981)[a]	IT	78	54	53	42
	OI	61	41	80	66
Roberge (1978)	IT	—	—	66	74
	OI	—	—	84	83

[a]Data averaged across rules in which the presence of negated components was permuted.

representation of *if then* includes only the explicit model of the situation where both *p* and *q* occur, whereas their initial representation of *only if* includes explicit modelling of the case where *neither* occur. This is roughly equivalent to the argument that *only if* emphasises the necessity of the consequent—subjects think about the fact that *p* cannot occur without *q*. The mental models theory does not, however, address the finding of more Affirmation of the Consequent inferences with *only if* rules (see Evans, in press).

The striking difference in inference rates between these two rule forms illustrates clearly the role of linguistic factors when logically equivalent variants are used, and reinforces the caution already expressed concerning the assumption that the linguistic *if* should be regarded as a natural expression of material implication. Further interesting differences between the usage of the two forms emerge when temporal factors are considered.

If an event *p* is said to be the cause of the event *q*, then in line with the laws of physics *p* will also occur prior to *q*. Hence, commonly the statement *if p then q* is used to refer to two real-world events that occur in temporal sequence. However, conditionals can be temporal without being causal and logical implications can run counter to the temporal sequence. Whenever an event *q* is a *necessary* condition for an event *p*, then *p* implies *q* even if *q* occurs first in time. Evans (1977a) asked subjects to construct examples of *if then* and *only if* sentences and noticed that they were used differently according to the temporal relations of the implication. For example, subjects would make statements such as the following:

If the train is late then I will miss my appointment
The match will be played only if the weather improves

but not with the alternative syntax:

The train will be late only if I miss my appointment
If the match is played then the weather will have improved

Evans developed the hypothesis that where temporal relations are involved, if the sufficient condition (e.g. a later train) occurs first in time, then the *if then* form will be used, whereas if the necessary condition (e.g. improving weather) occurs first, then the *only if* form will be preferred. Hence *if* is always associated with the earlier temporal event and *only* is used to modify the logical implication when required. This was tested in two studies reported by Evans and Newstead (1977) using the conditional inference task described in the next section and by Evans and Beck (1981) using a conditional inference task. In each case, non-causal temporal statements were used which were in either *if then* or *only if* syntax and either forward or backward temporal order. For example, an *only if*, backward order sentence used by Evans and Newstead (1977) was as follows:

The second letter is a B only if the first letter is a T

where "first" and "second" referred to the order of presentation in a two-field tachistiscope. It was predicted that subjects would find a forward order more natural in the *if then* form and backward order more natural in the *only if* form. Evans and Newstead (1977) and Evans and Beck (1981) reported similar findings using the inference task. In either case, analyses of response *latencies* produced a crossover interaction of the type predicted: *if then* rules were processed faster if the time order was forwards and slower if the order was backwards. However, in neither case were the reasoning frequencies affected by temporal order. Presumably, the hypothesised linguistic effect did influence ease of understanding the sentences but had no effect on the reasoning process as such.

Conclusions

We have looked at a number of studies in which subjects are asked to make the four inferences associated with conditional statements. We find overall that Modus Ponens is a very easy inference made most of the time, whereas Modus Tollens is much more difficult. The two fallacies, Denial of the Antecedent and Affirmation of the Consequent, occur with roughly equal frequencies but with considerable variation in the rates reported across different studies. Studies of children's reasoning show a similar pattern except that the fallacies occur more frequently with young children and decline with age. We also saw that two linguistic variables have a marked effect on responding. When negative components are introduced into the rules, the data suggest that subjects will more often endorse a given logical inference when the conclusion is negative rather than affirmative. We also found that phrasing the rule in an *if then* or an *only if* form has a major impact on the frequency of the inferences drawn.

THE CONDITIONAL TRUTH TABLE TASK

While most studies of conditional reasoning have used the inference paradigm discussed above or the Wason selection task to be considered in the next chapter, some research has also involved truth table tasks. The most common form is the truth table evaluation task in which subjects are shown conditional rules along with instances which correspond to the cases TT, FT, FT or FF, and are asked to judge whether the cases conform to the rule, contradict the rule or neither. The task was first used with an explicit third truth category for "irrelevant" or "indeterminate" by Johnson-Laird and Tagart (1969). They found, as hypothesised by Wason (1966), that when implication was expressed by the form *if p then q*, then subjects tended to conform to the defective truth table shown in Table 2.1. Hence,

TT cases are judged "true", TF cases "false" and FT and FF cases as irrelevant.

Evans (1972) replicated this study using a truth table construction task. Subjects were shown an array of coloured shapes and were asked exhaustively to identify cases which made the rule true and cases which made the rule false. Thus any case not selected on either the verification or falsification task could be inferred to be irrelevant without cueing the subject. Evans also introduced the four rules which can be produced by permuting negative components. The effect this has on the task is systematically to rotate the combination of affirmed and negated values of the items in the rule (*p* and *q*) required to produce each truth table case. These patterns are shown in Table 2.9 along with illustrative concrete examples. For simplicity, we use letter–number content as commonly adopted in later studies.

The use of rules with negative components lead to the discovery of one of the major biases in the conditional reasoning literature, which Evans described as "matching bias". Again, we use the term "bias" to describe systematic attention to a logically irrelevant feature of the task and do not beg any theoretical issues. We emphasise this point, since there is a tendency for some authors to leap from an empirical description of bias to judgements about human rationality. For example, Oaksford and Stenning (1992, p. 849) state baldly that "Matching bias implies that humans are

TABLE 2.9
Truth Table Cases for Conditional Rules with Negative Components Permuted with Concrete Examples of Letter–Number Rules

	Logical Case			
Rule	*TT*	*TF*	*FT*	*FF*
If p then q	pq	p¬q	¬pq	¬p¬q
If the letter is T then the number is 4	T4	T6	G4	H2
If p then not q	p¬q	pq	¬p¬q	¬pq
If the letter is A then the number is not 3	A7	A3	B9	L3
If not p then q	¬pq	¬p¬q	pq	p¬q
If the letter is not D then the number is 7	P7	X1	D7	M7
If not p then not q	¬p¬q	¬pq	p¬q	pq
If the letter is not Y then the number is not 5	E2	U5	Y6	Y5

irrational." This is not, however, an implication that has been drawn by Evans in his recent writing (e.g. 1989) about the phenomenon, nor one that would be accepted, for example, by Johnson-Laird and Byrne (1991), who account for the bias within the same mechanisms of mental model processing that they use to explain deductive competence. We will return to the implications of reasoning biases for human rationality in the final chapter of this volume.

Put simply, matching bias consists of a tendency to prefer to select (or evaluate as *relevant*) items which match the values named in the rule. In the case of the truth table task, items can match on both antecedent and consequent values (*p, q*) match on neither (*not-p, not-q*) or on one or the other (*p, not-q* and *not-p, q*). Thus Evans (1972) noticed than on the falsification task, the correct TF case was identified most often on the rule *if p then not q*, where it constitutes a double match (*p* & *q*), and the least often on the rule *if not p then q*, where it constitutes a double mismatch (*not-p* & *not-q*). For example, on the rule

If the letter is G then the number is not 9

the TF case is a G with a 9, whereas on the rule

If the letter is not G then the number is 9

the TF case is something like B7, i.e. a letter which is not a G together with a number which is not a 9. Subjects are much more likely to think of TF as a falsifying case in the first rule where it involves matching the content of the rule. Similarly, the FT case was frequently given as a falsifying case on the latter rule where it consisted of a double match, and much less often elsewhere and so on.

On the verification task, however, Evans found no matching bias, since most of the subjects chose the TT case on all rules. It appears that the conjunction of a true antecedent with a true consequent is so evidently conveyed by the *if then* form as to be impervious to bias. This observation is supported by the lack of negative conclusion bias for the Modus Ponens inference on studies of conditional inference (see Table 2.7). MP is again based upon the subject thinking of the conjunction of the true antecedent and the true consequent. Curiously, the study of Evans (1972) was not replicated until very recently. Oaksford and Stenning (1992) repeated the study as part of their Experiment 1 and found essentially similar results to those of Evans.

Matching bias has, however, been reported a number of times on a truth table *evaluation* task in which subjects are presented with all logical cases and asked to decide whether each conforms to the rule, contradicts the rule or is irrelevant to it. Evans (1975) demonstrated that a near identical distribution of results could be obtained by use of an evaluation task using the same four rule forms as with the construction task. In other words, subjects describe as *irrelevant* on the evaluation task precisely those cases they would *not* have selected on the construction task. Other demonstrations of matching bias on the evaluation task include those of Evans and Newstead (1977) and several experiments reported by Brooks (1984).

The matching bias effect has also been generalised to *only if* rules by, for example, Evans (1975) and Evans and Newstead (1977). (Matching bias does *not*, however, occur with disjunctive statements of the form *either p or q*: see Chapter 5.) In these studies, when matching cases are compared with the logic of the case controlled, a significant matching bias was observed with both *if then* and *only if* rules. When the logical cases are considered across all four rules (i.e. with matching controlled), the general pattern fits Wason's (1966) hypothesis of a "defective truth table", with TT rated as true, TF as false and more irrelevant ratings being given to the FT and FF cases. However, substantial numbers of subjects do rate FT as a falsifying case, especially on the *only if* form. This suggests that at least some subjects regard the rules as expressing a biconditional or equivalence relationship, a finding compatible with the generally quite high rates of DA and AC inferences found in studies of conditional inferences discussed earlier.

What could be the cause of the matching bias effect? Explanations have been offered within the heuristic/analytic framework of Evans (1983; 1984a; 1989) and within the mental models theory of deductive reasoning (Johnson-Laird & Byrne, 1991). Evans suggests that the linguistic function of negatives affects the comment rather than the topic of a sentence. Whether I say "I am working on my book today" or "I am not working on my book today" I am still talking about the same subject. Thus a rule of the form "If the letter is (not) a T then the number is (not) a 3" is about the T and the 3 whether the negatives are there or not. Evans actually suggests that there are two linguistic cues to *relevance*, i.e. the features of the task to which subjects attend. One of these is associated with *not* and the other with *if*. While *not* directs attention to the proposition it negates, *if* focuses attention on the antecedent condition specified (for related discussions of the nature of *if*, see Braine, 1978; Rips & Marcus, 1977).

What we might term the *if*-heuristic arguably explains a number of the phenomena in conditional reasoning, including the high acceptance rate for Modus Ponens inferences, the common evaluation of TT cases as true on the truth table task, and the almost universal selection of True Antecedent cases on the Wason selection task (see Chapter 4). It can also explain why AC and MT inferences occur more frequently on *only if* rules, where the placement of the word *if* shifts attention towards the consequent of the rule.

The explanation of matching bias offered by Johnson-Laird and Byrne (1991) is again based upon their idea that representations of conditionals are only partially formulated unless fleshed out by further processing. In particular, they suggest that subjects are more likely to include affirmative (matching) than negative (mismatching) cases in their initial stage of mental modelling. A more detailed exposition of their explanation of matching is given in our discussion of the effect on the Wason selection task (Chapter 4).

Some research has tested the explanation of matching bias in terms of the *not*-heuristic directing attention to the propositions denied. In the usual truth table paradigm, truth table cases negate rule values implicitly by providing an alternative value as in the concrete examples shown in Table 2.9. Evans (1983) compared this task with one using explicit negations. For example, given the rule:

If the letter is a B then the number is not a 4

the FT case for the control group might be given as:

The letter is a G and the number is a 7

but for the experimental group would be given as:

The letter is not a B and the number is not a 4

Evans argued that with explicit negations, the conditional sentence and the instance concern the same topic and hence that all instances should appear equally relevant. The experiment showed that the use of explicit inferences substantially and significantly reduced the size of the matching bias effect, but did not remove it altogether.

Oaksford and Stenning (1992) conducted a further investigation of the causes of matching bias. As mentioned above, their first experiment replicated Evans' (1972) findings using his methods of analysis. They also used an alternative measure which they called a "pure matching score", which they claim provides evidence against Evans' theory. A second group in the experiment were given a thematic form of the truth table construction task and showed no matching bias. This could be due to suppression of the bias by realistic content, as has been reported in studies of the Wason selection task (see Chapter 4). Their thematic task, unlike the abstract task, also described cases with the use of explicit negatives—a manipulation which, as we saw above, has been shown to inhibit the bias. Oaksford and Stenning's other experiments used the selection task problem and so will be considered in Chapter 4.

In summary, the truth table task provides evidence for the defective truth table hypothesis, but as with the conditional inference task is very susceptible to linguistic variants in the rules used. Thus significant differences in truth table classification occur between *if then* and *only if* rule forms, just as they did on inference frequencies. The permuting of negative components in conditional rules is also once again the cause of a major bias in responding when abstract content is employed; the negative conclusion bias of the inference task is now replaced by a matching bias. We will return to matching bias and its interpretation in the discussion of the Wason selection task in Chapter 4.

CONDITIONALS IN CONTEXT

While we have discussed conditional reasoning with reference to its natural language usage, all the experimental studies discussed so far have used abstract or arbitrary problem content. Although the effects of content and context in conditional reasoning have received increasing attention in the recent literature, most of this work has been conducted using the Wason selection task. In this section, we will look at effects of context on inference and truth table tasks only. First, we look at some general studies of the influence of content and context on conditional reasoning patterns, and then we will examine some recent studies that have focused specifically on the suppression of conditional inferences by contextual information.

Context and the Interpretation of Conditionals

As we shall see, the way in which people reason with *if* can be manipulated by changing the content—and therefore the meaning—of the antecedent or consequent, or the experimental context in which it appears. Most of the research here builds upon the issues about the linguistic nature of *if* discussed at the outset of this chapter, and in particular addresses the question of whether conditionals are interpreted as conveying implication or equivalence.

Many authors—especially those in the mental logic tradition of Piaget—have attempted to analyse effects of context and content in terms of a conditional or biconditional (equivalence) pattern. This is because Piagetian theory has the underlying assumption that reasoning will be *truth-functional*, i.e. consistent with some logical truth table. A related argument concerns the question of whether *if* has a fixed meaning or not. For example, Marcus and Rips (1979) found that biconditional response patterns were more frequent in a context describing a machine-like context (direction of the roll of a ball affects which light bulb is lit) than in a context describing contingencies between letters and numbers on a card, possibly due to the nature of the former. In discussion, they suggest three possible implications for the meaning of *if*: (1) that it is interpreted as a material implication (conditional) with all deviant responses due to processing errors; (2) that it has no fixed meaning and can be read as an implication or equivalence (biconditional) according to context; and (3) that it has a fixed meaning but that reasoning is not necessarily truth-functional. They specifically reject (2) and favour (3) without giving it very clear definition.

The notion that *if* has a changeable meaning was dubbed the "chameleon theory" by Braine (1978) in the context of his inference rule theory (see Chapter 3 for a discussion of the recent development of Braine's theory by Braine and O'Brien, 1991). While, Braine was critical of the chameleon theory, one of the pioneer's of research on reasoning with conditionals in context, Fillenbaum (1975; 1976; 1978), has advocated strongly the view that the word *does* have different meanings in different contexts. Thus, Fillenbaum (1975, p. 246) states:

> Whilst linguists may take it for granted that the conditional IF can be quite variously employed, psychologists have often written as though the formula *If p, q* always has some single analysis, regardless of the properties of the *p* and *q* connected in the formula, and much of the controversy about the interpretation of IF has been as to whether it could be better represented by material equivalence or a biconditional than by material implication. . . . Perhaps the most characteristic usage of the conditional by experimental psychologists is precisely one in which the propositions involved are general and abstract and the connection between them a completely arbitrary one.

Following Geis and Zwicky (1971), Fillenbaum emphasised the notion that certain inferences—for example, Denial of the Antecedent—are *invited* by the context, though not logically necessary. He was particularly concerned to show that the meaning and usage of *if* is dependent upon its context, and to introduce a new approach to studying conditional reasoning. He introduced the novel, if rather messy, methodology of asking subjects to paraphrase sentences, and also asked them to draw inferences with conditionals of different kinds. For example, he showed that conditionals used as threats or promises such as:

If you mow the lawn then I will give you $5

tend to invite the DA inference (if you don't mow the lawn then I won't give you $5), which as indicated earlier can be interpreted as conformity to the *principle of relevance* developed by Sperber and Wilson (1986).

A comprehensive attempt to compare conditional reasoning performance across contexts, using both inference and truth table tasks, has recently been made by Ellis (1991). He identified a total of eight distinct linguistic uses of conditional statements which he labelled temporal, causal, promise, threat, tip, warning, universal and intentional. All Ellis' conditionals were presented in a context provided by a short paragraph and all were statements presented by particular characters. The inferences drawn may therefore take into account linguistic conventions of dialogue, reliability of certain kinds of statements, explicit and hidden intentions of the speakers and so on.

With the conditional inference task, Ellis found that rates of all inferences, even Modus Ponens, varied considerably between contexts. In most contexts, the rates of the two fallacies, DA and AC, were high but were much lower with contingent universal rules which are similar to those used in abstract reasoning tasks. Corresponding to this was a high frequency of rating FT as false in the truth table tasks in many of the domains. The contexts which produced the strongest indications of equivalence interpretation on either task were promises, threats and intentions, the kinds of context which Fillenbaum argued would induce subjects to draw invited inferences.

Recent studies of conditionals in context have mostly been concerned with the investigation of contexts which suppress conditional inferences, both valid and invalid. This line of work is examined in detail in the following section.

The Suppression of Conditional Inferences

In our earlier review of the conditional inference task, we established that in the absence of obvious pragmatic influences (i.e. using abstract problem content), Modus Ponens is almost always made, whereas subjects often fail to draw the equally valid Modus Tollens inference. In addition, the two so-called invalid or fallacious inferences, Denial of the Antecedent and Affirmation of the Consequent, are often drawn. Of course, they are not fallacious if the conditional is interpreted as a biconditional. Thus correct "truth-functional" patterns are MP and MT for an implication reading, and all four inferences for an equivalence reading. As a further reminder, for a conditional the antecedent is a sufficient condition for the consequent and the consequent is a necessary condition for the antecedent. For a biconditional, both antecedent and consequent are necessary and sufficient conditions for the other.

Staudenmayer (1975) provides an early example of thinking about the conditions which might suppress conditional inferences. He found that subjects tended to make all four inferences more often in accordance with a biconditional interpretation (44%) than with a conditional interpretation (8%) for a premise such as:

If the switch is turned on then the light will go on.

However, they tended to make only Modus Ponens and Modus Tollens in accordance with a conditional interpretation (37%) rather than a biconditional interpretation (30%) for a premise such as:

If I turn the switch then the light will go on.

Why have the fallacious inferences (DA and AC) been suppressed—to an extent—in the latter case? Staudenmayer suggested that the second sort of premise allows individuals to think more readily of alternatives to the antecedent (e.g. other people might turn the switch), which enables them to appreciate that it is not a necessary antecedent, and so to reach the conditional interpretation. He conjectured that other *qualifying conditions* (e.g. that the light bulb is not burned out) could lead subjects to make an interpretation of the antecedent as necessary but insufficient: the consequent may fail to occur even when the antecedent occurs. He also described a final possible interpretation of the antecedent as not necessary and insufficient: the consequent may occur when the antecedent does not, and it may fail to occur even when the antecedent occurs.

Since individuals sometimes make all four inferences, perhaps inference rule theorists should propose that they are equipped with formal inference rules in their minds corresponding to each of the inferences. Rule theorists have, however, avoided this manoeuvre (Braine, 1978; Osherson, 1975; Rips, 1983) and have relied instead on Geis and Zwicky's (1971) distinction between a *necessary* inference, such as Modus Ponens, and an *invited* inference, such as the Denial of the Antecedent. They have suggested instead that the fallacies arise from valid inference rules, applied to misinterpreted premises (Rumain et al., 1983). Subjects misinterpret a premise such as:

If there is a dog in the box then there is an orange in the box

to mean also its invited obverse:

If there is not a dog in the box then there is not an orange in the box

Hence, given the minor premise:

There is not a dog in the box

the fallacious conclusion emerges from the application of the valid Modus Ponens rule to the misinterpreted premises. Rumain et al. showed that if this misinterpretation is *blocked*, subjects no longer make the fallacious inference. They blocked the misinterpretation by presenting subjects with a second conditional premise that contained an alternative antecedent of the following sort:

If there is a tiger in the box then there is an orange in the box

They then gave children and adults a new set of premises:

If there is a pig in the box then there is an apple in the box
If there is a dog in the box then there is an orange in the box
If there is a tiger in the box then there is an orange in the box
There is not a dog

and asked them, for example,

Is there an orange in the box?

The frequency with which the adults made the Denial of the Antecedent fallacy dropped from 73% with the simple premises to just 25% with the expanded set of premises, and the frequency with which they made the affirmation of the consequent fallacy dropped from 65% to just 23% with the expanded set of premises. The expanded set of premises had no effect on the valid inferences. Rumain et al. argued that since the fallacies can be suppressed, individuals do not have rules of inference in their minds corresponding to them.

Markovits (1984) emphasised that the ability to go beyond the presented information to be aware of alternative possibilities may differ from individual to individual. He tested subjects' ability to generate multiple alternatives by asking general questions, such as:

When David has homework to do, he gets into a bad mood
I saw David after school today and he was in a bad mood
Can you imagine what could have put David into a bad mood?

The subjects who could imagine many possible alternatives tended to make fewer of the fallacies, and their solution patterns were classified as conditional (45%) more often than biconditional (11%), whereas subjects who imagined just a single possibility tended to make the fallacies, and their solution patterns were classified as biconditional (41%) more often than conditional (15%; see also Markovits, 1985; 1988).

Figure 2.2 illustrates the suppression of the fallacies. As it shows, the provision of an alternative reduces the rate with which individuals endorse the fallacies, and has no effect on the rate with which they endorse the valid inferences. Does the suppression of the fallacies show that people do not have a formal inference rule corresponding to them? If so, then they must not have formal rules corresponding to the valid inferences either, because it has recently been found that even the valid inferences can be suppressed. Byrne (1989b) showed that it is possible to suppress the valid inferences as well as the fallacies, using the same technique. She suggested that individuals only make the valid Modus Ponens and Modus Tollens inferences when they can safely assume that other necessary background conditions, or presuppositions, have been met. When subjects suspect that the antecedent is not sufficient for the consequent, they no longer make the inferences.

She gave subjects pairs of conditional premises in which the second conditional contained an *additional* antecedent of the following sort:

If she meets her friend then she will go to a play
If she has enough money then she will go to a play

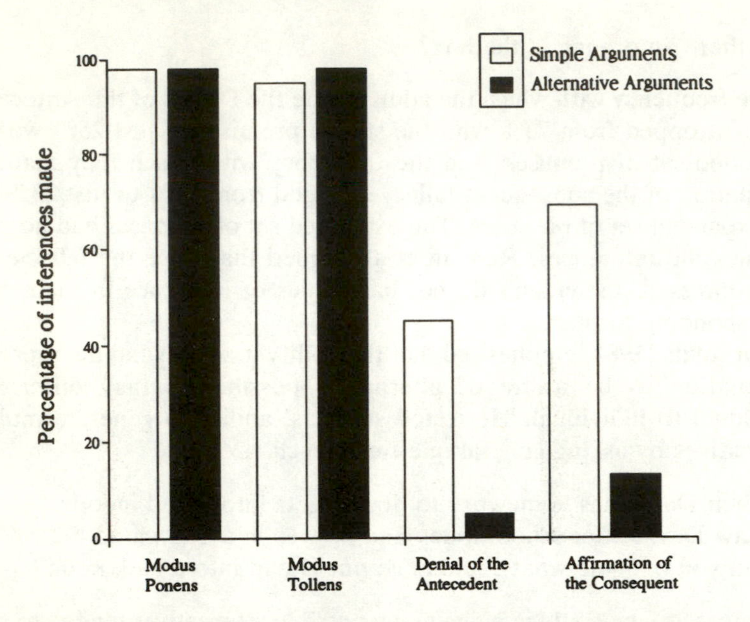

FIG. 2.2 The suppression of the fallacies (data from Byrne, 1989b).

Given the minor premise:

She meets her friend

the frequency with which subjects endorsed the Modus Ponens conclusion:

Therefore, she will go to a play

dropped from 96% on simple arguments (those containing just the first of the two conditionals) to just 38% on the expanded arguments. Given the minor premise:

She will not go to a play

the frequency with which subjects endorsed the Modus Tollens conclusion:

Therefore, she did not meet her friend

dropped from 92% on simple arguments to just 33% on the expanded arguments. The results show that if individuals are reminded of additional background conditions, they no longer make the valid inferences. Figure 2.3 illustrates the suppression of the valid inferences. As it shows, the provision of an additional condition dramatically reduces the rate with which individuals endorse the valid inferences, and it has no effect on the rate with which they endorse the fallacies.

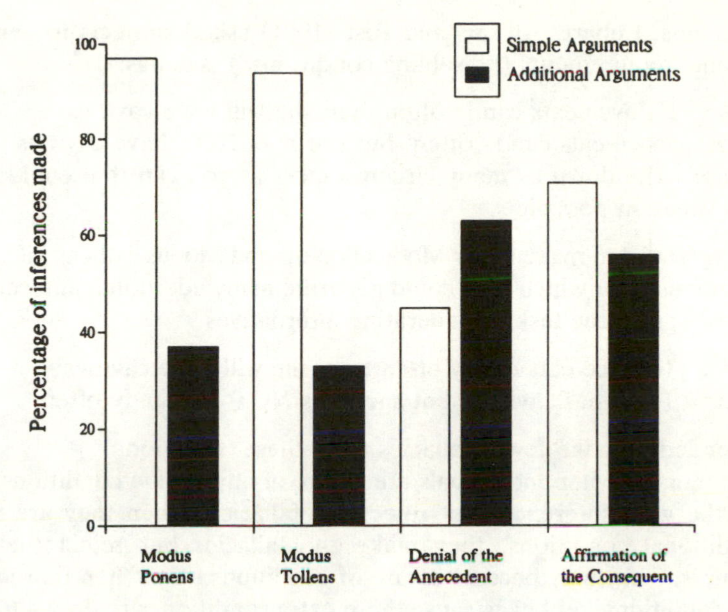

FIG. 2.3 The suppression of the valid inferences (data from Byrne, 1989b).

Byrne also found that both the valid inferences and the fallacies could be suppressed indirectly. She gave subjects contextual information about the duration of an event which was designed to prompt them to imagine alternative or additional conditions. For example:

> During the student protest the policeman said to the student:
> "If you enter the building I will arrest you."
> The student entered the building.
> Did the policeman arrest the student?

The valid inferences were suppressed in the context of a short duration (e.g. Modus Ponens dropped from 72% on no-duration problems such as the one above to 41% for short-duration problems that contained the information "during the 15-minute student protest . . ."). Byrne suggested that the short duration reminds subjects that there may be background conditions that might not be met, e.g. the protest may no longer be in progress. The fallacies were suppressed in the context of a long duration (e.g. the Denial of the Antecedent inference dropped from 44 to 19% for long-duration problems that contained the information "during the two-week student protest . . ."), presumably because the long duration prompted subjects to think of alternatives that may lead to the student being arrested.

Cummins, Lubart, Alksnis and Rist (1991) asked subjects to generate additional requirements ("disabling conditions"), such as:

> *Rule*: If Joyce eats candy often then she will have cavities
> *Fact*: Joyce eats candy often, but she does NOT have cavities
> Please write down as many circumstances as you can that could make this situation possible.

Subjects tended to make fewer Modus Ponens and Modus Tollens inferences from premises for which they could generate many additional antecedents. Likewise, given the task of generating alternatives:

> Rule: If Joyce eats candy often then she will have cavities
> Fact: Joyce has cavities, but she does NOT eat candy often

they tended to make fewer fallacies from these conditionals.

In summary, when individuals are aware of alternative conditions, they make the valid inferences but reject the fallacies; when they are aware of additional conditions, they make the fallacies but reject the valid inferences. They may become aware of conditions other than those in the target conditional, either because these extra conditions are drawn to their attention (Byrne, 1989b; Rumain et al., 1983) or because the content of the conditional or contextual information invites their generation (Byrne, 1989b; Cummins et al., 1991; Markovits, 1984; Staudenmayer, 1975).

The suppression of the valid inferences is released when individuals are told that both the additional conditions are jointly fulfilled, and the suppression of the fallacies is released when they are told that neither of the alternative antecedents has been fulfilled (Byrne, 1989b, experiment 2). Byrne (1989b) proposed that the alternative or additional antecedent in the second conditional alters the interpretation of the first conditional. Both sorts of premises have the same form:

> If p then q
> If r then q

but with additionals, the antecedents are interpreted in such a way that they are jointly necessary:

> If p *and* r then q

and with alternatives, they are interpreted in such a way that they are individually sufficient:

> If p *or* r then q

When individuals were asked to combine the two conditionals, they used different paraphrases for alternatives than for additional antecedents (Byrne & Johnson-Laird, 1992). They spontaneously used disjunctive combinations for conditionals that contained alternative antecedents (68%, e.g. If she meets her friend *or* she meets her family then she will go to a play), whereas they used conjunctive combinations for conditionals that contained additional antecedents (86%, e.g. If she meets her friend *and* she has enough money then she will go to a play).

Byrne (1989b) suggested that the suppression of the valid inferences and of the fallacies is consistent with the mental models theory, and there has been some debate about the proper interpretation of the suppression effect (Bach, 1993; Byrne, 1991a; Grandy, 1993; Over, 1993; Politzer & Braine, 1991; Savion, 1993). We will examine the implications of this controversy in the next chapter. There is no doubt, however, that the suppression effect provides insight into everyday reasoning with conditionals. Conditionals in everyday life are elliptical (Byrne, 1989b; Rips, 1990a), and "in real life situations, people are unlikely to be told all of the relevant conditions, and so they would not know whether all of the alternative or additional antecedents are satisfied" (Byrne, 1989b, p. 72). Thus, the suppression effect may provide us with a more realistic glimpse of the frequency with which individuals make conditional inferences in everyday life. The effect illustrates the non-monotonicity of reasoning: individuals can withdraw conclusions on foot of further evidence that suggests the conclusion is not warranted. Fillenbaum's (1993) judicious review of the suppression effect concludes that the interpretative component is so crucial to reasoning that any theory needs to explain, in full and rigorous detail, exactly how it works.

SUMMARY AND CONCLUSIONS

In this chapter, we have concentrated on discussing the experimental evidence concerning reasoning with conditional statements and have not looked in too much detail at the theoretical arguments about the underlying mechanisms. We attempt a brief summary of the findings before moving on.

Much of the research discussed in this chapter has concerned the four basic inferences that may be drawn from a conditional statement, two of which are logically valid for an implication reading of the rules and all four of which are valid for a biconditional or equivalence. While Modus Ponens is almost universally observed with abstract materials, the equally valid Modus Tollens is not, so that reasoning performance is not in practice truth-functional, i.e. consistent with an underlying truth table. Explanations for the difficulty of Modus Tollens have been considered. With abstract tasks, subjects also quite often endorse the "fallacies" of Denial of the Antecedent and Affirmation of the Consequent, which many authors have taken to mean that they read the sentence as a biconditional or equivalence. Endorsement of DA and AC is even more common in children as a brief survey of some developmental studies has revealed.

Further evidence for a non-logical component of performance comes from studies in which negated components are introduced into the conditional rules. With the inference task paradigm, a number of studies have shown a negative conclusion bias, i.e. a tendency to endorse inferences more often when their conclusion is negative rather than affirmative. The presence and absence of negative components also permits demonstration of a systematic bias when subjects are asked to construct or evaluate truth tables for conditional rules. This effect, known as "matching bias", comprises a tendency to select or consider relevant instances whose features match those explicitly identified in the conditional rule. Explanations of matching bias in terms of both heuristics and mental models have been considered.

A number of studies have compared reasoning with the standard conditional form *if p then q* with its linguistic alternative, but logical equivalent, *p only if q*. These studies have revealed some similarities (e.g. matching bias is manifest with either rule form) but also some clear differences in the frequencies of the inferences drawn. We have discussed possible explanations in terms of the differences in linguistic usage of the two forms and also within the framework of mental models theory.

In the final part of the chapter we have concentrated on studies using thematic content and/or context for the conditional reasoning. These studies suggest that in many but not all contexts, subjects' reasoning corresponds more closely to the pattern to be expected for a biconditional rather than conditional reading of the rules. As with the abstract reasoning tasks, however, the phenomena are more complex than can be explained simply in terms of switching from an implication to an equivalence pattern of reasoning. In particular, a number of recent studies have shown that manipulation of subjects' beliefs about possible alternative or additional qualifying conditions can cause suppression of the fallacies *or* of the valid inferences independently. These conditions evidently affect subjects' perception of the necessary and sufficient conditions exerted by the antecedent on the consequent and vice versa.

Of the four main theoretical approaches identified in Chapter 1, three have been mentioned at points during this chapter, namely those based upon heuristics, mental models and inference rules. The theory of pragmatic reasoning schemas and related proposals of domain-sensitive reasoning procedures have been almost entirely investigated with studies of the Wason selection task and will hence be considered in Chapter 4, together with further discussion of the heuristic theory. First, however, we must attend to the major theoretical debate that has developed between the mental models theory of propositional reasoning and that based upon the proposal of formal inference rules. While we have alluded to some of the arguments involved, we have not had space in this chapter either to elaborate the nature of these theories in detail, or to consider the debate between the two camps. The next chapter is devoted to this enterprise.

3 Theories of Conditional Reasoning: Rules Versus Models

What goes on in your mind when you make a conditional inference? What sorts of mental representations and cognitive processes could give rise to the range of experimental phenomena described in the previous chapter? The phenomena of conditional reasoning have been explained in several alternative ways. Two general theories of propositional reasoning have been so extensively researched and discussed in the recent literature that we will devote a chapter to the theoretical debate between them. The two theories are that reasoning depends on formal rules of inference, and that it depends on mental models.

These theories comprise only two of the four major approaches identified in the introduction (Chapter 1). The other two theories are considered in this book within the reviews of the particular phenomena to which they have been applied. For example, we have encountered the proposals of heuristic processes in conditional reasoning in Chapter 2, and will do so again in Chapter 4. In Chapter 4 we will also examine theories of domain-sensitive rules which have been developed to account for performance on the Wason selection task. Where specific accounts from either school have been proposed for phenomena considered in later chapters, we will return to the theories as appropriate.

We will discuss each of the two theories— formal inference rules and mental models—by considering the following central points:

- the tenets of the theory;
- its account of competence and errors;
- the evidence its proponents adduce to support it;

- the criticisms of the theory by its opponents, and the replies to these criticisms by its proponents.

The debate continues to flourish between the proponents of the two theories of conditional reasoning. We focus on the most recent contributions to our understanding of propositional reasoning in general, and conditional reasoning in particular, by proponents of formal inference-rule theories (e.g. Braine & O'Brien, 1991; Rips, 1990a) and mental model theories (e.g. Johnson-Laird & Byrne, 1991; Johnson-Laird, Byrne & Schaeken, 1992a).

FORMAL INFERENCE RULES

The Tenets of the Formal Rule Theory

The view that the mind contains a mental logic consisting of formal inference rules has appealed not only to psychologists but also to philosophers (e.g. Boole, 1847/1948), linguists (e.g. Sperber & Wilson, 1986) and artificial intelligence workers (e.g. Pollock, 1989). Psychological interest in formal inference rules was initiated in the 1950s and early 1960s (e.g. Henle, 1962; Inhelder & Piaget, 1958), and gained momentum during the 1970s and early 1980s (e.g. Braine, 1978; Macnamara, 1986; Rips, 1983; Taplin & Staudenmayer, 1973).

According to the formal inference-rule view, people rely on representations which are language-like, and on cognitive processes akin to the natural deduction method developed by logicians (see, e.g. Copi, 1981), where there are separate rules of inference for each logical connective, such as "and", "if", "not" and "or". Rips (1983, p. 40) explains this method in the following way:

> Deductive reasoning consists in the application of mental inference rules to the premises and conclusion of an argument. The sequence of applied rules forms a mental proof or derivation of the conclusion from the premises, where these implicit proofs are analogous to the explicit proofs of elementary logic.

Reasoners engage in three steps when they make an inference. First, they uncover the logical form of the premises; second, they access their mental repertory of inference rules to construct a mental derivation or proof of a conclusion; and third, they translate the content-free conclusion into the content of the premises (Braine, 1978; Braine & O'Brien, 1991; Johnson-Laird, 1975; Osherson, 1975; Rips, 1983).

Consider the following conditional premise:

If Buster wakes up then she moves about

Given the further information:

Buster wakes up

reasoners first uncover the logical form of the premises:

If p then q
p

They access a content-free inference rule corresponding to the Modus Ponens inference, and construct a proof of the conclusion which consists of a single step:

Therefore, q.

They translate this conclusion to the content of the premises:

Therefore, she moves about.

The heart of inference-rule theories is the repertory of inference rules that reasoners possess in their mental logic. The repertory differs from standard logical accounts in that it consists only of elementary rules. A rule is elementary if problems that are considered to require that inference alone are solved without errors, and if a chain of putatively more elementary rules to solve the problem would sum to a greater difficulty (Braine et al., 1984). The lexical entry for a connective defines information about it, and consists of inference rules that:

> provide instructions about how truth may be inherited from premises to conclusions. . . . No separate "semantics" is needed (Braine & O'Brien, 1991, p. 184).

For example, in Braine and O'Brien's system, the lexical entry for *if* consists of two inference rules, Modus Ponens and a rule for conditional proof (see Table 3.1). The rules mean that:

> an *if* sentence is true when the antecedent, taken with other things the speaker knows, leads to the consequent (Braine & O'Brien, 1991, p. 192).

In Rips's (1983) system, there are three rules for a conditional (see Table 3.1). The first allows a standard Modus Ponens inference from the appropriate premises to a conclusion, the second incorporates a strategy for using Modus Ponens to reach a subgoal, and the third, similar to Braine and O'Brien's conditional proof, incorporates a strategy to introduce a conditional to reach a subgoal.

Several well-formulated theories of propositional inferences based on inference rules have been advanced (Braine, 1978; Johnson-Laird, 1975; Osherson, 1974–76; Rips, 1983). Johnson-Laird and Byrne (1991) suggest

TABLE 3.1
The Rules for Conditionals in Two Formal Inference Rule Systems

Braine and O'Brien (1991)

1. Given *if p then q* and *p*, one can infer *q* (Modus Ponens).
2. To derive or evaluate *if p then* . . ., first suppose *p*, for any proposition *q* that follows from the supposition of *p* taken together with other information assumed, one may assert *if p then q* (schema for conditional proof).

The application of the conditional proof rule is limited by three constraints:

(a) nothing follows from a contradiction except that the initial supposition is wrong,
(b) suppositions must be consistent with prior assumptions, and
(c) subsequent assumptions cannot contradict the supposition which is the antecedent of the conditional.

Rips (1983)

1. *Modus Ponens (forwards):*
   Conditions: 1. Assertion tree[a] contains proposition x = *if p, q*
   2. x has not been used by the Modus Ponens rules
   3. Assertion tree contains the proposition *p*
   Actions: 1. Add *q* to the assertion tree
2. *Modus Ponens (backwards):*
   Conditions: 1. Current subgoal = *q*
   2. Assertion tree contains *if p then q*
   Actions: 1. Set up a subgoal to deduce *p*
   2. If subgoal 1 is achieved, add *q* to assertion tree
3. *If Introduction (backwards):*
   Conditions: 1. Current subgoal = *if p, q*
   Actions: 1. Add new subordinate node to assertion tree containing assumption *p*
   2. Set up corresponding subgoal node to deduce *q*
   3. If subgoal 2 is achieved, add *if p, q* to superordinate node of assertion tree

[a] See text for explanation.

that what they have in common outweighs their differences, and we reproduce here their table summarising the rules included in three of the theories (see Table 3.2). Detailed comparisons of these theories are made in Rips (1983) and Braine et al. (1984).

A theory of reasoning based on formal inference rules consists of several components: one is the repertory of inference rules; a second component is the reasoning program that controls the way in which a proof is constructed, how the inference rules are selected to apply at different stages in the proof, and how to move from one step to the next; and the third component is the comprehension component that decodes the premises into the logical form prior to reasoning, and recodes the conclusion to the content of the premises subsequent to reasoning.

Braine et al. (1984) specify a reasoning program that contains direct and indirect reasoning. Direct reasoning routines start with the premises, as they are construed, match rules to the form of propositions in the premise

TABLE 3.2
The Principal Formal Rules of Inference Proposed by Three Psychological Theories of Deduction

	Johnson-Laird	*Braine*	*Rips*
Conjunctions			
A, B .·. A & B	+	+	+
A & B .·. A	+	+	+
Disjunctions			
A or B, not-A .·. B	+	+	+
A .·. A or B	+		+
Conditionals			
If A then B, A .·. B	+	+	+
If A or B then C, A .·. C		+	+
A ⊢ B .·. If A then B	+	+	+
Negated conjunctions			
not (A & B), A .·. ¬B	+	+	
not (A & B).·. not-A or not-B			+
A & not-B .·. not (A & B)	+		
Double negations			
not not-A .·. A	+	+	
DeMorgan's laws			
A &(B or C) .·. (A & B) or (A & C)		+	
Reductio ad Absurdum			
A ⊢ B & not-B .·. not-A	+	+	+
Dilemmas			
A or B, A ⊢ C, B ⊢ C .·. C		+	+
A or B, A ⊢ C, B ⊢ D .·. C or D		+	
Introduction of tautologies			
.·. A or not-A		+	+

Notes: "+" indicates that a rule is postulated by the relevant theory. "A ⊢ B" means that a deduction from A to B is possible. Braine's rules interconnect any number of propositions, as we explain in the text. He postulates four separate rules that together enable a Reductio ad Absurdum to be made. Johnson-Laird relies on procedures that follow up the separate consequences of constituents in order to carry out dilemmas.

From Johnson-Laird and Byrne (1991). Reproduced with permission.

set, apply any that can be applied (excluding ones that introduce suppositions and with restrictions on infinite loops) and add each inference to the premise set, until a conclusion is reached, or a proposition that is incompatible with the given conclusion is reached. When the direct reasoning routine fails, indirect reasoning strategies are applied, which depend on heuristics to find a successful line of reasoning. Indirect reasoning is required for some inferences, and for making suppositions generally. For example, the conditional proof described earlier is realised in the reasoning program in the following way:

> if the conclusion given is an *if-then* statement, add the antecedent to the premise set and treat the consequent as the conclusion to be tested (Braine et al., 1984, p. 351).

Individual differences may arise from the variability in the available strategies.

Rips (1983) specifies a reasoning program which has been computationally modelled in LISP, and is nicknamed ANDS (for A Natural Deduction System). ANDS has a proof structure that contains an assertion tree, that is, a working memory structure to store temporarily the premises and the inferences derived from the premises. Any temporary suppositions are placed in a subordinate node of the assertion tree. The ANDS proof structure also contains a subgoal tree, to store the conclusion and the subgoals that will help to reach the conclusion, in order to keep the program directed towards the conclusion. These working memory tree structures are filled when the inference routines inspect the trees and respond to the appropriate patterns by applying inference rules. ANDS proves its theorems from the "outside in" working, alternately, backwards from the conclusion in the subgoal tree and forwards from the premises in the assertion tree. A proof succeeds if a match is found between the subgoals and the assertions, and it fails if it runs out of applicable rules.

The third component is the comprehension component. In most inference-rule theories, this interpretative mechanism has been left unspecified (e.g. Braine, 1978; Rips, 1983). Braine and O'Brien (1991) describe the nature of three pragmatic principles (not necessarily independent of one another) that govern how *if* is likely to be interpreted in context: (1) the content of the proposition affects the way it is construed, and a plausible interpretation is determined by world knowledge; (2) Grice's (1975) cooperative principle, whereby people are assumed to communicate in an informative, truthful, relevant and clear way leads to conversational implicatures that give rise to non-necessary inferences; and (3) logical particles can have attached to them "invited inferences" (Geis & Zwicky, 1971) as we will see in the next section.

Competence and Errors

Rule theorists propose that easy valid inferences are made by accessing a corresponding elementary inference rule. Difficult valid inferences have no corresponding inference rule, and reasoners must construct a proof of several steps to derive the conclusion. The difficulty of a problem is predicted from the rules in the repertory required to solve it, and assumptions about how the reasoning program selects the rules (e.g. Braine & O'Brien, 1991; Rips, 1983). For example, difficulty arises with the Modus Tollens inference. Given the premises:

If Buster wakes up then she moves about
Buster does not move about

reasoners must construct a mental proof of the conclusion (see Table 3.3). They do not have a rule in their repertory that matches these premises, and some people may infer mistakenly that nothing follows from the premises. Others manage to construct a derivation, which requires the use of several rules, including a rule for creating suppositions, the rule for Modus Ponens, a rule for conjoining two assertions and so on. Because it requires several steps in its derivation, it is a difficult inference to make and reasoners will make errors. It requires a difficult proof structure, since it is an indirect line of reasoning (Braine et al., 1984), or requires the creation of subordinate nodes in the assertion tree (Rips, 1983).

The purpose of making some valid inferences may lead to errors because, although reasoners possess a rule corresponding to the inference in their mental repertoire, it is difficult to access (Rips & Conrad, 1983). Valid inferences are difficult when reasoners do not have an available inference rule, or when the inference rule is available but inaccessible. The reasoning program may fail to find a line of reasoning that solves the problem, and undecidability judgements may require non-logical heuristics.

Errors may arise because of the comprehension component that precedes reasoning and is responsible for uncovering the logical form of the premises. Henle (1978) has asserted: "I have never found errors which

TABLE 3.3
A Proof for Modus Tollens

Premises:	If Buster wakes up then she moves about	
	Buster did not move about	
Step 1:	*Uncover the logical skeleton of the premises*	
1.	If p then q	(premise 1)
2.	not-q	(premise 2)
Step 2:	*Construct a mental derivation of the conclusion*	
3.	p	(supposition-creating rule)
4.	therefore, q	(Modus Ponens rule applied to step 3 and premise 1)
5.	q and not-q	(conjunction rule applied to step 2 and 4)
6.	not-p	(Reductio ad Absurdum from steps 5 and 3)
Step 3:	*Translate the conclusion to the content of the premises*	
	Therefore, Buster does not wake up	

could unambiguously be attributed to faulty reasoning." She proposed that many errors arise because of a failure to accept the logical task, that is, to distinguish between a conclusion that is valid and one that is true or agreeable (Henle, 1962). She identified other errors in a qualitative analysis of subjects' protocols, such as the restatement of a premise or conclusion with the intended meaning changed, resulting in reasoning from material other than that presented by the experimenter. Likewise, an error may result from omitting a premise, or from slipping in an additional premise, such as a commonplace assumption (cf. Evans, 1993b).

A comprehension deficit has been used to explain why reasoners sometimes make invalid inferences (e.g. Braine & O'Brien, 1991; Rumain et al., 1983). Consider the two common fallacies we encountered in the previous chapter. Given the premises:

If Buster wakes up she moves about
Buster does not wake up

the correct conclusion to these premises is that she may or may not move about, but many reasoners make the Denial of the Antecedent fallacy that she does not move about. Likewise, given the premises:

If Buster wakes up she moves about
Buster moves about

many reasoners make the Affirmation of the Consequent fallacy that she wakes up. Why do reasoners make these inferences? Few researchers have proposed that there are invalid inference rules in the mind (Von Domarus, 1944). Early researchers assumed that reasoners who made only the valid Modus Ponens and Modus Tollens inferences from a conditional had interpreted it as a material implication, whereas those who made all four inferences had interpreted it as a biconditional, or material equivalence, *if and only if* (e.g. Marcus & Rips, 1979; Staudenmayer, 1975; Taplin, 1971; Taplin & Staudenmayer, 1973). This avenue of research has been shown to be fraught with interpretational difficulty, and many responses have to be discarded since they cannot be categorised as falling into either group (see Chapter 2). More recent researchers have rejected the idea that *if* is interpreted as a biconditional, and instead they suggest that the fallacies arise from the valid inference rules, applied to misinterpreted premises, as we saw in the previous chapter when we considered the suppression effect (e.g. Rumain et al., 1983). As we saw in Chapter 2, they suggest that the fallacies are inferences that are invited by our conversational processes (see Geis & Zwicky, 1971), rather than inferences which are logically necessary (Braine & O'Brien, 1991).

Inference-rule theories have been developed to account for higher-level deductions, based not only on propositional inferences, but on inferences about the truth and falsity of assertors and their assertions. Rips (1989) extended his theory to encompass "knight–knave" puzzles, in which knights always tell the truth and knaves always lie, such as:

A says: B is a knave
B says: A is a knight if and only if C is a knight
Is C a knight or a knave, or undetermined?

The theory is based on the protocols of subjects, and it is modelled in a computer program written in PROLOG. It combines a subset of ANDS rules, that is, those that work forwards rather than those that work backwards, with a set of content-specific rules for the meaning of knight and knave:

1. says (x, p) and knight (x) entail p
2. says (x, p) and knave (x) entail NOT p
3. NOT knave (x) entails knight (x)
4. NOT knight (x) entails knave (x)

Rips's theory assumes a control structure in which subjects suppose that the first assertor is telling the truth, and they follow up the consequences of this assumption, making inferences from the truth or falsity of individuals to the truth or falsity of what they say (but not working backwards from the truth of what they say to their status). Table 3.4 illustrates the inference rule theory of knight–knave puzzles.

Supporting Evidence for the Formal Rule Theory

Braine et al. (1984) propose that their suggestion that the simplest inference problems have solutions which follow directly from the lexical entry is supported by the few errors made on such problems. They also found that problems which led to a conditional conclusion were rated as more difficult than matched problems which led to an atomic conclusion, and this finding supports their claim that a requirement of the conditional proof rule is mentally to add the antecedent to the premise set.

The development of accuracy on the Modus Tollens inference supports their claims that it requires an indirect line of reasoning. They suggest it is made correctly for the wrong reason by unsophisticated reasoners, such as children, who accept the biconditional ("if and only if") interpretation. Reasoners of intermediate sophistication do not accept the invited inference to the biconditional, but fail to find the indirect Reductio ad Absurdum line of reasoning, and so respond erroneously that nothing follows. Sophisticated reasoners succeed in resisting the biconditional interpretation and in finding the indirect line of reasoning (Braine & O'Brien, 1991). The theory also explains the "defective truth table" found

TABLE 3.4
An Inference Rule Derivation of a Knight–Knave Puzzle by Rips' Model[a]

Premises:	
1. A says: B is a knave	
2. B says: A is a knight if and only if C is a knight	
Supposition and consequences	
3. A is a knight	[supposition-creating rule]
4. B is a knave	[knight rule 1, from step 3 and premise 1]
5. Not (A is a knight if and only if C is a knight)	[knight rule 2, from step 4 and premise 3]
6. C is a knave	[propositional rule, from steps 3 and 5]
Conclusions	
7. B is a knave	[from assumption that B is a knight, and conflict with step 4]
8. C is a knave	[from assumption that C is a knight, and conflict with step 6]
Suppositions and consequences	
9. A is a knave	[supposition-creating rule]
10. NOT (B is a knave)	[knight rule 2, from step 9 and premise 1]
11. B is a knight	[knight rule 3, from step 10]
12. A is a knight if and only if C is a knight	[knight rule 1, from step 11 and premise 2]
13. C is a knave	[propositional rule, from steps 9 and 12]
Conclusion	
14. B is a knight	[from assumption that B is a knave, and conflict with step 11]
15. C is a knave	[from assumption that C is a knave, and consistency with step 13]
Overall conclusions:	
A is a knight, and B and C are knaves, *OR* B is a knight and A and C are knaves, i.e. A is uncertain; B is uncertain; C is a knave	

[a] See Rips (1989, pp. 92–93).

in truth judgements. To evaluate whether a conditional is true requires an individual to suppose the antecedent is true and to try to derive the consequent in that state of affairs. If the antecedent is true, the judgement that the conditional is true requires a judgement of whether the consequent is true in that state of affairs. If the antecedent is false, the conditional proof rule cannot be applied without changing the state of affairs (which would violate one of the constraints on its application) and so there is no way to evaluate the conditional. They support their proposal that fallacies arise from a comprehension error by demonstrating that the fallacies are suppressed when the invited inference is blocked (Braine & O'Brien, 1991; Rumain et al., 1983).

Inference-rule theories predict that inferences that require more steps in their derivation are more difficult than those that require fewer steps (see, e.g. Braine, 1978; Osherson, 1975; Rips, 1983; Smith, Langston & Nisbett, 1992). This prediction has been corroborated, for example, by Braine et al. (1984), who gave one-step and multi-step problems to subjects in several experiments and used three measures of difficulty: subjective rating of the difficulty of a problem on a 9-point scale, latencies to solve the problem and errors on the problems. They expected error-free performance on simple rules, and they used a set of data from such rules to predict the difficulty of problems that required short chains of reasoning. They considered the ratings data to provide the most reliable information, and they examined the relation of the difficulty ratings to the length of the problem, the number of steps the problem required according to the theory, and the different weightings given to the steps estimated from the data. They found that the difficulty was a function of the number of steps and the number of words in the problem.

Rips (1983) corroborated his theory using protocol data, memory for proofs and validity judgements. Subjects' "thinking aloud" protocols, collected while they were solving problems, were used to guide the overall design of the theory. For example, protocol analysis was employed to distinguish the use of forward and backward chains of reasoning. These protocols, when recast in a common format and rated for similarity by two judges on a 5-point scale (where 5 = the same) to the proofs produced by ANDS and by Osherson's (1974–76) model, achieved a high similarity rating for ANDS (3.64), reliably more than for Osherson's model (3.21). Subjects' memory for lines of proofs supports the proposed hierarchical proof structure in ANDS. The subjects recalled arguments that contained suppositions and matched arguments that contained no suppositions (Marcus, 1982). Since ANDS stores suppositions at a subordinate node, it was predicted that they should be recalled less often. This prediction was corroborated: suppositions were recalled less often (25%) than matched definite assertions (45%). Rips (1983) evaluated the ANDS model by mathematically modelling it. He assessed subjects' accuracy in evaluating the validity of given conclusions to deductions, where they achieved an average of 51% correct on the valid problems, with a range of 17–92%, and an average of 23% correct on the invalid problems. He found that his model provided a reasonable fit to the data, on the assumption that rules are unavailable on some proportion of trials, either because subjects fail to retrieve the rule, fail to recognise it as applicable or fail to apply it properly.

Rips (1989) corroborated his knight–knave inference-rule theory by showing that subjects are more likely to make mistakes and to take longer to solve these puzzles when they require a large number of steps (suppositions and inferences) in their derivation. He found that a set of large-step problems that required on average 24 steps to solve were more difficult (20% correct) than small-step problems that required on average 19 steps to solve (32% correct). In a second experiment, for problems matched on number of speakers, clauses, connectives and so on, he found that large-step problems took longer to solve (29.5 sec) than small-step problems (23.9 and 25.5 sec for two sorts of small-step problems), although the percentage of correct inferences did not follow this trend (large-step problems, 14%; small-step problems: type 1, 16%; type 2, 9%).

Criticisms of the Formal Rule Theory and Rebuttals

One of the primary criticisms of the inference-rule theory has been its failure to account for the effects of content on reasoning (e.g. Cheng & Holyoak, 1985; Griggs, 1983), and we will consider content effects in the selection task in the next chapter. Two of the eight criteria proposed by Smith et al. (1992) for determining whether or not people use abstract rules in reasoning are that performance is as accurate on unfamiliar as on familiar materials, and that it is as accurate on abstract as on concrete materials. However, performance is often *better* on familiar materials and on concrete materials (see Chapter 4 for a detailed discussion of such facilitation effects). Content effects have been attributed to the comprehension component, but as we have seen this component has been left unspecified. Critics point out that little attempt has been made to specify the complex processes involved despite several decades of research on formal inference rules (Byrne, 1991a; Evans, 1989). The comprehension component has worked as a buffer against data that could potentially falsify the theory (e.g. Johnson-Laird, 1983; Johnson-Laird & Byrne, 1991). Recently, rule theorists have proposed that the formal inference rules can be supplemented with content-sensitive rules (Braine & O'Brien, 1991; Rips, 1989). However, Manktelow and Over (1991) consider that attempts to account for content effects by such constraints on the formal rules fatally weakens the theory's parsimony and testability. Rips (1990a) suggests that what is needed may not be content-sensitive rules but, for example, modal logics, non-logical operations and so on.

The most direct empirical examination of the comprehension component was undertaken by Rumain et al. (1983) in their examination of the suppression of the fallacies. But, as we saw in the previous chapter, the suppression of the valid inferences undermines the use of the comprehension component to explain fallacies (Byrne, 1989a). Byrne (1989b) argued that the suppression of the valid inferences places rule theorists on the horns of a dilemma: If they conclude from the suppression of the fallacies that there are no inference rules in the mind corresponding to the fallacies, then they should conclude from the suppression of the valid inferences that there are no inference rules in the mind corresponding to valid inferences either. The suppression does not cast doubt on the validity of Modus Ponens as an inference, but on the idea that individuals make the inference by applying automatically a formal rule of inference, which applies equally well to any content. Byrne suggested that the results are consistent with the mental model theory (Johnson-Laird, 1983), and we will consider this possibility shortly. The debate on the suppression effect highlights the difficulty for formal rules theories to incorporate non-monotonicity (Byrne, 1989a; Chater & Oaksford, 1991; Holyoak & Spellman, 1993).

Braine and O'Brien argue that the lexical entry for *if* must include abstract versions of rules such as Modus Ponens and the conditional proof rule to explain the commonality in our understanding of *if*: the abstract versions are used for default interpretations when the content of *if* falls outside of content-sensitive rules. But, critics have identified problems with the operation of some of the rules, especially the conditional proof rule. It is intended to apply to any argument—causal, psychological, or one based on a scenario or model. Byrne and Johnson-Laird (1992, p. 107) argue that the conditional proof schema leads to a vicious circle: "in order to generate a conditional of the form *if p then q* for the constituents *p* and *q* one needs such a conditional to establish that *q* follows from *p*". Moreover, they showed that reasoners can generate a conditional to paraphrase sets of assertions even though none of the assertions could be said to validly imply the other. The conditional proof rule leads to an impasse, and so cannot account for the data (see also Holyoak & Spellman, 1993).

Alternative explanations have been proposed for the data provided by Braine et al. and Rips in support of their theories. Johnson-Laird, Byrne and Schaeken (1992a) presented the direct problems used by Braine et al. to their computer program based on mental models (described below). All of the problems required only simple (initial) models to be constructed, and they found that problems that required more models were rated as more difficult than those that required fewer models. They also reported a confounding factor in the problems used by Rips (1983): half of the problems threw away semantic information, whereas the other half maintained it, and the former were reliably more difficult than the latter.

Critics have also tested the predictions of rule theories and failed to find support for them. Rule theories cannot explain why Modus Tollens is easier from a biconditional than from a conditional, when there is no difference between Modus Ponens in either case (Johnson-Laird et al.,

1992a). The number of steps required for the mental derivation of Modus Tollens is the same whether *if* is interpreted as a conditional or a biconditional. Likewise, Smith et al. (1992) predict that a problem which requires a single Modus Ponens inference should be easier than one that requires two Modus Ponens inferences. But Byrne (1989b) has shown the opposite: Subjects produce conclusions more readily, without modal qualifiers, to a sequence of premises that requires two Modus Ponens inferences (85%) than to separate component premise sets (50%). She suggests that reasoners construct a unified representation of the sequence which highlights its transitivity. An alternative explanation is suggested by Smith et al.'s fifth criterion, that the application of a rule may subsequently prime the use of the same rule. But this criterion conflicts with the proof strategy employed by rule theorists that once a rule has been invoked it is not used again immediately, to avoid endless loops (Braine et al., 1984; Rips, 1983; 1989).

Rule theories cannot explain the difference in difficulty between inclusive and exclusive disjunctions found in the "double disjunction" task (described below), since they both require the same derivation. These inferences are extremely difficult, yet the derivations are no longer than one for Modus Tollens. Rule theories can describe effects such as the difference found between conditionals and exclusive disjunctions ("either . . . or . . . but not both"), by asserting *ad hoc* that the rule for one inference is more accessible than the rule for another (Johnson-Laird et al., 1992a). But this tactic does not explain the difference, nor does it enable one to predict *a priori* which inferences will be easy, which will be hard, or the nature of the errors that reasoners will make. In general, rule theories have been tested using conclusion evaluation tasks (but see Rips, 1989, for an exception). Evaluation tasks may fail to engage subjects' reasoning and lead them to guess or use some other non-logical strategy (Johnson-Laird et al., 1992a). Indeed, some rule theorists have queried the engagement of subjects' reasoning in such tasks themselves (Braine et al., 1984), and concede that their theories do not account for inference production (Rips, 1983).

Rips' (1989) knight–knave theory has been criticised for the inflexibility of its single deterministic procedure, which places an impossible load on working memory (Johnson-Laird & Byrne, 1990; see also Evans, 1990b). Johnson-Laird and Byrne (1990) argue that reasoners do not come to these complex puzzles with a ready-made procedure and instead they spontaneously develop strategies to solve them. They re-analysed Rips' data and found, for example, that subjects made more correct conclusions (28%) to problems that could be solved by one of their proposed simple strategies (described later) than to problems that could not be solved by a simple strategy (14%). Rips (1990b) countered that only one of the four strategies outlined by Johnson-Laird and Byrne (1990) produced reliably more correct conclusions, when problems were matched for clauses, connectives, speakers and so on.

However, Byrne and Handley (1993) found that subjects made more correct conclusions to matched problems that could be solved by the simple strategy (44%) than to problems that could not be solved by it (18%). Rips (1990b, p. 301) argues that his proposal is about how subjects solve the puzzles at a steady-state of performance, and that they may take some time to hit upon a stable solution path. This stable solution path rests on the main feature of natural deduction systems, which is a "suppose-and-deduce" control structure. However, Byrne and Handley (1993) showed that making suppositions is one of the most difficult aspects of these puzzles; for problems for which subjects had no simple strategy, they made more correct conclusions when they were given an appropriate supposition (58%) than when they were not given one (18%). They were not simply guessing, since problems for which they were given an inappropriate supposition did not result in a corresponding deterioration of performance (25%) (see also Byrne & Handley, 1992; Byrne, Johnson-Laird & Handley, in press).

Rule theorists acknowledge the incompleteness of their theories with regard to both an account of invalid inferences, and an account of how subjects cut short an exhaustive search for a derivation and decide simply that there is no valid conclusion (Rips, 1983).

In addition to empirically based criticisms, theoretical "in-principle" criticisms have been advanced by opponents of inference rules. Critics have argued that a reliance on language-like structures and a mechanism of pattern matching places too much emphasis on syntactic structures (e.g. Johnson-Laird & Byrne, 1991). The theory is concerned with the relation of truth between sentences, rather than between sentences and the world. Rips (1986, p. 265) argues that:

> cognitive psychology must do without semantic notions like truth and reference that depend on the relationship between mental representations and the outside world . . . what's cognitively relevant are representations, . . . people can compare these representations in various ways, but . . . they don't have cognitive access to the external relations these representations bear to the world (see also Oden, 1987).

But many cognitive scientists (e.g. Hofstadter & Dennett, 1981; Johnson-Laird, 1983) argue that without such concepts there could be no cognitive psychology. Rips (1990a, p. 297) proposes that "representations have causal ties to the situations they represent, but these external causal connections are not the ones that cognitive psychologists invoke in explaining performance".

MENTAL MODELS

The Tenets of the Mental Models Theory

The idea of models has gained importance in logic (e.g. Tarski, 1956), linguistics (e.g. Barwise, 1989), artificial intelligence (e.g. Bundy, 1983; Levesque, 1986) and psychology (e.g. Johnson-Laird, 1983; Marr, 1982). Johnson-Laird and Byrne (1991) provide a theory of propositional reasoning based on models. They characterise reasoning both at the computational level (i.e. what the mind is doing when it makes a deduction) as well as at the algorithmic level (i.e. how the mind makes a deduction) (see Marr, 1982). At the computational level, they propose that reasoning competence meets three constraints: "To deduce is to maintain semantic information, to simplify, and to reach a new conclusion" (Johnson-Laird & Byrne, 1991, p. 22). They describe three extra-logical constraints that govern the deductions people make from the infinite number of possible deductions that they could make (see Johnson-Laird, 1983). First, people usually do not throw away semantic information (the proportion of possible states of affairs that an assertion rules out). A conjunction, *p and q*, rules out three states of affairs, whereas a disjunction, *p or q*, or both rules out only one state of affairs; hence, the conjunction contains more information than the disjunction. A valid deduction by definition does not increase semantic information, but it may decrease semantic information, and reasoners avoid such deductions. Second, conclusions should be simple or parsimonious; for example, people do not draw conclusions that re-assert something that has just been asserted. Third, the conclusion should be informative, i.e. contain information that is not stated explicitly in the premises. The deductions that people make meet these three constraints, even though they may not be mentally represented, conscious constraints.

At the algorithmic level, Johnson-Laird and Byrne propose that human mental logic does not consist of formal rules of inference. Instead, the mind contains procedures that manipulate mental models (Johnson-Laird, 1983). A mental model of a premise is a representation that corresponds to the way the world would be if the premise were true. Consider once again the conditional:

If Buster wakes up then she moves about

Recall from Chapters 1 and 2 that the situations the conditional describes can be captured in a truth table (see Table 3.5). Each entry indicates the possible combinations of Buster waking up and moving about. For example, in the first row it is true that she wakes up and true that she moves about, whereas in the second row it is true that she wakes up and false that she moves about, i.e. she does not move about. The truth-functional meaning of the logical connective *if* connecting two situations

TABLE 3.5
A Truth Table for the Conditional: *If Buster wakes up then she moves about*

1. A Truth Table for Two Assertions:

Buster wakes up	*Buster moves about*
True	True
True	False
False	True
False	False

2. A Truth Table for Two Assertions Conjoined by if:

Buster wakes up	*Buster moves about*	*If Buster wakes up then she moves about*
True	True	True
True	False	False
False	True	True
False	False	True

rules out the second combination. The conditional is true in the first row where Buster wakes up and moves about, and it is false in the second row where she wakes up and does not move about. The conditional is true in the two remaining situations, where Buster does not wake up, and in these situations she may either move about or not move about.

It is unlikely that people construct truth tables in their minds. When they are presented with truth tables, they seem overwhelmed by the amount of information in them, and have difficulty solving problems based on them (see Osherson, 1975; Wason & Johnson-Laird, 1972). But truth tables contain the kernel of a psychologically plausible mechanism of reasoning, which Johnson-Laird and Byrne (1991) have developed to account for propositional reasoning (see also Johnson-Laird et al., 1992a). Because of the constraints on reasoners' limited working memories (see Baddeley, 1990), they represent as little information as necessary to capture the meaning of a premise. They represent just those situations where the premise is true, and not the situations where it is false. They do not represent the situation that is inconsistent with the conditional, described in the second row of the truth table, but they represent the remaining situations that are consistent with it, described in the first, third and fourth rows:

Buster wakes up	she moves about
Buster does not wake up	she moves about
Buster does not wake up	she does not move about

Each line corresponds to an alternative situation in the world, and each separate model is represented on a separate line, as a convenient notation (see Johnson-Laird & Byrne, 1991). The specific information in models may turn out to be images, propositional tags or some other symbol. The content may be enriched with concrete retrieved information about who Buster is, where she sleeps and why she moves about, depending on the background knowledge of the reasoner. However, these features are not crucial for the theory of reasoning: the structure of the models is crucial. The information is usually abbreviated, again for notational convenience, into the following sort of diagram:

```
  w    m
 ¬w    m
 ¬w   ¬m
```

where "w" stands for Buster waking up, "m" stands for her moving about and "¬" is a symbol to represent negation, i.e. "¬m" stands for her not moving about.

Because people have limited working memories and cannot keep many alternatives in mind, the model theory proposes that the procedures for constructing models build an initial set of models which maintains as much information as possible implicitly:

```
[w]  m
 ...
```

The first model represents explicitly the situation where Buster wakes up and moves about. The second model, represented by the three dots, contains implicit information: it indicates that there are alternative models to the first one, but they have not been "fleshed out" yet. In the first model, the possibility of Buster waking up has been represented exhaustively in relation to her moving about: Buster waking up cannot be represented in any other situation unless in that situation she is also moving about. The square brackets indicate the exhaustive representation of all instances of this contingency. The information that Buster moves about has not been exhaustively represented and it may occur in other models, with or without Buster waking up:

```
[w]  m
     m
 ...
```

Because Buster waking up has been exhaustively represented, it may not occur in other models, and so the fully fleshed-out set of models is as follows:

```
  w    m
 ¬w    m
 ¬w   ¬m
```

TABLE 3.6
Models for the Propositional Connectives[a]

1. *p and q*				
Initial model:	p	q		
Explicit model:	[p]	[q]		
2. *p or q*				
Initial models:	p			
		q		
Explicit models:	*Inclusive*		*Exclusive*	
	[p]	[$\neg$q]	[p]	[$\neg$q]
	[$\neg$p]	[q]	[$\neg$p]	[q]
	[p]	[q]		
3. *if p then q*				
Initial models:	p	q		
	. . .			
Explicit models:	*Conditional*		*Biconditional*	
	[p]	[q]	[p]	[q]
	[$\neg$p]	[q]	[$\neg$p]	[$\neg$q]
	[$\neg$p]	[$\neg$q]		
4. *p only if q*				
Initial models:	[p]	q		
	$\neg$p	[$\neg$q]		
	. . .			
Explicit models:	*Conditional*		*Biconditional*	
	[p]	[q]	[p]	[q]
	[$\neg$p]	[$\neg$q]	[$\neg$p]	[$\neg$q]
	[$\neg$p]	[q]		

[a]Each line represents an alternative model, and the square brackets indicate that the set of contingencies has been exhaustively represented.
From Johnson-Laird and Byrne (1991).

We reproduce here a table from Johnson-Laird and Byrne (1991) outlining both the initial and fleshed-out sets of models for various connectives (see Table 3.6).

The model theory of propositional reasoning specifies that reasoning requires three stages (Johnson-Laird & Byrne, 1991). First, it requires model-constructing procedures that take the premises and any background knowledge as their input and produce models of the premises as their output, and that flesh out models to be more explicit if necessary. The second stage of reasoning depends on model-combining procedures, that take two or more sets of models as input, and produce the combined set as output, revising them to eliminate any inconsistencies. This step also requires model-describing procedures that take models as their input and produce a parsimonious description of the models as their output. The third stage is one of validation that requires model-revising procedures, to take a premise or putative conclusion and a set of models as their input and produce a revised model and conclusion as their output, which falsifies the putative conclusion if this is possible. The theory has been modelled as a psychological algorithm in a computer program written in LISP (Johnson-Laird & Byrne, 1991, ch. 9), and the principles by which models are constructed and combined have been described in detail (Johnson-Laird et al., 1992a).

Competence and Errors

The theory proposes that reasoners are rational in principle but that they err in practice (Johnson-Laird & Byrne, 1993c). It explains why some valid inferences are easy and others are difficult in the following way. Consider the premises:

If Buster wakes up then she moves about
Buster wakes up

The first stage of making an inference requires procedures or rules that construct models. These procedures construct an initial set of models corresponding to the first premise:

[w] m
...

and a model corresponding to the second premise:

w

The second stage of making an inference requires procedures for combining models. They add the information from the second model to the first model in the initial set, and eliminate the implicit model:

w m

This stage also requires procedures for describing models. The model can be described as:

Buster wakes up and moves about

Since the second premise contains the information that Buster wakes up, the procedures should produce the parsimonious conclusion:

Buster moves about

since there is no need to state the obvious (Grice, 1975).

The Modus Ponens inference is easy because the initial set of models does not need to be fleshed-out to make it. The Modus Tollens inference is more difficult. Given the premises:

If Buster wakes up then she moves about
Buster does not move about

reasoners represent the first premise in an initial set of models:

[w] m
. . .

and the procedures for combining information attempt to add the information from the second premise to this initial set:

¬m

Because the information in the models cannot be combined, some reasoners may conclude that nothing follows from the premises. If the set of models is fleshed-out to be explicit:

w m
¬w m
¬w ¬m

the procedures for combining models can add the information from the second premise to the information in the third model. They will eliminate the first two models, which contain the information about Buster moving about, and leave the final model:

¬w ¬m

The procedures that describe models will produce the parsimonious conclusion that Buster does not wake up. The Modus Tollens inference is difficult because it requires the set of models to be fleshed-out, and multiple models to be kept in mind. Reasoners make these inferences not by applying rules of inference, but by applying rules which construct and revise mental models (see also Byrne, 1989c; 1992; Johnson-Laird, 1992).

The theory also explains why reasoners make invalid inferences. Reasoners may make errors by failing to flesh out the set of models, or by fleshing out the set of models in different ways. Reasoners make the Denial of the Antecedent and Affirmation of the Consequent fallacies if they consider that there are no alternatives to Buster waking up which could lead her to move about, in other words, they interpret it to mean the biconditional:

If and only if Buster wakes up then she moves about

This premise is represented in an initial set of models in which both components are exhaustively represented:

[w] [m]
. . .

Given the information that Buster moved about, the procedures will eliminate the second model above and lead to the Affirmation of the Consequent conclusion that Buster wakes up. Given the Denial of the Antecedent information that Buster does not wake up, reasoners may erroneously get the right answer for the wrong reason: they may say accurately that nothing follows, simply because they cannot combine the information in the second premise with the initial set of models, regardless of whether those models are for the conditional or biconditional interpretation. If reasoners flesh out the models for the biconditional:

w m
¬w ¬m

they will make the inference, since the second premise rules out the first model. Hence the theory explains the difference in difficulty between the invalid inferences—the Denial of the Antecedent is made less often than the Affirmation of the Consequent because reasoners can get the right answer for the wrong reason.

Johnson-Laird and Byrne (1990) extend the theory to account for higher-level meta-deductions that are based on propositional inferences, such as the knight–knave puzzles we encountered earlier. The meta-deductive theory is based on the protocols of subjects solving such puzzles, and it was simulated by adding a new meta-deductive component to their computer program for propositional inference. The new component contains four simple strategies that guide the construction of models: reasoners may develop many other strategies depending on the particular puzzles they encounter. Table 3.7 illustrates the way in which one simple strategy guides the construction of models for a knight–knave puzzle. The simple strategies are designed to minimise the number of models a reasoner must keep in mind in order to reach a solution.

Supporting Evidence for the Model Theory

Johnson-Laird and Byrne (1991, p. 52) specify that:

> The theory makes three processing assumptions. The first is that the greater the number of explicit models that a reasoner has to keep in mind, the harder the task will be . . . The second assumption is that a deduction that can be made from the initial models will be easier than one that can be made only by fleshing out the models with explicit information . . . The third assumption is that it takes time to detect inconsistencies between elements of models.

TABLE 3.7
The Hypothesise-and-Match Strategy Guides the Construction of Models[a]

Premises:			
A asserts:	I am a knight and B is a knight		
B asserts:	A is not a knight		
Models for A			
A			[a model in which A is a knight]
A	B		[a model of A's assertion as true]
A:	A	B	[final model: combination of the two models]
Models for B			
B			[consequences of final model for A above: a model of B as a knight]
not-A			[a model of B's assertion as true]
B:	not-A		[final model: combination of the two models]
Models for A and B:			
A: A	B	**B**: not-A	[combination of the models for A and B]
nil			[from contradiction between A and not-A in models]
Match:			
not-A			[model from assumption that A is true, and resulting contradiction]
B:	not-A		[model of B and B's assertion]
B:	not-A		[final model: combination of both models]
Conclusions:			
B is a knight and A is a knave			[description of final model]

[a] See Johnson-Laird and Byrne (1990, p. 76).

Furthermore, erroneous conclusions are expected to correspond to a proper subset of the possible models (Johnson-Laird et al., 1992a). These predictions have been corroborated for propositional inferences (as well as for the other main domains of deduction).

Johnson-Laird and Byrne (1991) demonstrate that the theory can account for many of the established phenomena of propositional reasoning. For example, it explains the difference in difficulty between Modus Ponens and Modus Tollens: Modus Ponens can be made from the initial set, whereas Modus Tollens requires fleshing-out of the models. It explains why there is no difference in difficulty for Modus Ponens and Modus Tollens for *p only if q*, because the initial set of models for *only if* contain explicit information about the affirmative and negative cases (see Table 3.6). It accounts for the initial ambiguities in reasoners' interpretations of *if* as a conditional or biconditional, because the initial set of models can be fleshed-out to be either. Likewise, it accounts for the ambiguity of the exclusive ("but not both") and inclusive ("or both") disjunctive interpretations in the same way. It explains the difference in difficulty between inferences based on inclusive and exclusive disjunction—exclusive disjunctions require fewer models than inclusive ones.

The theory explains the "defective" truth table judgements for neutral conditionals (see Chapter 2). The initial set of models for a conditional has nothing to say about alternatives where the antecedent fails to hold, hence these cases appear, at least initially, to be "irrelevant" to the subject. It also explains the similarity between a conditional with a negated antecedent such as *if not p then q* and to a disjunction *p or q*. The conditional is initially represented by the following set of models:

[¬p] q
. . .

Negation calls to mind the affirmative alternative, and so this element may be made explicit in the model. Since the antecedent is exhausted, the other cases will exhaust the alternatives:

[¬p] q
[p]

which correspond to the models for the disjunction *p or q*. A conditional with a negated consequent *if p then not q* is represented by the following set of models:

[p] ¬q
. . .

The affirmative case may be represented as:

[p] ¬q
q
. . .

but since the negated consequent is not exhaustively represented, affirmative or negative cases may occur in the subsequent models. This set does not correspond to a disjunction.

We have encountered the phenomenon of "matching bias" in the conditional truth table task (Chapter 2) and will find that this bias is also characteristic of responses on the abstract selection task (Chapter 4). It refers to selective attention to the items named in the conditional assertions, irrespective of the presence of negative components. The mental model theory accounts for matching bias in the following way. Reasoners attend to those elements that they have explicitly represented, for example, *if p then q* is represented by the following set of models:

[p] q
. . .

which represent explicitly *p* and *q*. A conditional with a negated component, e.g. *if not p then q*, leads to the representation of the affirmative case:

q
[p]

and reasoners once again have explicitly represented *p* and *q*. Hence, the matching values will appear more relevant to the subject (Evans, 1989) or be more likely to be selected on a construction or selection task.

The suppression effect (discussed in detail in Chapter 2) is difficult for the formal rule theory to explain as we have seen, but it is consistent with the model theory. Byrne (1989b) proposed that the extra information leads to a different interpretation of the premises that contain alternatives and those that contain additionals; the premises call for a set of models that are of a different structure for alternatives than for additionals. The procedures that revise models find the alternative antecedent to be a counterexample to the fallacies, and they find the additional antecedent to be a counterexample to the valid inferences. This proposal is supported by the spontaneous use of conjunctions and disjunctions to combine alternatives and additional conditions (Byrne & Johnson-Laird, 1992; see also Braine & O'Brien, 1991; Grandy, 1993; Holyoak & Spellman, 1993).

Byrne and Johnson-Laird (1992) corroborated their proposal that the representation for a conditional contains an explicit model in which the events occur, and an implicit model in which alternative events may occur. They found that individuals more often use a conditional to paraphrase three assertions when the outcome contains a modal (e.g. "Mark can eat in a restaurant": 36%) than when it does not ("Mark eats in a restaurant": 5%).

The theory predicts a difference in the difficulty of inferences from conditionals and biconditionals. Modus Ponens for conditionals requires just one explicit model (in the initial set) and Modus Tollens requires three explicit models. Modus Ponens for biconditionals again requires just one explicit model, but Modus Tollens requires two explicit models. Johnson-Laird et al. (1992a) showed that Modus Tollens is easier with a biconditional (59%) than a conditional (38%), and there is no difference between Modus Ponens in either case (97%).

The model theory predicts that deductions from conditionals, which require one explicit model initially, should be easier than those from exclusive disjunctions, which require two explicit models to be constructed. For example, Modus Ponens from a conditional requires a single model, and the analogous affirmative inference from an exclusive disjunction requires two explicit models, and the former is easier (91%) than the latter (48%). "Double disjunctions", that is, inferences based on pairs of disjunctive premises, require multiple models to be kept in mind and lead to a breakdown in performance. An inclusive double disjunction requires five models to be kept in mind (4% correct) and is more difficult than an exclusive double disjunction that requires three models (15%). The errors people make are consistent with constructing just one of the many possible models, and few of their conclusions are not consistent with any models.

Conjunctions are easier than disjunctions (e.g. Osherson, 1974–76) and the model theory explains why this difference arises, in terms of the number of models these connectives require in their initial set. In fact, Johnson-Laird et al. (1992a) predicted the order of difficulty of different connectives, and corroborated their prediction using the difficulty ratings from Braine et al. (1984): *and* (1.79), *if* (1.88), *or* (2.66), and *not both* (3.18, where 1 = easy and 9 = hard). They also showed that the number of elements in models contributes to their difficulty.

Individual differences may arise because some individuals flesh-out their models readily whereas others fail to, or some individuals readily keep multiple models in mind whereas others fail to. Manktelow and Over (1991) suggest that the theory explains performance on deontic inferences (discussed in the next chapter), and Markovits (1988) extends the model theory to a range of conditional tasks.

The meta-deductive theory is supported by data from Rips (1989), which shows that problems that can be solved by a simple strategy are easier than problems that cannot (Johnson-Laird & Byrne, 1990; see also Byrne & Handley, 1993; Rips, 1990b). The idea that reasoners do not come to these problems with a fixed strategy is supported by the finding that they improve spontaneously on these problems, without feedback (Byrne & Handley, 1993). Likewise, the idea that they develop specific strategies to suit individual problems rather than settle into a stable solution path is supported by the finding that their performance improves on problems that can be solved by a very specific strategy (a "same-assertion-and-match" strategy) when they receive the same problems again, but not when they receive problems that require a different strategy (see Byrne & Handley, in press; Byrne, Handley & Johnson-Laird, 1992).

Criticisms of the Model Theory and Rebuttals

A wide range of criticisms of the model theory have been discussed recently (see the commentaries following Johnson-Laird & Byrne, 1993a; see also Johnson-Laird & Byrne, 1991, chs 2 and 10) and we summarise the primary ones here. The theory was originally proposed to account for syllogistic inference only (see Chapter 7), and as a result it was criticised for its limited scope (e.g. Braine et al., 1984; Braine & O'Brien, 1991; Evans, 1987; Rips, 1986). The criticism is obsolete since the theory has been developed to account for reasoning in the primary domains of deduction (Johnson-Laird & Byrne, 1991). It extends to propositional inference (Byrne & Johnson-Laird, 1990b; 1992; Johnson-Laird et al., 1992a) and to meta-deduction (Johnson-Laird & Byrne, 1990), as we have already seen. As we will see in forthcoming chapters, it also extends to relational inference (Byrne & Johnson-Laird, 1989) and to quantificational inference (Johnson-Laird & Byrne, 1989; see also Byrne & Johnson-Laird, 1990a; Greene, 1992; Johnson-Laird, Byrne & Tabossi, 1992). In fact, the theory can now claim to account for a wider range of deductive phenomena than any current theory of deduction.

Critics have tested the predictions of the model theory and failed to find support for them. Rips (1990b) found no difference between multiple model problems such as:

not (p and q)
if not p then r
if not q then r
Therefore, r?

and single model problems based on the same premises but with a disjunction, *or*, in the first premise (approximately 65% correct for both). The negation of a conjunction leads to three models, so the model theory predicts that this problem should be harder than the negation of a disjunction which leads to a single model. Rips's rule theory predicts the lack of a difference, since it includes rules to deal directly with such sentential negations (DeMorgan's laws; but for reservations about their status as elementary rules, see Braine et al., 1984). Byrne and Handley (1992) showed that reasoners rarely made the correct interpretation of the negation of a conjunction (25%) compared to a disjunction (43%). The most common error (25%) was to interpret the negated conjunction in exactly the same way as the negated disjunction: *not p and not q*. Subjects who misinterpreted the conjunction would none the less reach the correct answer to Rips's problems: it follows whether they have made a correct or incorrect interpretation of the first premise, and the presentation of conclusions to evaluate is too insensitive a measure to discriminate between them. Hence, both problems are single model problems, for the bulk of subjects who fail to interpret the negated conjunction accurately. In fact, Rips (1983) mentions a case of a subject whose protocol indicated a similar error, interpreting *if not (p and q) then r* to mean *if not p and not q then r*. Rips discusses the possible need for pathological rules to deal with such cases, but the model theory explains the phenomenon without sacrificing logical competence (see Byrne & Handley, 1992).

Another empirical criticism of the model theory is that its application to meta-deduction fails to account for errors through the mechanism of model construction, but relies instead on *ad hoc* strategies independent of the model framework (Rips, 1989; 1990b). But, the strategies are motivated by the need to minimise the number of models that reasoners consider during the course of solving meta-deductions (Johnson-Laird & Byrne, 1990; 1991).

The predictions of the model theory have been pitted against the predictions of rule theories and the data have corroborated the model theory in each of the primary domains of deduction (Johnson-Laird & Byrne, 1991). The comparisons between rules and models may have been unfair: they should have been based on measures such as the number of direct and indirect proofs (Fetzer, 1993) or the number of embedded assumptions (Crawford, 1993). But the measures used were those proposed by formal rule theorists, that the number of steps in a derivation corresponds to the difficulty of an inference (Braine et al., 1984; Braine & O'Brien, 1991; Rips, 1983; 1989; Smith et al., 1992). Some critics argue that the model theory is too flexible to be testable, but Johnson-Laird and Byrne point out that the results of their experimentation in each of the domains of deduction could have falsified the theory. We discuss other empirical criticisms of the model theory, for example in the domains of the selection task, multiple quantification and so on, in subsequent chapters. We turn now to the bulk of the criticisms of the model theory, which have been primarily of a theoretical rather than an empirical nature.

Rips (1986) suggests that the theory cannot explain the generality of inference: it explains content effects but not reasoning with unfamiliar material. Johnson-Laird and Byrne (1991) contend that reasoners can construct models of unfamiliar domains—all they need is a knowledge of the meaning of the connectives and quantifiers. Conversely, how the theory deals with content effects, in particular how people retrieve counterexamples, and when they can incorporate available world knowledge to flesh-out their models, remains unclear (Eysenck & Keane, 1990; Green, 1993; Holyoak & Spellman, 1993; Inder, 1993; Legrenzi & Sonino, 1993; Stevenson, 1993). There are glimpses of the process of retrieval in reasoning, for example, Keane (1987) discovered that reasoners retrieving analogies tend to retrieve semantically close analogues based on surface features such as similar objects, rather than semantically remote analogues (see also Holyoak & Koh, 1987; Keane, 1988; Keane, Ledgeway & Duff, 1991). Models may be unworkable because the amount of knowledge needed to simulate real phenomena is unrealistic (Rips, 1986), but Johnson-Laird and Byrne argue that models can be incomplete. They concede that there are aspects of the theory that remain unspecified, such as the way in which reasoners search for alternative models, how the models are generated and how the search is terminated.

More information about how knowledge becomes available would help to clarify the use of counterexamples in non-monotonic inference, and obviate any suggested need for a logic to constrain the construction of models (*pace* Chater, 1993; see also Oaksford, 1993). The suppression effect may arise because individuals combine the alternatives or additional conditions in models and find counterexamples to the conclusions in the ways described above. Alternatively, it may arise because the second conditional causes individuals to doubt the truth of the first conditional (Politzer & Braine, 1991), to reject it (Bach, 1993), to consider it uncertain (Over, 1993) or even to consider it false (Savion, 1993). Do individuals doubt the truth of one of the premises? Byrne (1991a) disputed Politzer and Braine's (1991) suggestion that reasoners reach the conclusion that one of the premises is false. She argued it makes predictions that are falsified by data from the experiment it is designed to explain. Moreover, the suppression effect is found even when individuals are not given an explicit second conditional (Byrne, 1989a; Cummins et al., 1991). Hence, it cannot result purely from doubt in the premises. Byrne and Handley (reported in Johnson-Laird & Byrne, 1993c) carried out an experiment in which subjects judged whether both sentences could be true together, or whether if the first sentence was true then the second sentence was false, or vice versa. Their most frequent judgement was that the conditionals containing additional antecedents can both be true at the same time.

The search for counterexamples lies at the heart of the model theory. It appears to underlie few predictions (Polk, 1993), to be very difficult for reasoners (Bara, 1993; Fetzer, 1993). The specific theory of propositional reasoning appears to rest on an algorithm that does not involve refutation by counterexample (Rips, 1990a). Johnson-Laird and Byrne (1993b) suggest that the search for counterexamples is not a self-conscious one, and so reasoners frequently make mistakes and fail to complete it. It is this very difficulty of searching for counterexamples which underlies the prediction that the more models a reasoner must examine, the more difficult an inference will be.

Critics claim that models capitalise on a visual metaphor, they are image-like and must contain only perceptual tokens (Ford, 1985; Inder, 1987; Stenning and Oberlander, 1993; ter Meulen, 1993; see also MacLennan, 1993). Moreover, "vivid representations" (Levesque, 1986) can contain only definite items, and so the notion of an implicit model is contradictory (Holyoak & Spellman, 1993). Johnson-Laird and Byrne (1991) contend that the computer programs that simulate the theory do not rely on any visual metaphor, and there is good experimental evidence for the use of propositional-like tags (Johnson-Laird & Byrne, 1989; Polk & Newell, 1988) and for the existence of implicit models (Byrne & Johnson-Laird, 1992). They suggest that:

> . . . there are distinctions between the two sorts of representation, e.g. vivid representations cannot represent directly either negatives or disjunctions . . . The tokens of mental models may occur in a visual image, or they may not be directly accessible to consciousness. What matters is, not the phenomenal experience, but the structure of the models. This structure . . . often transcends the perceptible (Johnson-Laird & Byrne, 1991, pp. 38–39).

Images may be a special case of models, but models can represent many assertions that cannot be visualised. They can represent multiply-quantified relations, unlike Euler circles, and since reasoners can move freely between singly and multiple quantified relations, it is unlikely that they rely on Euler circles (*pace* Stenning & Oberlander, 1993).

Critics argue that there is an anomaly between models being unconscious but in working memory (e.g. Braine & O'Brien, 1991; Braine, 1993; Rips, 1989; Wetherick, 1993). But, presence in consciousness may be a matter of degree for models (MacLennan, 1993), and the content of models may be available to consciousness. Introspective evidence from protocols has guided the construction of both sorts of inference theory—rules and models—and it can weigh equally against either (Johnson-Laird & Byrne, 1993b). The process of inference and the format of mental representations are never fully accessible (Johnson-Laird & Byrne, 1993b). An underlying mechanism of reasoning cannot be expected to be introspectible (Evans, 1990b).

What is the relation of the model theory to logic? Some critics suggest that mental models are irrational, since they do not contain formal inference rules. Johnson-Laird and Byrne (1991) show that the theory provides a mental logic that depends on a model-theoretic rather than a proof-theoretic logic. Is there a genuine difference between formal rules and mental models? According to some critics, the procedures needed to specify how models work *are* inference rules, at least "tacit inference rules" (Braine, 1993; Goldman, 1986; Rips, 1990a).Johnson-Laird and Byrne (1991; 1993c) contend that the procedures that manipulate models are not *inference rules*. The confusion is similar to confusing the semantic method of truth tables with the syntactic method of proof in propositional logic. For example, to add a new connective to the system, a rule theory must add an inference rule for it, whereas the model theory must add its meaning to the lexicon, that is, the structure of the models that are to be constructed. The rules for constructing models, revising them and so on, remain exactly the same. Some authors suggest that mental models may be unnecessary, and the underlying representation may be propositional, e.g. syntactic strings of symbols (Rips, 1986), or neural. However, Johnson-Laird and Byrne (1991) argue that mental computations can rely on high-level structures, just as programming languages can. The theory does not argue against rules *per se* (*pace* Andrews, 1993; Braine, 1993; Stenning & Oberlander, 1993; ter Meulen, 1993), only against rules of inference. Theories based on formal rules and on mental models posit different sorts of mental representations and different sorts of cognitive processes, and they lead to different empirical predictions (Johnson-Laird & Byrne, 1991).

Are mental models like the models made familiar to logicians by Tarski? Reasoners cannot construct infinitely many models: they examine a finite number of models to validate a deduction (see Barwise, 1993; Bundy, 1993; Inder, 1993; Johnson-Laird & Byrne, 1993b; ter Meulen, 1993). Johnson-Laird and Byrne (1991) show that the model theory, unlike the predicate calculus, applies only to finite sets of models, it has a decision procedure and it works directly with finite models. Are mental models based on syntactic procedures (e.g. Bundy, 1993; Holyoak & Spellman, 1993; Inder, 1993)? Rules for manipulating models are syntactic in the computer programs modelling the theory: "The application of the adjective 'semantic' to any existing computer program is an oxymoron. Models in programs, however, should not be confused with the real thing" (Johnson-Laird & Byrne, 1993b). Humans can have access to the meanings of their expressions. As we saw earlier, dispute surrounds the question of whether theories should do without semantic notions like truth and reference that depend on the relation between mental representations and the world (see Oden, 1987; Rips, 1986). Rips (1990b, p. 297) proposes that the debate centres on "a confusion between truth in the actual world and truth with respect to a representation . . . mental models are just representations too; so you can always ask in turn whether they are true or false". In fact, Johnson-Laird and Byrne (1991) argue that it is exactly through asking whether a mental model is a representation of an actual state of affairs, a real possibility, a real impossibility, or a counterfactual situation, that one keeps track of the metaphysics of everyday situations, either factual or fictional. Without such notions, there would be little left of mental life to study.

It may be the case that people reason by use of both inference rules *and* mental models (Braine, 1993), although no proposals have been made about when each would be used (Smith et al., 1992), and there are inherent problems in experimentally distinguishing them as strategies (Roberts, in press). Johnson-Laird and Byrne (1991) argue that mental models do not supplement inference rules but are a distinct algorithm that renders rules superfluous. Perhaps the theory needs to be combined with some fundamental, automatic rules such as the rule for Modus Ponens

(Falmagne, 1993; Pollard, 1993; Wetherick, 1993)? On the contrary, Johnson-Laird and Byrne (1993b) show that the models for conditionals are constructed without the rule for Modus Ponens, and the computer program that models the theory uses only the "truth conditions" of the connective.

The theory may overestimate the importance of logical ability (e.g. Fisher, 1993; Galotti & Komatsu, 1993; Luchins & Luchins, 1993; Savion, 1993). The experimental evidence is founded on a presupposition of rational competence without which the theory would collapse (Cohen, 1993). Johnson-Laird and Byrne (1991) agree that without the semantic principle of validity, the argument would collapse—as would any argument—and they suggest that "a world without deduction would be a world without science, technology, laws, and social conventions" (p. 3). There are many sorts of thinking to which the theory has yet to be extended. However, attempts are underway to apply the theory to inductive reasoning (Johnson-Laird, 1993), probabilistic inference (see Rodrigo, deVega & Castaneda, 1992), argumentation (e.g. Keane, Byrne & Johnson-Laird, 1993), explanation (Byrne, 1991b) and conceptual combination (Costello & Keane, 1992). Moreover, the theory may encompass phenomena on goal-directed thinking (Baron, 1993), scientific thinking (Tweney, 1993), children's thinking (Bara, 1993; Markovits & Vachon, 1990) and animal cognition (Davis, 1993).

Johnson-Laird and Byrne (1991) acknowledge that the theory is incomplete and can appear piecemeal (Polk, 1993). More information is needed on the components out of which deduction is assembled, they suggest, as well as on such questions as, what counts as a mental model, what other forms of mental representation are there, how does the theory apply to modal reasoning, and do two people have the same models when they reach the same inference?

CONCLUSIONS

In this chapter, we have described two theories of conditional reasoning: the theory that it depends on formal rules and the theory that it depends on mental models. Our aim has been to provide a clear exposition of these theories, to indicate the range of evidence for which they can or cannot claim to account, and to provide the reader with the arguments proposed for and against each position. We will return to the model theory from time to time to examine its application to the particular phenomena reviewed in the chapters which follow. It will at times be contrasted with the heuristic account and the domain-sensitive rule theory. Of these two remaining theories, we have seen applications of heuristic accounts already in Chapter 2 and will see more of this theory in the following chapter. Our discussion of research on the Wason selection task is also the appropriate place in which to describe the domain-sensitive rules theory. It is to the Wason selection task that we now turn.

4 The Wason Selection Task

The four card selection task was first described by Wason (1966), who can hardly have suspected that in the next quarter of a century it would become the most intensively researched single problem in the history of the psychology of reasoning. At the time of writing, there is no sign that interest in the task is abating, and submissions of papers on the problem to learned journals continue with great regularity.

Early research on the selection task (see Evans, 1982; Wason & Johnson-Laird, 1972) lead to the development of a standard abstract formulation of the problem which is shown in Fig. 4.1. In this form, the subjects are shown four cards drawn from a pack which all have a capital letter on one side and a single figure number on the other side. They are then given a conditional statement variously described as a rule or a claim which makes a statement such as: "If there is an A on one side of the card, then there is a 3 on the other side of the card." The facing values of the cards always include one letter and one number that match those in the rule and one letter and number that differ. In the example shown, the four cards are "A", "D", "3" and "7". These are often referred to as the *p*, *not-p*, *q* and *not-q* cards for a rule of the general form *If p then q*.

The task set is one of hypothesis testing, although it requires deductive reasoning based on the logic of conditionals. Subjects are asked to decide which cards they would need to turn over in order to decide whether the rule is true or false. Logical analysis indicates that the correct answer is the A (*p*) and 7 (*not-q*) cards. In order to see this, one has to project the possible consequences of turning each card. The A card might have a 3 on the back which conforms to the rule, or a number other than a 3 which

Subjects are shown a set of cards, each of which is seen to have a capital letter on one side and a single figure number on the other side. The experimenter then hides the cards and selects four which are placed on the table. The subject can then see the four facing sides as follows:

The subject is then told that "the following rule applies to these four cards and may be true or false"

If there is an A on one side of the card, then there is a 3 on the other side of the card

The subject is then asked to decide which of the four cards would need to be turned over in order to decide whether the rule is true or false.

TYPICAL CHOICES

A alone, or A and 3

CORRECT CHOICE

A and 7, because the rule can only be falsified if a card is found which has an A on one side and does not have a 3 on the other side.

FIG. 4.1 The Wason selection task (standard abstract presentation).

clearly contradicts the rule. Hence, it must be turned over. Unless you interpret the rule as a biconditional, the D card need not be turned because the rule has no implications for cards with letters other than A. The 3 card may have an A on the back, but if it does not, then the rule is not contradicted since there is no claim that there must be an A on the back of a 3. Finally, the 7 might have an A on the back; this would be a case of an A together with a number which is not a 3, which clearly contradicts the rule. Hence, the 7 card must be turned. If the rule is interpreted as biconditional, then all four cards should be turned over.

The interest in the task lies in the fact that despite its apparent simplicity, the great majority of intelligent adult subjects fail to solve it. Early studies (e.g. Wason, 1968; 1969; Wason & Johnson-Laird, 1970) reported that most subjects chose either the *p* cards alone or the *p* and *q* cards, and that few subjects selected *not-q*. Thus there are two characteristic logical errors: (1) selection of the unnecessary *q* card and (2) failure to select the logically required *not-q* card. The correct combination of *p* and *not-q* was reported to occur less than 10% of the time in these early studies (Wason & Johnson-Laird, 1972). As we shall see, this very low base rate performance depends upon (1) the standard form of presentation of the task and (2) the testing of subjects on a single task in a between-groups design.

In the original Wason studies, real packs of cards were used, which the subjects were allowed to inspect prior to the four cards being secretly drawn. Most recent studies, however, have relied on descriptions of the cards and pictorial representations of the facing sides of the cards either on pencil and paper or on a computer screen. These procedural evolutions of the task have made very little difference in themselves to baseline responding, and the two errors described above persist in forms of the task in which (1) the rule used is an affirmative *if p then q* conditional and (2) the content remains abstract rather than thematic. Many studies in the past 10–15 years have investigated thematic content and this work will be reviewed later in the chapter. We concentrate first, however, on studies using abstract materials.

STUDIES USING ABSTRACT CONTENT

The Early Wason and Johnson-Laird Studies

Wason's (1966) introduction of the selection task was followed by several journal articles which established the reliability of the phenomenon and its robustness in the face of minor procedural variations (Wason, 1968; 1969; Wason & Johnson-Laird, 1970). These and other early studies of the selection task will receive comparatively brief treatment here and the reader is referred to Wason and Johnson-Laird (1972) and to Evans (1982) for more detailed review and discussion.

The theoretical account of the basic errors was based upon confirmation bias, although Wason preferred the term "verification bias" in his early papers. Essentially, it was suggested that subjects were trying to prove the conditional statement true rather than false and that consequently they chose the confirming combination of True Antecedent (*p*) and True Consequent (*q*) and avoided the potentially falsifying False Consequent (*not-q*). Wason (1966) realised that this account would not work if the subject was assumed to possess a truth table for material implication and hence proposed the "defective" truth table for conditionals (see Chapter 2). Subjects are not, in consequence, predicted to select the False

Antecedent (*not-p*) card, since this will lead to a combination which is irrelevant to the truth of the rule rather than a confirmation of it.

Johnson-Laird and Wason (1970) expanded this confirmation bias account into a formal model in which it was proposed that subjects were in one of three states of insight as follows:

- *No insight*. Subjects in this state attempted to verify the rule and chose either *p* alone or *p* and *q* depending upon whether they held a conditional or biconditional reading of the conditional.
- *Partial insight*. Subjects in this state look for choices which both verify and falsify the rule and are predicted to select the cards *p*, *q* and *not-q*.
- *Complete insight*. Subjects here attempt only to falsify the rule and choose the correct cards, *p* and *q*.

This paper was followed by others proposing variants of the insight model, the most ambitious of which was that of Smalley (1974). Evidence for insight models was based partially upon introspective reports of subjects (e.g. Goodwin & Wason, 1972, discussed below) and partially upon transitions in responding noted in studies using "therapeutic" procedures aimed at inducing insight into the need for falsification. Therapy experiments (e.g. Wason, 1969; Wason & Johnson-Laird, 1970; Wason & Golding, 1974) involved attempts of varying strength to make subjects aware of the falsifying potential of the *not-q* card. For example, subjects might be asked to consider what could be on the back of this card and asked to comment on the effect that such hidden values could have on the rule. In some experiments, subjects were actually asked to turn over the *not-q* card and discovered the falsifying *p* value on the back.

It turns out that subjects have no difficulty in seeing that a *p* card with a *not-q* on the back, or vice versa, will falsify the rule. This should not surprise us, since we saw that research on the truth table task discussed in Chapter 2 shows that subjects readily identify TF as a falsifying combination for a conditional statement. What is surprising is that in some cases prompting subjects to say that a *p* on the back of the *not-q* card would falsify the rule did not lead them to change their decision about the need to select it. Perhaps the most fascinating aspect of these papers is the verbal protocols which show apparently marked degrees of inconsistency and self-contradiction in the intelligent adult subjects employed.

A statistical argument against the validity of insight models was proposed by Evans (1977b; see also Krauth, 1982), who argued that such theories attach significance to the particular combinations of cards that subjects choose. In a re-analysis of a number of published experiments, Evans showed that the frequency of choice of cards *q* and *not-q* were statistically independent. Hence, he argued, the combinations were mere statistical outcomes of no special significance. Whether subjects' choices on the selection task reflect a confirmation bias is also highly moot for other reasons, as we shall see shortly. There is both evidence of an alternative factor called "matching bias" and reason to question the validity of subjects' introspective accounts of their card selections (see below). What these early studies do demonstrate, however, is a markedly persistent logical error on an apparently simple task which is difficult to eliminate and which may be defended by some tortuous rationalisations on the part of the subjects.

The Reduced Array Selection Task (RAST)

It was mentioned above that the early Wason and Johnson-Laird studies demonstrated robustness of selection rates over procedural variations. These included such manipulations as the use of a quantified rather than conditional rule ("Every card which has an A on one side . . ."), the use of binary materials so that a card either does or does not have a given symbol, and the presentation of problems with antecedent and consequent items on the same side of (partially concealed) cards.

It was, however, discovered quite early on that logical performance could be enhanced if subjects were induced to think only about the consequent choices. Johnson-Laird and Wason (1970) asked subjects to try to verify or falsify statements describing the contents of two boxes such as *If they are triangles then they are black*. To do this, they could ask for objects from a box containing black figures and one containing white figures. Logically, the white box needs to be searched exhaustively and the black box not at all. In all cases, the contents of the white box was exhaustively examined and in no case was this done with the black box—so all subjects appeared to gain insight at some point. An instructional set to falsify produced better performance (less black choices) than instructions to verify. This task has become known as the RAST: reduced array selection task.

Subsequent research on the RAST has often used one-trial versions, which is essentially a standard selection task with the *p* and *not-p* cards omitted. In fact, Roth (1979) has shown that facilitation can occur if just the *p* card is left out and replaced by a second *not-p*. [Wason and Green (1984), in addition to replicating the facilitatory effect of the RAST, have also shown that use of rules which refer to a single entity, e.g. "All circles are black", facilitates performance compared with the usual kind of rule.] The effect of the RAST manipulation is substantially to increase the number of correct selections of the *not-q* card, although Wason and Green (1984) have shown that this does not transfer to a subsequently presented standard selection task. There are several possible explanations of this effect, but it seems to provide evidence that the failure to select *not-q* in the standard task is due to giving it insufficient attention and/or to a fallacious belief that choice of *p* precludes the need to examine *not-q*. The finding is thus broadly supportive of the interpretations of the selection task which are proposed by Evans (1984a; 1989) and by Margolis (1987), each of which is discussed below. It has also been taken as support for the mental models account of the selection task (Green, 1992; Johnson-Laird & Byrne, 1991).

Effects of Instructional Manipulations

The wording of the selection task instructions has attracted attention from time to time in the subsequent literature on the selection task. One issue has been the use of terms such as "truth" and "falsity" in the instructions. The instruction shown in the standard version of the task (Fig. 3.1) is typical—but not universal—in asking subjects to decide whether the rule is true or false. The issue of these instructions was raised by Yachanin and Tweney (1982) in connection with the alleged thematic facilitation effect in which use of realistic rather than abstract problem material is supposed to induce correct logical responding on the selection task. The use of thematic materials is discussed later in the chapter, but we will consider the issue of instructions here. What Yachanin and Tweney specifically proposed was that while abstract versions of the task typically used the true–false instruction shown in Fig. 4.1, most successful realistic variants of the task asked subjects to decide whether or not the rule had been *violated*. They claim that the testing task is more difficult than the violation task and that this change in instruction could be responsible at least in part for the facilitation observed. Yachanin (1983, experiment 1) actually found some evidence that abstract selection task performance could be facilitated by use of the violation form of instruction.

Yachanin's hypothesis was investigated in an experiment reported by Griggs (1984). He used both abstract and thematic content with both true–false and violation instructions. By "abstract", Griggs means that the content does not provide any cues to the logical solution from previous experience of the content. The abstract problem was as follows:

> On this task imagine you are a "widgit" inspector. The cards below have information about four widgits on a table. On one side of a card is the widgit's letter and on the other side of the card is a widgit's number.
>
> Here is a rule you heard: *If a widgit has an "A" on one side, then it must have a "3" on the other side.*
>
> Since you left your list of widgit rules at home, you must find out if the rule is true or false. Consider each card, one at a time, selecting the card or cards that you definitely need to turn over to determine if the rule is true or false.

In the violation version, the last sentence was replaced by the following:

> Consider each card, one at a time, selecting the card or cards that you definitely need to turn over to determine whether the rule is being violated.

The thematic materials used by Griggs were those of the Drinking Age Rule (Griggs & Cox, 1982) discussed later in this chapter. He found no facilitation, in fact no logically correct choices of *p* and *not-q*, with abstract content regardless of instruction, whereas facilitation was observed in both instruction groups on the thematic content version. However, with thematic content, correct choices were significantly more often observed using the violation instruction. A later paper by Valentine (1985) included further investigation of the instructional set in abstract selection tasks, and supported Griggs' finding that violation instructions produce no facilitation in such cases.

Chrostowski and Griggs (1985) suggested that the discrepancy with Yachanin's (1983) results might reflect procedural differences. In particular, Yachanin's subjects were asked to think aloud while solving the task, a procedure shown by Berry (1983) to improve selection task performance in itself. Chrostowski and Griggs therefore repeated the study of Griggs (1984) with the additional manipulation of presence and absence of verbalisation. In fact, no effect of verbalisation was recorded, whereas the effects of content and instruction were essentially the same as those of Griggs (1984). A further study by Yachanin (1986) himself confirmed the findings of Griggs that thematic content was necessary in order for the violation instruction to have an effect. In conclusion, then, this set of studies does not support the hypothesis that induction of a falsification set by the use of violation instructions is either sufficient or necessary to produce facilitation of responding on the selection task. It does, however, appear to enhance the level of facilitation observed on the thematic versions such as the Drinking Age Rule, described later in this chapter.

Hoch and Tschirgi (1983; 1985) reported modest facilitation of performance on the abstract selection task when the conditional rule was explicated. For example, the rule "If there is an A on one side of the card, then there is a 2 on the other side of the card" was clarified by the following: "Cards with the letter A on the front may have only the number 2 on the back, but cards with the letter B on the front may have either a 1 or a 2 on the back." Platt and Griggs (in press a) replicated this finding but also showed that the effect is stronger if (a) the explication replaces the standard rule rather than accompanying it and (b) if—as was the case in Hoch and Tschirgi's experiments—subjects are asked to provide verbal justifications for their choices. In their third experiment, Platt and Griggs also showed that—in contrast with standard abstract problems—the level of performance on the explicated rule with reasons procedure was enhanced significantly further by use of the violation rather than true–false form of instruction. In conjunction with the interaction of instructions with abstract/thematic content reported above, it appears that the violation instruction facilitates performance only in conjunction with another facilitating factor.

Some striking effects of instructional manipulations on selection task choices have also been observed in some recent papers of Griggs (1989; Griggs & Jackson,1990) designed to test hypotheses put forward by Margolis (1987). Margolis presented a hypothesis of scenario ambiguity to explain the usual pattern of erroneous choices on the selection task. He suggested that subjects mistakenly impute an open scenario context to the selection task while it is in fact closed. He gives an open scenario version of the selection task to demonstrate the difference. In this task, the rule concerning a collection of cards is: *If it says "swan" on one side of a card then it must say "white" on the other*. Of the four *categories* "swan", "raven", "white" and "black", you are asked to check any which may lead to a violation of the rule. In this case, the correct answer is "swan" (*p*) or "black" (*not-p*) but *not both*, since an exhaustive search of either category will lead to discovery of any counterexample to the rule.

The crucial difference between this and the standard selection task is that when you choose "swan" you get to see every card which has a swan on it rather than just the particular card which has a swan on its facing side. Margolis suggests that this open scenario, in which you decide which *categories* to investigate, is more likely to occur in real life than the closed scenario of the selection task in which you must decide which particular *exemplars* to investigate. Could a misinterpretation of the selection task as an open scenario problem then account for the usual error of *p* alone, or *p* and *q* (which follows from a biconditional reading of the rule)? As Griggs (1989) points out, the hypothesis is consistent with findings on the RAST. If subjects are denied the usual choice of the *p* card, then they are much more likely to choose *not-q*, since these choices would be perceived as alternative methods of achieving the same goal.

Margolis argues that the following task removes the scenario ambiguity:

> Four cards have been picked from a mixed pack (some red backs, some blue). The person who chose the cards was told to obey the following rule: *Pick any four cards . . . except that if a card has a red back, it must be at least a 6.*
>
> You see the cards lying on a table, with two face down and two face up. Circle each card that must be turned over in order to be sure that it violates the rule.

Griggs (1989) presented this problem to subjects in two experiments and found the remarkably high correct selection rates of 80 and 73% for red backs and numbers less than 6, respectively. In a third experiment, he changed the last sentence to produce a true–false version of the instruction. Correct responding dropped to 50%, but this is still well above the 10% or less which is typical of abstract selection task experiments. Moreover, in this condition, a further 25% showed the "partial insight" pattern of *p*, *q* and *not-q*.

Griggs and Jackson (1990) tested more of Margolis' hypotheses. First, if scenario ambiguity is not resolved (an otherwise standard task) but the subject is constrained to choose exactly two cards by the instruction "Circle two cards to turn over in order to check whether the rule has been violated", then it is expected that the number of *p* & *q* choices will increase. This is because *p* is deemed to provide the same information as *not-q*, so the subjects can only gain new information with a second choice by assuming the rule to be an equivalence. More interesting is the following prediction: when the instruction is "Figure out which two cards could violate the rule, and circle them", Margolis predicts that there will be an increase in the number of *not-p* and *not-q* cards selected—an extremely infrequently observed combination under standard instructions, which runs counter to the matching bias effect discussed below. Margolis claims that the emphasis on violation in the second phrasing shifts subjects' attention towards the cards not specified in the rule. The procedure differs from that of other studies of the violation form of instruction in again specifying exactly two cards. Griggs and Jackson (1990, experiment 1) found dramatic support for these predictions. The first instructional variant produced 80% *p* & *q* selections compared with 40% under standard instructions, and the second produced 65% *not-p* & *not-q* choices compared with 10% under standard instructions.

In conclusion, then, instructions which simply direct subjects towards violation rather than a search for truth and falsity do not facilitate selections on the abstract task, although they may enhance responding on already effective thematic content. The instructional variants proposed by Margolis (1987) have, however, been shown to have marked effects on selection task responses in line with his surprising predictions, and must therefore command some serious attention to the interpretation of selection task performance that he proposes.

Effects of Intelligence, Education and Training

The final set of studies we consider using the affirmative abstract selection task concern the question of whether performance depends upon intelligence and whether it can be improved by education or special training. We know that the logical error is very common among intelligent adults (undergraduate students) but what of professional scientists, mathematicians or professors of logic? There are few studies in the literature which bear on this issue.

Valentine (1975) looked at the relationship between a general measure of intelligence and performance on the selection task in a group of undergraduate psychology students. Even using a population with such a restricted range of intelligence, she did find a significant positive correlation. Hoch and Tschirgi (1985) compared groups with three levels of educational attainment: high school, bachelor's degrees and master's degrees. They found a significant association between educational level and correct selections on the task, and also reported more evidence of matching bias in groups of lower educational attainment. The correct selection rates in the masters group were observed at the extraordinarily high rate of 48%. Although attainment covaried with exposure to teaching formal logic, this factor proved not to be predictive of performance when it was separated out.

Jackson and Griggs (1988) were puzzled by Hoch and Tschirgi's findings with masters students which are out of line with findings of several studies on professional scientists. For example, Griggs and Ransdell (1986) found correct solution rates on the standard abstract task of under 10% by doctoral scientists. They hypothesised that it was not the educational level of Hoch and Tschirgi's subjects *per se*, but their specialism in technical areas such as mathematics and engineering that was responsible for the findings. Jackson and Griggs compared four areas of expertise (social science, technical engineering, computer science and mathematics) and two levels of education (bachelor's and master's degrees). Their findings showed no effect of educational level but a significant effect of subject expertise: mathematicians performed better than subjects with other areas of specialism and achieved solution rates of well over 50%.

The area of training that one might expect to be of most help is that of formal logic, despite the negative findings of Hoch and Tschirgi (1985). A relevant major study is reported by Cheng, Holyoak, Nisbett and Oliver (1986). A study of statistical reasoning known to the authors had recently shown that the use of statistical concepts in everyday reasoning can be enhanced both by laboratory training and by attendance at formal classes in statistics (Fong, Krantz & Nisbett, 1986). Cheng et al. set out effectively to replicate these findings with logic and the selection task but came up with rather different results. Laboratory-based training was only effective in reducing error when rule-based training was used in conjunction with examples training, whereas Fong et al. found each to be effective individually. In a second study, Cheng et al. compared the performance of subjects who had received a course of formal training in logic and found no effect on ability to solve the selection task—again in contrast with the analogous work on statistics classes reported by Fong et al.

We know that there are individual differences in ability to solve the selection task, since a small minority of typical student samples do get it right. The studies reviewed in this section suggest that it may be related to intelligence or educational attainment—which are in any case correlated —and that it is related to ability in mathematics. It is certainly interesting that no apparent benefit derives from training in formal logic. This could be taken as evidence for the view of Evans (1989) that subjects do not so much reason badly on the selection task, as perhaps not reason at all. For example, if subjects are choosing cards which appear relevant without analysis of the logical consequence of turning them over, then no amount of training in logic will help them.

Effects of Negation: Matching Bias Revisited

In Chapter 2, the matching bias effect on the truth table task was discussed in some detail. Since the standard selection task uses an affirmative form of the conditional statement, and the common responses are to choose *p* and *q*, rather than *not-p* and *not-q*, it may well be argued that subjects' choices reflect matching bias rather than the confirmation or verification biases originally proposed by Wason and Johnson-Laird. As with the truth table task, the separation of matching from logic requires the use of rules with negated components. The effect of negated components on the logical status of card choices is illustrated in Table 4.1.

TABLE 4.1
The Four Logical Choices on the Wason Selection Task with Negative Components Permuted and with Concrete Examples of Letter–Number Rules

	Logical Case			
Rule	*TA*	*FA*	*TC*	*FC*
If p then q If there is a T on one side then there is a 7 on the other side	*p* T	*not-p* Y	*q* 7	*not-q* 5
If p then not q If there is a B on one side then there is not a 2 on the other side	*p* B	*not-p* D	*not-q* 4	*q* 2
If not p then q If there is not an M on one side then there is a 3 on the other side	*not-p* S	*p* M	*q* 3	*not-q* 9
If not p then not q If there is not a J on one side then there is not a 6 on the other side	*not-p* G	*p* J	*not-q* 1	*q* 6

Abbreviations: TA, True Antecedent; FA, False Antecedent; TC, True Consequent; FC, False Consequent.

Once negations are introduced, reference to card choices as *p*, *not-p*, etc., is ambiguous with regard to their logical status. For this reason, we introduce the terminology True Antecedent (TA), False Antecedent (FA), True Consequent (TC) and False Consequent (FC), which correspond to the *p*, *not-p*, *q* and *not-q* choices in the case of the affirmative rule. As Table 4.1 illustrates, the manipulation of negative components allows the matching and verification bias hypotheses to be separated. If subjects are verifying, then they should choose TC and FC on all rules, regardless of negatives. If they are matching, then they should choose a given logical case more often on the rule where it matches (i.e. corresponds to a card named in the rule) than where it mismatches.

The first study to test this hypothesis was that of Evans and Lynch (1973). They made four specific and statistically independent predictions:

- there will be more TA choices on rules with affirmative antecedents;
- there will be more FA choices on rules with negative antecedents;
- there will be more TC choices on rules with affirmative consequents;
- there will be more FC choices on rules with negative consequents.

All four predictions were confirmed and these findings have since been replicated in a number of studies (though see Oaksford & Stenning, 1992). Figure 4.2 summarises the data from four independent experiments reported by Evans and Lynch (1973), Manktelow and Evans (1979; two experiments) and Evans (1992a). While experimenters in other laboratories have also in general observed matching bias with comparable methodology, there have been claims that verification bias is shown as well as

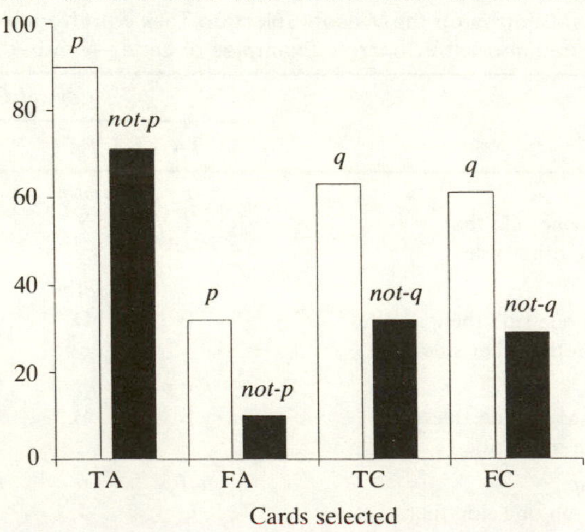

FIG. 4.2 Frequency (%) selections of the four cards where they do and do not match the items in the rules aggregated from four experiments (see text).

matching when negation is controlled (e.g. Krauth, 1982; Reich & Ruth, 1982). This would imply an overall preference for TC over FC, which is not found in the Evans studies summarised in Fig. 4.2.

What Fig. 4.2 illustrates clearly is that there are two main findings to be explained when negated components are introduced. First, there is a clear matching effect on all four logical cases; second, with matching controlled (i.e. averaging over rules with and without negative components), there is a clear preference for TA over FA with TC and FC choices intermediate. The latter trend is consistent with the finding on the truth table task discussed in Chapter 2 that TT tends to be selected or evaluated as confirming the conditional rule regardless of the presence of negatives, and Evans (1984a; 1989) offers a similar explanation discussed in the next section.

Research on matching bias in the truth table task (Chapter 2) lead to the finding that the phenomenon was only present with conditional (*if then* or *only if*) and not disjunctive statements and that its effect was considerably reduced by the introduction of explicit negatives into the instances (Evans, 1983). Explicit negatives have been introduced into the standard abstract selection task by Jackson and Griggs (1990) and by Kroger, Cheng and Holyoak (in press) without finding any facilitation of logical responding. However, whereas Evans (1983) looked at conditionals with negated components, these experiments used only affirmative rules and so could not be given a standard analysis for matching bias. Jackson and Griggs have also demonstrated facilitatory effects of explicit negatives with an alternative kind of abstract rule (see the Theory of Pragmatic Reasoning Schemas, below).

It has also been shown that the introduction of thematic contents, even when they are non-facilitatory, removes the matching bias effect on the selection task (Evans, 1992a; Griggs & Cox, 1983; Oaksford & Stenning, 1992). An exception to this finding is that of Manktelow and Evans (1979), who reported matching bias on arbitrary food and drink rules such as "If I eat haddock then I drink gin." It is possible that these materials—which were entirely non-facilitatory—are in fact so arbitrary as to function effectively as an abstract problem content. The normal loss of matching with thematic content suggests that such materials induce a different kind of thinking on the part of the subjects. For example, subjects might engage in more analytical reasoning, or alternatively pragmatic cues to the relevance of cards could be seen as dominating the merely syntactic influence of negatives.

The first report of matching bias on the selection task by Evans and Lynch (1973) was puzzling in the light of evidence from subjects' verbal protocols and introspections which always appeared to explain their choices in the context of the instructions, i.e. an attempt to prove the rule true or false. For example, Goodwin and Wason (1972) had used the evidence of subjects' verbal justifications to support the insight model of Johnson-Laird and Wason (1970). Subjects choosing the correct *p* and *not-q*, for example, explained their choices on the grounds that they might falsify the rule. However, Wason and Evans (1975) showed that while subjects showed apparent insight in their verbalisations on the rule *If p then not q* where matching leads to correct responses, the same subjects showed no transfer or apparent insight in their verbalisations when attempting a subsequent standard *If p then q* rule. They hypothesised that subjects were rationalising choices determined by an unconscious bias and claimed evidence for a "dual process" theory (see also Evans & Wason, 1976). A detailed account of this work and the theory is provided by Evans (1982).

The dual process theory has obvious links with the heuristic/analytic theory of Evans (1984a; 1989) discussed below. The most recent evidence for the original theory, however, is claimed by Beattie and Baron (1988), using both a selection task and an interesting modification of it which they call the multi-card task. Subjects proved vulnerable to matching bias on both tasks, and an analysis of verbal protocols confirmed that most subjects who gave matching responses did so without having considered alternative solutions to the problem (this was recently replicated by Evans, 1992a). Concurrent verbal protocols of this type are widely regarded as more informative about the processes responsible for decisions than are retrospective reports of the type discussed above (see Ericsson & Simon, 1980).

Contemporary Theories of the Abstract Selection Task

As stated earlier, most recent research—and theorising—has been concerned with the thematic selection task discussed in the second half of this chapter. So far as the abstract selection task is concerned, the two main contemporary theories are the heuristic-analytic or relevance theory of Evans (1984a; 1989) and the mental models account proposed by Johnson-Laird and Byrne (1991). In a development of the Wason and Evans (1975) dual process theory, Evans (1984a; 1989) argued that all reasoning tasks involve selective attention to relevant items which are selected at a preconscious heuristic stage and subject to a subsequent (unspecified) analytic reasoning stage. In the case of the selection task, however, he argued that only the heuristic stage is involved: subjects simply choose the cards which appear relevant. On the abstract selection task, the perceived *relevance* of the cards is determined by two linguistic factors: *not* directs attention to the proposition which it negates and *if* directs attention to the hypothetical circumstance which it concerns. Oaksford and Stenning

(1992) refer to these proposals as an *if*-heuristic and a *not*-heuristic. On thematic selection tasks, relevance is cued by pragmatic rather than linguistic factors, which is why the matching bias effect normally disappears.

In one test of the heuristic-analytic theory, Evans, Ball and Brooks (1987) used a computer-presented selection task and measured the order in which subjects made decisions about the cards. As predicted, subjects made decisions about matching cards significantly earlier than about mismatching cards, and about TA before FA cards (in line with the *not*- and *if*-heuristics). Overall, there was a high correlation between the frequency of selection of card and the order in which it was chosen. Although this appears to support the attentional hypothesis, it is possible that subjects consider all cards equally but have a response bias to signal selection decisions before non-selection decisions.

A more direct test of the heuristic-analytic theory is provided in some experiments reported by Evans (1992a). In these experiments, subjects were given selection tasks either under standard instructions for reasoning, or else under alternative, judgement instructions. The latter groups were told that the experiment was concerned with natural language understanding and were asked only to make judgements of relevance. They were asked to judge "to which of the following cards does the above rule appear relevant". Contrary to predictions, the relevance judgements differed markedly from selections under normal reasoning instructions. In particular, judgement groups showed no matching bias, instead giving a very strong verification pattern of TA and TC choices. With hindsight, it seems that subjects may have interpreted "relevance" to mean that they should identify the cards which make the rule *true*. We saw in Chapter 2 in discussing the truth table construction task that subjects will construct the True Antecedent–True Consequent case to verify a conditional rule, regardless of the presence of negatives.

A methodological innovation in Evans' (1992a) study, however, did produce evidence favourable to the heuristic-analytic theory. In one experiment using computer presentation, subjects were asked to point with the mouse to any card that they were *considering* selecting, and cumulative "inspection times" were logged by the microcomputer. As predicted by the notion of relevance within the theory, subjects spent far longer considering the cards which they ended up selecting than the ones they did not select under both reasoning and judgement instructions. In some cases, very little time indeed was spent considering cards which were not selected. This finding cannot be easily be reconciled with a view that subjects consider each card in turn and decide whether to turn it by reasoning about the hidden values.

In the study of Platt and Griggs (in press a) discussed earlier, the authors offer an interpretation of their findings in terms of the heuristic-analytic theory. They suggest that while subjects' card selections are normally determined only by heuristic processes, as Evans proposes, certain manipulations can induce analytic-processing and hence better logical performance. In particular, they suggest that their finding of a facilitatory effect in the abstract selection task when subjects are asked to provide verbal justifications (see also Berry, 1983; Hoch & Tschirgi, 1983; 1985) is because this manipulation induces analytic processing. The supposition that subjects in this condition are reasoning about hidden card values would also help to explain the fact that violation instructions enhance their performance further, while providing no benefit on the standard abstract task.

The heuristic approach, like all the theories discussed in this book, has attracted a number of criticisms. One common comment is that Evans' heuristic-analytic theory appears to render people inherently irrational, with responses governed by unconscious biases rather than reasoning processes (e.g. Johnson-Laird & Byrne, 1991; Oaksford & Stenning, 1992), and another is that the theory is seriously incomplete in not describing the mechanism for deductive competence implied in the analytic stage (Johnson-Laird & Byrne, 1991; Oakhill, 1991, Oaksford & Chater, 1993). Several authors have argued that the proposals of the heuristic theory are not sufficiently well formulated, and do not lead to clear predictions (e.g. Oaksford & Chater, 1993; O'Brien, 1993). For example, O'Brien (1993) cites as an example inconsistencies between different authors in their application of the concept of matching bias to Wason's THOG problem (described in Chapter 5). O'Brien also takes exception to Evans' argument that preconscious heuristics precede and pre-empt attempts at logical reasoning, arguing to the contrary that subjects may fall back on heuristics only if they are unable to find an effective means of reasoning. Oaksford and Chater (1993) also doubt that an appropriate set of heuristics can be proposed to deal with the problem of computational intractability which they claim afflicts all current theories of deduction.

Evans has responded to some of these points in recent publications. He argues (Evans, 1993b) that people *are* rational, but with two important qualifications. First, he defines rationality in terms of achievement of goals and *not* in terms of logicality and, second, he suggests that a number of cognitive constraints prevent subjects applying their understanding of logical principles in many situations. (The rationality issue is discussed further in Chapter 9.) Evans is also well aware of the lack of specification of a mechanism for deductive competence (Evans, 1991a) and has suggested recently (e.g. Evans, 1993a) that the mental models theory provides a plausible account of reasoning with novel problems. However, he regards the manipulation of mental models as a high effort, first principles approach and suggests that subjects are likely to switch to domain-sensitive rules and schemas when they reason with problems in familiar contexts.

The account of the abstract selection task offered by Johnson-Laird and Byrne (1991) suggests that the underlying mechanism that gives rise to matching bias lies in the construction of mental models, in particular initial incomplete models. Their theory of conditional reasoning in general assumes that subjects form initial, incomplete models of conditional statements which are later "fleshed out" as necessary. They account for matching bias by the suggestion that subjects tend to represent positive items. For example, the initial representation of the rule "If there is an A on one side of the card then there is a 2 on the other" is proposed to be:

[A] 2
. . .

meaning that they explicitly represent the fact that all occurrences of an A will be accompanied by a 3, and leave other possibilities implicit. For the rule "If there is *not* an A on one side of the card then there is a 2 on the other", Johnson-Laird and Byrne (1991, p. 80) suggest that subjects may form the initial representation:

2
[A]

and argue that subjects will be more likely to select cards which are included in such initial representations, thus accounting for matching bias. To solve the selection task with the standard affirmative rule, subjects would first have to flesh out the model in the form:

[A] 2
¬2

and perhaps explicitly represent the case which must *not* occur:

[A] [¬2]

This last proposal takes the mental models theory into new territory, since all other proposals assume that subjects model what may be true rather than what must be false. Evans (in press) has argued that Johnson-Laird and Byrne's account fails to take into account the *if*-heuristic and the associated finding of high TA selection regardless of the presence of negatives. Thus, for example, Evans suggests a modification of the representation of the negative antecedent rule (*If not A then 2*) which Johnson-Laird and Byrne (p. 76) propose is represented by the models:

2
[A]
. . .

which should instead be represented by the models:

[¬A] 2
[A]

In other words, Evans proposes that subjects tend to represent the True Antecedent case as well as the matching case in their explicit models, thus explaining the selection preference for TA over FA as well as the matching bias which is typical of the data (see Fig. 4.2).

Johnson-Laird and Byrne argue that performance is facilitated by any manipulation which induces subjects to build explicit models which include the *not-q* card, such as the RAST and certain forms of thematic content to be discussed later in the chapter. It should be apparent that this account—with the modification suggested by Evans (1992a)—is essentially similar to the relevance theory of Evans (1989) and that similar predictions can be deduced from either. In fact, Evans (1991a) proposes a possible reconciliation of the theory in which relevance is equated with explicit representation in a mental model.

The findings discussed earlier in support of the heuristic-analytic theory can then equally be taken as evidence that subjects do not think about cards which are not explicitly represented in models. A recent experimental study motivated specifically by the mental models account, however, was presented by Green (1992). Green argued that an experimental procedure conducted prior to the selection task should facilitate performance if it induced subjects to flesh out the initial model or expand, in Evans' terms, the relevant content of the representation. He found a clear relation between the number of counterexamples (*p & not-q* combinations) generated and subsequent success on the selection task. It appeared that production of one or more counterexamples was a necessary but not sufficient condition for success. That is, most subjects solving the task had identified counter-examples in the pre-task, but the converse was not true. Green concludes from this that subjects cannot simply be selecting relevant cards (in Evans' sense) or those which are present in the mental model, but there must be some further evaluation stage as well. This is similar to Platt and Griggs' proposal that analytic reasoning is responsible for facilitation effects.

At present, there is evidence to support both of the accounts—or a combination of the two—discussed in this section, but by no means extensive or unequivocal support. We turn now to studies of the thematic selection task which have attracted more theoretical interest and experimental test in the recent literature.

SELECTION TASK STUDIES USING THEMATIC CONTENT

Despite the considerable bulk of research so far considered, the majority of more recently published studies on the selection task have used so-called thematic, concrete or "realistic" materials. A large number of different problem contents have been used since the first study of this kind (Wason

& Shapiro, 1971) appeared. To assist the reader, a summary of the main thematic versions and their effects on card selections is shown in Table 4.2. The organisation of this section is broadly chronological, so we start

TABLE 4.2
Examples of Different Contents Used on the Selection Task

Name	*Original Study*	*Example Rule*	*Comments*
Towns and Transport	Wason and Shapiro (1971)	Every time I go to Manchester I travel by train	Early claims of facilitation; later reports of non-replication
Postal rule	Johnson-Laird et al. (1972)	If the letter is sealed then it has a 50 lire stamp on it	Strong facilitation in original study; does not replicate on groups (e.g. US students) who have no experience of rule in real life
Food and drinks	Manktelow and Evans (1979)	If I eat haddock then I drink gin	No facilitation, due to arbitrary nature of "realistic" rules
Sears problem	D'Anrade (described by Griggs, 1983)	If a purchase exceeds $30 then the receipt must be signed by the departmental manager	Reliable facilitation, despite lack of direct experience of rule by the subjects
Drinking Age rule	Griggs and Cox (1982)	If a person is drinking beer then that person must be over 19 years of age	Reliable facilitiation, unless policeman scenario is removed (see Pollard & Evans, 1987)
Clothing Age rule	Cox and Griggs (1982)	If a person is wearing blue then that person must be over 19 years of age	Facilitation only if preceded by Drinking Age rule
Abstract Permission rule	Cheng and Holyoak (1985)	If one is to take action "A" then one must first satisfy precondition "P"	Strong facilitation despite abstract nature, provided that explicit negatives are used on the cards
Standard Social Contract	Cosmides (1989)	If a man eats a cassava root then he must have a tattoo on his face	Context established social contract; facilitates *p* and *not-q* selections
Switched Social Contract	Cosmides (1989)	If a man has a tattoo on his face then he eats cassava root	Context as above; subjects choose same cards, now *not-p* and *q*
Deontic conditionals	Manktelow and Over (1991)	E.g. (Mother to son): "If you tidy your room then you may go out to play"	Subjects select *p* and *not-q* if checking whether mother has broken the rule, but select *not-p* and *q* if checking whether son has broken the rule

the story with the early work of Wason, Johnson-Laird and others, which appeared to establish a thematic facilitation effect and with subsequent evidence which challenged this. Next we discuss the particularly influential theory of pragmatic reasoning schemas and associated experimental research. Finally, we will discuss recent work motivated by alternative theoretical accounts of how pragmatic factors influence performance on the task.

The Thematic Facilitation Effect

The thematic facilitation effect—or rather *alleged* effect—is that it is easier to reason with problems which have concrete or thematic content than with those which have abstract, unfamiliar content. One clear counterexample to this claim is provided by the phenomenon of belief bias, first discovered by Wilkins (1928) and discussed in our review of reasoning with quantifiers (Chapter 8). It is known, for example, that subjects are much more likely to declare the conclusion of an argument to be valid if they believe it to be true than if they think it false. Nevertheless, when beliefs do not conflict with logic in this way, there might be a thematic facilitation effect and it certainly appeared that way at the time of Wason and Johnson-Laird's (1972) textbook on reasoning. Their conclusions were based upon two early experiments on the selection task.

Wason and Shapiro (1971) reported an experiment using a problem content which became known as "Towns and Transport". The subjects were presented with cards each of which represented a journey made by the experimenter. On one side of the card was the destination and on the other the means of transport used. The experimenter claimed that she followed the rule "Every time I go to Manchester I travel by car". The exposed sides of the four cards were "Manchester" (*p*), "Leeds" (*not-p*), "car" (*q*) and "train" (*not-q*). The subjects were required to decide which cards they would need to turn over in order to decide whether the experimenter's claim was true or false. Significantly more subjects chose the correct answer—Manchester and train—than in a control group using abstract materials.

The second study was that of Johnson-Laird, Legrenzi and Legrenzi (1972), which produced a very strong facilitation effect. Subjects were asked to imagine that they were Post Office workers sorting letters and testing the rule "If a letter is sealed then it has a 50 lire stamp on it". They were shown a display including four envelopes, two address side up and two address side down. Of the first two, one had a 50 lire stamp on it (*q*) and the other a 40 lire stamp on it (*not-q*). Of the latter, one was sealed (*p*) and the other unsealed (*not-p*). There was actually a fifth, blank envelope as well which is rarely mentioned in citations of this study (see

Griggs & Cox, 1982, for a discussion of the methodological problems this raises). The Postal rule was very effective, producing a staggering 81% correct selection rate.

Following early replications of facilitation by the Towns and Transport problem (Bracewell & Hidi, 1974; Gilhooly & Falconer, 1974; see also Pollard, 1981), doubts about the thematic facilitation effect did not set in until publication of a paper by Manktelow and Evans (1979), who reported several experiments which look—with hindsight—to be rather naïve. They were attempting to test whether the matching bias effect would hold up with thematic materials (it does not: see Evans, 1992a; Griggs & Cox, 1983) by combining thematic content with negative components. The only problem was that the thematic content they used failed to produce any facilitation at all on the standard affirmative rule (or any other) in four separate experiments. The content, known as Food and Drinks, was based upon an individual's preference for eating certain foods with certain drinks. A now notorious example of a non-facilitating rule was "Every time I eat haddock then I drink gin".

After eliminating various explanations of their non-facilitation in the first four experiments, Manktelow and Evans then raised the question of whether the thematic facilitation effect was as reliable as was generally believed at the time. In their fifth experiment, they repeated Wason and Shapiro's original Towns and Transport task and found no facilitation. In their discussion, they suggested that the Postal rule material used by Johnson-Laird et al. (1972) was unsound as it was more a test of memory than of reasoning, so closely did the rule resemble that which subjects were accustomed to using in their everyday experience. At the time in England there was a Post Office rule in force that higher value stamps were required on sealed letters. Thus subjects could well have read the rule as "If a letter is sealed then it *must* have a 50 lire stamp on it". It is significant also that the *not-q* card involved a stamp of lower rather than higher value, which would thus violate the rule familiar to the subjects unless the envelope was left unsealed. Manktelow and Evans' argument was dubbed the "memory cue" hypothesis by Griggs and Cox (1982).

The study of Griggs and Cox (1982) was an excellent piece of clearly motivated and designed experimentation which helped clarify the issues considerably. In their first experiment, they produced an adapted version of the Towns and Transport material ("Every time I go to Miami I travel by airplane") which their University of Florida students failed to solve any better than an abstract selection task. This confirmed Manktelow and Evans' failure to replicate facilitation with this material as have a number of other studies (Brown, Keats, Keats & Seggie, 1980; Reich & Ruth, 1982; Yachanin & Tweney, 1982). However, Cosmides (1989) recently found a relatively high (compared with abstract materials) solution rate of 46% with a version of this material.

In a second experiment, Griggs and Cox then administered the Postal rule, arguing that if the Manktelow and Evans memory cue explanation was correct, then no facilitation should be observed: the real-world Postal rule was unknown to the Florida students. There was, again, no facilitation whatever. In their third experiment, they produced a new content, the Drinking Age rule (Fig. 4.3), which they predicted *would* facilitate on the basis of memory cueing. Subjects were asked to imagine that they were a police officer checking whether people conform to certain rules. The rule given was "If a person is drinking beer then the person must be over 19 years of age", which corresponds to the law in the state of Florida. The cards had information about the person's drink on one side and their age on the other: "beer" (*p*), "coke" (*not-p*), "22 years of age" (*q*) and "16 years of age" (*not-q*). The material proved massively facilitatory with 74% of the subjects correctly checking the beer drinker and the person under 19 years of age.

The findings of Griggs and Cox (1982) have proved reliable, with several replications of the facilitation by the Drinking Age rule subsequently being published (e.g. Griggs & Cox, 1983; Griggs, 1984). Pollard and Evans (1987) have, however, shown that the police officer scenario is essential: if the rule is presented without context, then subjects perform at abstract

On this task imagine that you are a police officer on duty. It is your job to ensure that people conform with certain rules. The cards in front of you have information about four people sitting at a table. On one side of a card is a person's age and on the other side of the card is what a person is drinking. Here is a rule: "IF A PERSON IS DRINKING BEER, THEN THE PERSON MUST BE OVER 19 YEARS OF AGE". Select the card, or cards that you definitely need to turn over to determine whether or not people are violating the rule.

DRINKING A BEER	DRINKING A COKE	16 YEARS OF AGE	22 YEARS OF AGE

TYPICAL AND CORRECT CHOICES

"DRINKING A BEER" (*p*) and "16 YEARS OF AGE" (*not-q*)

FIG. 4.3 The Wason selection task (Drinking Age rule of Griggs & Cox, 1982).

task level. The argument that the facilitation effect of the Postal rule is population specific has also been confirmed. Cheng and Holyoak (1985) showed that when no rationale was provided, subjects from Hong Kong showed large facilitation on the Postal rule, whereas those from Michigan did not (the rule had recently been used in Hong Kong). Moreover, in a study of British subjects, Golding (1981) showed that only older subjects who could still remember the rule (abolished shortly after Johnson-Laird and colleagues' experiment!) showed facilitation with this content.

Memory cueing can be combined with the proposals of Pollard (1982) and other specific suggestions (e.g. those of Manktelow & Evans, 1979) in order to characterise a general availability theory of content effects (see Cosmides, 1989; Gigerenzer & Hug, 1992). The availability theory assumes that subjects' responses are influenced by the retrieval of specific information and associations from memory. When the correct responses are "available", subjects' logical performance will be facilitated, but not due to a process of reasoning as such. We consider in the next section some research which has been presented in support of this position and the more recently developed relevance theory.

Availability and Relevance in the Thematic Selection Task

The availability approach places emphasis on prior beliefs and associations which are evoked by the problem content. One relevant factor which has received some attention is plausibility or believability of the conditional rule itself. Van Duyne (1976) proposed that subjects might be more likely to attempt to falsify a rule which they believed *a priori* to be false rather than true. In a variant of the selection task procedure, using self-generated sentences, he claimed that more correct selections were given for unbelievable than believable rules. However, as Pollard and Evans (1981) pointed out, he only scored subjects as correct if they gave the right selections and also "gave the correct reason for this selection"—a dubious method in view of Wason and Evans' (1975) demonstrations of rationalisation in retrospective protocols. In a re-analysis of Van Duyne's data, Pollard and Evans showed that only the reasons given and not the actual selections were affected by the believability of the rules.

Pollard and Evans (1981) performed a similar experiment in which subjects were asked to generate four classes of sentence: always or usually true or false. They found that falsity *did* significantly facilitate selections of *not-q* and inhibit selections of *q* even when verbal justifications were disregarded, thus supporting Van Duyne's original hypothesis with stronger data. In a follow-up study, Pollard and Evans (1983) were able to produce a similar finding using letter–number rules whose truth value was established in a probability learning experiment conducted immediately prior to the selection task. Pollard and Evans interpreted their findings at the time on the grounds that with false rules the *p & not-q* case is "available" to the subjects (see also Pollard, 1982) since it corresponds to the subjects' real-world experience of the materials. For example, if you believe that the rule "If you work hard then you will fail your exams" to be normally false, it is because you can more easily think of examples of people working hard and passing their exams. Thus, the falsifying case of an unbelievable rule is easily available.

The availability explanation is a cognitive type of explanation. As with some other phenomena in the reasoning literature (e.g. confirmation bias: see Evans, 1989), a motivational explanation is also possible. Subjects may be more motivated to disprove a rule which they believe to be false. A relevance account incorporates aspects of both approaches: subjects select relevant (not simply available) cards, but relevance can be determined by motivational significance. A recent study which utilises this concept of relevance is that of George (1991), which suggests that where goals are specified the utility of different outcomes—satisfactory or unsatisfactory—will become a determinant of relevance and therefore selections. Specifically, outcomes which are satisfactory or have positive utility will be more relevant.

In George's experiment 1, problems all start with the statement of a goal, followed by a rule. For example:

> Your goal is to buy a car.
> Somebody states:
> "If one buys a K-make of car, one is always satisfied."
> You need to know if this assertion is true or false.

The subject is shown four cards which display the make of car on one side and the consequence (satisfied, dissatisfied) on the other. A negative form of this problem would include the rule "If one buys a K-make of car, one is always dissatisfied". George used several contents with positive and negative versions associated with satisfactory and unsatisfactory outcomes. He found a strong bias to investigate satisfactory outcomes, such that *q* was more often selected on positive rules and *not-q* more often selected on negative rules. In a second experiment, he manipulated the presence and absence of a goal statement. The findings were replicated when the goal statement was present, but no significant effects of positive/negative rules occurred when the goal statement was absent. George concludes that the statement of a goal has a major influence on the perceived relevance of the cards.

While relevance is a concept of current interest in the field—as we saw in discussion of the abstract selection task—the same cannot really be said of availability, and to some extent the papers of Cosmides (1989) and Gigerenzer and Hug (1992) are attacking a theory "made of straw". For example, the memory cueing account of Griggs and Cox (1982) was short-lived as an account of thematic facilitation effects. It soon transpired that facilitation can occur which cannot be attributed to direct retrieval of the correct solution from memory. Consider, for example, the Sears problem of Roy D'Andrade (discussed by Rumelhart, 1980). Subjects are told to imagine that they are managers in a Sears department store checking sales receipts for compliance with the rule "If a purchase exceeds $30 then the receipt must be approved by the departmental manager". The "cards" are receipts which show on the front the amount spent, and on the back the presence or absence of the departmental manager's signature. This problem is easily solved by most people to whom it is given: they check the receipt for over $30 (*p*) and the *unsigned* receipt (*not-q*). Few people have any direct real-world experience of the problem content, however, so facilitation cannot be simply due to memory cueing.

The other major findings which showed that availability of memory cueing was too simple an explanation of content effects in the selection task came from various studies of transfer effects, which we now consider.

Transfer Effects with Facilitatory Materials

A number of studies have looked at the question of whether performance on an abstract selection task could be enhanced if it is preceded by presentation of a rule with thematic and facilitatory content. Such transfer effects were strikingly absent in early studies (e.g. Johnson-Laird et al., 1972; Wason & Shapiro, 1971). Subjects normally regress to the usual low performance on the abstract task following successful completion of a facilitatory thematic task.

Transfer effects were, however, successfully demonstrated by Cox and Griggs (1982) with a problem content that does not facilitate when presented without a prior task. They used the Drinking Age rule, a standard letters and numbers abstract rule, and a third content, the Clothing Age rule. This content used an arbitrary rule of similar structure to the Drinking Age rule but lacked the real-world reference: "If a person is wearing blue then the person must be over 19". This rule is presented with the same policeman scenario as the Drinking Age rule. When given as the first task, subjects show no facilitation on the Clothing Age rule. There was, however, a significant transfer effect when it was preceded by the Drinking Age problem. No transfer, however, was observed with the letters and numbers task. Cox and Griggs suggested that subjects were reasoning by analogy between the two age rules, which clearly goes beyond simple memory cueing.

Transfer from a thematic to abstract task has remained elusive in most other studies and can be seen as evidence that facilitation, when it occurs, does not reflect any general logical insight or imply the presence of abstract reasoning. Berry (1983) did report thematic to abstract transfer but only when subjects were instructed to verbalise aloud while attempting the problems. However, Klaczynski, Gelfand and Reese (1989) claim that Berry's verbalisation manipulation was confounded by the provision of an explanation of correct responding which could instead account for the transfer effects. In their own study, Klaczynski et al. found no effect of verbalisation, although they did find that providing explanations of choices produced transfer among problems *of the same type* (abstract/thematic) and especially on abstract rules. A key factor here—and in the Cox and Griggs study—seems to lie in the structural similarity of the problems, which was high among abstract rules, low between abstract and thematic rules, and moderate among the thematic rules. The last type consisted of the Drinking Age rule and an assortment of other analogous rules devised by the authors, all of which were strongly facilitatory. The Clothing Age rule of Cox and Griggs had, of course, high structural similarity to the Drinking Age rule, which would have facilitated mapping between the two.

Some further evidence concerning transfer effects is provided by developmental studies of the selection task and RAST problem. In a developmental study using selection tasks with rather similar materials to Klaczynski et al., Overton et al. (1987) noted the lack of transfer from their facilitatory deontic conditionals to abstract rules which is typical of adult studies. In contrast, the study of RAST performance in young children (10–11 years old) reported by Girotto, Light and Colbourn (1988) did find a transfer effect from a permission rule—which facilitated performance—to a formal rule, but one which again had high structural similarity (a similar effect is reported by Light, Blaye, Gilly & Girotto, 1990). We will return to the studies of Girotto, Light and colleagues in the next section, since they also bear upon the theory of pragmatic reasoning schemas.

To summarise, by the early 1980s, it was already clear that there was no general thematic facilitation effect. Merely making a problem content concrete did not guarantee facilitation. Some contents, such as the Postal rule, facilitate only for populations with relevant real-world experience, but this does not apply to all (e.g. the Sears problem). There was also evidence of transfer and "reasoning by analogy" which clearly go beyond solutions by direct memory retrieval.

The Theory of Pragmatic Reasoning Schemas

The most recent research on the thematic selection task needs to be viewed in the context of the major theories which have motivated this work. In contrast with the heuristic and mental models accounts, which dominate explanations of findings on the abstract selection task, thinking on the thematic selection task is strongly influenced by two theories which propose domain-specific reasoning mechanisms. In this section, we deal with the theory of pragmatic reasoning schemas, which is the earlier theory, while in the next section we look at social contract theory and also compare its performance with that of schema theory. Both theories have focused primarily on accounting for the conditions under which facilitation of responding is observed on the selection task.

The notion that facilitation by realistic content on the selection task might reflect the induction and application of schemas was mooted by Rumelhart (1980) but first formalised as a specific account by Cheng and Holyoak (1985). The concept of "schemas" as dynamic knowledge structures has a long history in cognitive psychology, dating at least from Bartlett's (1932) work on very long-term memory. Schemas contain generalised abstracted knowledge which has been learnt or induced from experience in particular domains. They are more than concepts, however, as they can include rules for action or inference. If thematic contents which facilitate performance do so by inducing schemas, then we can explain the results discussed above which create difficulties for the memory cue hypothesis. Schemas facilitate reasoning by analogy, since they have an abstract structure which can be mapped on to different but related problems. Schemas have slots or variables that can be instantiated to particular cases. Hence the construct can be used to explain the transfer between structurally similar versions of the selection task or RAST problems.

Cheng and Holyoak proposed the existence of pragmatic reasoning schemas and in particular the *permission schema* to account for thematic facilitation effects on the selection task. The permission schema is learnt from situations in which we require permission to perform actions and is applicable to any conditional of the general type: *If an action is to be taken then a precondition must be satisfied*. Cheng and Holyoak propose that the schema includes four production rules as follows:

Rule 1: If the action is to be taken then the precondition must be satisfied
Rule 2: If the action is not be be taken then the precondition need not be satisfied
Rule 3: If the precondition is satisfied then the action may be taken
Rule 4: If the precondition is not satisfied then the action must not be taken

As applied to the selection task, p is the action and q is the condition. The rules tell you respectively that you need select p (Rule 1) and *not-q* (Rule 4), since these rules contain the modal (deontic) imperative *must*.

For example, the Drinking Age problem uses a permission rule in which drinking beer is the action and being over 19 years of age is the condition. Subjects select the *not-q* card because Rule 4 (when instantiated) tells them that if you are not over 19 years of age then you must not drink. Hence, it is imperative to check the underage drinker. The error of selecting *q*—common on the abstract task—is avoided, since Rule 3 says only that you *may* drink beer if you are over the age limit.

This theory appears to resolve the problems of the memory cue or availability explanations described above and also does seem able to account for most of the thematic materials effects discussed so far in this chapter. Of the contents shown in Table 4.2, Towns and Transport is not a permission rule, but as we have also seen it is only a weak and unreliable facilitator of correct selections. The totally ineffective Food and Drinks content also does not comprise a permission rule. Of the reliable facilitators, the Drinking Age rule and Postal rule problems can both be regarded as permission problems: you must fulfil the precondition of being over 19 years of age in order to drink alcohol in a bar; you must fulfil the precondition of using a stamp of sufficient value in order to post a sealed letter.

The once mysterious Sears problem can also be explained. We may not have experience as managers but we identify the permission rule (action: make purchase over $30; condition: approval by departmental manager), so we can retrieve and apply the schema. The essential presence of the policeman scenario in order to achieve facilitation with the Drinking Age problem (Pollard & Evans, 1987) can also be explained by the schema theory. The rule (out of context) is insufficient to evoke the permission schema, so the problem remains arbitrary. In the same way, the Postal rule remains arbitrary for those subjects who lack the relevant real-world experience to see it as a permission rule. Similarly, the arbitrary Clothing Age rule has a permission structure (Cox & Griggs, 1982). Once the permission schema has been elicited by the more familiar Drinking Age rule, one could argue, then it will be applied also to the Clothing Age rule—but not to a subsequently presented letters and numbers rule—thus accounting for the differential transfer effects found.

Cheng and Holyoak (1985), however, attempt to go beyond explanation of findings in the literature and to predict new results from their own experiments designed to test the theory. One study, mentioned earlier, was the comparison of reasoning with the Postal rule between Hong Kong and US subjects. The critical manipulation was the presence or absence of a rationale which said that the purpose rule was to increase profit from personal mail which was nearly always sealed. When the scenario was present, the performance of US subjects was now as good as that of the Hong Kong subjects despite their lack of personal experience of the rule—presumably because this facilitated retrieval of a schema.

In a second experiment, Cheng and Holyoak attempted to demonstrate facilitation on an abstract version of the selection task, also by evoking a permission schema. Subjects were told that they were an authority checking regulations all of which had the form "If one is to take action 'A' then one must fulfil precondition 'P'." The cards were labelled as follows:

has taken action A (*p*)
has not taken action A (*not-p*)
has fulfilled precondition P (*q*)
has not fulfilled precondition P (*not-q*)

This problem is clearly lacking thematic content but should evoke the permission schema. In total, 61% of subjects gave the correct answer compared with 19% on the usual abstract letters and numbers content. In a third study, Cheng and Holyoak showed that when conditionals are rephrased by subjects, then deontic terms such as *must* and *may* were far more often introduced into permission statements than arbitrary rules. Further evidence for the theory was claimed by Cheng et al. (1986), who showed that abstract training with schemas—but not training in abstract rules of logic—was sufficient to produce facilitation on the selection task. This finding not only supports the theory but is also apparently inconsistent with the formal rules theory of deductive competence. Cheng et al. introduced obligation schemas which are the other main kind of deontic conditional rule. An obligation rule has the form, "If an event occurs then an action must be taken".

Pragmatic schema theory has attracted both supporters and critics. Notable among the supporters are Girotto and Light who, together with other colleagues, have run a number of experiments on young children which they argue to support the schema theory (for a review and discussion, see Girotto, 1991). Studies of children's reasoning have traditionally been conducted within the Piagetian approach which is a form of mental logic. The selection task is problematic from a Piagetian point of view, since even intelligent adults who should be well into formal operational thought usually fail to solve the standard abstract task. However, it has been shown that performance on thematic versions of the selection task systematically improves with age from around 10 to 18 years (Overton et al., 1987; Ward & Overton, 1990).

Girotto and co-workers argue that if it is possible to demonstrate competent reasoning in young children with the kind of content that assists adults, then this would favour the theory of pragmatic reasoning schemas and be hard to account for in Piagetian theory. Girotto et al. (1988) first demonstrated that 10-year-olds could solve a permission version of the RAST task. This was followed by two more striking findings: (a) that children as young as 6 or 7 can produce quite reasonable performance on a permission version of RAST [and significantly better than on a formal version (Light et al., 1990)] and (b) that 10- to 11-year-olds as well as 14- to 15-year-olds can give high selection rates to permission versions of the full four card selection task (Girotto, Gilly, Blaye & Light, 1989). Whether or not you favour the pragmatic reasoning schema theory, the findings of Girotto and co-workers certainly confirm how strikingly content dependent is the reasoning ability of both children and adults: A task which defeats most university students in its abstract form is comparatively easy for a 10-year-old in a permission context.

Most critics of schema theory favour alternative (especially social contract theory) or more general accounts which are covered below. Jackson and Griggs (1990), however, criticised Cheng and Holyoak on methodological grounds. Their first experiment was encouraging for the theory, not only replicating the facilitation of the abstract permission rule used by Cheng and Holyoak (1985) but also extending this to a facilitation of an abstract obligation schema rule ("If situation 'C' arises then action 'I' must be done"), previously shown to facilitate in a thematic form (Cheng et al., 1986). However, Jackson and Griggs then pointed out that the use of explicit negatives for *not-p* and *not-q* (e.g. "has not taken action 'A'") was methodologically dubious, since Evans (1983) had shown on a truth table task that explicit negatives reduce matching bias and increase logical performance (see Chapter 2). The standard letters and numbers rule—used as a control by Cheng and Holyoak—uses implicit negatives. In further experiments, Jackson and Griggs showed that facilitation on the abstract permission and obligation rules disappears when implicit negatives are introduced, thus apparently invalidating an important piece of evidence for the schema theory. However, they also showed that introducing explicit negatives is not sufficient to facilitate performance with the abstract letter and numbers rule. These findings have recently been replicated by Griggs and Cox (1992). Jackson and Griggs argued that their findings provide strong support for the Evans heuristic-analytic theory, although they erroneously imply that the latter account precludes the use of schemas.

Girotto, Mazzacco and Cherubini (1992) have, however, provided a response to Jackson and Griggs' paper. First, they point out that the erroneous choice in the abstract permission rule with implicit negatives is *p* alone rather than *p* and *q*; thus subjects are not responding to the linguistic relevance of *q* which Evans (1989) uses to explain abstract selection task performance, and appear instead to be judging relevance *pragmatically* in the schema condition [this is quite compatible with Evans' (1989) own account of thematic selection tasks, e.g. p. 89]. They explain the omission of *not-q* due to ambiguity of the implicit negative: fulfilling precondition R does not necessarily preclude fulfilling precondition Q, whereas stating that Q did not occur is quite unambiguous. In Girotto and co-workers' own experiments, they demonstrated facilitation of the abstract schema rule with a procedure which disambiguated the implicit negative. Their account of the effects of negation are supported by the arguments and experiments reported by Kroger et al. (in press) and appear to have been accepted also by Griggs and Cox (1992).

Research on Cheng and Holyoak's schema theory has further advanced our understanding of the conditions under which facilitation effects occur, but has not produced any direct support for the authors' claim that subjects are reasoning by use of production rules. For example, from the viewpoint of the Evans' heuristic-analytic theory, it can be argued that subjects are still making judgements of relevance on thematic as well as abstract tasks: it is only that they switch from linguistic to pragmatic sources of relevance. Similarly, Johnson-Laird and Byrne (1991) account for these findings in terms of the fleshing-out of initial models in different ways, prompted by background knowledge.

The question of whether conditional *reasoning per se* is facilitated by the use of a permission rule has been investigated in one recent study by Markovits and Savary (1992). They showed that a permission rule (Postal rule) produced fewer correct responses on conditional inference tasks than did a causal rule (e.g. a significantly higher rate of Modus Tollens), but that the reverse was true when the same rules (and associated contexts) were compared on the selection task. The authors claim that the permission rule improves selection task performance without facilitating understanding of conditional logic.

Schema theory has been criticised on various grounds, the most obvious being that it cannot for either deductive competence or the systematic errors that are observed with abstract reasoning problems (e.g. Evans, 1991a). Some authors, however, have suggested that the theory might account for some of the data in conjunction with other mechanisms (e.g. Evans, 1993a; O'Brien, 1993). Others have suggested that there is no particular reason to favour schema theory, since there are a number of other ways in which prior knowledge may be represented or used in reasoning (Johnson-Laird & Byrne, 1991). As with most other theories in this area, there have been claims that schema theory is insufficiently clearly formulated. For example, Oaksford and Chater (1993) have argued that the theory provides inadequate specification of how beliefs are updated and how knowledge is compartmentalised. The specific empirical claims of schema theory in the field of the Wason selection task have also been challenged by the proponents of the rival social contract theory, to which we now turn.

Social Contract Theory

A new theory based on an evolutionary approach was proposed by Cosmides (1989). She proposes the presence of Darwinian algorithms which maximise achievement of goals in social situations, and concentrates on the situation of social exchange, i.e. cooperation between two individuals for mutual benefit. This gives rise to social contracts in which individuals are obliged to pay costs in order to receive benefits. She further claims that such social exchanges could not evolve without a mechanism for detecting cheaters. In the case of the selection task, she considers two rules of the following general type:

Rule 1: *Standard social contract*: "If you take a benefit then you must pay a cost"

Rule 2: *Switched social contract*: "If you pay the cost then you take the benefit'

Cosmides then argues that a "look for cheaters" algorithm would produce logical facilitation (i.e. *p & not-q* selections) on the standard rule, but produce *not-p & q* selections on a switched rule. She contrasts her approach both with the schema theory of Cheng and Holyoak and with the generalised "availability" theory described earlier, and attributed to such authors as Manktelow and Evans (1979), Griggs and Cox (1982) and Pollard (1982). Availability theory, she claims, is based upon the notion that selection task responses are facilitated by associational links in subjects' past experiences.

Before looking at Cosmides' own experiments, consider again the list of facilitatory and non-facilitatory contents in Table 4.2. On consideration, we can see that social contract rules are a subclass of permission rules. Hence, if the permission rules which facilitate are also social contracts, then Cosmides' theory can provide an alternative account of these. Presumably, a law such as the Drinking Age rule or Postal problem is a formalisation of a social contract and so can be accounted for in the theory. It is arguable whether or not the Sears problem constitutes a social contract. The finding reported in the first part of this chapter that instructions to find *violators* rather than to decide the truth or falsity of the rule enhances facilitation on the Drinking Age rule, supports the notion of a cheater detection algorithm. On the other hand, it does not account for the facilitation which occurs relative to the abstract problem on the True/False version.

Cosmides argues that Cheng and Holyoak's work was intended to reject availability theory but failed to do so for methodological reasons. She goes on to present experiments of her own which demonstrate the predicted patterns of responses for both standard and switched social contract rules. Her problem contents involve quite elaborate scenarios. To summarise one example, a tribe are described whose men crave cassava root—which is an aphrodisiac—but they are only allowed to eat it, by tribal custom, if they are married. A married man is distinguished by a tattoo on his face. The scenario indicates that attempts to cheat on this rule are rife. The standard social contract rule is, then, "If a man eats cassava root, then he must have a tattoo on his face", whereas the switched SC rule is "If a man has a tattoo on his face then he eats cassava root". The point is that the contexts are unfamiliar and therefore not explainable by availability theory.

Cosmides argues that her experiments refuted availability theory on the grounds that her effects could be demonstrated, albeit with the use of detailed scenarios, by use of materials previously unfamiliar to subjects as in the example discussed above. In the case of pragmatic reasoning schemas, she argues that all existing facilitatory contents, including those used by Cheng and Holyoak, were social contracts. In her own experiments 5 and 6, she produced non-social contract versions of permission rules and showed that they produce significantly less facilitation than do social contract equivalents in the same domain. A similar finding is claimed by Gigerenzer and Hug (1992). In both cases, however, it transpired that the non-social contract permission rules produce levels of correct responding well above the 10% or so to be expected on abstract selection task problems. Cosmides found solution rates of 30 and 34%, whereas Gigerenzer and Hug reported rates of 36, 52 and 44% for non-social contract permission problems in different domains. Neither study included abstract task control groups.

Cheng and Holyoak (1989) identify the essence of Cosmides' claim for superiority of the social-contract theory: "In Cosmides' view, the evidence she offers in support of her prediction that only social-contract rules will yield facilitation in the selections indicates that such knowledge is not the product of general inductive mechanisms" (p. 289). Cheng and Holyoak go on to argue that many facilitating contents on the selection task, including the Drinking Age rule and the Sears problem, cannot correctly be seen as social exchanges; they also dispute some of her own experimental evidence. Cheng and Holyoak, of course, see social contract rules as examples of the application of schemas. Pollard (1990) defends availability theories on the grounds that none had claimed that *all* facilitation effects could be explained on the basis of direct experience. He also agrees with Cheng and Holyoak that Cosmides has failed to demonstrate that there is a specialised reasoning mechanism for social contracts.

Platt and Griggs (in press b) conducted a series of experiments in order to try to identify which features of Cosmides' (1989) rather complex problems were responsible for the effects she observed. First, they showed that her main findings were robust when much shorter and simpler instructions were used and when subjects were tested on single problems rather than multiple problems. In line with social contract theory, they found reduced facilitation when reference to cost–benefit information was removed from the problem scenarios. They also found some evidence that performance was better when the deontic term *must* was included in the rules (see below) and when explicit negatives were used to describe the cards, but neither finding extended across all the problems investigated.

Manktelow and Over (1991) declare themselves to be dissatisfied with both schema and social contract theory accounts of thematic effects in the selection task. They distinguish between selection tasks involving indicative conditionals of the form *if there is a p then there is a q* and deontic conditionals of the form *if you do p then you must do q*. In general, abstract and non-facilitatory thematic rules have the indicative form, whereas successful facilitators including permission and social contract rules have the deontic form. However, where Manktelow and Over wish to go beyond either theory is in suggesting that deontic conditionals involve assessment of the utilities of actions which go beyond the cost–benefit analysis of social contract theory, which is seen as a special case. In effect, they propose that subjects approach the problem as a decision-making rather than reasoning task (see also Evans, Over & Manktelow, in press).

Manktelow and Over used a rule given by a mother to a son: "If you tidy your room then you may go out to play". When subjects were asked to evaluate this from the viewpoint of the son to check whether the mother had followed their rule, they selected "tidy room" and "did not go out to play" (*p & not-q*), but when asked to play the role of the mother checking if the son had followed the rule, they chose "did not tidy room" and "went out to play" (*not-p & q*). The latter combination has rarely been observed except on Cosmides' switched social contract problem. It is apparent from reading the above that each checks the method by which the other could cheat on the rule.

In an independently designed study, Politzer and Nguyen-Xuan (1992) reported essentially the same effect. They compared managers' and consumers' approaches to the rule "If the purchase exceeds 10,000 francs, then the salesman must stick on the back of the receipt a voucher gift for a gold bracelet". Subjects playing the manager checked for customers cheating by examining more *not-p & q* cards, whereas consumers checked significantly more *p & not-q* cards. These authors found an additional new result: a neutral tester tended to check all four cards.

An interesting feature of this parallel discovery is that both sets of authors predict their findings, but on the basis of different theoretical principles! Neither are very sympathetic with Cosmides' social contract theory but differ on the issue of schemas. Manktelow and Over dismiss schema theory on the grounds that it does not represent the utilities of actions, and suggest instead an extended mental models theory with utilities incorporated in representations. Politzer and Nguyen-Xuan consider explanations based on schemas, social contracts, availability and relevance, but favour an application of the schema theory. A conditional permission rule, they argue, involves an obligation rule from the viewpoint of the promisor ("If over 10,000 francs is spent, you *must* give a gift voucher") but a reversed permission rule from the viewpoint of the promisee ("If you claim a gift, then you must spend more than 10,000 francs"). Each role checks for violations of the rule which the *other* role implies using a set of production rules spelt out in the paper. The neutral tester checks both rules, hence treating the relation as biconditional and selecting all four cards.

Johnson-Laird and Byrne (1992) agree that mental models can explain the findings on reasoning with deontic conditionals, but dispute Manktelow and Over's proposal that an extended form of the mental models theory is needed to account for their findings. Instead, they suggest that the use of deontic rules and familiar domains assists subjects in fleshing out their models or what is permissible—and also what is impermissible—and hence determine their card selections in line with the theory of Johnson-Laird and Byrne (1991). In response, Manktelow and Over (1992) remain unconvinced and argue that subjects are expressing *preferences* and hence must in some way represent utilities associated with their actions.

To muddy the theoretical waters still further, another recent paper on social contract reasoning by Gigerenzer and Hug (1992) also investigated perspective shifts but interpreted this as evidence *for* social contract theory, albeit revised and extended from Cosmides' original proposals. Gigerenzer and Hug were concerned to separate the search for cheaters algorithm from other aspects of social contract theory. One of their manipulations was devising social contract rules in which the search for cheaters algorithm would not be relevant. This was done by providing the perspective of an outside investigator (e.g. an anthropologist) whose task was to discover whether or not a social contract rule was in existence. This lead to a massive reduction in correct responding, a finding which they claim identifies the cheating algorithm as critical and which also militates against schema theory since permission or obligation rules were involved.

Gigerenzer and Hug also investigated social contract problems which involve unilateral or bilateral obligations for the two parties involved. As predicted in both cases, switching perspectives between the parties involved reducing the numbers of correct *p & not-q* choices, but only in the case of bilateral obligations was there a marked increase in *not-p & q* choices. This finding is consistent with those of Manktelow and Over (1991) and of Politzer and Nguyen-Xuan (1992) whose problems involved bilateral obligations.

Although Gigerenzer and Hug claim that their experiments support a revised social contract theory, their own explication of the difference between a cheating and non-cheating version of a social contract story suggest the more general distinction between indicative and deontic selection tasks proposed by Manktelow and Over (1991, p. 143):

> Note that in both stories the rule was explicitly identified as the same social contract. The difference was that in the cheating version the subject was cued into the perspective of one party in a social contract, and the other party . . . had the cheating option. In the no-cheating version, the subject was cued into the perspective of a third party who is not engaged in the social contract, but who attempts to determine whether the social contract rule exists.

In the work discussed in this section, only availability theory seems constantly to have been in retreat. Schemas, social contract theory and to a lesser extent relevance theory and mental models all have their supporters in the attempt to explain pragmatic influences on the Wason selection task. It is not our purpose, however, to arbitrate between these conflicting theoretical explanations, but rather to record the progress of research in this area and summarise the basic findings arising. While authors disagree about the precise theoretical mechanism best suited to explaining the results, there is actually much common view about the phenomena in more general terms. None of the authors appear to be equating rationality with logical reasoning, but rather assume that selections are rational in the sense of achieving goals or maximising utility (see also Evans, 1993b; Evans et al., in press; Gigerenzer & Hug, 1992). All assume that the pragmatic influences on reasoning reflect some broadly adaptive mechanisms and that social contracts induce subjects to check for violations or cheating from the perspective made relevant in the context. The work discussed in this section should also serve to illustrate how far the study of thematic content on the Wason selection task has now advanced beyond the original claim of a thematic facilitation effect in reasoning.

CONCLUSIONS

Evans' (1982) review of the selection task began its conclusion with the comment: "It is arguable that research on the Wason selection task has been more productive of psychologically interesting findings and theories than work on any other reasoning paradigm." Bearing in mind the number of post-1980 references (not included in the earlier review) that have appeared in this chapter, and the nature of the recent theoretical debate, it would be hard to argue that this conclusion did not still apply, and perhaps more strongly than before. The abstract selection task, though less intensively researched, continues to provoke theoretical interest and is the subject of several very recent papers. Work on the thematic selection task has snowballed dramatically in the past decade and has made the selection task the principal focus at the current time for debate about the issue of pragmatic factors in reasoning. If anything, interest in the task is currently on the increase in the psychology of reasoning.

In the Introduction, we described four main classes of reasoning theory based on inference rules, heuristics, mental models and domain-sensitive rules. We will return to an overall evaluation of these in our discussion (Chapter 9). However, it is worth noting here that all of these except for formal rule theory have been heavily involved in accounts of findings on the selection task. Heuristic theories based on availability and more especially on relevance have provided explanations for findings with the abstract task, such as matching bias, and have also been adduced in account of thematic effects. While selection task research has not been a major focus of attention for mental models theorists, we have nevertheless seen that mental models accounts for a number of the phenomena involved have been proposed. It is theories based on domain-sensitive mechanisms such as schema theory and social contract theory which have, however, been most heavily developed in this field of work. They have, however, been little applied to most of the other phenomena which we review in this book.

5 Disjunctive Reasoning

As we have seen in the last three chapters, there has been an enormous amount of research on conditional reasoning; similarly, as will emerge in Chapters 7 and 8, there is a large and rapidly growing body of research on reasoning with quantifiers. In contrast, there has been relatively little work on disjunctive reasoning, though the causes of this discrepancy in research interest are not immediately obvious. It is true that disjunctive reasoning does not have its roots in antiquity in the same way that syllogistic reasoning does, but then neither does conditional reasoning. Nor is it likely to be due to the relative infrequency of disjunctives in everyday language, since the word *or* is just as common as the word *if* or the quantifiers used in syllogisms. Disjunctives are ambiguous, but this can hardly be the source of their unpopularity, since conditionals are equally ambiguous. Regardless of the reasons, however, an inspection of the published research will readily reveal that the literature on disjunctives is nothing like as voluminous as that on syllogisms, conditionals or even relational reasoning.

Many of the themes that will be discussed in this chapter are similar to those which we have already covered in Chapter 2. In order to facilitate comparisons between the literatures in conditional and disjunctive reasoning, the organisation of this chapter will follow as closely as possible that adopted in Chapter 2.

DISJUNCTIVES IN LOGIC AND LANGUAGE

Disjunctives are probably best understood in terms of their defining truth tables. Whenever just one of the disjuncts is true, the overall disjunctive is true, and whenever both disjuncts are false, the disjunctive itself is false;

however, the case in which both disjuncts are true is ambiguous, being true in the case of inclusive disjunction but false in the case of exclusive disjunction. This is best illustrated by an example. The disjunctive statement "Either Mary is rich or John is foolish" is clearly true in the situation where Mary is rich and John is not foolish and also in the situation where Mary is not rich and John is foolish; these correspond to the cases where just one of the disjuncts is true. Equally clearly the statement is false in the situation where Mary is not rich and John is not foolish, i.e. when both disjuncts are false. Ambiguity surrounds the situation where Mary is rich and John is foolish; under inclusive disjunction this would be true but under exclusive disjunction it would be false. The full truth tables for the two types of disjunction are presented in Table 5.1.

Everyday examples of these two types of disjunction are not hard to find. The statement "You can either have the money or the free gift" would normally be taken to be an exclusive disjunction, since there is the clear expectation that the person being addressed could not have both the money and the free gift. On the other hand, the statement "You must be over 18 or accompanied by an adult to be allowed entry" would surely not preclude someone who was both over 18 and accompanied by an adult.

There are striking similarities between disjunctives and conditionals. As can be seen from a comparison of the truth tables presented in Tables 5.1 and 2.1 (see Chapter 2), it is possible to translate disjunctives into conditionals and vice versa. An exclusive disjunctive has the same truth table as *If not p then q* when this latter is given a material equivalence interpretation, while inclusive disjunctives have the same truth table as *If not p then q* when this is given a material implication interpretation. As an example of this latter, "Either you give me the money or I will hit you" seems to translate readily into "If you do not give me the money I will hit you". Hence the ambiguity that exists between the two possible interpretations of conditionals has an exact parallel in the ambiguity between exclusive and inclusive interpretations of disjunctives.

TABLE 5.1
Truth Tables for the Disjunctive Statement *p or q*

p	*q*	*Exclusive Disjunction*	*Inclusive Disjunction*
T	T	F	T
T	F	T	T
F	T	T	T
F	F	F	F

Abbreviations: T, true; F, false.

Linguists have for some years studied the interpretations given to disjunctives. A central concern has been to ascertain which meaning is the basic one, though there is no consensus as yet as to which this is. The most commonly argued view is that the inclusive interpretation is the basic one, perhaps inspired by logicians who also typically adopt this stance. Pelletier (1977, p. 63) says, quite categorically, that "*or* in English is always inclusive". He claims that no utterance using *or* ever completely disallows the inclusive interpretation. A less extreme position is that of Gazdar (1979) who also argues that the inclusive interpretation is basic, but acknowledges that exclusive interpretations sometimes occur. He claims that such occurrences can be explained in terms of contextual factors and conversational implicatures modifying the basic meaning.

The exact opposite of this view has been put forward by Lakoff (1971). She states: "except for a very few possible exceptions, *or* must be exclusive" (p. 142). She cites as evidence for this view the fact that in most naturally occurring contexts, *or* does seem to demand an exclusive interpretation. In contrast to both Pelletier and Lakoff, some linguists (e.g. Hurford, 1974) have claimed that *or* has two meanings, the one to be adopted being determined primarily by pragmatic factors. We will return to this issue of the basic interpretation of *or* in the next section when we consider the effects of contextual factors on disjunctives.

Psychological research into the interpretation of disjunctives has been carried out mainly by Fillenbaum (1974a; 1974b). He utilised a variety of techniques to investigate subjects' interpretations, including memory, paraphrasing and strangeness judgements. In logic, *or* is unordered, can connect any two propositions and is inclusive; Fillenbaum's research suggests that the *or* used in language is none of these. When used in threats, disjunctives seem to have a natural order. Fillenbaum's (1974a) subjects found it perfectly natural to say "Get out of my way or I'll hit you", but the reverse of this, "I'll hit you or get out of my way", seemed distinctly odd. Also strange were disjunctives which did not share a common topic (cf. Lakoff, 1971). An example of such a sentence was "He will wear sandals or sell cokes", where the two disjuncts seem to be referring to quite unrelated events. Subjects often paraphrased these to make them more normal, for example by rendering this sentence as "He will sell cokes while wearing sandals". Finally, the supposedly inclusive disjunctives used by Fillenbaum (1974a), such as "He will write his father or call his mother", were judged to be rather strange, leading Fillenbaum to state that "in natural language it may, ordinarily, be quite difficult to interpret *or* in an inclusive sense" (p. 914). Hence this research lends support to the claim of Lakoff (1971) that *or* is normally interpreted exclusively.

THE DISJUNCTIVE TRUTH TABLE TASK

Truth table tasks typically involve subjects evaluating instances as to whether or not they conform to a disjunctive rule. For example, the subject might be given the rule "Either the letter is A or the number is 3" and asked to evaluate whether the instance A4 conforms to this description. This would be classified as a TF instance, since the first disjunct is true while the second is false. Other cases involve TT, FT and FF instances. Several studies of disjunctive truth tables have been conducted on adults, while others have taken a developmental perspective. Some studies have used abstract material such as the letters and numbers given in the example above, while others have used more concrete material. A technique commonly used with children has been to use disjunctive statements to describe the contents of a box and to ask children to indicate whether the statement is an appropriate description of the contents.

Adult Studies

A representative selection of the results using this paradigm on adult subjects (college students in each case) is presented in Table 5.2. In these studies, the disjunctive rules are presented in the form *(Either) p or q* without the qualifying *or both* or *but not both*. It is immediately clear from this table that subjects almost universally regard the FF case as being inconsistent with the rule. Further, about 80% of the time they indicate that the cases involving one true and one false disjunct (TF and FT) conform to the rule. It is perhaps a little surprising that this figure is as low as 80% given the apparent simplicity of the task. One possible reason for this may be that subjects simply failed to spot that one of the disjuncts was false, something they would be less likely to do in the FF case.

Perhaps the most interesting aspect of the findings is with respect to the TT case. Under inclusive disjunction this should be regarded as true, while under exclusive disjunction it should be considered false. In the studies presented in Table 5.2, a surprising number of subjects—more that 60% overall—responded according to the truth table of inclusive disjunction. This may, however, be something of an overestimate. When researchers have looked at the overall truth tables adopted by subjects, rather than looking at the responses to individual instances, there seems to be a preference for exclusive disjunction. Braine and Rumain (1981) found 41% exclusive truth tables as opposed to 32% inclusive; and Sternberg (1979) found 82% exclusive as opposed to just 16% inclusive. The high number of true responses seen in Table 5.2 may be due in part to subjects adopting truth tables quite different to those of inclusive and exclusive disjunction, for example that of conjunction.

TABLE 5.2
Percentage of True and False Judgements to Different Types of Instances on Truth Table Tasks

	TT	*TF*	*FT*	*FF*
Paris (1973)				
Or				
True	75	72	80	0
False	25	28	20	100
Either . . . or				
True	67	87	90	0
False	33	13	10	100
Evans and Newstead (1980)				
True	57	83	83	0
False	43	17	17	100
Braine and Rumain (1981)				
True	50	73[a]	73[a]	0
False	50	18[a]	18[a]	100

[a] These do not sum to 100 because there were some ambiguous responses.

Developmental Studies

A number of the adult studies just reported also looked at developmental trends. In Table 5.3 we present the results from two such studies, those of Paris (1973) and Braine and Rumain (1981). The general picture is of a pattern of responding which gradually approaches that of adults. The few true responses to FF soon disappear; and there is an increasing tendency to indicate that the instances containing just one of the disjuncts (TF and FT) are false. However, even the older children still said, incorrectly, that these were false on a sizeable number of occasions. This is not surprising, since this pattern of responding remains even in adults.

Responses to the TT case show a general trend towards giving fewer true responses over age. This could be interpreted as indicating that young children adopt an inclusive interpretation of *or*, while older children have a growing preference for exclusive interpretations. This is reinforced by the findings of Sternberg (1979) and Braine and Rumain (1981), who studied the individual truth tables demonstrated by each child. There was a shift over time from a preponderance of inclusive truth tables to a preponderance of exclusive ones. However, this finding has to be tempered by the possibility of alternative explanations. It is possible that young children respond to the disjunctive statements as if they were conjunctions, responding true whenever both elements of the statement occur. There

TABLE 5.3
Percentage of True Responses on Two Developmental Truth Table Tasks

	TT	*TF*	*FT*	*FF*
Paris (1973)				
Or				
7-year-olds	98	32	27	3
9-year-olds	77	30	37	3
11-year-olds	85	50	52	3
14-year-olds	75	70	62	0
Either . . . or				
7-year-olds	92	50	37	5
9-year-olds	75	42	55	18
11-year-olds	75	65	62	10
14-year-olds	72	90	90	0
Braine and Rumain (1981)				
5- to 6-year-olds	95	38[a]	33[a]	0
7- to 8-year-olds	81	77[a]	66[a]	0
9- to 10-year-olds	78	68[a]	68[a]	0

[a] These percentages are based only on the responses classifiable as either true or false.

was some evidence for such a tendency in the conditional reasoning literature (see Chapter 2), and it cannot be ruled out in the present situation. However, even allowing for this occurring in the younger children, there does seem to be a tendency for older children to develop a preference for exclusive truth tables.

Taking the results from adult and child studies together, it seems reasonable to conclude that the exclusive interpretation is the normal one. It is the one that is marginally preferred by adults, and it is also the interpretation that is progressively more often adopted by children. Fillenbaum's research, mentioned above, also supported this conclusion. In addition, as we shall see in a later section, the exclusive interpretation seems to be the preferred one in the great majority of realistic contexts.

STUDIES OF DISJUNCTIVE INFERENCES

The types of inference that can be drawn from disjunctives follow from the truth tables presented above. From the falsity of one disjunct, one can deduce the truth of the other, hence the following inferences are valid:

p or q	p or q
not p	not q
Therefore,	Therefore,
q	p

Both of these involve deducing from the denial of one of the disjuncts the truth of the other; hence we shall refer to this inference as the denial inference. It is valid under both inclusive and exclusive disjunction. With exclusive disjunction the following inferences are also valid:

p or q	p or q
p	q
Therefore,	Therefore,
not q	not p

Since this involves deducing from the affirmation of one disjunct the falsity of the other, we shall refer to it as the affirmation inference. It is valid because, under exclusive disjunction, only one of the disjuncts can be true. This is not, of course, the case with inclusive disjunction, where both disjuncts are permitted to be true. Hence the affirmation inference is not valid under inclusive disjunction, where nothing follows from the truth of one of the disjuncts.

Hence, the denial inference from either component is always valid, and the affirmation inference in either direction follows only from an exclusive interpretation of the rule.

Studies of the Denial Inference

The denial inference (deducing the truth of one disjunct from the falsity of the other) seems almost trivially easy but it is nevertheless one on which errors are made. With abstract or arbitrary material, surprisingly high error rates have been obtained. A selection of results is presented in Table 5.4. On average, subjects correctly accept this inference between 80 and 85% of the time. The figure is slightly higher for exclusive disjunctives, and the two studies that have used both types of disjunction have both found exclusive disjunctives to be easier. In these studies, inclusive disjunction is indicated by the tag *or both* at the end of the disjunctive statement, exclusive disjunction by the tag *but not both*.

TABLE 5.4
Percentage of Subjects Making the Denial Inference

	Type of Disjunctive	
	Inclusive	*Exclusive*
Roberge (1976a)	70	84
Roberge (1976b)		84
Roberge (1977)	83	
Roberge (1978)	84	93
Johnson-Laird et al. (1992a)		48
Weighted mean	80	84

Much of the research on this inference was carried out by Roberge and his colleagues in the 1970s, and it is noteworthy in Table 5.4 that the more recent study by Johnson-Laird et al. (1992a) has found a rather lower acceptance of this inference. These latter authors gave their subjects premises such as:

Either Steven is in Donegal or Jenny is in Princeton, but not both
Jenny is in London

and were asked to indicate what conclusion followed. This is a conclusion production task as opposed to the conclusion evaluation task used by most other researchers. However, this is not likely to be the major source of the low level of acceptance of the inference in this study, since at least one other study, that of Roberge (1978), also used a conclusion production task and found much higher levels of performance. The reason for the discrepancy between this study and the others is not entirely clear, but may be attributable to the use of different materials or different subject populations (Johnson-Laird et al. used subjects drawn from the general population rather than college undergraduates).

Studies of the Affirmation Inference

The affirmation inference involves deducing the falsity of one disjunct from the truth of the other, an inference which is valid only with exclusive disjunction. The results from a number of studies which have investigated this inference are presented in Table 5.5. This inference is correctly accepted more than 80% of the time with exclusive disjunctives, but is accepted less than 40% of the time with inclusive disjunctives, where it would constitute an error. Hence once again inclusive disjunctives produce fewer logically correct responses, though in this case their greater difficulty may be due to the fact that the inference is indeterminate rather than false. For example, given the problem:

Either Joan is athletic or she is rich, or both
Joan is athletic
Therefore, Joan is rich

the conclusion is neither determined nor falsified by the premises: Joan could be rich or poor given these premises. In contrast, all the other inferences we have considered produce definitely true or definitely false conclusions, and it is possible that the ambiguity inherent in this inference with inclusive disjunctives contributes to its difficulty.

As with the studies of the denial inference, there is a marked difference between the findings of Johnson-Laird et al. (1992a) and other research in this area, with the former finding comparatively low levels of performance.

TABLE 5.5
Percentage of Subjects Drawing the Affirmation Inference

	Type of Disjunctive	
	Inclusive	*Exclusive*
Roberge (1974)	40	
Roberge (1976b)		92
Roberge (1977)	34	
Johnson-Laird et al. (1992a)		30
Weighted mean	36	83

Note: the affirmation inference is valid under exclusive disjunction, invalid under inclusive disjunction.

The Relative Difficulty of Exclusive and Inclusive Disjunctives

Another finding to emerge from studies of disjunctive inference is that it is in general easier to draw inferences from exclusive than from inclusive rules. Tables 5.4 and 5.5 present results pertinent to this claim. There is a fairly large difference with the affirmation inference, but as we have seen, this may be due to this inference being valid under exclusive disjunction but indeterminate under inclusive disjunction. Only two analyses of the denial inference have used both types of disjunction in the same study, and both of these found greater accuracy with exclusive disjunctions, though this appears to have been significant only in the study by Roberge (1976a).

A relatively straightforward explanation of this finding is that exclusive interpretations are the more common and hence people find it easier to reason with this form. However, other explanations have been put forward. Newstead and Griggs (1983a) suggest that it might be due to the fact that exclusive disjunctions lead to symmetrical inferences, in that one can deduce the truth of one disjunct from the falsity of the other and the falsity of one disjunct from the truth of the other. In contrast, with inclusive disjunctives, nothing can be deduced from the truth of either disjunct. However, Newstead and Griggs provide no reason as to why such symmetry should be easier than the non-symmetrical inferences required with inclusive disjunctives (Johnson-Laird & Byrne, 1991), and hence this can be no more than an interesting possibility.

Johnson-Laird and Byrne (1991) claim that the mental model for exclusive disjunction is simpler than that for inclusive disjunction and that this is the source of the differential difficulty. They claim that the representation of the disjunctive *p or q* will be a very simple one:

p
        q

This representation involves two models, in one of which *p* occurs and in the other of which *q* occurs. This representation, which is ambiguous with respect to inclusive or exclusive interpretation, will in many instances remain ambiguous, but if it needs to be fleshed out it will result in the following models:

[p] ¬q
¬p [q]
(exclusive disjunction)

[p] [q]
[p] ¬q
¬p [q]
(inclusive disjunction)

As can be seen from these representations, there are more models to be constructed with the inclusive interpretation resulting from the possible model, indicated on the first line, in which both *p* and *q* occur. While mental models provide an explanation of the results, it is too early to rule out the alternative explanation in terms of the preferred interpretation.

Double Disjunctions

Johnson-Laird et al. (1992a) have recently investigated a more complicated type of disjunctive reasoning problem which they term double disjunctions. The following is an example of such a problem:

June is in Wales or Charles is in Scotland, or both
Charles is in Scotland or Kate is in Ireland, or both
What, if anything, follows?

The premises support the conclusion that June is in Wales and Kate is in Ireland, or Charles is in Scotland, or both. The reasoning goes as follows: if Charles is not in Scotland, then, by the denial inference, June is in Wales and Kate is in Ireland. Hence either this statement is true or it is the case that Charles is in Scotland, which is the inference that we have just seen may be drawn. (Since this is an inclusive disjunctive, it is also possible that both statements may be true.)

Perhaps not surprisingly with such a complex problem, few people got it correct (6% on the type of problem presented). Johnson-Laird et al. also found that these problems were significantly harder with inclusive disjunctives than with exclusive ones, a finding they explain in terms of the more complex mental models required with inclusive disjunctives. In addition, these authors point out that the vast majority of erroneous conclusions were ones which were consistent with a subset of the models that could be produced from the premises.

While these results are clearly explicable in terms of the mental models theory, they do not rule out alternative explanations. As we saw in the previous section, it is possible that the difficulty of inclusive disjunctives stems at least in part from their relative infrequency. Nevertheless, this is a clear example of a prediction derived from the mental models theory which has gained empirical support.

The Relative Difficulty of Conditionals and Disjunctives

One other finding concerning disjunctive inferences has recently attracted attention, i.e. the claim that disjunctives are harder to reason with than conditionals. Johnson-Laird et al. (1992a) cite this as evidence in favour of the mental models approach, since disjunctives have a more complex mental model. Their own research found, in a conclusion production task, that disjunctives were indeed more difficult than conditionals. However, a number of other studies have failed to find such an effect. Roberge (1974; 1978) found no difference in difficulty, and Roberge and Antonak (1979) found differences that varied in both direction and magnitude as a function of the content used. Given the potential importance of these findings, research is needed to determine how robust the effect is.

REASONING WITH NEGATED DISJUNCTIVES

The previous sections have focused on affirmative disjunctives in order to establish performance on the basic truth table and inference tasks, and in general it would appear that these are within the competence of most adults. We now turn to disjunctions using negatives, where, as we shall see, things get rather more complicated. However, at least part of the difficulty may stem from the fact that negatives are seldom used with disjunctives, and hence some discussion of this issue is in order.

It is actually quite difficult to find realistic disjunctives in which one or both of the disjuncts are negated. Perhaps the only situation in which they are genuinely acceptable is that of threat, as in the sentence: "Either you do your homework or you will not get your pocket money". The point about such threats is that they stress the negative consequences of the second disjunct and hence the negative form seems perfectly acceptable. It is even possible to think of doubly negated threats which approach acceptability, as in "Either you don't go out again or you won't pass your exams". Such examples seem to be of only marginal acceptability, and yet they are probably as near as one can get to forms that might actually occur. It is possible that negated disjunctions scarcely ever occur in everyday language—in stark contrast to conditionals where negation is perfectly acceptable (see Chapter 2). This has not, however, prevented researchers from systematically investigating the effects of negatives on disjunctive reasoning. Indeed, this has actually been one of the most popular manipulations in studies of disjunctives and, despite the artificiality, results of interest have emerged.

The first finding, which will surprise no-one, is that negatives are more difficult than affirmatives (Evans & Newstead, 1980; Johnson-Laird & Tridgell, 1972; Johnson-Laird et al., 1992a; Roberge, 1974; 1976a; 1976b; 1978; Wason & Johnson-Laird, 1969). However, the relative difficulty of the negative forms does hold some surprises. Table 5.6 presents results from a representative set of studies, involving both exclusive and inclusive disjunctives and both the denial and the affirmation inference. The pattern of results is remarkably consistent. The double affirmative instance always produces the highest level of accuracy, and there is very little difference between the two cases where just one of the disjuncts is negated (AN and NA). Interestingly, the doubly negated instance (NN) does not produce

TABLE 5.6
Percentage of Correct Responses in Studies Involving Negated Disjunctives

	AA	*AN*	*NA*	*NN*
Inclusive disjunction				
Denial inference				
Roberge (1974)	59	38	33	48
Roberge (1976a)	85	86	81	84
Roberge (1978)	84	51	47	41
Affirmation inference				
Roberge (1974)	62	51	49	50
Exclusive disjunction				
Denial inference				
Roberge (1976a)	92	72	69	80
Roberge (1976b)	92	47	49	73
Roberge (1978)	93	37	48	64
Affirmation inference				
Roberge (1976b)	84	40	42	65

Abbreviations: AA, both disjuncts affirmative; AN, first disjunct affirmative, second negative, etc.

any poorer performance than the singly negated ones and, in the case of exclusive disjunctives, it actually produces better performance.

Roberge (1976a; 1976b) explains this finding by suggesting that subjects actually drop the negatives when these are present in both disjuncts. Thus subjects treat the statement *Either not p or not q* as if it were *Either p or q*. This is not as bizarre as it might seem at first sight, since under the exclusive interpretation this conversion is actually logically valid. And, as can be seen in Table 5.6, the double negative is easier with exclusive disjunction where this conversion is valid than with inclusive disjunction where it is not. Evans and Newstead (1980) confirmed the finding that double negatives are no more difficult than single negatives, this time in a truth table task, and also argued in favour of the explanation in terms of conversion.

The second finding of interest is the absence of a phenomenon that might have been expected to occur—matching bias. In studies of conditional reasoning, as we have seen, subjects have consistently been found to have a tendency to select the items named in the rule, regardless of whether these have been negated or not. It seems entirely reasonable to expect such findings to be found also with disjunctives, but this is simply not the case.

Matching would be demonstrated on a disjunctive reasoning task by subjects selecting the items named in the rules. For example, if subjects were asked to construct a situation which verified the rule "Either the letter is A or the number is not 3", then there are two logically acceptable ways of doing this: the first is to produce A3, the second to produce a letter other than A and a number other than 3. The first of these is a perfect match, since it contains both the items named in the rule (negatives are ignored in matching), whereas the second is a complete mismatch. The predictions are quite clear, but the results do not bear them out. Using a verification task, Evans and Newstead (1980) actually found a slight (but not significant) tendency for subjects to construct more instances that were complete mismatches than ones which were complete matches. There was no support in their data for the existence of matching bias, and other studies too have failed to find any (Van Duyne, 1974; Wason & Johnson-Laird, 1969).

One quite recent study has, however, claimed to find matching bias in a disjunctive reasoning task. Krauth and Berchtold-Neumann (1988) used a version of the selection task in which the rules were phrased as either inclusive or exclusive disjunctions. They modelled the performance of their subjects on this task, and one of the parameters (following Krauth, 1982) was the tendency to match the items named in the rule. Since their model gave a reasonable fit to the data, they conclude that matching bias does occur. However, their model is a complicated one, and it is not clear whether a simpler model not involving matching might not be able to provide an equally good fit. In the light of all the other negative evidence, it seems sensible to conclude that matching bias simply does not occur with disjunctives.

This, of course, raises the issue of why the effect disappears with disjunctives. One possibility is that matching bias is restricted to conditionals and does not generalise to other situations. Another possibility discussed by Evans and Newstead (1980) is that negatives alter the interpretation of disjunctives, thus confounding the analysis of matching, which assumes constancy of interpretation. A final possibility raised by these authors is that disjunctives lead to a different sort of matching compared to that found with conditionals. Conditional statements lead to an expectancy that the two items mentioned in the rule will occur together; in other words, the two items are positively associated. Disjunctives, however, lead to an expectancy that the two elements will not co-occur, since the presence of one item is associated with the absence of the other. This would lead to a tendency for subjects to choose verifying cases in which one of the named items occurred and the other did not. In terms of matching cases, this means that there should be a tendency to choose *p* plus *not-q* and *not-p* plus *q*, and these combinations were in fact chosen more frequently than either the double match (*p* plus *q*) or the double mismatch (*not-p* plus *not-q*). Hence what may have happened is that the positive matching found with conditionals has been replaced in disjunctives by a kind of negative matching.

More recently, Evans (1989, p. 33) has argued for an interpretation of the discrepancy between the conditional and disjunctive task, which supports his theory that matching reflects linguistically cued relevance:

> I believe that the absence of matching bias in disjunctive reasoning is due to the different linguistic context which they induce relative to conditionals. A conditional . . . is essentially hypothetical in nature, so that it seems to subjects that the rule might or might not apply. That is why subjects use three truth values—true, false and irrelevant for the evaluation of such sentences. It was noticeable in the Evans & Newstead (1980) experiment that the proportion of irrelevant or non-constructed cases was much lower than with conditionals.

A third finding to emerge from studies of the introduction of negatives into disjunctives concerns plausible denial. In Johnson-Laird and Tridgell's (1972) study, subjects found it easier to make logical deductions when the second premise negated something that had been asserted in the first premise. To illustrate, they found the first argument given below easier than the second:

(i) Either p or q
Not q
Therefore, p

(ii) Either p or not q
q
Therefore, p

The authors believe that this finding occurs because in the first example the negative is used to deny something that might plausibly be true. In the second, however, the negative is used in an unusual way since the second disjunct (*q*) would not normally have been negated if there had been reason to expect that it might be true. This finding has been replicated by Roberge (e.g. 1976b) and again explained in terms of inappropriate negation. An alterative explanation is that disjunctives containing negatives are highly unusual and scarcely ever occur in everyday language. The first example contains two affirmative disjuncts which is, we have argued, virtually the only form in which disjunctives normally occur. The second example involves a negated disjunct and it is possible that this accounts for its difficulty.

A final issue is whether the negative conclusion bias which features in abstract conditional reasoning (see Chapter 2) generalises to disjunctives. This consists of a preference for negative over affirmative conclusions when logic is controlled by rotation of negative components in the rules. Unlike matching bias, the preference for negative conclusions does appear to be a pure response bias, or at least we are not aware of other explanations for this finding. This being the case, we should expect it to be observed with disjunctives also. The way most authors report their results, as in Table 5.6, does not enable us to check for the bias, since we need to know whether the inference is being made from first to second component or vice versa. However, in one study, Roberge (1976b) checked specifically for negative conclusion bias with exclusive disjunctive reasoning and found that the bias did generalise to disjunctives, especially in the case of affirmation inferences. In these inferences, drawing an affirmative conclusion is more difficult because the subject has to reason from the affirmation of one component to deny a negative in the other. Consider the inference:

Either p or q but not both
p
Therefore, not q

This seems straightforward enough. Now we add a negative into the second component:

Either p or not q but not both
p
Therefore, q

This is logically equivalent to the first case (affirmation inference with exclusive disjunctive) but much more difficult. The subject must infer that *q* is true because *not-q* is false, i.e. *not not-q*. This double negation problem might also account for the negative conclusion bias on conditional rules so far as the Modus Tollens and Denial of the Antecedent inferences are concerned. However, it is also possible that the extra difficulty of the second inference stems from the presence of a negated disjunctive in the first premise.

DISJUNCTIVES IN CONTEXT

We have examined a large number of studies of disjunctive reasoning, but virtually all of those so far considered have used abstract or arbitrary material. Not all of the authors would agree with our designation of their material as being arbitrary. Roberge (1977; 1978) set out specifically to examine the effects of concrete material to see if it led to improved performance over abstract material. He found no such improvement, and Roberge and Antonak (1979) actually found that abstract material lead to significantly better performance. However, it is revealing to examine just what is meant by concrete material in these studies. An example taken from Roberge (1978) is: "Either Joan is athletic or she is rich (but not both)". As with many other examples of concrete disjunctives that we have examined, this seems to be a rather strange thing to say. It is clumsy because of the "but not both" tag at the end, and it also relates two quite disparate elements: in Lakoff's (1971) terms, it breaches the principle of common topic. It is difficult to conceive of any real-life situation in which the sentence would be uttered. Hence we would argue that this material is to all intents abstract and arbitrary, in just the same way that Manktelow and Evans' (1979) food and drink content was in the selection task (see Chapter 4).

One of the few studies to have used genuinely realistic material is that of Newstead, Griggs and Chrostowski (1984). They used disjunctives that might well occur in everyday conversation rather than being contrived and artificial as in some of the previous studies. This was one of the contexts they used:

> Tom was in debt to his brother. He told him: "I will either pay you back next week or mow the lawn for you"

The sentence in quoted speech is the key disjunctive sentence, but it is embedded in a vignette to make it appear more natural. In one of their experiments, Newstead et al. (1984) used a truth table task in which subjects had to indicate whether certain outcomes (e.g. "Tom mowed the lawn; he did not pay his brother back") were consistent or inconsistent with the disjunctive statement. The data were analysed in terms of the individual truth tables demonstrated by the subjects. Over all the contexts, 76% of the truth tables corresponded to that of exclusive disjunction, 18% to inclusive disjunction, while 6% fell into other patterns. Furthermore, there were consistent differences between the various contexts, as can be seen in the first column of numbers in Table 5.7. Exclusive interpretations were much the most preferred in all of the contexts except that of Qualification. Inspection of the types of material used in this context readily reveals why this should have been the case. For example, this was one of their passages:

> A computer firm was trying to recruit a new programmer. In the advertisement it said: "The successful applicant must have either a degree or experience in computing"

It is easy to see why appointing a candidate having both a degree and computing experience would be seen as consistent with the disjunctive statement. By and large, however, there was a very strong preference for the truth tables corresponding to exclusive disjunction, and it is difficult to avoid the conclusion that this is the normal interpretation in most contexts. It is interesting to note that Ray, Reynolds and Carranza (1989), in one of the few other studies to attempt to use genuinely realistic material, also found a general preference for exclusive interpretations.

Newstead et al. (1984) also looked at the inferences that subjects drew from disjunctives embedded in contexts. In the first example given above, they might be given the additional premise:

Tom paid back his brother
Therefore,
Tom did not mow the lawn

TABLE 5.7
Percentage of Inclusive and Exclusive Truth Tables and Inferences as a Function of Context[a]

Context	*Inclusive Interpretation*	*Exclusive Interpretation*	*Denial Inference*	*Affirmation Inference (inc.)*	*Affirmation Inference (exc.)*
Threat	2	97	93	0	93
Promise	14	85	100	1	96
Choice	6	85	97	0	99
Qualification	53	47	88	45	46
Uncertainty	8	83	93	4	94
Abstract	18	67	80	13	74
Concrete	23	71	91	14	80
Mean	18	76	92	11	83

[a]After Newstead et al. (1984).

By permuting the affirmation and denial of the disjunct and the affirmation and denial of the conclusion, they were able to investigate the types of inferences that subjects drew. Responses corresponding to the denial inference are presented in the second column of numbers in Table 5.7. Such response patterns would involve indicating that the denial of one of the disjuncts implied the truth of the other disjunct, but that the falsity of the other disjunct did not follow. The great majority of subjects drew this inference in all the contexts.

The affirmation inference has two forms, corresponding to the inclusive and exclusive forms of the disjunctive. With exclusive disjunction, the truth of one disjunct implies the falsity of the other, but this is not a valid inference with inclusive disjunction. The fourth and fifth columns of Table 5.7 show the frequency of these inference patterns. It is striking that the inference pattern for inclusive disjunction occurred predominantly with the Qualification context, precisely the one which evoked an inclusive interpretation as measured in the truth table task. In the other contexts, there was a very strong tendency to draw the inferences permitted under exclusive disjunction. It would appear that subjects are consistently drawing the permitted logical inferences in the light of the interpretations that they have adopted.

THOG: A DISJUNCTIVE REASONING PROBLEM

The THOG problem is another of those irritating problems devised by Peter Wason—irritating in the sense that they are superficially rather simple but most of us manage to get them wrong. This problem was devised a little later than the selection task (see Chapter 4) and has not generated the same voluminous literature, but it has still been the subject of considerable—and continuing—interest.

The classic version of the problem as presented by Wason and Brooks (1979) is shown in Fig. 5.1. The subjects' task is to classify the designs into the appropriate category.

The correct answer is that the white diamond and the black circle are definitely not THOGs, whereas the white circle definitely is a THOG. The reason for this is that the particular shape and colour could be either black plus circle or white plus diamond, and the same conclusion follows in each case. For example, if black plus circle had been written down, then the white diamond could not be a THOG since it contains neither of the properties, and the black circle could not be a THOG because it contains both; only the white circle is a THOG since it contains just one of the designated properties. Precisely the same conclusion follows from the other pair of properties that could have been written down.

Typically, only about one-third or fewer of subjects produce the correct response. The most common response is actually almost a mirror image of the

In front of you are four designs: black diamond, white diamond, black circle, and white circle.

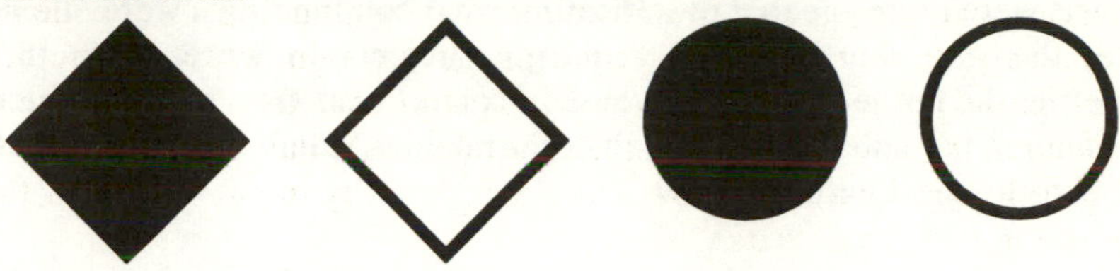

You are to assume that I have written down one of the colours (black or white) and one of the shapes (diamond or circle). Now read the following rule carefully:

If, and only if, any of the designs includes either the colour I have written down, or the shape I have written down, but not both, then it is called a THOG.

I will tell you that the black diamond is a THOG.

Each of the designs can now be classified into one of the following categories:

A) Definitely is a THOG
B) Insufficient information to decide
C) Definitely is not a THOG

FIG. 5.1 Designs used in the abstract THOG problem.

correct one: subjects say that the white diamond and the black circle either are or might be THOGs, whereas the white circle is definitely not a THOG. Wason and Brooks (1979) have called these responses "intuitive errors".

The Source of the Difficulty of the THOG Problem

Research on the THOG problem has arguably told us more about the factors that do *not* contribute to the problem's difficulty than those that do. One possibility is that subjects fail to understand the rule; in other words, they do not realise what exclusive disjunction involves. This seems somewhat implausible given that this is probably the normal interpretation of a disjunctive, and was eliminated as an explanation in the study by Wason and Brooks (1979). They showed that subjects had no difficulty in indicating what followed when they themselves generated the two defining properties. What is more, even after subjects had demonstrated their understanding of the disjunction, they were still unable to solve the standard THOG problem.

Wason and Brooks (1979) also eliminated another plausible explanation for the difficulty of the THOG problem, i.e. that subjects might have difficulty in generating hypotheses as to what properties might be written down. In their second experiment, they showed that the majority of subjects were quite capable of indicating what combinations were allowed under the rule. Furthermore, requiring subjects to write down these properties did not lead to any increase in correct responses to the problem. This finding has subsequently been confirmed by Smyth and Clark (1986) and Girotto and Legrenzi (1989).

The Effects of Realistic Material

Research on the realism of the material used in the THOG problem has revealed that use of abstract material is not a major source of the problem's difficulty. Griggs and Newstead (1982) and Newstead, Griggs and Warner (1982) devised a number of realistic versions of the problem which failed to improve performance. It is possible to cue in the correct answer but this seems to have little to do with an increased understanding of the underlying logic of the problem. Newstead et al. (1982) used a version of the problem involving combinations of food, in which the subjects' task was to indicate which combinations were acceptable ones for the experimenter to eat. Use of such material in itself did not lead to any improvement in performance, but when the correct answer was to say that the experimenter would eat ice cream with chocolate sauce but would not eat meat with chocolate sauce or ice cream with gravy this did, not surprisingly, lead to more correct solutions.

Smyth and Clark (1986) devised an ingenious realistic version of the problem in which the relationship of half-sister was used. This relationship can be defined in terms of exclusive disjunction, since a half-sister is someone who has one parent in common but not both. The half-sister problem is as follows:

> At the bottom of the page are the descriptions of the parents of four women. You are to assume that I have written down one of the mothers (Jane or my mother) and one of the fathers (my father or George). Now read the following rule carefully: If, and only if, the description of a woman's parents includes either the mother I have written down, or the father I have written down, but not both, then that woman is my half-sister. I now tell you that Robin is my half-sister.

Although some simplified forms of this problem led to improved performance, when this material was used in a version similar to the normal THOG problem, no significant difference was found. Girotto and Legrenzi (1989) and O'Brien et al. (1990) also used realistic versions of the problem which failed to affect performance. Hence phrasing the problem in realistic terms does not in itself lead to any improvement in performance, although, as we shall see, some realistic versions lead to an increased number of correct answers for other reasons.

The first versions of the THOG problem which were reliably found to improve performance were those produced by Griggs and Newstead (1982). One of the problems which produced facilitation is the DRUG problem, which is presented here in full:

> Dr. Robinson was instructing some trainee nurses on how to administer drugs. He was talking about kidney diseases and told the nurses that renal patients required carefully controlled intakes of calcium and potassium. The best way of administering these was by two injections daily, but patients became very sore with this number of injections. Thus, it was hospital policy to administer one drug intravenously and one orally. The doctor emphasized: "You must give the patients potassium either in an injection or orally every day, but of course you must not give them both the potassium injection and the potassium pill. Similarly, you must give the patients calcium but not both the calcium injection and the calcium pill."
>
> The nurses were then told, as a class exercise, to decide what brand name of drugs they would select to administer to patients. They were told to choose some combination of the drugs Deroxin and Altanin (which are intravenous drugs, one containing calcium and the other potassium) with the drugs Prisone and Triblomate (which are orally administered drugs, one of which contains calcium, the other potassium).
>
> At the next class, Dr. Robinson was surprised to find that the class had produced as answers all the possible combinations of the drugs:

	Injection	*Drug*
Answer 1	Deroxin	Prisone
Answer 2	Deroxin	Triblomate
Answer 3	Altanin	Prisone
Answer 4	Altanin	Triblomate

> Dr. Robinson got as far as telling the class that the combination in Answer 1 conformed to his instructions when he was called away to do an emergency operation. Hence the students had to work out for themselves whether they were right or wrong.

The subjects had to classify the remaining combinations as to whether they conformed to Dr. Robinson's instructions.

At first sight, this seems somewhat removed from the original version of the THOG problem, but Griggs and Newstead (1982) show, by an analysis of the underlying structures, that the problems are isomorphic and require the same logical operations in their solution. The structural tree for the problem can be seen in Fig. 5.2. The DRUG problem led to correct solutions from more than 70% of the subjects attempting it, well in excess of what is found with the standard version of the problem. Griggs and Newstead explain this improvement in terms of problem representation. They point out that the underlying problem space can be envisaged as

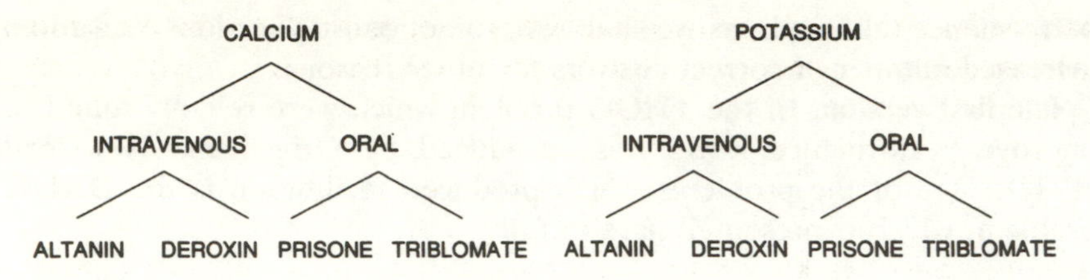

FIG. 5.2 The DRUG problem.

having two branches (see Fig. 5.2). They claim that their version makes the existence of the second branch very clear, since it is given a verbal label and this enables subjects to represent the problem properly. The standard THOG problem, on the other hand, does not make the second branch at all explicit, since this corresponds to the properties not written down. Griggs and Newstead found support for this explanation by devising abstract versions which made the structure very clear and which also produced significant facilitation. Other research has also found that giving labels to negative concepts can lead to improved performance (e.g. Tweney et al., 1980), and there are also clear analogies to the tendency to focus on positive instances that has been claimed to underlie a number of cognitive phenomena (Evans, 1989).

Confusion Theory

The explanation put forward for their results by Griggs and Newstead (1982) has recently been challenged. Girotto and Legrenzi (1989) and O'Brien et al. (1990) point out that the DRUG problem differs in a number of ways from the standard THOG. They claim that the DRUG problem may clarify the problem structure in a rather different way to that originally claimed. More specifically, the problem may help overcome possible confusion between the properties written down and those present in the positive exemplar. Although people are perfectly capable of generating hypotheses as to what the written-down properties are (Wason & Brooks, 1979), it seems that they have great difficulty in using these hypothesised properties in a combinatorial analysis, and this may well stem from confusion between the properties written down and those possessed by the positive exemplar.

The first research to investigate this was carried out by Girotto and Legrenzi (1989). They found facilitation on a version of the problem called the spy problem in which certain combinations of descriptions were required on passports in order to secure safe passage out of a foreign country. The interesting feature of the problem is that the spies had to change the descriptions on the passports, and the positive exemplar was also a combination that was successful only after it had been changed. Hence subjects were not actually told what the properties of the positive exemplar were and it was assumed that this helped avoid confusion.

These authors were also able to produce facilitation in a version of the THOG problem which used the same designs as the original:

Five friends meet every night in the pub. One night, Charles decides to play a game: "I have brought a deck of cards. It contains only these four types of card: [The subjects were at this point shown the designs in Fig. 5.1.] I deal one for myself from the deck, and I won't show it to you. Now, I'll deal each of you a card, and I'll pay for a dinner for each person who has a card including either the colour of my card, or the shape of my card, but not both."

The following are the cards of Charles's friends:

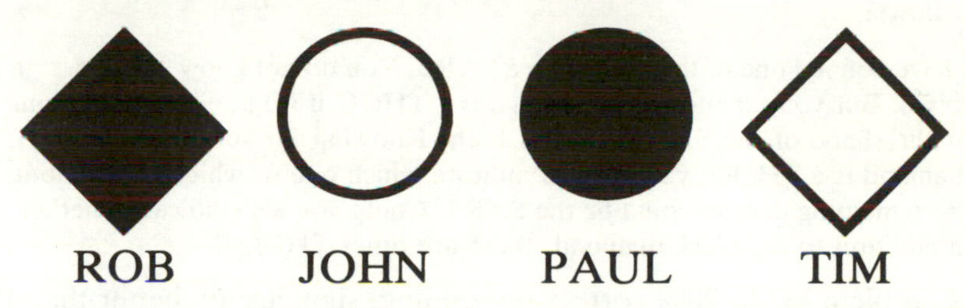

Charles continues: "Without showing you my card, I can tell you that I owe Rob a dinner. Which card do you think I could have? And do you think that I have to pay for a dinner for someone else? If so, for whom?"

FIG. 5.3 Designs used in Girotto and Legrenzi's (1989) Pub problem.

This problem produced significant facilitation which the authors attribute to the fact that there is a clear distinction between the properties of the positive exemplar and the properties on the selected card, and that there is also a clear indication that hypotheses need to be generated and tested. Unfortunately, however, a slight variant on the problem in which the original designs were described verbally rather than presented visually failed to produce facilitation. This surprising result is difficult to explain and casts doubt on the generality of the finding.

Newstead and Griggs (1992) investigated this problem further and were able to shed some light on the results. In particular, they found that it made no difference whether the properties were presented verbally rather than visually. Paradoxically, while this finding contradicts that of Girotto and Legrenzi, it lends support to their explanation of their findings in terms of confusion between the properties of the exemplar and the hypothesised properties that need to be tested.

A similar finding has emerged from a study by O'Brien et al. (1990). They found facilitation in a version of the problem in which separate labels were given to the colour and the shape that the experimenter had chosen. They explain this as being due to the fact that these labels serve to distinguish clearly between the properties written down and the properties of the positive exemplar, thus removing any possible confusion between these [which is, of course, essentially the same explanation as that put forward by Girotto and Legrenzi (1989)].

Perhaps the most convincing evidence in favour of confusion theory comes from research on an abstract version of the problem. Girotto and Legrenzi (1992) have devised yet another version of the problem which they call the SARS problem. This involves the basic designs as used in the original THOG problem (see Fig. 5.1) but subjects are given instructions as follows:

> I have defined one of the designs as a SARS. You do not know which design this is. But you do know that a design is a THOG if it has either the colour or the shape of the SARS, but not both. Knowing for sure that the black diamond is a THOG, you have to indicate which one or which ones among the remaining designs could be the SARS. Could you also indicate whether, in addition to the black diamond, there are other THOGs?

This problem led to 70% correct responding, significantly better than the standard THOG. Girotto and Legrenzi (1992) interpret this as indicating that clear separation of the properties in the positive exemplar and the properties in the hypothesis can produce facilitation even in an abstract version of the task.

It would thus appear that a consensus is emerging that confusion theory provides an appropriate explanation of the difficulty of the THOG problem. However, the theory is not without its problems. Newstead and Griggs (1992) found that separation of the properties in the positive exemplar from those in the hypothesis was not on its own enough to produce facilitation. They found that it was also necessary to ask subjects to write down the properties in the hypothesis (something that was required in all of the versions used by Girotto and Legrenzi in their research). In the absence of such a requirement, no facilitation occurred. This seems to indicate that subjects need to both name the possible properties and have these clearly differentiated from the positive exemplar for facilitation to occur.

The Source of Intuitive Errors

Another aspect of the THOG problem which has generated a sizeable amount of research is the explanation of the occurrence of intuitive errors. Griggs and Newstead (1983) propose two main explanations for these, the first in terms of the "common element fallacy", the second in terms of matching bias. According to the common element fallacy, subjects assume that the properties in the positive example of the THOG are in fact those which define the concept of THOGness. The idea is derived originally from work on concept formation (Bruner, Goodnow & Austin, 1956) in which it has been found that disjunctive concepts are difficult to acquire and that many subjects assume that commonly occurring attributes define the concept. The matching bias explanation proposes that subjects match examples to the known positive instance and respond according to how close the match is. In the original version of the problem, they would say that the white circle is not a THOG since it shares no properties in common with the black diamond, while the other two designs could be THOGs since they each share one property in common with the black diamond. Note that both the common element and the matching bias explanations are related to the confusion theory discussed above, since both claim that subjects are failing to distinguish properly between the properties written down and those in the positive instance.

The research reported by Griggs and Newstead (1983) involved some highly complicated variants on the THOG task, including a number which introduced negatives. The majority of the results (but not all of them) favoured the matching bias explanation. Subsequent research has also supported this conclusion. O'Brien et al. (1990) found that a number of subjects did seem to assume that the properties written down were the same as those in the positive exemplar, just as the common element explanation predicts; but these subjects were not those who made intuitive errors! The common element fallacy does not provide a good account of the observed findings, and an explanation in terms of perceptual matching seems the most plausible. It is perhaps a little paradoxical that the THOG problem, which involves disjunctive reasoning, should provide support for a type of matching bias when other research on disjunctives has led to some questioning of the generality of the phenomenon.

It is arguable that the THOG problem has not taught us a great deal about disjunctive reasoning *per se*, but has nevertheless taught us something about more general aspects of reasoning. We have learned that subjects have some difficulty with the combinatorial analysis required by the THOG problem, which runs contrary to certain theories of competence which claim that such combinatorial analyses are well within the capabilities of adult subjects (e.g. Inhelder & Piaget, 1958). It would also seem that subjects can be confused by the presence of a positive instance that does not correspond to one of the hypothesised combinations—so much so that they abandon hypothetical reasoning and resort to a more primitive matching strategy. In these respects, the THOG problem is similar to the selection task, which could also be claimed to have thrown little light on conditional reasoning but which has produced a number of findings which are highly relevant to an understanding of reasoning in general.

OVERVIEW

It may now be becoming apparent why disjunctive reasoning has attracted less attention than other types of reasoning. For one thing, it would appear that there are fewer errors to explain: subjects make fewer errors on disjunctive inferences than on conditional inferences or syllogisms, and the THOG problem produces better performance than the selection task. But the most important factor is surely that studies of disjunctives have thrown up fewer theoretical issues and fewer findings of real interest than have other types of reasoning. In fact, much of the research has been essentially atheoretical, aimed at finding out what happens rather than addressing theoretical questions. The theoretically motivated research that has been carried out has been largely inspired by ideas drawn from other areas rather than from disjunctive reasoning itself. There is a hint of a resurgence of interest in disjunctive reasoning as new problems are devised and become a testing ground for theories; but there is a long way to go before disjunctives even start to approach the level of research that conditionals have attracted.

6 Relational Inferences

Many everyday inferences depend on relationships between entities. Suppose you are trying to choose which one of several textbooks to buy. You hear the following information from a friend:

Textbook A is worse than Textbook B.

You read the following information in a review:

Textbook C is better than Textbook B.

You can put these pieces of information together and make the following inference:

Textbook C is best.

The inference that Textbook C is best is based on the transitivity of the relation "better than" and its antonym "worse than". In the previous chapters, we examined inferences that depended primarily on the relations between propositions, for example, we outlined the sorts of inferences people make, based on their understanding of the connective *if*, from premises, such as:

If Textbook C is better than Textbook B
then Ann will read Textbook C

In this chapter, we begin our examination of inferences that depend on relations internal to propositions, based on relational terms such as "better than" and "worse than". Some relations are intransitive. For example:

Ann is the mother of Belle
Belle is the mother of Cass
Therefore, Ann is *not* the mother of Cass.

Other relations are atransitive, that is, they support neither transitive nor intransitive inferences. For example:

Ann is next to Belle
Belle is next to Cass

If the women are standing in a line then Ann is not next to Cass, but if they are arranged in a circle then Ann is next to Cass. Neither inference can be made conclusively.

Relational inferences and, in particular, transitive inferences, have received attention from psychologists interested in everyday reasoning skills. These simple, immediate inferences underlie many of our more complex, abstract skills, such as mathematical, scientific and probabilistic thinking (e.g. Kahneman, Slovic & Tversky, 1982). They enable us to navigate through the environment, and to establish the spatial location of entities (Denis & Cocude, 1989; Maki, 1981). Transitive inference skills develop early in childhood, but in this chapter we will focus on our understanding of the cognitive processes that underlie relational reasoning in adults. To begin, we will examine the sorts of problems that adults have been asked to solve in experimental studies.

THE THREE-TERM SERIES PROBLEM

A series of three terms can be arranged in a linear order, such as:

A
B
C

We can describe this layout in the following *linear syllogism*, sometimes called a *three-term series*:

A is higher than B
B is higher than C.

The premises in the description describe the layout unambiguously—they cannot be interpreted in such a way that they do not describe it, or in such a way that they describe an alternative layout. But, in fact, there are numerous other ways to describe the same layout: almost 100 simple descriptions can be formed by changing the order of the terms in the description (A, B and C) and by changing the words used to describe the relations between them. For example, the same layout can be described in the following way:

B is not as high as A
C is lower than B

The ease with which individuals can make inferences about a layout is affected by the way it is described, as we will see in the next section. Psychologists have studied alternative descriptions to get clues about the ways in which individuals represent such information, and how they process it. The layout above can be described in eight different ways, using affirmative relations, that is, "higher" and "lower", with the terms arranged so that the description is determinate, that is, it describes this array and no other. These eight descriptions have been studied extensively in experimental research, and they are outlined in Table 6.1.

The premises with which we began:

A is higher than B
B is higher than C

support certain valid inferences. Given the question:

Which letter is highest?

the premises support the answer:

A

and given the question:

Which letter is lowest?

they support the answer:

C.

Likewise, the premises support the inferences:

A is higher than C

or equivalently:

TABLE 6.1
Determinate Affirmative Descriptions of a Single Three-term Array:
A
B
C

1. A higher than B B higher than C	2. C lower than B B lower than A	3. B higher than C A higher than B	4. B lower than A C lower than B
5. A higher than B C lower than B	6. C lower than B A higher than B	7. B lower than A B higher than C	8. B higher than C B lower than A

C is lower than A.

These conclusions are valid—there is no situation in which the premises could be true and the conclusions false. In fact, every one of the eight descriptions in Table 6.1 support the same valid inferences about the array, as interested readers can verify for themselves.

We can introduce negative relations into the description, such as "not as high as" and "not as low as", and form another eight determinate descriptions based on two negative premises. For example:

A is not as low as B
B is not as low as C

In addition, there are eight descriptions based on an affirmative first premise and a negative second premise, e.g.

A is higher than B
B is not as low as C

and eight based on a negative first premise and an affirmative second premise, e.g.

A is not as low as B
B is higher than C.

In total, then, there are 32 pairs of premises that uniquely describe the single layout introduced earlier, and every one of these descriptions is determinate, that is, it describes only this layout, and it gives rise to the valid inferences outlined. These determinate descriptions have received the most extensive attention in the study of relational inferences, and we will see shortly the differences in the ease and speed with which individuals make inferences from the different descriptions.

There are still other ways to describe the layout. Consider the following premises:

A is higher than C
B is higher than C

They describe the layout, but they could describe other layouts as well. In fact, the description is consistent with three alternative layouts:

1	2	3
A	B	A B
B	A	C
C	C	

The description is *indeterminate*, that is, it fails to provide sufficient information to refer uniquely to one layout. There is an indeterminacy in establishing the exact location of each term with reference to the other terms. The indeterminacy becomes most apparent when you try to make an inference about the relative location of some of the terms. Indeterminate descriptions do not support valid conclusions relating the two unrepeated terms; for example, it could be the case that *A is higher than B*, or it could be the case that *B is higher than A*. Neither inference can be made for certain. Likewise, the question:

Which letter is highest?

cannot be answered with certainty, since either A or B, or both, may be highest. On the other hand, the question:

Which letter is lowest?

can be answered:

C

The layout with which we began can be described by a range of *indeterminate* descriptions, and Table 6.2 illustrates 16 such descriptions based on affirmative premises alone. These descriptions describe the layout, but they could be construed in such a way that they describe an alternative layout. There are a further 16 indeterminate descriptions based on two negative premises, 16 based on an affirmative first premise and a negative second premise, and 16 based on a negative first premise and an affirmative second premise. In total, then, there are 64 indeterminate descriptions that correspond, in one of their interpretations, to the layout above.

TABLE 6.2
Indeterminate Affirmative Descriptions of a Three-term Array:
A
B
C

C is the repeated term			
1′. A higher than C B higher than C	2′. C lower than B C lower than A	3′. B higher than C A higher than C	4′. C lower than A C lower than B
5′. A higher than C C lower than B	6′. C lower than B A higher than C	7′. C lower than A B higher than C	8′. B higher than C C lower than A
A is the repeated term			
1″. A higher than B A higher than C	2″. B lower than A C lower than A	3″. A higher than B A higher than C	4″. B lower than A C lower than A
5″. A higher than B C lower than A	6″. A higher than B C lower than A	7″. B lower than A A higher than C	8″. B lower than A A higher than C

A picture may paint a thousand words, and in this case, there are 96 possible descriptions for the single layout with which we began. Some of the descriptions are *determinate*, and some are *indeterminate*; some are based on *affirmative* premises and some are based on *negative* premises. We have considered just a single layout, but in fact three terms can be arranged in a vertical series in six different orders:

1	2	3	4	5	6
A	A	B	B	C	C
B	C	C	A	B	A
C	B	A	C	A	B

and so there is a wealth of possible three-term series problems. We have information on the inferences that people make from just a selected few of these possible descriptions.

THE PHENOMENA OF RELATIONAL REASONING

Individuals find some relational inferences more difficult than others: they take longer to make some inferences, and they make more errors when they must make the inference in a short time. We will review the key phenomena established in previous research. First, we will consider two phenomena that preoccupied early researchers attempting to distinguish between alternative theories of the representations and processes used in solving three-term series problems:

- Markedness: directional spatial arrays or linguistic compression?
- End-anchoring or question congruence?

Next, we will consider four phenomena that have helped clarify the nature of the representations individuals construct for a range of relational problems:

- The integration of the premises.
- The continuity of the information.
- The determinacy of the description.
- Presented and inferred information: the distance effect.

Finally, we will consider two curious phenomena that have puzzled researchers on relational reasoning, and we will consider the resolution of them from our contemporary understanding of the mechanisms underlying reasoning:

- Problem imageability.
- Strategies in reasoning.

Two Phenomena to Challenge Early Theories of Relational Reasoning

Descriptions of a single array can differ in the difficulty with which people make the inferences they support. Each description may describe the same layout, but the order of the terms in the description, and the relations used to express the arrangement, lead to differences in the ease with which people make inferences. The four sets of data in Table 6.3 illustrate these differences in difficulty.

As Table 6.3 shows, individuals tend to make the correct inferences from these simple three-term series problems, ranging from 81 to 92% correct (Huttenlocher, 1968). When they must reach their conclusion within a 10-sec time limit, they produce fewer correct answers, ranging from 38 to

TABLE 6.3
The Difficulty of Different Three-term Series Problems

Relation Used	*De Soto et al. (1965) Better–Worse (%: 10 sec limit)*	*Huttenlocher (1968) Taller–Shorter (%:sec)*	*Clark (1969a) Better–Worse (sec)*	*Sternberg (1980, exp. 3) Taller–Shorter Better–Worse Faster–Slower (sec)*
1. A is better than B B is better than C	61	83:1.55	5.75 (6.34)	6.38 (7.12)
2. C is worse than B B is worse than A	43	86:1.61	6.40 (6.08)	7.85 (6.30)
3. B is better than C A is better than B	53	89:1.35	5.25 (6.85)	5.98 (8.67)
4. B is worse than A C is worse than B	50	92:1.42	5.47 (6.35)	6.57 (7.32)
5. A is better than B C is worse than B	62	90:1.41	5.34 (6.50)	6.20 (8.55)
6. C is worse than B A is better than B	57	91:1.42	5.32 (6.53)	6.09 (8.21)
7. B is worse than A B is better than C	42	82:1.57	5.49 (6.14)	6.81 (6.52)
8. B is better than C B is worse than A	38	81:1.57	5.77 (6.25)	6.84 (6.66)

Notes: % = Percentages of correct inferences.
sec = Latencies in seconds (the first set is for responses to the question only, the remaining 4 sets are for processing the premises and responding to the question).
Figures in parentheses are latencies to *negative* premises (see text for further information).

62% correct (De Soto, London & Handel, 1965). As a result of the ease with which individuals reach correct conclusions, research on three-term series problems, unlike other aspects of deductive reasoning, has tended to focus on the length of time it takes people to reach their correct conclusion. As Table 6.3 shows, latencies to solve the different problems vary: the time to respond to the question, once subjects have understood the premises, is about 1.5 sec, ranging from 1.41 to 1.61 sec (Huttenlocher, 1968). Overall, their latency to understand the premises and make an inference is about 6 sec, and ranges, for example, from 5.25 to 6.40 sec (Clark, 1969a). Table 6.3 also shows that latencies to problems based on affirmative relations are faster than the equivalent problems based on negative relations (in parentheses).

One of the striking features of the data in Table 6.3 is the variability in the relative difficulty of the different problems. No two researchers appear to have found exactly the same pattern of results. Nonetheless, some consistency is apparent in the latencies, and we can see, for example, that problem 3:

B is better than C
A is better than B

emerges as one of the easiest problems, and problem 2:

C is worse than B
B is worse than A

emerges as one of the most difficult problems. Why do the eight problems in Table 6.3 differ in their difficulty? Researchers have examined two alternative proposals about the mental representations and processes that individuals rely on to solve these problems, and that give rise to the pattern of difficulty in the inferences that they make.

One view of the representations and processes that underlie reasoning about relations is that people: "rely on spatial representations or 'thought-models' which they construct in some cognitive space" (De Soto et al., 1965, p. 518). This view can be considered an early precursor to the theory that people make inferences by constructing and revising mental models (Johnson-Laird, 1983; Johnson-Laird & Byrne, 1991). People use the linguistic description of the layout to construct a representation of the layout itself, and different descriptions enable the construction of a layout more readily than others. De Soto et al. proposed that a premise such as:

Al is better than Bob

requires people to construct a spatial array. They insert the entities mentioned in the description into the appropriate location in the array. They represent the meaning of the premise above by inserting a token, "A", corresponding to Al, into the top position of an array:

A
.
.

and then they insert a token, "B", corresponding to Bob, in the next position down:

A
B
.

A premise such as:

Bob is worse than Al

requires individuals to construct their array from the bottom-up. They insert B into the last position of the array:

.
.
B

and they insert A in the next position up:

.
A
B

(De Soto et al., 1965; see also Handel, De Soto & London, 1968).

An alternative view of the representations and processes that individuals rely on to make relational inferences is that they correspond to a linguistic representation that uncovers the underlying meaning of the premises (Clark, 1969a). This view can be seen as an early precursor to inference-rule theories (e.g. Braine, 1978; Cheng & Holyoak, 1985; Rips, 1983). Clark proposed that people represent the premise:

Al is better than Bob

by constructing a linguistic representation, based on a dimension of goodness:

A is more good, B is less good.

"Better" is an adjective which describes the relative *goodness* of two entities. In contrast, "worse" is an adjective which describes the relative *badness* of two entities. Hence, individuals represent the premise:

Bob is worse than Al

on a dimension of badness:

B is more bad, A is less bad.

These two alternative theories of relational reasoning give rise to different predictions about the relative difficulty of different three-term series, as we will now see.

Markedness: Directional Spatial Arrays or Linguistic Compression?

De Soto et al. (1965, p. 513) recount the following anecdote:

> Mickey Mantle tells of an exhibition baseball game in which he and Willie Mays, both superstars, were playing. Unhappily, the two superstars were having a bad day. Finally a leather-lunged fan shouted at Mantle, "I came to see which of you two guys was better, you or Mays. Instead, I'm seeing which is worse!"

The two relational terms, better and worse, seem to have different meanings. "Better" is an unmarked comparative: it describes the relative goodness of two entities, but it does not provide absolute information about whether they are both good or bad. The information:

Mickey Mantle is better than Willie Mays

describes their relative goodness in the game, but it could turn out that they both played well, or that they both played badly. The information:

Mickey Mantle is worse than Willie Mays

describes not only their relative goodness in the game, it also provides absolute information about their playing—it indicates that they both played badly (see also Clark, 1969a). How does this difference in the nature of the adjective used affect the ease with which individuals make their inferences?

According to the spatial array view, individuals prefer to construct arrays from the top-down, rather than from the bottom-up. A premise that contains an unmarked comparative, e.g.

A is better than B

requires the construction of a top-down array:

A
B
.

A premise that contains a marked comparative, e.g.

A is worse than B

requires the construction of a bottom-up array:

.
B
A

In support of this proposal, De Soto et al. found that problem 1 in Table 6.3:

A is better than B
B is better than C

which requires a wholly top-down construction of the array, is easier (61% correct) than problem 2:

C is worse than B
B is worse than A

(43% correct), which requires a wholly bottom-up construction of the array.

According to the linguistic view, individuals construct an economical linguistic representation of the premises. "Worse" describes the relative badness of the two entities, *and* it provides the absolute information that they are both bad, and so it requires more information to be stored than the unmarked adjective (Clark, 1969a). In support of this view, Clark found that problem 1 in Table 3:

A is better than B
B is better than C

and problem 3:

B is better than C
A is better than B

which are based on unmarked adjectives, were easier (5.75 and 5.25 sec, respectively) than problems based on marked adjectives, e.g. problem 2:

C is worse than B
B is worse than A

and problem 4:

B is worse than A
C is worse than B

(6.40 and 5.47 sec, respectively). In fact, individuals take longer to reach a solution depending on which adjective is marked, the one in the first premise (556 msec), the second premise (402 msec), or the question (358 msec: Sternberg, 1980).

In addition, the linguistic view explains the difference in difficulty between problems that contain the same sorts of adjectives, e.g. problems

1 and 3 above both contain unmarked adjectives. For example, the premise:

A is better than B

is represented in the linguistic representation:

A is more good, B is less good

Individuals *compress* the information in working memory as they process it (Clark, 1969a), and the representation is reduced to information about the most extreme of the two terms.

A is more good.

Given problem 1:

A is better than B
B is better than C

individuals construct the partially compressed representation:

A is more good
B is more good, C is less good.

They encounter difficulties in making an inference because the compression of the first premise has caused them to eliminate the repeated term, B. There is no way to compare the entities and so the repeated term must be recovered to make the inference. Compression does not lead to this difficulty for other descriptions. For example, problem 3:

B is better than C
A is better than B

leads to the representation:

B is more good
A is more good, B is less good

The repeated term is retained in the compressed form and so the inference can be made without backtracking. Since B is both more good and less good in the representation, it is discarded in favour of A. The theory explains the differential difficulty of premises based on similar relations but with the terms in different arrangements, by invoking a principle of economy in the linguistic representation.

Do individuals represent the two sorts of relational terms in a uniform spatial array, and have a preference for constructing arrays in a top-down direction, or do they represent them in two different linguistic formats, and compress the information? Both accounts seem to be supported by the results we have examined. They make the same predictions for affirmative problems, but their predictions appear to differ for the equivalent problems based on negative premises, that is, *negative-equative* problems, such as:

A is not as bad as B
B is not as bad as C.

According to Clark (1969a), the premises are equivalent to problem 1 in Table 3:

A is better than B
B is better than C.

But, their underlying linguistic representation is very different. The negative-equative problem is represented as:

B is more bad
C is more bad, B is less bad

The repeated term is preserved in the compressed representation and so the negative-equative problem should be easy. As we saw earlier, the repeated term is lost in the compressed representation for the affirmative problem, and so it is difficult to make an inference. In short, if individuals compress information in a linguistic representation, then the pattern of results for the negative-equative problems should be the *reverse* of the pattern for the affirmative problems. Moreover, Clark (1969a) argued that the spatial array view makes the *opposite* prediction. The negative-equative problem:

A is not as bad as B
B is not as bad as C

requires a spatial array to be constructed from the top-down, just as the equivalent affirmative problem does. Hence, if individuals have a directional preference for constructing arrays, then the pattern of results for the negative-equative problems should be the same as the pattern for the comparative problems. Clark found that the data support the linguistic view rather than the array view, as shown by the latencies for the negative-equative problems, reported in parentheses in Table 6.3. For example, the negative-equative problems 1′ and 3′ are more difficult (6.34 and 6.85 sec, respectively) than the negative-equative problems 2′ and 4′ (6.08 and 6.35 sec, respectively) (see also Huttenlocher, Higgins, Milligan & Kauffman, 1970; Jones, 1970; Keeney & Gaudino, 1973).

Do these data rule out the spatial array view? Their interpretation is based on the assumption that a negative-equative premise, such as:

A is not as bad as B

is psychologically equivalent to the affirmative premise:

A is better than B

and so the negative-equative premise requires a spatial array to be constructed in the preferred top-down manner. But, marked adjectives seem implicitly negative, and the negative-equative "not as bad as" seems to be a double negative (see Higgins, 1976; Huttenlocher & Higgins, 1971; cf. Clark, 1971; Jones, 1970). In fact, the negative premise above may be mentally equivalent to:

B is worse than A.

Hence, the negative-equative problem that Clark proposed was equivalent to problem 1:

A is not as bad as B
B is a not as bad as C

may in fact be equivalent to problem 4 instead:

B is worse than A
C is worse than B.

This problem requires an array to be constructed from the non-preferred bottom-up direction (Johnson-Laird, 1972), and so it should be a difficult problem. On this account, the spatial array predictions are the *same* as the linguistic predictions, not only for affirmative but also for negative-equative premises (see also Huttenlocher et al., 1970; Sternberg, 1980). The data can be taken to support the array view, as well as the linguistic view. The two theories cannot be distinguished empirically by examining the relative patterns of inferences for the negative-equative and affirmative problems.

However, a crucial difference between the two accounts remains, and it is whether marked and unmarked adjectives are represented in a uniform format or not. The spatial array view proposes that a marked adjective, such as:

A is worse than B

requires individuals to construct an array from the bottom-up:

.
B
A

whereas an unmarked adjective, such as:

B is better than A

requires individuals to construct an array from the top-down:

B
A
.

A bottom-up array is more difficult to construct than a top-down array. But, once the array is constructed, the difference between the marked and unmarked adjectives used to construct the array evaporates: they have been represented in exactly the same format. If people discard the linguistic information, and retain only their spatial array, they should be unaffected by whether marked or unmarked adjectives were used to construct the array. In contrast, the linguistic view proposes that marked and unmarked adjectives are represented in different formats. The premise:

A is worse than B

is represented on the linguistic dimension of badness:

A is more bad, B is less bad

whereas the premise:

B is better than A

is represented on the linguistic dimension of goodness:

B is more good, A is less good

The difference in representation may lead to a loss or retention of the middle term, which can help or hinder the process of making an inference. But, in addition, the underlying representation of the two premises preserves the differences in their surface expression. If people retain this linguistic information, then they should be affected by the markedness of the adjectives even after they have constructed the representation.

Are marked and unmarked adjectives represented in a uniform format, as the spatial array view suggests, or in different formats, as the linguistic view suggests? Potts and Scholz (1975) carried out an experiment which suggests that individuals represent marked and unmarked adjectives in a uniform way. They compared the latencies of subjects presented with the premises and question simultaneously, to the latencies of subjects who were given the premises to peruse first, and then timed for their solution to the question. The second group of individuals were given time to represent the premises: if they represented them in a spatial array, then they would represent the marked and unmarked adjectives in a uniform format, and they would not be affected in their subsequent inference by whether the adjectives in the premises were marked or unmarked. On the other hand, if they represented the premises in a linguistic representation, then they *would* preserve the marked and unmarked adjectives in different formats, and they would be affected in their subsequent inference by whether the adjectives in the premises were marked or unmarked.

Potts and Scholz found that the time to answer a question was *not* affected by whether the relations in the premises were marked or unmarked. They gave individuals problems such as:

Tom is worse than Dick
Dick is worse than Sam
Who is best?

The time to answer the unmarked question, "Who is best?", was faster than the time to answer the marked question, "Who is worst?", but the effect did not interact with the markedness of the adjectives used in the premises. In other words, subjects were not affected by whether the premises contained marked or unmarked adjectives once they had had time to represent the premises. This result suggests that their representation did not preserve the difference between the adjectives in different formats, as the linguistic view suggests, but instead they discarded the linguistic information once they had represented the adjectives in a uniform format, as the spatial array view suggests.

End-anchoring or Question Congruence?

So far, we have concentrated on the data from the first four problems in Table 6.3: these problems use homogeneous adjectives, for example, both premises contain "better than" or both premises contain "worse than". The next four problems (5–8) contain heterogeneous adjectives, for example, one premise contains "better than" and the other premise contains "worse than". This mixture of different adjectives is informative, as we will now see. One of the easiest problems, as Table 6.3 shows, is problem 5:

A is better than B
C is worse than B

whereas one of the hardest problems is problem 7:

B is worse than A
B is better than C

The two theories provide alternative explanations for this difference in difficulty.

The spatial array view proposes that individuals find it easier to process information from the reference point of an extreme term. This *end-anchor* effect ensures that problems based on premises that proceed from an extreme term (A or C) to the repeated term are easier than problems that proceed in the other direction. Consider, for example, problem 5:

A is better than B
C is worse than B

The first premise requires an array to be constructed from the top-down, working from the term at the top extreme, A, to the term in the middle, B:

A
B
.

The second premise requires an array to be constructed from the bottom-up, working from the term at the bottom extreme, C, to the term in the middle, B:

.
B
C

Other problems are based on premises that proceed in the opposite direction. Consider, for example, problem 7:

B is worse than A
B is better than C

The first premise requires an array to be constructed from the bottom-up, working from the term that will turn out to be in the middle, to the term at the top extreme, A:

.
A
B

The second premise requires an array to be constructed from the top-down, working from the term in the middle, B, to the term at the bottom extreme, C:

B
C
.

In support of their proposal of an end-anchor effect, De Soto et al. found that problems 5 and 6, based on premises that proceed from an extreme term to the repeated term, are easier than problems 7 and 8, based on premises that proceed in the other direction (see also Potts, 1972). In fact, problems that contain a second premise that proceeds from an extreme term to the repeated term (e.g. problems 3, 4, 5 and 6) are easier than the others (Huttenlocher, 1968; see also Smith & Foos, 1975; but cf. Mynatt & Smith, 1977). Why would individuals have a preference for processing information from an extreme end of an array to the middle of the array? Some physical placement tasks indicate that placing a moveable object in relation to a fixed one is easier when the instruction proceeds from the moveable object to the fixed one (see Huttenlocher, 1968; Huttenlocher & Higgins, 1971; 1972; and cf. Clark, 1971; 1972). It may be easier to process information from the reference point of an extreme term than the reference point of the middle term, because the middle term is seen as a "fixed" object, whereas the extreme terms are "moveable".

The alternative linguistic view attributes the difference in difficulty of problems such as 5 and 7 to the *congruence* of the questions asked to elicit the inferences based on these premises (Clark, 1969a). Consider the premises of problem 5:

A is better than B
C is worse than B

They can be represented (fully) as:

A is more good, B is less good
C is more bad, B is less bad

The question:

Who is best?

is represented as:

Who is most good?

A search for the entity that is most good will succeed in locating the correct entity in the above representation: "A". "A" occurs once in the representation, indicated by a single token, showing that "A" is more good. Likewise, the question:

Who is worst?

is represented as:

Who is most bad?

and a search for the entity that is most bad will succeed in locating the correct entity: "C". "C" also occurs once in the representation, indicated by a single token, showing that "C" is more bad. Problem 5 is easy because its representation contains information required to answer both sorts of question. In contrast, problem 7 is hard because its representation does not contain the information required to answer either question accurately. The premises of problem 7:

B is worse than A
B is better than C

result in the representation:

B is more bad, A is less bad
B is more good, C is less good

The question:

Who is best?

requires a search for the entity that is most good. One token of "B" occurs in the representation showing "B" as more good, but a second token also occurs showing "B" as more bad. The search for the "most good" entity will not succeed in locating the correct entity in the above representation: "A", which is represented, non-congruently, as "less bad". Likewise, the question:

Who is worst?

requires a search for the most bad entity. Once again, "B" may be considered a candidate since one token of it is represented as more bad, but the second token representing it as more good eliminates it from consideration. Once again, the search for the most bad entity will not succeed in locating the correct entity in the above representation, "C", which is represented, non-congruently, as "less good".

Do individuals construct spatial arrays and have an end-anchoring preference, or do they construct linguistic representations that may or may not contain information congruent with the questions they are asked? Once again, the results from the negative-equative problems initially seemed to support the linguistic view and go against the spatial array view. According to the linguistic view, the pattern of the difficulty of the affirmative and the negative-equative problems should reverse; according to the spatial array view, the pattern should be the same, for the same sorts of reasons we described in the previous section. The data support the linguistic view: the pattern of latencies for the negative-equative problems is the reverse of the pattern for the affirmatives (see Table 6.3; see also Clark, 1969a; Keeney & Gaudino, 1973; Potts & Scholz, 1975; Sternberg, 1980), at least for problems based on the relation "better–worse" (cf. Huttenlocher et al., 1970). Once again, the proper interpretation of the negative-equative premises may account for the reversal (Johnson-Laird, 1972). The negative premises considered equivalent to problem 5 in Table 6.3 are:

A is not as bad than B
C is not as good than B

and since they are end-anchored they should be easy. But, if they are transposed they become:

B is worse than A
B is better than C

Then, because these premises are not end-anchored, they should be difficult. As a result, the negative-equative problems cannot be used to distinguish between the two accounts.

Do individuals have an end-anchoring tendency, or are they susceptible to the congruence of the question? Table 6.4 shows the latencies of individuals to respond to the two sorts of questions for different problems. The solution latencies show that non-congruent questions take longer to answer, for example, individuals can answer the question:

Who is best?

for the premises:

A is better than B
B is better than C

faster than they can answer the question:

Who is worst?

and the phenomenon occurs even with two-term series problems (Clark, 1969a). Individuals make inferences faster when the question is suited to the problems, whether the problems are based on affirmative or negative premises, e.g. the question "Who is best?" is suited to problems based on the adjectives "better" and "not as good as". This question is not suited to problems based on "worse" or "not as bad as". The latencies in bold type in Table 6.4 are those latencies that are expected to be faster in each pair. In Clark's data, 7 of the 8 comparisons follow the predicted direction. In Sternberg's data, 5 of the 8 comparisons follow the predicted direction, when the question was asked after the premises were presented, and 6 of the 8 comparisons when the question was asked before the premises were presented. The typical errors that people made to indeterminate problems also corresponded to the answer that was congruent with the question (Clark, 1969b).

However, Potts and Scholz (1975) showed that the congruence of the question only affects the speed of the inference when subjects were presented with both the premises and the question at the same time. They gave subjects the separated-stages paradigm that we described earlier: subjects read the premises first, and then they were subsequently presented with the question, after they had had time to mentally represent the premises. In this situation, their latencies to respond were exactly the

TABLE 6.4
The Solution Latencies (sec) to Problems for which the Question is Congruent (Bold Type) or Non-congruent with the Relation in the Premises

	Clark (1969a)		Sternberg (1980) Question Last (Exp. 1)		Sternberg (1980) Question First (Exp. 2)	
Question	*best?*	*worst?*	*best?*	*worst?*	*best?*	*worst?*
A is better than B B is better than C	**5.42**	6.10	**6.40**	6.29	**5.98**	6.30
B is better than C A is better than B	**4.98**	5.52	**5.84**	6.59	**6.16**	6.99
C is not as good as B B is not as good as A	**5.58**	6.33	**6.24**	6.72	**6.52**	7.81
B is not as good as A C is not as good as B	**6.11**	6.60	**7.66**	7.94	**7.68**	7.24
C is worse than B B is worse than A	6.27	**6.53**	6.39	**7.34**	7.17	**7.14**
B is worse than A C is worse than B	5.93	**5.04**	6.93	**6.07**	7.65	**7.02**
A is not as bad as B B is not as bad as C	6.77	**5.95**	8.09	**7.52**	7.97	**6.88**
B is not as bad as C A is not as bad as B	7.16	**6.56**	9.28	**9.49**	8.94	**9.51**

same for problems with congruent questions and non-congruent questions (see also Ormrod, 1979). Once again, the data suggest that individuals represent the premises in a uniform format, such as an array, that dispenses with linguistic information about goodness or badness. As a result, the questions are all equally congruent with an underlying representation that does not retain the superficial language of the premises.

Finally, although checking the congruity of the question is not required for a spatial array representation, the most recently understood adjective may be more accessible (Huttenlocher & Higgins, 1971; cf. Clark, 1971; 1972). When an array is constructed, the last insertion may be at the top or bottom of the array. For example, consider the premises:

A is taller than B
B is taller than C

The construction of an array results in the representation:

A
B
C

and the last inserted item is C, at the bottom of the array. If the answer to the question lies in the same part of the array, then it can be produced more readily (Sternberg, 1980; see also Hunter, 1957). Johnson-Laird (1972) proposed that individuals read the question first, and use this to guide their answer. They may check the congruity of the question in a linguistic representation of the premises only if they have not formed a sufficiently "sharp" spatial representation (Sternberg, 1980). If they have formed a sharp spatial representation, because they were pre-cued by the presentation of the premises or the question separately, then they do not need to check the question congruence.

In summary, the two early theories of the mental representations and cognitive processes required to make relational inferences in three-term series problems are that they depend on procedures that construct and manipulate spatial arrays or models, and that they depend on procedures that construct and manipulate linguistic representations. The two theories predict the differences in difficulty between a range of affirmative and negative determinate descriptions. The spatial array account proposes that individuals construct a uniform array for marked and unmarked adjectives. The differences in difficulty arise because individuals have a preference for constructing arrays from the top-down rather than from the bottom-up. They also have an end-anchoring preference, that is, a preference for constructing arrays from an extreme term to a middle term, rather than in the opposite direction. The linguistic representation account proposes that individuals represent marked and unmarked adjectives in different formats. The differences in difficulty arise because they compress the information in their linguistic representation, sometimes eliminating information that must be recovered subsequently to make an inference. They also may be asked a question which is congruent or non-congruent with the information they have included in their representation. Unfortunately, the empirical predictions of the two theories mirror each other for many problems: the same predictions about the difficulty of problems are made by the spatial array theory's top-down preference hypothesis as by the linguistic theory's compression hypothesis. Likewise, the same predictions about the difficulty of problems are made by the spatial array theory's end-anchoring hypothesis as by the linguistic theory's question-congruence hypothesis. However, the underlying difference in the two theories rests on the representation of marked and unmarked adjectives: the spatial array theory proposes that they are represented in a uniform format, whereas the linguistic theory proposes that they are represented in different formats. The data corroborate the spatial array theory and go against the linguistic theory: they suggest that individuals represent relational terms in a uniform format.

FOUR CLUES TO THE NATURE OF REPRESENTATIONS

A crucial difference between the spatial and linguistic accounts is whether an integrated representation of the two premises is constructed (De Soto et al., 1965; Huttenlocher, 1968), or whether the representations of the two premises are held separately in memory (Clark, 1969a). Recent evidence, to which we now turn, indicates that the representations of the two premises are integrated. Factors that interfere with their integration, such as discontinuity in the order of the terms, or indeterminacies in the description, dramatically affect reasoning performance. The integration of the representations of the premises also leads to the curious inferential-distance effect. In this section, we discuss each of these clues to the sorts of representations that individuals construct of relational terms.

The Integration of the Premises

One of the earliest theorists of relational reasoning emphasised the importance of integrating the premise information. Hunter (1957) suggested that individuals mentally transform problems with non-adjacent repeated terms. For example, the premises of problem 5 in Table 6.3:

A is taller than B
C is shorter than B

must be transformed by converting the order of the terms in the second premise, and changing the adjective accordingly:

A is taller than B
B is taller than C.

And so Hunter proposed that this problem should be harder than problem 1, which does not require this operation. Problem 4:

B is shorter than A
C is shorter than B

requires the reordering of the premises to make the repeated terms adjacent:

C is shorter than B
B is shorter than A

and so it should be harder than either problem 5 or 1. Even more difficult than these three problems is problem 7:

B is shorter than A
B is shorter than C

which requires reversing to convert the first premise. Unfortunately, there is little evidence to support the idea that individuals make these specific transformations: the theory predicts that problems 1 and 2 should be easier than the rest, and, in fact, problem 2 is one of the hardest problems. Moreover, it predicts that problems 3–8 should be homogeneously intermediate, whereas problems 7 and 8 are harder than the others (De Soto et al., 1965).

Nonetheless, there is evidence that the order of the terms affects the conclusions individuals produce. For example, when subjects are given problems of the form:

A is related to B
B is related to C

they tend to generate spontaneously more conclusions of the form:

A is related to C

than conclusions of the form:

C related to A.

However, when they are given premises of the form:

B is related to A
C is related to B

they tend to generate spontaneously more conclusions of the form:

C is related to A

than conclusions of the form:

A is related to C

(Johnson-Laird & Bara, 1984). This "figural effect" may arise because of the need to carry out mental operations to bring the middle terms (B) into contiguity (Hunter, 1957; Johnson-Laird & Bara, 1984), as research on this effect has shown for categorical syllogisms (see Chapter 7). The integration of the premises in working memory may be easier for certain orders (see also Trabasso, Riley & Wilson, 1975). If individuals construct an array, then the easiest premises are those which result in reaching the repeated term or pivot, which is then immediately available for use in adding the information from the next premise (Sternberg, 1980).

Premise integration has been examined directly by assessing the length of time it takes individuals to respond to a probe (a tone to which they must say "beep") when they hear it during the presentation of the first premise, the second premise, or the question (Maybery, Bain & Halford, 1986). Subjects were given a three-term series problem:

A is above B
C is below B

and were asked to judge the truth of an array based on it, e.g.

C
A

To carry out the task, they had to integrate the information in the two premises. They were given two other sorts of problems that did not require the integration of the premises. They were given premises that could not be integrated, e.g.

A is above B
C is below D

and they judged the truth of an array based on them:

C
D

They were also given premises, such as the ones we encountered earlier:

A is above B
C is below B

but they were given arrays to judge that did not require them to integrate them, e.g.

A   B
B   C

The length of time they took to respond to the probe when they were perusing the second premise was measured. The first task, the genuine three-term series problem, is the only one which requires the premises to be integrated at this point. They took longer to respond to the probe for the first task than for the other two tasks. This result suggests that people do attempt to integrate the information in the two premises of a three-term series problem, rather than holding the two pieces of information separately in working memory.

Individuals find three-term series problems, such as:

A is better than B
B is better than C
Who is best?

harder than two-term series problems:

A is better than B
Who is best?

(Clark, 1969a; Sternberg, 1980). But, five-term series problems, such as:

The knife is on the right of the vase [A is on the right of B]
The glass is on the left of the vase [C is on the left of B]
The cup is in front of the glass [D is in front of C]
The book is in front of the vase [E is in front of B]
What is the relation between the cup and the book?

are just as easy as three-term series problems:

The knife is on the right of the vase [A is on the right of B]
The glass is on the left of the vase [C is on the left of B]
What is the relation between the knife and glass?

(Byrne & Johnson-Laird, 1989). This curious result may be explained by the demands of premise integration. Individuals find three-term series problems harder than two-term series problems, because only the three-term series problems require premise integration. They do not find five-term series problems any more difficult than three-term series problems, because both require premise integration.

These experimental phenomena—the "figural effect", the length of time it takes to respond to a probe when processing the second premise of a three-term series problems, and the differential difficulty of two-, three- and five-term series problems—all indicate that individuals combine the information in the premises of a series rather than hold the pieces of information separately in working memory.

The Continuity of the Information

Further evidence that individuals construct integrated representations is found in the difficulty of problems that are presented in a discontinuous order. Potts (1972, p. 730) gave individuals problems such as the following:

> In a small forest just south of nowhere, a deer, a bear, a wolf, and a hawk were battling for dominion over the land. It boiled down to a battle of wits, so intelligence was the crucial factor. The bear was smarter than the hawk, the hawk was smarter than the wolf, and the wolf was smarter than the deer. On a small pond in the middle of the same forest, another contest for dominion was being waged. The contenders were a frog, a clam, a duck, and a fish. In this case, however, the battle was to be decided by an election, and friendliness was the crucial factor. The fish was friendlier than the frog, the frog was friendlier than the clam, and the clam was friendlier than the duck. In the end, each of the battles was decided in its own way and tranquillity returned to the area.

Subjects in one group received information about the two linear orders in a continuous order, as in the example above:

The bear was smarter than the hawk	[A is smarter than B]
The hawk was smarter than the wolf	[B is smarter than C]
The wolf was smarter than the deer	[C is smarter than D]

They were subsequently presented with a premise, e.g.

A is smarter than B

or an inferable sentence, e.g.

A is smarter than C

They were also presented with the converse of a premise, e.g.

B is smarter than A

or the converse of an inferable sentence, e.g.

C is smarter than A.

Their task was to judge the sentences as "true", i.e. previously presented or inferable, or "false", i.e. not presented or inferable. Subjects in the second group were given the initial set of premises in a discontinuous order, e.g.

C is smarter than D
A is smarter than B
B is smarter than C

The subjects made more correct inferences to the continuous premises (85% correct) than to the discontinuous ones (75%). If individuals construct an array, then the discontinuous order forces them to construct the array corresponding to the first premise:

C
D

and the array corresponding to the second premise:

A
B

and to keep these arrays separately in mind until they construct an array for the third premise:

B
C

It is only at this point that they can integrate the premises into an overall array:

A
B
C
D

Potts' subjects took notes—usually writing places for each entity from top to bottom or left to right. The group who received the discontinuous premises made more notes (94% notes on at least one relation) than the continuous group (79% notes). However, the group who received the continuous premises made notes that were more often accurate (81% at least one note correct) than the discontinuous group (66%).

Subjects recall the order of sentences more accurately from descriptions presented in a continuous order (60% correct) than descriptions presented in a discontinuous order (39%) even when they have written down the terms (Smith & Foos, 1975). Some discontinuous orders are more difficult than others. Subjects made inferences faster from a discontinuous order from the top-down, e.g.

The doctor is taller than the farmer	[A is taller than B]
The soldier is taller than the teacher	[C is taller than D]
The farmer is taller than the soldier	[B is taller than C]

(13.07 sec) than a discontinuous order from the bottom-up, e.g.

C is taller than D
A is taller than B
B is taller than C

(17.63 sec: Mynatt & Smith, 1977). Nonetheless, they made inferences faster on problems presented in a continuous order, both top-down (10.79 sec) and bottom-up (11.88 sec):

Top-down	*Bottom-up*
A is taller than B	C is taller than D
B is taller than C	B is taller than C
C is taller than D	A is taller than B

than on problems presented in a semi-continuous order, both top-down (11.40 sec) and bottom-up (12.94 sec):

Top-down	*Bottom-up*
B is taller than C	B is taller than C
C is taller than D	A is taller than B
A is taller than B	C is taller than D

The discontinuous orders were harder than either the continuous or semi-continuous ones, and bottom-up orders were harder than top-down ones for each of the three sorts of descriptions. Individuals may integrate information from incoming premises into an existing array, rather than construct separate arrays for each premise prior to seriation (cf. Sternberg, 1980).

Finally, let us look more closely at semi-continuous orders, such as:

The knife is in front of the pot	[B is in front of C]
The pot is on the left of the glass	[C is on the left of D]
The dish is on the left of the knife	[A is on the left of B]

They introduce a discontinuity only in the second and third premises, which do not share any terms in common (Ehrlich & Johnson-Laird, 1982). But, the discontinuity does not interfere with the construction of an integrated array. Individuals can represent the first premise:

C
B

and add the information from the second premise to this array:

C D
B

and, finally, they can add the information from the third premise to the array:

   C D
A B

Individuals drew as many correct diagrams from a semi-continuous description (61% correct) as from a continuous one (57% correct), and both were easier than a discontinuous description (33% correct: Ehrlich & Johnson-Laird, 1982). This results suggests that it is not simply whether the order of terms is continuous or not that affects the ease with which individuals understand and reason about a relational series, but whether the order of terms interferes with the construction of an array. Moreover, Ehrlich and Johnson-Laird found that the length of time to read a continuous description (6.1 sec) and a semi-continuous description (6.3 sec) was shorter than the length of time to read a discontinuous one (7.1 sec). Readers tended to spend a longer time (9.4 sec) reading the crucial third premise of the discontinuous description than the third premise of the other two sorts of descriptions (5.4 and 6.5 sec, respectively). It is this third premise in a discontinuous order that provides the integrating information.

Consider the premises:

C is on the left of D
A is on the left of B
B is in front of C

The first premise requires the construction of an array:

C D

The second premise requires the construction of a separate array, which cannot be joined to the first array because they do not share any terms in common:

A B

It is only with the information in the third premise, that the two arrays can be integrated together:

      C D
A B

The considerably long length of time that individuals spend processing the information in the third premise in a discontinuous description supports the idea that they are using the third premise to integrate the information in the premises into a unified representation. Sentences which cannot be immediately integrated may be held temporarily in propositional form (Ehrlich & Johnson-Laird, 1982; see also Foos, Smith, Sabol & Mynatt, 1976; Ohlsson, 1984).

Individuals find it easier to understand and reason from descriptions that present the information in a continuous or semi-continuous order rather than in a discontinuous order. The advantage of a continuous or semi-continuous presentation over a discontinuous one is seen in that subjects make more correct inferences, they make their inferences faster, they recall the order of the premises better, they draw more correct diagrams and they are faster to read the descriptions. The differences in difficulty between continuous, semi-continuous and discontinuous descriptions indicate that individuals attempt to combine the information in a series into an integrated representation. In fact, the pattern of results is difficult to explain if individuals are *not* constructing integrated representations.

The Determinacy of the Description

We have seen that relational inferences are difficult when people cannot construct an integrated representation. They are also difficult when individuals can construct more than one representation. In several of the previous chapters, we have seen that problems that require multiple models are more difficult than problems that require a single model, a phenomenon which corroborates the predictions of the model theory (e.g. Johnson-Laird, 1983; Johnson-Laird & Byrne, 1991). We will see a similar phenomenon in this section, because relational inferences that require more than one representation are more difficult than those that require a single representation.

Indeterminate premises give rise to alternative interpretations of the array they describe. De Soto et al. (1965, p. 520) observed: "the tendency to treat a given set of elements as having only one ordering, with strong aversion to multiple orderings of the set, has been noted as a phenomenon and problem in diverse realms of thought".

Consider the premises:

A is bigger than B
C is bigger than B

They contain an indeterminacy in the relative location of some of the entities. They are consistent with three alternative layouts, as we saw earlier:

A	C	A C
C	A	B
B	B	

They do not support a valid inference interrelating the un-repeated terms: A may be bigger than C, or C may be bigger than A. They do not support a determinate answer to the question "Who is biggest?", since either A or C may be biggest. However, they do support a valid answer to the question "Who is smallest?"—in every representation B is smallest.

Individuals do not make as many correct inferences from indeterminate as from determinate problems, even for the answerable (determinate) questions (Clark, 1969b; see also Hayes-Roth & Hayes-Roth, 1975; Moeser & Tarrant 1977). For example, the following determinate three-term series problem:

The knife is on the right of the vase [A is on the right of B]
The glass is on the left of the vase [C is on the left of B]

supports the valid answer:

The knife is on the right of the glass [A is on the right of B]

The indeterminate three-term series problem:

The vase is on the right of the knife [B is on the right of A]
The glass is on the left of the vase [C is on the left of B]

does not support any valid answer interrelating the knife and the glass. Individuals made more correct inferences from the determinate problems with a valid answer (69% correct) than from the indeterminate problems with no valid answer (19%: Byrne & Johnson-Laird, 1989).

Interestingly, individuals make correct inferences faster from indeterminate, invalid three-term series problems (7.97 sec), than from determinate, valid ones (8.89 sec: Sternberg, 1981). Inferences from indeterminate problems may be faster because people superimpose the indeterminate terms in the final array. They may construct the two-term array for the first premise:

A
B

and the array for the second premise:

C
B

and they may superimpose the indeterminate terms in a final single array, as a sort of short-hand notation:

A C
  B

rather than maintain separate alternative arrays:

A	C
C	A
B	B

(Sternberg, 1981). *Determinate* problems require a determinate location to be established for each of the three items, and individuals may develop short-cut heuristics to identify indeterminate problems more readily than determinate ones (cf. Maybery, 1990; Sternberg, 1990).

Individuals remember the *gist* of determinate descriptions better than indeterminate ones. But, they remember the verbatim description of indeterminate descriptions better than determinate ones (Mani & Johnson-Laird, 1982). Subjects were given determinate and indeterminate descriptions, and an example of an indeterminate description is as follows:

The bookshelf is to the right of the chair	[A is to the right of B]
The chair is in front of the table	[B is in front of C]
The bed is behind the chair	[D is behind B]

They judged the consistency of diagrams with the descriptions, for example, the description is consistent with at least two alternative diagrams:

D		C	
C		D	
B	A	B	A

They were then given an unexpected memory test, in which they had to rank-order the original verbatim description, as well as a paraphrase (with letters substituted here for clarity), such as:

A is to the right of B
C is behind B
B is in front of D

and two confuser descriptions, such as:

A is to the right of C
B is in front of C
C is behind D.

They rank-ordered the original description and the paraphrase higher than the two confuser descriptions more often for the determinate descriptions (70%) than the indeterminate ones (39%). But, they ranked the verbatim description above a paraphrase more often for indeterminate descriptions (88%) than for determinate descriptions (68%). Individuals may construct a model of the determinate descriptions, and keep the indeterminate ones in propositional form (Mani & Johnson-Laird, 1982).

The indeterminacy of the premises and the validity of the inference is confounded for three-term series problems: indeterminate premises never give rise to a valid conclusion interrelating the end terms. The two factors are not confounded for the following sort of five-term series problems:

The vase is on the right of the knife	[B is on the right of A]
The glass is on the left of the vase	[C is on the left of B]
The cup is in front of the glass	[D is in front of C]
The book is in front of the vase	[E is in front of B]

The premises are consistent with at least two alternative arrays:

	1			2	
C	A	B	A	C	B
D		E		D	E

Despite the indeterminacy, the premises support a valid conclusion interrelating D and E. In both of the arrays, D is on the left of E. For five-term series problems, it is possible to examine the effects of the determinacy and indeterminacy of the description, independently of the effects of the validity and invalidity of the inference. Byrne and Johnson-Laird (1989) gave subjects three sorts of five-term series problems: one sort was based on determinate descriptions and supported a valid conclusion; a second sort was based on indeterminate descriptions but nonetheless supported a valid conclusion; and the third sort was based on indeterminate descriptions that did not support a valid conclusion. Table 6.5 illustrates some of these five-term series problems. They made more correct inferences from the problems that were determinate and valid (70%), such as problem 1 in Table 6.5, than from those that were indeterminate and invalid, such as problem 4 (15%). Most interestingly,

TABLE 6.5
Examples of Four Sorts of Five-term Series Problems[a]

1. *Determinate valid problem*	*Models:*		
A is right of B	1. C	B	A
C is left of B	D	E	
D is front of C			
E is front of B			
What is the relation between D and E?			
2. *Indeterminate valid problem*	*Models*		
B is right of A	1. C	A	B
C is left of B	D		E
D is front of C			
E is front of B	2. A	C	B
What is the relation between D and E?		D	E
3. *Determinate valid problem*	*Models*		
A is right of B	1. C	B	A
C is left of B	D		E
D is front of C			
E is front of A			
What is the relation between D and E?			
4. *Indeterminate invalid problem*	*Models*		
B is right of A	1. C	A	B
C is left of B	D	E	
D is front of C			
E is front of A	2. A	C	B
What is the relation between D and E?	E	D	

[a]From Byrne and Johnson-Laird (1989).

the problems that were indeterminate but valid were intermediate in difficulty (e.g. problem 2, 46%; Byrne & Johnson-Laird, 1989). Their errors to the indeterminate problems corresponded to constructing just a single array for the description (Byrne & Johnson-Laird, 1989).

The effects of the determinacy of the description suggest that individuals construct an integrated representation of the premises. When the nature of the premises requires them to construct more than one integrated representation, this requirement can lead them into difficulty. The data go against the idea that individuals hold the separate pieces of information in memory separately. But, could a linguistic theory be constructed to account for the data? Hagert (1984) proposed that premises are represented linguistically and integrated by inference rules. Consider the premises:

B is on the left of A
C is in front of B

The first premise is represented linguistically as:

Left (B, A)

and the second premise is represented as:

Front (C, B)

The information from the two premises is integrated according to rules such as:

Left (x, y) *and* Front (z, x) *implies* Left (Front (z, x) y)

In other words, the representation of the two premises can be coded into the rule:

Left (B, A) *and* Front (C, B) *implies* Left (Front (C, B) A)

and the conclusion is then what is implied by the premises (referred to on the right-hand side of the rule):

Left (Front (C, B) A)

Further rules can be used to make further inferences, and at each step the information is integrated into a linguistic representation.

Do individuals construct integrated representations that are based on procedures that construct alternative models, or based on inference rules that construct linguistic representations? Byrne and Johnson-Laird (1989) pitted the predictions of the two theories against one another in two ways. First, the model theory predicts that problem 1 in Table 6.5 should be easier than problem 2 because problem 2 requires multiple models to be kept in mind. Hagert's linguistic rule theory predicts that there should be *no* difference between the problems. The crucial point is that the first premise in both problems is entirely irrelevant in the mental derivation using inference rules—the inference is made on the basis of the remaining three premises—and these three premises are *identical* for the two problems. The same steps must be followed for both problems. Both of them require individuals to reach an inference about the relation between D and E. As interested readers can verify from Table 6.5, the inference depends on noticing that D is linked to C, and E is linked to B, and that C and B are themselves linked. The relation between D and E will be the same one as the relation between C and B. Using Hagert's rules, individuals first interrelate D and B (D is in front and to the left of B), and then E and C (E is in front and to the right of C), and with this information they can interrelate D and E (D is to the left of E). Because the three crucial premises are identical, the same steps are followed for both problems, and so the linguistic theory predicts no difference between them. However, the data corroborate the model theory: problem 1 is reliably easier (61%) than problem 2 (50%: Byrne & Johnson-Laird, 1989).

Second, Byrne and Johnson-Laird showed that the two theories make the opposite predictions about the relative difficulty of some problems. Consider problem 3 in Table 6.5: it is a valid determinate problem which supports a single model. The model theory predicts it should be easier than problem 2 which requires multiple models. According to the linguistic theory, it should be *more difficult* than problem 2. In this problem, the first premise is relevant: the inference requires individuals to interrelate D and E, which are related to C and A, respectively. But there is no premise directly interrelating C and A. The first two premises:

A is right of B
C is left of B

must be used to derive the conclusion:

C is left of A

Individuals can then interrelate D and A, then interrelate E and C and, with this information, they can then interrelate D and E. Because the first premise is relevant, and must be used to make an inference, the final conclusion takes more steps than problem 2 and so the rule theory predicts it should be more difficult. Once again, the data corroborate the model theory: problem 3 is reliably easier (70% correct) than problem 2 (46%: Byrne & Johnson-Laird, 1989).

The determinacy of a description affects the number of models that individuals must keep in mind. When individuals must keep multiple representations in mind, they make fewer correct inferences, but they make them faster, perhaps because of short-cut heuristics. They remember the gist of determinate descriptions better than indeterminate ones, and they remember the verbatim description of indeterminate descriptions better than determinate ones. The difficulty of indeterminate problems does not arise simply because they support no valid conclusions: for five-term series problems, they make more correct inferences to determinate valid problems than to indeterminate but valid problems, and they find indeterminate invalid problems hardest of all. The results suggest that individuals construct more than one representation when they detect an indeterminacy in the description of a series. The data suggest that these integrated representations are models based on the structure of the situation that the premises describe, rather than linguistic representations based on the language used to describe the situation.

Presented and Inferred Information: The Distance Effect

One of the most curious findings on relational inferences is that individuals are faster and more accurate in their judgements of the truth of *inferred* information than of *presented* information. Consider a fragment of the problem we encountered earlier, presented to subjects by Potts (1972):

> In a small forest just south of nowhere, a deer, a bear, a wolf, and a hawk were battling for dominion over the land. It boiled down to a battle of wits, so intelligence was the crucial factor. The bear was smarter than the hawk, the hawk was smarter than the wolf, and the wolf was smarter than the deer.

Potts' (1972) subjects read an ordering, such as:

A is smarter than B
B is smarter than C
C is smarter than D

and then they were given sentences that were true, presented ones, e.g.

A is smarter than B

or true, inferable ones, e.g

A is smarter than C

They were also given sentences that were false, based on the converse of the presented sentences, e.g.

B is smarter than A

and ones that were false, based on the converse of the inferable sentences, e.g.

C is smarter than A

Curiously, they made more correct judgements, and were faster to make their judgements, for the *inferable* non-adjacent pairs, such as:

A is smarter than C

than for the presented adjacent pairs, such as:

A is smarter than B

This *inferential distance* effect has puzzled researchers for many years.

Potts' subjects made their judgements faster for pairs that contained an end-term, i.e. A or D, than for the other pairs. In fact, they made their judgements for the true sentences faster for the terms that contained an A term first in the pair, and their judgements for the false sentences faster for the terms that contained a D term first in the pair (see also Newstead, Pollard & Griggs, 1986). But, the inferable pairs contained an end-term, whereas not all the presented ones contained an end-term. Perhaps the distance effect is simply an end-term effect? This explanation is ruled out by the results from problems for which the two variables are not confounded, e.g.

A is taller than B
B is taller than C
C is taller than D
D is taller than E
E is taller than F

(Potts, 1974). Some of the inferable pairs contained an end-term (e.g. A is taller than F) but others did not (e.g. B is taller than E). Individuals still made inferences faster to the inferable pairs, even when they did not contain an end-term (2.38 sec), than to the presented pairs (2.67 sec). They also made fewer errors to the inferable pairs (Potts, 1974; Scholz & Potts, 1974; see also Polich & Potts, 1977; cf. Hayes-Roth & Hayes-Roth, 1975; Moeser & Tarrant, 1977). Once again, for true sentences, pairs containing the first end-term, A, were the fastest, whereas for false sentences, pairs containing the last end-term, F, were the fastest (see Potts, 1974).

People seem to know the difference between the presented and inferred information. They can identify sentences as ones they were previously given (50% correct), although they sometimes mistake them for paraphrases (18%) or for implications (20%). Likewise, they identify implications correctly (50%), but they sometimes mistake them for sentences that were presented to them (20%) or for paraphrases (21%). In contrast, they tend to fail to identify paraphrases (23% correct), mistaking them for sentences that were presented to them (48%) or for implications (21%). They usually correctly identify false sentences (80%: Lawson, 1977; see also Barclay, 1973; Mani & Johnson-Laird, 1982). Hence, the data suggest that people can keep track of what has been presented to them and what they have inferred.

Individuals may keep track of the number of times each entity is encountered as the greater or lesser item, and respond on the basis of frequency alone (Humphreys, 1975; cf. Moeser & Tarrant, 1977). But, consider numeric passages based on sentences such as:

The hawk got five times as many votes as the rabbit.

The distance effect is found only when the questions are comparative ones:

Did the hawk get more votes than the rabbit?

and not when they are numeric ones:

Did the hawk get five times as many votes as the rabbit?

(Mayer, 1978; 1979). The distance effect is also found when individuals are given the inferable, non-adjacent pairs instead of the usual adjacent pairs (the adjacent pairs are deducible from the non-adjacent ones only for such numeric premises—they are indeterminate for non-numeric premises). There are similar effects with stored symbolic information, such as the alphabet (Moyer & Bayer, 1976). Hence, it is unlikely that individuals are simply using short-cut heuristics, such as a frequency estimate.

The distance effect is *not* found when the relation fails to support certain logical properties. When the relation is specified only by a tag, e.g.

A–B

individuals tend to assume it is symmetrical:

B–A

(Newstead et al., 1986; Tsal, 1977; see also Potts, 1976; 1978). In fact, most relational terms studied are *asymmetrical*, for example, the premise:

A is smarter than B

does not support the symmetrical inference:

B is smarter than A.

It may be necessary to resist this inference in order to be able to distinguish between presented premises and their converses. The distance effect is not found for set inclusions (see Chapter 7). Whereas people rarely assume that an ordering relation is symmetrical, e.g.

A is better than B

is not mistaken to mean:

B is better than A

they do sometimes assume that an inclusion relation is symmetrical, e.g.

All A are B

is mistaken to mean:

All B are A.

If individuals make this symmetrical inference, then they may find it difficult to distinguish presented premises from their converses, and so they will not exhibit a distance effect. In fact, those individuals who make few errors on inclusion relations—that is, they resist the symmetrical inference—do tend to exhibit a distance effect (Potts, 1976). Moreover, individuals tend to assume that the unspecified relation is not transitive, i.e. from the premises:

A–B
B–C

they do not make the transitive inference:

A–C

Most relational terms studied are transitive. For example:

A is smarter than B
B is smarter than C

supports the transitive inference:

A is smarter than C

It may be that making this inference interferes with distinguishing between presented adjacent pairs, and their non-presented, non-adjacent pairs. The effect is found when individuals are told to imagine the letters stand for boys' names and the relation stands for height, and not when they are given no information about the terms or the relation (Mayer, 1979; see also Potts, 1977).

What causes this curious pattern of results? The distance effect suggests that individuals are not "cognitive misers" storing only the necessary given information and not the deducible information. If they were, they should be faster and more accurate on the given information than on the deducible information—the reverse of what has been found. Nor are they simply storing the inferable pairs *as well as* the presented ones. If they were, they should be *just as* fast and accurate on the inferable information as on the given information, but instead they are *faster* and *more* accurate on the inferable information. The results make sense if individuals are constructing an integrated representation such as a spatial array. The array contains implicit information about the relations between each element, e.g.

A
B
C
D
E
F

The procedures that manipulate arrays may be more efficient in processing information about a pair the further apart the pair is in the array (Potts, 1972). Hence judgements about inferred relations, such as:

B is smarter than E

can be made more readily than judgements about presented relations, such as:

B is smarter than C

When subjects make judgements about any relation, whether it is presented or inferred, they must inspect the array. The farther apart the two terms are, the easier it is to compute their distance, and so judgements about the inferable entities are faster and more accurate than judgements about the presented entities, and they are easiest if individuals can begin at an extreme end of the array. This curious phenomenon turns out to be further support for the idea that individuals construct an integrated representation such as a model-like array.

In summary, four strands of research clarify the nature of the representations that reasoners construct of a relational problem. They construct representations that integrate the information in the premises into a unified seriation, rather than hold the separate pieces of information in working memory. They find it easier to understand and reason from descriptions that present the information in a continuous or semi-continuous order (rather than in a discontinuous order), which facilitates the combination of the information in a series into an integrated representation. They find it easier to deal with determinate descriptions, which require a single representation to be kept in mind, rather than indeterminate descriptions, which require multiple representations. Finally, the inferential-distance effect shows that individuals are faster and more accurate in their judgements about inferable relations than presented relations, because they construct an integrated representation that makes explicit the relations between the terms. These four clues to the sorts of representations that individuals construct support the idea that they rely on models based on the structure of the situation that the premises describe, rather than on linguistic representations based on the language used to describe the situation.

TWO CURIOUS PHENOMENA

Two phenomena, investigated using relational inferences, have puzzled researchers. The first phenomenon is that although there is ample evidence for the use of spatial arrays in relational reasoning, there appears to be little evidence for the use of imagery. The data caused confusion because early researchers assumed spatial arrays must be represented as images. They make sense given the current conceptualisations of spatial arrays as models rather than as images (e.g. Johnson-Laird & Byrne, 1991). The second phenomenon concerns the use of strategies in relational reasoning. More research has been carried out on strategies in the domain of relational reasoning than in any other domain of deduction. The proper interpretation of the results remains a challenge for contemporary researchers on reasoning.

Problem Imageability

We have seen considerable evidence that individuals construct an integrated representation, such as a spatial array. An early view of the nature of spatial arrays was that they were closely related to images (e.g. Huttenlocher, 1968). If individuals construct an image-like representation, then it is to be expected that they would be affected by the imageability of the relations. But, the role of imagery in relational reasoning is unclear.

Individuals impute a spatial direction to some adjectives, such as better–worse, in a consistent way. For example, they tend to allocate the better entity to a location at the top of a vertical axis, and the worse entity to the bottom of the axis, when they are required to insert them into a two-dimensional horizontal–vertical axis (De Soto et al., 1965; see also Handel et al., 1968). They are less consistent in their allocation of locations for terms connected by other adjectives, such as "lighter" and "darker". The preferred axis for affirmative relations, such as "better than", is not always the same as for negative-equatives, such as "not as bad as" (Jones, 1970).

People may imagine the arrangement of different relations differently, but does this affect the ease with which they reason from them? De Soto et al. (1965, p. 519) found that linear syllogisms based on left–right were harder than others and noted that the "momentary inability to decide which direction is left and which is right is a common failing—certainly more common than ignorance of which way is up and which is down". However, experiments on a variety of relations have produced conflicting results. Some studies have found no differences in the ease with which individuals make inferences from imageable and less imageable relations (e.g. Clark, 1969a; Johnson-Laird et al., 1989; Mynatt & Smith, 1977; Newstead et al., 1986; Sternberg, 1980), whereas other studies have found some differences (e.g. Egan & Grimes-Farrow, 1982; Hunter, 1957; Ormrod, 1979).

The evidence is mixed concerning whether the ease with which an individual can process a premise, such as:

Al is better than Bob

depends on the ease with which they can construct an image corresponding to the *relation* "better than". But, could it depend on the ease with which they can construct an image of the *terms*, "Al" and "Bob"? Individuals may adopt a strategy of forming concrete images of the terms (Egan & Grimes-Farrow, 1982). However, subjects were no better at making inferences when they had been pre-trained to link a name with a face for the terms of a linear ordering (Richardson, 1987). The pre-trained subjects who could put a face to the name were slower to make inferences (1.72 sec) than the non-trained ones who could not (1.39 sec). The pre-trained subjects who were subsequently tested on the names were slower (1.72 sec) than the ones tested on the faces (1.36 sec). It seems unlikely, then, that individuals must construct concrete images to carry out relational inferences.

If individuals rely on images, then interfering with the construction of images should interfere with their reasoning. Subjects made fewer errors in repeating a message verbatim (about the location of entities in a matrix) when they listened to the message, than when they listened and read it (Brooks, 1967). The results indicate that the visual demands of reading interfered with the imaginal demands of the matrix task. But, is reasoning performance on three-term series problems similarly affected? Some studies show that reasoning performance is better by subjects of high spatial ability, on imageable materials, following imagery instructions, and with auditory rather than visual presentation (e.g. Shaver et al., 1975; see also Ormrod, 1979). Other studies have failed to find interference effects, even when individuals had to attend selectively to the premises, either verbally or visually (e.g. Newstead, Manktelow & Evans, 1982). There is also conflicting evidence for correlations with spatial and verbal IQ tests. Sternberg (1980) has shown that both sorts of test correlate highly overall with performance on linear syllogisms, but differently with different components of the task.

The results about the use of imagery in relational reasoning are mixed. Overall, the evidence that there is a central role for imagery in relational reasoning is not compelling. This bifurcation of evidence—strong evidence for the role of a spatial array-like representation, but conflicting evidence for the role of an image-like representation—initially caused dispute among early researchers who tended to equate the two sorts of representation (Clark, 1969a; Huttenlocher, 1968). However, Johnson-Laird (1972, p. 75) suggested that the identification of spatial arrays with images may be misguided:

> In blindfold chess, for example, some kind of visual representation of the pieces seems to be vital in order to keep track of the moves. But this representation no more determines which move should be made then would the use of an actual chessboard. Similarly, making an inference requires the reasoner to construct an underlying representation of the premises . . . But, regardless of the form of the representation, the process of inference requires a number of steps in information-processing; and it is a specification of these processes, not whether the representations are abstract symbols or concrete images, which constitutes an explanation of the phenomena.

Current conceptualisations of spatial array-like representations identify them as models that are close to the structure of the world, rather than to the structure of the language that the world is described by. As we have seen elsewhere in the book (e.g. Chapter 3), models are not necessarily equated with an experiential image. Johnson-Laird and Byrne (1991, pp. 38–39) suggest: "The tokens of mental models may occur in a visual image, or they may not be directly accessible to consciousness. What matters is, not the phenomenal experience, but the structure of the models. This structure . . . often transcends the perceptible."

Strategies in Reasoning

We have reviewed evidence that examines the role of spatial and linguistic processes in relational reasoning, and we have tacitly assumed that individuals rely on one or the other of these sorts of processes. Is this assumption warranted? Research on the development of strategies based on spatial or linguistic processing appears to cast a shadow of doubt on the assumption.

One possibility is that individuals progress from one sort of representation to another as they gain expertise. They may progress from spatial to linguistic processing (e.g. Johnson-Laird, 1972; Wason & Johnson-Laird, 1972) or from linguistic to spatial processing (e.g. Shaver et al., 1975; see also Mynatt & Smith, 1977; Trabasso et al., 1975). For example, whether or not subjects can readily answer a question about the relation between two internal terms, rather than a question about the relation between the end-terms, depends on how well-used they have become in the experiment to answering one sort of question rather than the other. They could answer the unexpected question about the internal terms more accurately on the first problem (55%), and after 1, 2 or 5 problems (35%), than they could answer it after 10 or 15 problems (25%) or 20 problems (10%: Wood, Shotter & Godden, 1974). The results suggest that the subjects may have abandoned a flexible strategy that enabled them to answer either sort of question early on in the experiment, in favour of a quicker, short-cut strategy suited to answering only the expected question.

Another possibility is that different individuals use different strategies. Individuals who use linear arrays can be identified from their retrospective reports and their drawings (Egan & Grimes-Farrow, 1982). For example, some subjects represented the premises:

A is bigger than B
B is bigger than C

by the linear array:

A
B
C

These individuals exhibited the sorts of spatial-array effects discussed earlier, such as a preference for constructing arrays from the top-down rather than from the bottom-up. Other subjects seemed to rely on concrete images, identifiable from their retrospections and their drawings. For example, they represented the premises above by the following sort of diagram:

A B C

These subjects did not exhibit the spatial-array effects (Egan & Grimes-Farrow, 1982).

The strategies people adopt may be influenced by the instructions they are given (e.g. Barclay, 1973) or by the presentation of the information. For example, subjects who received the premises and question in a sequential order, either auditorily or visually, tended to adopt a verbal strategy (according to their introspections) when they received the question first. Those who were given the question last adopted a spatial strategy (Ormrod, 1979). Subjects who received simultaneous (visual) presentation adopted a spatial strategy regardless of whether the question came first or last, perhaps because they could access the question first in both cases. Some people may maintain a representational strategy, be it spatial or linguistic, whereas others may quickly develop a short-cut "heuristic" strategy (e.g. Quinton & Fellows, 1975; see also Ohlsson, 1984).

A third possibility is that all subjects use a mixture of spatial and linguistic processes. Sternberg (1981, p. 417) suggests that "the irresolubility of the long-standing debate as to whether the internal representation subjects use during the solution of a linear syllogism is linguistic or spatial has derived in part from the fact that both kinds of representation are used at different points during the solution process" (see also Maybery, 1990; Sternberg, 1980; 1990). Individuals may construct two representations, a propositional one and a model-based one (Ehrlich & Johnson-Laird, 1982; Mani & Johnson-Laird, 1982). But, to reason accurately from determinate and indeterminate problems, they may require access to a model representation (Byrne & Johnson-Laird, 1989; cf. Sternberg, 1980).

Thus, the underlying mechanism of reasoning may depend exclusively on spatial or linguistic processes, as we have considered throughout this chapter, or it may depend on a mixture of both spatial or linguistic processes. The underlying mechanism may be the same for all people or it may differ for different people. The underlying mechanism may be overlain, as people gain experience with problems, with spontaneously developed strategies based on spatial or linguistic processes or on heuristic short-cut processes. Considerable research was carried out on strategies in relational reasoning, especially during the 1970s, but there has been a dearth of research on strategies in deduction since, in part because of the conflicting results that emerged from the research on relational reasoning. An interest in strategies in reasoning is beginning to re-emerge (e.g. Roberts, in press; Byrne & Handley, 1992; Johnson-Laird & Byrne, 1990; Rips, 1989) and their role in understanding and reasoning from relational premises remains a challenging problem in contemporary research.

In summary, two puzzling effects underscore our understanding of the representations and processes that reasoners use to solve relational problems. One of these phenomena is clarified by our contemporary understanding of representations: the findings that spatial arrays appear to have a central role in relational reasoning, but that imagery appears to have little part to play, is easy to understand if the spatial arrays that reasoners construct are model-like structures which need not necessarily give rise to an image. The second idea, that different reasoners may rely on different processes, or they may develop strategies to overlay their underlying processes, remains a controversial challenge in contemporary research.

CONCLUSIONS

Relational inferences underlie many of our everyday reasoning skills. Individuals find some relational inferences more difficult than others. The two early theories of the mental representations and cognitive processes required to make relational inferences in three-term series problems are that they depend on procedures that construct and manipulate spatial arrays or models, and that they depend on procedures that construct and manipulate linguistic representations. The spatial array view proposes that individuals construct a uniform array for marked and unmarked adjectives, they have a preference for constructing arrays from the top-down, and from an extreme "end-anchored" term. The linguistic representation view proposes that individuals represent marked and unmarked adjectives in different formats, they compress the information, and it may be congruent or non-congruent with the questions they are asked. It is difficult to distinguish the two theories empirically, but the data appear to corroborate the spatial array theory's proposal that marked and unmarked adjectives are represented in a uniform format, and to go against the linguistic theory's proposal that they are represented in different formats.

Four strands of research have clarified further the nature of the representations that subjects construct of a relational problem. They construct representations that integrate the information in the premises into a unified seriation, and so, for example, they find it easier to understand and reason from descriptions that present the information in a continuous rather than in a discontinuous order, and they find it easier to deal with determinate descriptions, which require a single representation to be kept in mind. Subjects appear to rely on models based on the structure of the situation that the premises describe, rather than linguistic representations based on the language used to describe the situation. These models need not necessarily give rise to an image, and so imagery may have little part to play in relational reasoning. The role of strategies in reasoning remains an outstanding challenge for contemporary researchers to consider.

7 Syllogistic Reasoning

Traditional syllogisms were first devised by Aristotle, and for centuries were believed to be the basis of all rational thought. Countless generations of students of logic must have been required to learn the mnemonic device for remembering valid syllogisms, which goes:

Barbara, Darii, Celarent, Ferio
Camestres, Baroco, Cesare, Festino
Darapti, Datisi, Felapton, Ferison, Disamis, Bocardo
Bramantip, Camenes, Dimaris, Fesapo, Fresison

To modern-day readers, this approach to learning about the laws of thought seems archaic, even quaint. It is probable that most readers of this book have never come across the above mnemonic which formed such an important part of the education of so many people. Its significance will be explained shortly, following a description of the nature of syllogisms.

THE NATURE OF SYLLOGISMS

We have already come across syllogisms in Chapter 1. The following is an illustrative example of a syllogism:

No musicians are Italians
All barbers are musicians
Therefore,
No barbers are Italians

All syllogisms are like this in that they have two premises and a conclusion. The premises contain three terms (musicians, Italians and barbers in the above example), one of which, the middle term, occurs in both premises (musicians). The conclusion connects the other two terms. The premises and the conclusion each contain one of the quantifiers *all, no, some* and *some . . . not*. The quantifiers *all* and *no* are universal, since they refer to all the members of a set. *Some* and *some . . . not* are particular, since they may refer to less than the entire set: *some* is technically defined as meaning *at least one and possibly all*. Additionally, two of the quantifiers (*all* and *some*) are positive, while the others (*no* and *some . . . not*) are negative. It should be pointed out at this stage that these four quantifiers are the ones that have traditionally been used as the English-language equivalents of the logical quantifiers, but that others may serve as well or even better. *At least one and possibly all* would certainly be a more precise translation, but it would also be considerably more cumbersome than *some*.

Figure

Syllogisms fall into one of four figures, as can be seen in Table 7.1, based on the location of the terms. In Table 7.1, M indicates the middle term, S the subject of the conclusion and P the predicate of the conclusion. The example syllogism given above clearly falls into figure 1. An example of a syllogism in figure 3 is:

Some doctors are archers
No doctors are farmers
Therefore,
Some farmers are not archers

Mood

The mood of a syllogism is determined by the quantifiers used in the premises and conclusion. By convention, each of these quantifiers is referred to by a letter:

TABLE 7.1
The Four Syllogistic Figures

Figure 1	*Figure 2*	*Figure 3*	*Figure 4*
M-P	P-M	M-P	P-M
S-M	S-M	M-S	M-S
S-P	S-P	S-P	S-P

A = all
E = no
I = some
O = some . . . not

If a syllogism contained the quantifier *all* in both the premises and the conclusion, then its mood would be AAA; if the first premise contained *no*, the second premise *some* and the conclusion *some* . . . *not*, then its mood would be EIO (with apologies to Old MacDonald).

How Many Syllogisms are There?

This apparently simple question does not have a simple answer. According to traditional logicians such as Cohen and Nagel (1934), there are four figures, and the premises and conclusion can each contain four different quantifiers. Hence by simple arithmetic there are 4*4*4*4 = 256 syllogisms. However, Aristotle himself did not acknowledge this number. Apparently, he did not believe that figure 4 was a genuine one, and so presumably he only recognised the existence of 192 syllogisms.

The issue is complicated further when one considers syllogisms not from a logician's point of view but from that of a psychologist. According to the logicians, the first premise should always contain the predicate of the conclusion and the second premise the subject. Reversing the premises does not affect the logic but it might affect the way in which people reason with syllogisms. Reversing the order of premises doubles the number of syllogisms and hence (*pace* Aristotle) there are to all intents and purposes 512 possible syllogisms.

How Many of the Syllogisms are Valid?

Again, this question defies a straightforward answer. The logicians' answer is contained in the mnemonic given at the beginning of this chapter. The four so-called "strong" syllogisms in figure 1 are given by the first line of the verse. The three vowels in Barbara indicate that AAA syllogisms are valid in this figure, and the remaining words indicate that AII, EAE and EIO syllogisms are also valid. However, there are also two weak conclusions that are valid in this figure: AAI and EAO. These are weak conclusions in that they draw particular conclusions (*some* or *some* . . . *not*) when universal conclusions (involving *all* or *no*) are permissible. To illustrate, the premises:

All men are mortal
All Greeks are men

warrant the conclusion that "All Greeks are mortal". The conclusion that "Some Greeks are mortal" is also valid, but is clearly not the strongest conclusion available.

Allowing for the validity of both weak and strong conclusions, there are reckoned by traditional logicians to be 24 valid syllogisms (see, e.g. Cohen & Nagel, 1934). We can immediately double this to 48, since we have accepted that syllogisms with reversed premises should be acknowledged to be different syllogisms. [Some readers may be aware that Johnson-Laird (e.g. 1983) claims that there are 27 valid syllogisms. There is no real discrepancy here, since Johnson-Laird allows for conclusions in both directions (in effect going from predicate to subject as well as from subject to predicate) and also omits some conclusions, in particular the weak ones.]

Logicians might not let the matter rest there. They might well go on to discuss whether this number of 48 valid syllogisms is correct, since it can change depending on the assumptions made about the existence of members of the sets described by the syllogisms; but there, for present purposes, we will let the matter rest. (The interested reader might wish to look ahead to Table 7.2 to see a full listing of the valid syllogisms.)

A comment is in order about the terminology used to describe syllogisms. Traditionally, the first premise is the one containing the predicate of the conclusion, the second premise the one containing the subject, and only conclusions going from subject to predicate are allowed. Thus an AI1 syllogism has the first premise in mood A, the second in mood I and is in figure 1. Traditionally, one would also have had to specify the mood of the conclusion, but in order to allow for open-ended syllogisms where no conclusion is indicated, we will frequently exclude the conclusion from our notation. Most of the research up until the last decade used this terminology, and it is the one adopted here. However, Johnson-Laird and his colleagues (e.g. Johnson-Laird & Bara, 1984) have adopted a different way of describing syllogisms, based on the fact that they allow conclusions in both directions, and conclusions going from the predicate term to the subject term can alter the figure of the syllogism. This leads to some problems in comparing the results of different studies. Johnson-Laird talks, for example, of an AB–BC syllogism, which means that the first premise contains the items A and B, in that order, while the second contains B and C in that order. Such a syllogism does not fall automatically into one of the classical figures, since conclusions going from both A to C and from C to A are permitted. The comparisons in this chapter are based on the fact that, assuming conclusions going from A to C, then Johnson-Laird's AB–BC figure is the classical figure 1 with the premises reversed; AB–CB is figure 2 with reversed premises; BA–BC is figure 3 with reversed premises; and BA–CB is figure 4 with reversed premises.

THE PSYCHOLOGY OF SYLLOGISMS

Most people, when they have it explained to them, will accept the validity of the logic underlying syllogisms. However, when actually confronted by exercises in syllogistic reasoning, people make a large number of errors. Not that this is a recent phenomenon; the fact that students over the ages have had to learn by rote the valid syllogisms suggests that our forebears did not find the task any easier than we do. Much research in psychology over the past century has sought to understand the source of such errors.

Before discussing the various theories, it is necessary to say a few words about methodology. The most frequent way of presenting a syllogistic reasoning task is to give the premises followed by all the possible conclusions and to ask subjects to indicate which conclusion follows. Even here, there are wide variations in procedure, with some studies presenting just the four recognised propositional conclusions (A,E,I,O), others permitting subjects to indicate that no valid conclusion follows, and others presenting the conclusions in both directions. Some studies present subjects with complete syllogisms (i.e. two premises and a conclusion) and ask them to judge their validity. To our knowledge, this is always done on a subset of the total number of syllogisms: no-one has ever tested all 512 syllogisms in a single study. A significant number of recent studies have used a novel variant on the task, in which subjects are presented with two premises and are asked to generate their own conclusions. Studies also vary with respect to the instructions given, in particular how (or indeed whether) they define logical validity, and in how they instruct subjects to interpret the quantifiers. It is by no means obvious that all these tasks are equivalent to each other, and it must be borne in mind that some of the conflicting findings may owe more to the task used than to the theoretical question they were designed to address.

In order to provide some flavour of the type of results that are obtained, the data from a study by Dickstein (1978) are summarised in Table 7.2. This study is one of the few which used all 64 premise pairs, and in this case subjects were asked to choose one of the four conclusions permitted in traditional theory (i.e. going from subject to predicate) or to indicate that no valid conclusion followed. It is immediately obvious from inspection of the third column of Table 7.2 that people make a considerable number of errors in this task. Overall, just 52% of the responses were logically correct. Since subjects had just five responses to choose from, one would expect them to be correct 20% of the time purely by chance. One of the main themes in research has been an attempt to explain why people do so badly, especially on some of the syllogisms, and why they produce the responses they do.

Conceptually, the task of solving syllogisms can be broken down into three stages. First, it is necessary to interpret the premises (and the

TABLE 7.2
Results Obtained by Dickstein (1978)

Syllogism	*Correct Response*	*Percent Correct*	*Preferred Conclusion*	*Syllogism*	*Correct Response*	*Percent Correct*	*Preferred Conclusion*
AA1	A(I)	95(3)	A	AA3	I	29	A
AE1	N	37	E	AE3	N	18	E
AI1	I	90	I	AI3	I	90	I
AO1	N	37	O	AO3	N	18	O
EA1	E(O)	92(5)	E	EA3	O	24	E
EE1	N	61	N	EE3	N	82	N
EI1	O	68	O	EI3	O	55	O
EO1	N	55	N	EO3	N	45	O
IA1	N	24	I	IA3	I	84	I
IE1	N	68	N	IE3	N	40	N
II1	N	55	N	II3	N	63	N
IO1	N	53	N	IO3	N	45	N
OA1	N	29	O	OA3	O	79	O
OE1	N	82	N	OE3	N	53	N
OI1	N	58	N	OI3	N	47	N
OO1	N	61	N	OO3	N	66	N
AA2	N	21	A	AA4	I	21	A
AE2	E(O)	95(3)	E	AE4	E(O)	90(3)	E
AI2	N	11	I	AI4	N	24	I
AO2	O	74	O	AO4	N	16	O
EA2	E(O)	92(5)	E	EA4	O	5	E
EE2	N	61	N	EE4	N	74	N
EI2	O	58	O	EI4	O	24	N
EO2	N	63	N	EO4	N	82	N
IA2	N	24	I	IA4	I	90	I
IE2	N	18	E	IE4	N	34	O/N
II2	N	37	I	II4	N	58	N
IO2	N	40	O	IO4	N	45	O/N
OA2	N	16	O	OA4	N	29	O
OE2	N	58	N	OE4	N	58	N
OI2	N	34	O	OI4	N	58	N
OO2	N	47	N	OO4	N	47	N

Abbreviations: A, *all*; E, *no*; I, *some*; O, *some . . . not*; N, no valid conclusion.
The first letter indicates the mood of the first premise, the second letter the mood of the second premise, and the number of the figure of the syllogism. Weak conclusions are given in parentheses.

conclusion if one is given). Second, the information in the two premises must be combined. And, third, a response must be produced. Errors could occur at all three stages, and indeed theories of syllogistic reasoning have proposed all of them as the principal source of error. For ease of presentation, the various explanations will be categorised according to the stage of processing at which they suggest that errors occur. It should be recognised, however, that this categorisation is necessarily rather crude, and that some theories allow for errors at more than one stage. Nevertheless, all theories do seem to emphasise one stage over the others, and the following categorisation does not seem to do any real injustice to the various approaches. Hence in the following sections we discuss the major theories of syllogistic reasoning under the headings of interpretational explanations, premise combination explanations and response generation explanations.

INTERPRETATIONAL EXPLANATIONS

Interpretational theories attribute errors to misinterpretation of the premises. Two main kinds of explanation have been proposed. The first of these suggests that subjects illicitly convert the quantifiers *all* and *some . . . not*; the second that we interpret quantifiers according to their meaning in everyday language rather than according to the dictates of logic.

Conversion

The statement "All A are B" does not imply its converse, "All B are A". This can be demonstrated with a simple example: "All dogs are animals" does not imply that "All animals are dogs". Similarly, "Some A are not B" is not convertible: "Some animals are not dogs" does not imply that "Some dogs are not animals". In contrast, both *some* and *no* are convertible. If people incorrectly believe that statements using *all* and *some . . . not* are convertible then this will lead to errors. For example, the figure 2 syllogism:

Some C are B
All A are B

does not have a valid conclusion. However, if the second premise is converted, then this becomes a valid figure 4 syllogism:

Some C are B
All B are A

for which the conclusion "Some A are C" follows. Research has indicated that such conclusions are quite common (e.g. Dickstein, 1978, and syllogism IA2 in Table 7.2).

The idea of conversion is usually attributed to Chapman and Chapman (1959), though earlier researchers had also noted its existence (e.g. Wilkins, 1928). Chapman and Chapman did not offer any evidence for the existence of conversion other than that it explained several aspects of the results they had obtained. What is more, as has frequently been noted by subsequent researchers, their original formulation was extremely vague. It has been left to other researchers to spell out in more detail the precise details of the theory and to carry out empirical work on its validity.

In recent years, Revlin has been the foremost champion of the conversion theory. His version of the theory is highly specific and therefore relatively easy to test. Unfortunately, these tests have produced largely negative results. Revlis (1975a; 1975b) has made the counterintuitive claim that not only do subjects convert premises but that this is actually the preferred interpretation. In other words, subjects reason with the converted form of the premises rather than the non-converted form that was actually presented to them. This claim is almost certainly wrong; even Revlin's own evidence gave little support to the claim (Revlis, 1975a). Furthermore, Dickstein (1981) tested the predictions of the theory against various published sets of data. On the critical syllogisms where Revlin's theory gave different predictions to other theories, typically fewer than 10% of the responses favoured Revlin.

Other versions of the conversion theory stand up rather better to empirical test. In the same paper as that just cited, Dickstein tested the predictions of what he termed the "conversion-by-addition" theory. According to this, people do not substitute the converted form, as claimed by Revlin, but rather assume that both the original and the converted form are true. Hence, given the premise "All A are B", people will assume that "All A are B and all B are A". Specific predictions can be derived from this claim and, in the problems studied by Dickstein (1981), these were strongly borne out.

There is other evidence in support of the claim that some form of conversion plays a role in syllogistic reasoning. Dickstein (1975) found that instructions which warned subjects of the dangers of conversion were effective in reducing reasoning errors. Unfortunately, however, the instructions also warned about another source of error, probabilistic inference, and it is possible that this was the source of the improvement. Ceraso and Provitera (1971) tried a not dissimilar approach, in which they tried to block conversion. In effect, the premises were modified such that, for example, A premises where conversion was blocked became "All A are B and some B are not A". This manipulation had the effect of improving performance. Unfortunately, Ceraso and Provitera also changed the task in other ways, for example by showing subjects actual instances of the premises (e.g. a block which had a hole in it to illustrate the premise "All red blocks have holes") and hence we cannot be sure how general this finding is.

A further prediction is that syllogisms for which conversion will produce errors should be more difficult than others. This has generally been found, not only in the original study by Chapman and Chapman (1959) but also in subsequent research by Dickstein (1975; 1976). Revlis (1975a) has divided syllogisms into those where logic and conversion produce the same conclusion and those where they produce different conclusions. As predicted, those syllogisms where logic and conversion conflict proved to be more difficult.

Another way of testing the conversion hypothesis is to determine whether people do indeed systematically misinterpret quantified expressions. Two main tasks have been used to assess interpretation. The first of these, the immediate inference task, involves subjects indicating what is implied given the truth of a quantified statement. The second involves subjects selecting which Euler circles are appropriate for such statements.

In the immediate inference task, subjects are presented with a sentence containing a quantifier, for example "All A are B", and are asked to judge whether a number of other quantified statements logically follow from it. Conversion would be demonstrated if subjects indicated that "All A are B" logically implies the truth of "All B are A". Such responses are found to be quite common. For example, Newstead and Griggs (1983a) found that approximately 35% of subjects endorsed the conversion of *all* and more than 70% endorsed the conversion of *some . . . not*.

Studies of Euler circles produce a conflicting and more variable picture. Euler circles indicate the possible relationships between two sets, A and B, as shown in Fig. 7.1. In diagram 1 of this figure, the two sets are identical; in diagram 2, A is a subset of B; in diagram 3, B is a subset of A; in diagram 4, the two sets partially overlap; and in diagram 5, the two sets are completely disjoint. Logic defines which diagrams are appropriate for which quantifier, and the logically correct responses are given at the bottom of Fig. 7.1. "All A are B" has two possible interpretations, one in which the two sets are identical (diagram 1) and one in which A is a subset of B (diagram 2). Only in the identity relationship is the quantifier convertible, and hence conversion theory would presumably predict that this diagram will frequently be chosen on its own. The evidence indicates, however, that this choice is quite rare. Griggs and Warner (1982) found this response on fewer than 5% of the trials, which is fairly typical, though a study by Newstead (1989) obtained a slightly higher figure of around 20%.

How can the findings of the immediate inference and Euler circle tasks be reconciled, with the former providing strong support for conversion, in complete contrast to the latter? The answer may lie in the nature of the tasks used. It is possible that the tasks are not, as has been thought, both measuring the same thing, and indeed one (or even both) of them might not be measuring conversion at all. Consistent with such a suggestion is the finding of Newstead (1989) that there was no correlation between performance on the two tasks. But which, if any, of the tasks is providing

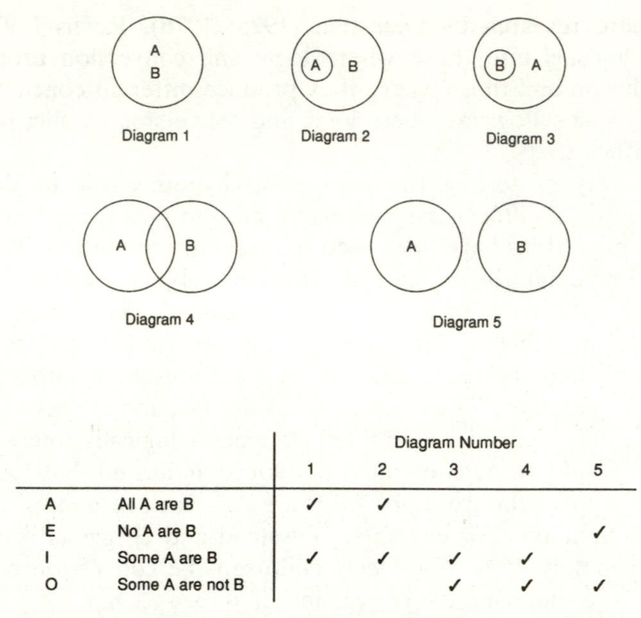

		Diagram Number				
		1	2	3	4	5
A	All A are B	✓	✓			
E	No A are B					✓
I	Some A are B	✓	✓	✓	✓	
O	Some A are not B			✓	✓	✓

FIG. 7.1 Euler circles and their relationship to quantifiers.

a measure of the type of conversion that might explain errors in syllogistic reasoning? Intuitively, the immediate inference task seems to be the strongest contender, since it is measuring the tendency to convert the verbal form of the statement. The Euler circle task involves translation into diagrams, and this task may have nothing to do with syllogistic reasoning (although as we shall see some researchers would contest this claim). Support for the claim that the immediate inference task measures the sort of conversion involved in syllogistic reasoning comes from the finding by Newstead (1989) that performance on this task correlated with the errors predicted by conversion theory in the solving of syllogisms.

Conversion has been extensively studied by researchers, but there is still an incomplete understanding of the role it plays. Part of the confusion may arise from the fact that different people mean different things by conversion. In addition to the conversion-by-substitution of Revlin and the conversion-by-addition of Dickstein, a number of other meanings can be detected in the literature (Newstead, 1990). It would appear that conversion does exist in the interpretation of quantifiers, and that such misinterpretation can explain some of the errors that occur in syllogistic reasoning. Any conclusion stronger than this would be unwarranted, and it would seem that conversion is only part of any comprehensive explanation of syllogistic reasoning behaviour.

Conversational Implicatures

Conversational implicatures are rules governing the use of language in everyday conversation. From the present perspective, the most important principle is the maxim of quantity, which states that speakers should be as informative as possible, and should not deliberately withhold information they know to be true (Grice, 1975). By extension from Grice's theory, it would be wrong of speakers to say *some* when they know *all* to be the case. But of course this is exactly what subjects in a syllogistic reasoning task are requested to do: they have to assume that "some A are B" can be true even in a situation when all As are Bs. If subjects fail to adopt the logical interpretation of *some*, despite instructions as to what this interpretation is, then this will obviously lead to errors.

There is ample evidence that people interpret quantifiers according to conversational implicatures rather than logic. Begg and Harris (1982) showed in a series of experiments that *some* and *some . . . not* are given similar interpretations, both being understood to mean *some but not all*. Newstead and Griggs (1983a) also present evidence to support the claim that *some* is not normally seen as being consistent with situations in which *all* is true, and *some . . . not* is not consistent with situations in which *no* is true. Begg (1987) has presented evidence which indicates that *some* typically means *fewer than half*, a claim that has much other research to support it (e.g. Newstead, Pollard & Riezebos, 1987). In fact, it is probable that no researchers in this area would deny that *some* is frequently interpreted in its conversational rather than its logical way.

However, it is one thing to show that such interpretations occur, another to show that they cause syllogistic reasoning errors. This latter claim has often been made (e.g. Begg & Harris, 1982; Politzer, 1986; 1990) but has rarely been backed up by empirical evidence. Furthermore, it has seldom been specified exactly what sorts of errors the theory predicts. Nevertheless, on the assumption that subjects make Gricean errors but otherwise reason logically, one can derive the following predictions:

(a) Whenever an I conclusion is permitted, subjects will often give an O conclusion in error (Politzer, 1990). Similarly, where an O conclusion is permitted, subjects will erroneously draw an I conclusion. This is because, according to the Gricean approach, these two conclusions imply each other—*some* implies *some . . . not* and vice versa.
(b) Whenever a specific conclusion is precluded only by the universal interpretation of O or I premises, then this conclusion will frequently be given in error. In other words, any conclusion which is valid under the assumption that *some* means *some but not all* will tend to be accepted.

These predictions can be tested against previously reported data. There are 14 classical syllogisms which produce valid I or O conclusions if we exclude those syllogisms which also permit stronger conclusions, for example where A is true (see Table 7.2). In the data of Dickstein (1978), which involved subjects evaluating conclusions as to their logical validity, errors involving the substitution of O for I conclusions constituted on average 25% of the errors made, while the substitution of I for O conclusions constituted 24% of the errors (see Table 7.3). Since there were four possible erroneous responses on each syllogism, by chance alone one would have expected 25% of the responses to be of this kind. Clearly, the frequency of this response does not exceed chance expectancies.

The occurrence of such errors can also be examined in studies in which subjects are required to produce their own conclusions. One of the more comprehensive databases derived from a study of this kind can be found in Johnson-Laird and Bara (1984). There are 21 pairs of premises which produce a valid I or O conclusion and for which no other conclusion is also valid. (The number differs from that in Dickstein's conclusion evaluation task, since the production task permits conclusions in either direction.) The frequency of such errors is presented in Table 7.3. Not one of the errors involved giving an O conclusion when I was valid, while just 6% of the errors when O was valid involved producing an I response. Both of these numbers are far less than would be expected by chance if subjects were simply choosing at random among the incorrect alternatives. (Chance levels of expectancy vary on this task depending on which quantifier is correct, but they never come below 1:8 or 12.5%; both of the above figures are clearly below this figure.) On the basis of this examination of published data, it would appear that the first prediction of Gricean theory is clearly disconfirmed.

Prediction (b) can be tested against the same databases. According to the calculations of the present authors, there are 10 classical syllogisms

TABLE 7.3
Gricean Substitution Errors (Responding O when I is Valid and vice versa)

	Dickstein (1978)	*Johnson-Laird and Bara (1984)*
Mean percentage of O conclusions on syllogisms where I is valid	25%	0%
Mean percentage of I conclusions on syllogisms where O is valid	24%	6%

which produce a different valid conclusion if Gricean interpretations are adopted. Consider, for example, the following syllogism of type AO1:

All Bs are Cs
Some As are not Bs

No valid conclusion follows from these premises. However, if subjects believe that the second premise is equivalent to "Some As are Bs", then the conclusion "Some As are Cs" is valid. This conclusion is excluded only by the situation in which no As are Bs, and Gricean interpreters will presumably not consider this possibility.

The 10 classical syllogisms which produce different responses when Gricean interpretations are adopted are shown in Table 7.4. Also given in Table 7.4 is the frequency of the error predicted by Gricean theory as found by Dickstein (1978). As can be seen, the predicted error occurred, on average, 47% of the time, which is more frequent than the 25% that would have been expected by chance. Curiously, however, if the data from Dickstein's first study rather than his second had been considered, the picture would have been rather different. In that sample, the average frequency of the predicted error was only 13%, which is actually below the chance level. There is no obvious explanation for this discrepancy, but it would suggest that this is not a highly reliable finding.

We can consider the same prediction with respect to the conclusion production task. In Johnson-Laird and Bara's (1984) study, the conclusions predicted on these 10 syllogisms accounted for just 14% of the errors made, which is near to the chance level (see Table 7.4). (Once again, the exact frequency predicted by chance varies but is never higher than

TABLE 7.4
Syllogisms where Gricean Errors Lead to Predictable Responses

Syllogism	*Response Predicted by Gricean Theory*	*Percentage of Errors Explained by Gricean Theory (Dickstein, 1978)*	*Percentage of Errors Explained by Gricean Theory (Johnson-Laird & Bara, 1984)*
AO1	I	4.1	36
EO1	O	58.8	22.2
AI2	O	23.6	0
EO2	O	42.9	0
AO3	O	19.4	31
EO3	I	85.7	0
IA3	I	50.0	0
OA3	O	87.2	15
EO4	I	28.8	0
OA4	O	70.3	40

12.5%.) On the conclusion production task, there are six more syllogisms which predict a different conclusion if Gricean interpretations operate. These hold no more comfort for the Gricean theory; just 6% of the errors on these corresponded to the predicted one. Overall, it must be concluded that prediction (b), like prediction (a), receives scant support in the published literature.

Another prediction that can be made on the basis of conversational implicatures is that those individuals who tend to adopt Gricean interpretations will also tend to produce more of the errors predicted by this theory. The only published study that has set out specifically to investigate this relationship seems to be that of Newstead (1989), and unfortunately this used only three syllogisms. There was, however, some suggestion of support for the theory since Gricean errors, as measured on an Euler circle task, correlated with the conclusions predicted by Gricean theory. However, interpretational errors as measured by the immediate inference task showed no correlation at all with the predicted syllogistic errors. Although this finding was based on just three syllogisms, there is some evidence that it may be a reasonably robust finding; Newstead (1993) found an identical pattern of results using all 10 syllogisms which lead to different conclusions when Gricean interpretations are adopted.

Are there any other data that allow us to assess the viability of the Gricean theory? Johnson-Laird and Bara (1984) called some of the responses they obtained Gricean ones. Some of the syllogisms are the same as those we have already considered but others are different. For example, given the syllogism:

Some B are C
Some A are not B

Johnson-Laird and Bara called a response of "Some A are C" a Gricean error. This may, in fact, result from another kind of Gricean error, the tendency to assume that the speaker is referring to the same entities in both premises. It is not, however, a response that logically follows from the interpretation of *some* in its conversational sense.

There is, then, conflicting evidence concerning the claim that Gricean errors are a major factor in explaining syllogistic reasoning performance. There is little doubt that Gricean errors of interpretation occur. Every study that has investigated them has had no difficulty at all in demonstrating their existence. However, there is little evidence in published data that such misinterpretations are a major source of syllogistic errors. There is, however, a small amount of evidence to support the theory coming from studies which have shown a correlation between Gricean interpretations and performance on a small set of syllogisms whose conclusion varies with the interpretation adopted. It would appear that Gricean errors are not perhaps as important as some theorists have claimed, and that they do not play a major part in explaining syllogistic reasoning performance; it would, however, be wrong to conclude that they play no role at all.

PREMISE COMBINATION EXPLANATIONS

Once the premises have been encoded, they have to be combined in some way if a conclusion is to be extracted. A number of theories have been put forward to explain how this is done and to explain how errors might creep into the process.

Euler Circles

We have already come across Euler circles in discussing premise interpretation. Some theorists, notably Erickson (1974; 1978) and Guyote and Sternberg (1981), have proposed that people use a mental analogue of Euler circles in carrying out syllogistic reasoning. This is, of course, a theory about how syllogisms are interpreted, and could therefore have been included in the previous section. However, it is also an important theory about how premises are combined, and seems best treated along with other such theories.

Erickson (1974; 1978) proposed a detailed process model of syllogistic reasoning. He assumes that people encode premises as Euler circles, but can only handle one diagram for each premise. Thus, if presented with the premise "All A are B", some subjects will encode this as an identity relationship (diagram 1 in Fig. 7.1), while others will encode it as a subset relationship (diagram 2 in Fig. 7.1). Few, if any, subjects will adopt both interpretations. [There is a problem here right away, since many studies using Euler circles to assess interpretation have found that people will quite readily adopt both interpretations (e.g. Neimark & Chapman, 1975).]

Once they have formed these representations, people have to combine the two diagrams they have constructed. Once again, Erickson assumes that subjects can handle no more than one composite representation. For example, if subjects have been given the premises:

All A are B
All C are B

they might adopt the identity relationship for both the premises, as shown in Fig. 7.2a. These could then be combined into a single composite representation in which all three sets are identical to each other (see Fig. 7.2b). In combining premises in this way, clearly a number of representations are overlooked, in this case all those in which the first term is a subset of

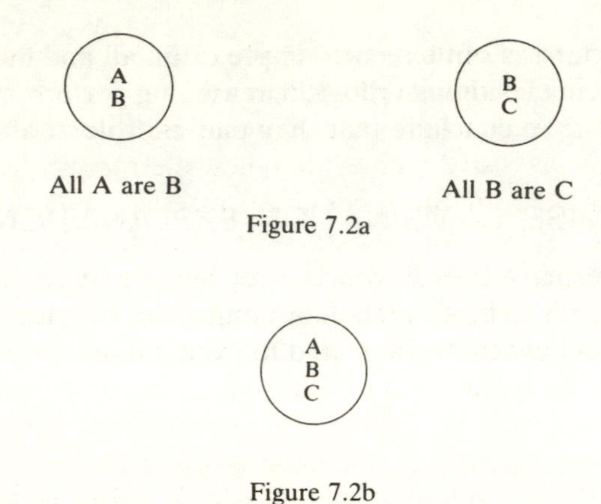

FIG. 7.2 Combinations of Euler circles.

the second. Such omissions will, of course, lead to errors. In the case above, it would lead to subjects concluding that "All A are C" or that "All C are A"; neither of these conclusions is justified by the premises.

The model also needs to specify which interpretations will be preferred by subjects, and which composite representation they will adopt. Erickson does this on the basis of empirical data collected by his colleagues and himself. For example, he assumes that, for the premise "All A are B", subjects will have a 0.4 probability of adopting the identity interpretation and a 0.6 probability of adopting that of subset. Using such estimates of the parameters in his model, Erickson (1974) found that it provided a reasonable fit to the data. However, the success of the model depends crucially on the parameter estimates adopted and, as we have seen for the assumptions concerning interpretation, these are almost certainly wrong.

A second theoretical approach based on Euler circles is that of Guyote and Sternberg (1981). This theory, like that of Erickson, assumes that the premises are represented in a form that is analagous to Euler circles. It also makes the surprising assumption that such representations are error-free, which we know from the discussion of premise interpretation not to be the case. The principal contribution of the theory is that it proposes a model of how the two premises are combined, something on which Erickson's theory is silent. According to Guyote and Sternberg, people try to construct transitive chains, which are essentially links between the two end-terms achieved using the middle term as a connecting device. These links can be positive or negative. A positive link is established when the first term has a positive connection with the middle term, which in turn has a positive connection with the third term. A negative (or more correctly ambiguous) link is established when no positive link can be made.

By repeated application of these two simple rules, all possible links can be determined and conclusions established.

This theory is difficult to evaluate. Guyote and Sternberg investigated it by carrying out extensive studies of syllogistic reasoning, estimating a number of parameters for the model, and assessing how well the model fitted the results. While the results were reasonably supportive, it is difficult to draw any general conclusions on the basis of them. The parameters were all derived in the context of the experiment and these parameters will presumably differ for different subject populations. This makes it difficult to evaluate the theory with respect to existing experimental findings, nor is it easy to derive testable predictions that can be tried out against new data sets. One claim of the theory we know to be wrong: it claims that encoding of premises is an error-free process, while it is known that this is not the case. Interestingly, a study by Sternberg and Turner (1981) found reasonably accurate interpretation by subjects, but this study is atypical. In general, we know that some of the claims of the transitive chain theory are wrong, and others seem difficult to test; hence this approach is no longer a strong contender.

Venn Diagrams

Venn diagrams are often confused with Euler circles, but are actually quite different. They involve three overlapping circles, each of which represents one of the sets in the syllogism (see Fig. 7.3). Syllogisms can be solved by marking these circles in specified ways for different premises. For example, "All A are B" would be encoded by shading the diagram as illustrated in Fig. 7.3. This shading indicates that the area covered—the members of set A that are not Bs—does not exist.

While Venn diagrams are recommended by many as a good technique for solving syllogisms, it has not often been claimed that they provide a

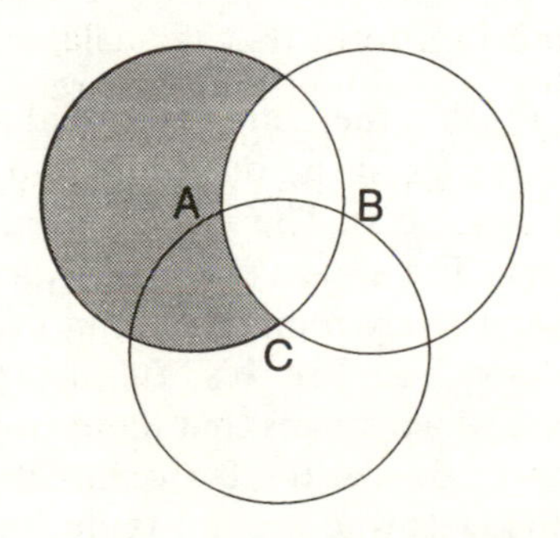

FIG. 7.3 Example of a Venn diagram.

means by which people actually do solve syllogisms. The only approach that does suggest this—and even here implicitly rather than explicitly—is that of Newell (1981). He claims that syllogistic reasoning can be regarded as a search through problem space, and that this latter is best characterised as involving representations analogous to Venn diagrams. However, he presents no empirical evidence to support this claim, and it is not easy to envisage what form such evidence might take. More recently, Newell (1990) has argued that Venn diagrams are used only rarely, and probably only by those who are expert in their use. Newell now seems to prefer the mental models approach, though translated into his preferred terminology of problem space.

Mental Models

Mental models have been discussed on a number of occasions in this book, though it is interesting to note that the theory was first developed in the context of syllogistic reasoning (Johnson-Laird & Steedman, 1978; Johnson-Laird, 1983). The ideas, and especially the notational system, have changed over the years; the presentation here is based on that of Johnson-Laird and Byrne (1991). It should be noted that this theory is one of the few that has something to say about all stages of syllogistic reasoning—interpretation, premise combination and response production. It has been included in this section partly for convenience and partly because it has probably made its major contribution to the debate in its detailed specification of how people combine premises into integrated representations.

The theory assumes that reasoners understand a premise by forming a mental model of it. These mental models consist of tokens which represent individual elements of the set. To illustrate, the premise "All A are B" would be represented as follows:

[a] b
[a] b
. . .

This representation means that there are individual members of the set A (shown as lower-case letter a's in the diagram) who are also members of set B (indicated by lower-case b's). The number of individuals represented in the diagram is arbitrary. The a's are enclosed by square brackets, which means that they are exhaustively represented; in other words, that there are no a's which are not b's. The b's, on the other hand, are not represented exhaustively, which means that there could exist b's which are not linked to a's. The three dots at the bottom of the model indicate that there may be other individuals who are not represented in the model, for example individuals who are not a's.

The crucial part of the theory comes in the building up of composite mental models which combine the models derived from each of the premises. This is in fact a fairly straightforward process of adding the model for the second premise to that of the first. For example, assume that the second premise is "All B are C" and that this has to be added to the first premise given above, "All A are B". This produces the following composite mental model:

[[a] b] c
[[a] b] c
. . .

What has happened here is that the second premise builds on the tokens existing in the model of the first premise. Whenever a b occurs, this has a c added to it, to indicate that there are b's that are c's. Furthermore, b is exhaustively represented with respect to c, and hence is surrounded by square brackets. On the other hand, there could be c's that are not b's, and so there are no brackets round the c's. Since there could also exist other entities, three dots are included at the bottom of the model.

In some situations, premise combination is more complicated than this, and in order to appreciate some of the predictions of the theory it is necessary to consider these. If the second premise (following the first premise "All A are B") had been "Some B are C", then one could build up the following representation:

[a] b c
[a] b c
. . .

The model simply incorporates c's into the model whenever b's occur, to indicate that there exist c's that are b's; however, they are not exhaustively represented since there could exist c's that are not b's and vice versa. From this composite model, the conclusion "Some A are C" follows, and this is a conclusion that is frequently but erroneously given. In order to establish that this conclusion does not follow, it is necessary to construct alternative models. The following model is consistent with the premises but in this case the conclusion "Some A are C" does not follow:

[a] b
[a] b
b c
. . .

This brings us to another important part of the theory—the attempt to construct falsifying models. Once people have established a possible conclusion, they must, if they are to test the validity of the conclusion, try to construct alternative models in which the premises are true but where the conclusion does not follow. If they fail, then they adopt the conclusion as valid; but if they succeed, they try to find another possible conclusion and, failing that, say that no conclusion follows.

One of the main predictions of the theory can now be specified—that the more mental models that can be produced consistent with the premises, but which falsify putative conclusions, the more difficult will the syllogism be. This prediction has been tested on numerous occasions by Johnson-Laird and his colleagues, and each time it has received overwhelming support (e.g. Johnson-Laird & Bara, 1984). It is usually claimed that some syllogisms require one model, some two and others three, and that there are large differences in difficulty between these. More recently, the emphasis has been on the simple distinction between one-model and multiple-model syllogisms (see Johnson-Laird & Byrne, 1991).

Since this is such a crucial prediction of the theory, it is worth examining it more closely. The initial example given above ("All A are B, All B are C") was a single-model syllogism, producing just the model:

```
[[a]  b]  c
[[a]  b]  c
   . . .
```

However, it might be argued that other models are possible, for example:

```
[[a]   b]  c
[[a]   b]  c
      [b]  c
   . . .
```

which simply indicates that there may be be b's which are not a's. From the point of view of solving the syllogism, this model is irrelevant, since it does not falsify the provisional conclusion. Hence this is presumably a model that subjects, guided by the principle that they are trying to falsify the putative conclusion that "All As are Bs", do not construct. Subjects try to construct a model in which there are a's which are not b's and, if they find this impossible (which they should do on this particular syllogism), accept the original conclusion.

It will be clear from the above that there are actually a large number of different models that can be constructed even from single-model syllogisms (an infinite number given that there can be any number of individuals represented in the model), but that subjects are assumed to construct only a small number of these. In order to test the predictions of the theory, it is necessary to indicate the principles governing model construction, specifying clearly the number of models required by each syllogism. A useful start has been made on this enterprise by Johnson-Laird and Bara

(1984) in the development of a computer program that produces models (see also Newell, 1990; Polk & Newell, 1988). A crucial test of the theory would involve testing whether subjects actually construct the models as predicted by the theory. To date this has been tested only rather indirectly, by examining the effects of number of models on syllogism difficulty, but this evidence is highly supportive of the predictions of the theory. The prediction has been confirmed not only with traditional syllogisms but also with syllogisms using the quantifier "only" (Johnson-Laird & Byrne, 1989). These authors made specific predictions about the difficulty of syllogisms involving this quantifier based on the number of mental models that needed to be constructed and these were uniformly supported.

However, it is wise to introduce a note of caution here concerning mental models theory. Some of the early predictions were not always confirmed (e.g. Lee & Oakhill, 1984). Furthermore, the main predictions deriving from the theory concern the relationship between the number of mental models and problem difficulty, and it is worthwhile considering just how risky these predictions are. Other theories would also predict that there are differences in difficulty between syllogisms, and in many cases these correspond closely to the predictions of mental models theory. For example, theories involving Euler circles (e.g. Erickson, 1974) predict that difficulty will be related to the number of Euler diagrams that need to be constructed. Since there are four diagrams needed for *some*, three for *some . . . not*, two for *all* and one for *no* (see Fig. 7.1), one can quite easily build up a measure of problem difficulty based on this. For example, an AI syllogism will involve 2 * 4 = 8 diagrams, while an EO syllogism will involve 1 * 3 = 3 diagrams. In general, the multiple-model syllogisms are also ones which involve a large number of Euler diagrams; all syllogisms which contain two particular premises (i.e. ones containing *some* or *some . . . not*) involve multiple models, and such syllogisms are typically rather difficult. Single-model syllogisms contain at least one and usually two universal quantifiers, and hence would be expected to be relatively simple according to Erickson's theory. There are, of course, exceptions, where two universally quantified premises prove to be psychologically complex or where two particular premises prove to be quite easy. But this does not alter the fact that Erickson's theory actually explains the data quite well. We do not wish to argue for Erickson's theory, which we believe to be flawed on other grounds; the point is that his theory, and indeed most of those that have been put forward, explain the relative difficulty of syllogisms quite well, and hence the fact that mental models theory does so too does not prove that it is correct.

Fortunately, research looking into predictions other than those relating to problem difficulty are now beginning to be conducted. Byrne and Johnson-Laird (1990a) investigated the recognition memory of subjects for conclusions that they had not produced during the solution of syllogisms. The idea behind this was that some of these conclusions corresponded to ones that, according to the mental models approach, subjects would have generated and then rejected during their solving of the syllogisms. Hence, although the subjects did not actually give these conclusions they might mistakenly think that they had. The results confirmed the predictions. As the authors acknowledge, there are alternative explanations of these findings, but it is nevertheless significant that a result predicted specifically on the basis of the theory has been empirically confirmed.

The mental models approach is in many ways still in its infancy. It is still not entirely specific as to how mental models are generated, nor as to how conclusions are generated. Nevertheless, it has much preliminary evidence in its favour, and must clearly be in contention as an explanation of syllogistic reasoning.

Formal Rules

Despite their popularity in other areas of deductive reasoning such as reasoning with conditionals (see Chapter 3), no fully-fledged account of the types of inference rules that might be used in syllogistic reasoning seems to have been developed. Braine and Rumain (1983) have put forward proposals concerning the form that such rules might take but have not yet developed this further. Indeed, Johnson-Laird and Byrne (1991) in their discussion of such approaches felt obliged to formulate their own version so that they could consider its potential for explaining the phenomena. Nevertheless, there has been at least one discussion of the validity of formal rule approaches in general, and this needs to be discussed briefly.

Galotti, Baron and Sabini (1986) claimed to have found evidence that formal rules could explain certain aspects of the performance of their subjects in a syllogistic reasoning task. They found that some subjects—generally those who had been classified as "good" reasoners—started formulating their own rules as the task progressed (it actually took something like 2 hours to complete the task!). For example, they came to realise that two premises containing the word *some* can never lead to a propositional conclusion; hence they responded that no valid conclusion followed whenever such premise combinations occurred. This is clearly a rule, but is it the kind of rule that formal rule theorists have proposed? We think not. Normally, subjects are assumed to possess formal rules when they start the reasoning task; the types of rules discovered by Galotti et al. seem better categorised as strategies developed in the experimental situation. Presumably, the subjects were able to carry out the syllogism task before developing these strategies, and it is the processes that they used at this stage which are of more importance. The results of Galotti and co-workers' experiment are of interest, but they do not provide convincing support for the formal rules approach. Indeed, until a coherent version of this theory is developed for syllogisms, no such support is likely to be forthcoming.

Directionality Effects

On occasions, subjects seem to prefer conclusions in one direction rather than another. Such effects were found originally in the form of figural effects—differences in accuracy between syllogisms in the four figures. Typically, it has been found that syllogisms in figure 1 are the easiest, those in figure 4 the hardest and those in figures 2 and 3 somewhere in between (e.g. Frase, 1968). The most plausible explanation for such effects seems to be in terms of direction of processing. In figure 1 syllogisms, the information is presented in the order A–B, B–C (or B–C, A–B in the traditional task) and subjects are required to draw the conclusion A–C. Dickstein (1978) assumes that it is easier to draw this conclusion in figure 1 than figure 4, where the premises are presented in the order C–B, B–A. The point is that in figure 1, the natural order for processing the information is from A to C, while in figure 4 it is from C to A. Figures 2 and 3 have one forward and one backward premise, and hence should be of intermediate difficulty, as indeed they are. Similar directionality effects have been found in relational reasoning (see Chapter 6).

Until recently, directionality effects had been found only in the differential difficulty of the four figures. More recently, researchers have become less hidebound by the constraints of classical syllogisms, and other interesting effects have emerged. Johnson-Laird and Steedman (1978) gave subjects pairs of premises and asked them to draw their own conclusions. This meant that subjects were free to draw conclusions in either direction, rather than being constrained by the classical convention that conclusions can only go in the direction S to P (see the introductory section of this chapter). Johnson-Laird and Steedman found definite preferences for the direction in which conclusions were drawn. Premises of the form A–B, B–C produced a strong preference for A–C conclusions, while premises of the form B–A, C–B produced a preference for C–A conclusions. The other two figures showed no strong preference for one direction over the other. Clearly, this finding closely parallels that of Dickstein (1978), demonstrating that subjects prefer to process information in a forward rather than backward direction.

A different kind of figural effect on the conclusion production task has been pointed out by Johnson-Laird and Byrne (1991). In their re-analysis of the Johnson-Laird and Bara (1984) data, they found fewer correct answers, and more erroneous conclusions that no valid conclusion follows, on figure 3 syllogisms.

What is the reason for the observed effects? Johnson-Laird and Steedman attribute the preferences to the way in which subjects construct mental models, since people tend to form a model of the first premise and then add the information in the second premise to this. If the conclusion is read off in a left-to-right direction, then the observed preferences would be expected. More recently, Johnson-Laird (e.g. Johnson-Laird & Bara, 1984) has claimed that the effects stem from the difficulty of rearranging the information so that the two middle terms occur together. This will be especially difficult with figures 2 and 3, where the middle terms appear in the same position in the two premises. Dickstein (1978), as we have seen, states simply that there is a general preference for forward processing. Frase (1968) likens the syllogistic figures to conditioning paradigms in his attempt to explain the differences between them. Wetherick and Gilhooly (1990) argue that the effects arise from the tendency to use as an end-term in the conclusion a term that has appeared as the subject of one of the premises. However, as Johnson-Laird and Byrne (1991) observe, this does not predict the precise order of difficulty actually found. It cannot explain, for example, why figure 3 (where there is no end-term as subject) is harder than figure 2 (where there are two end-terms), though this is not to say that such an explanation could not be found.

At the moment, there is no clear consensus as to which is the correct explanation of figural effects, and arguably there has been too little research aimed at distinguishing between the various explanations. What is clear, however, is that any adequate explanation of syllogistic reasoning will have to take the figural effects into account, since they are among the best established effects in the area. Any theory which ignores them—as most have done—will be incomplete.

RESPONSE GENERATION EXPLANATIONS OF SYLLOGISMS

Perhaps surprisingly, a significant number of theories focus on the response stage as the one at which errors mainly occur. We say surprisingly since such theories claim in effect that little reasoning is going on, and that subjects are responding largely on the basis of some response bias. Nevertheless, such theories exist in other areas of reasoning (see, for example, the discussion of negative conclusion bias in Chapter 2) and have also received substantial experimental support in studies of syllogistic reasoning. These theories range from the claim that people base their responses on the mood of the premises to the claim that they make their judgements according to the probability that certain properties are shared.

Atmosphere

Atmosphere refers to the overall mood created by the two premises. The idea was put forward by Woodworth and Sells (1935) and still has a number of proponents. The principles of atmosphere theory have been expressed most succinctly by Begg and Denny (1969). These are:

- *Principle of Quality*: whenever one or more of the premises is negative the preferred conclusion will be negative.
- *Principle of Quantity*: whenever one or more of the premises is particular, the preferred conclusion will be particular.

To illustrate the principles, consider the syllogism:

Some A are B
Some B are C

Since both the premises are positive and particular, there should be a strong preference for a positive, particular conclusion. The predicted I conclusion is in fact given regularly by subjects; in Johnson-Laird and Bara's (1984) study, it constituted fully 90% of the responses.

Inspection of any data from any syllogistic reasoning experiment will yield ample evidence to support the predictions of the atmosphere theory. Examination of the data of Dickstein (1978) reveals that 49% of all the responses produced were consistent with the predictions of atmosphere—far in excess of the 20% that would be expected by chance. The main discrepancies seem to be when the atmosphere produced is both particular and negative. The premise pairs EO, IE, OE and OO are all predicted to produce O conclusions, but these are seldom given by subjects. These are all syllogisms for which no valid conclusion follows, and in most instances this was the response that subjects gave. Atmosphere theory always predicts a propositional conclusion and hence cannot explain why "no valid conclusion" responses are given. Atmosphere theory also fares quite well in conclusion production tasks as well as in conclusion evaluation tasks; it correctly predicts 43% of the responses in Johnson-Laird and Bara's (1984) study, where chance expectancy would be 22%.

Whenever the atmosphere theory has been tested empirically, it has usually fared rather well. Begg and Denny (1969) compared the predictions of the atmosphere theory with those of conversion theory. On the few problems where the predictions of the two theories differed, it was the atmosphere theory that accorded best with the data. Similarly, Revlis (1975a) compared two information-processing models, one derived from atmosphere theory, the other from conversion theory. Although Revlis claims support for his preferred model, conversion theory, inspection of the data reveals that, if anything, its rival received stronger support. Jackson (1982) also found strong support for the theory.

Studies of the effects of instructions have produced ambiguous results. Simpson and Johnson (1966) found that instructions warning of the danger of atmosphere errors were successful in improving performance. However, Dickstein (1975) was unable to replicate this result. Since the instructions differed in the two studies, it is impossible to draw any firm conclusions.

Dickstein (1975) also reported other evidence which he claimed contradicted the atmosphere theory. He divided syllogisms into four groups: those that had the same quality and quantity (e.g. AA); those that had the same quality but different quantity (e.g. IA); those that had the same quantity but different quality (e.g. IO); and those that differed on both quantity and quality (e.g. IE). He assumed that syllogisms in the first group (i.e. those where both premises had the same quality and quantity) would produce the strongest atmosphere effect and hence would lead to the greatest number of errors. Syllogisms in the second and third groups should produce an intermediate number of errors, and those in the fourth group should produce the fewest. In fact, the results went in completely the opposite direction. It might be argued that atmosphere theory would not necessarily make this prediction. Nowhere is it claimed, at least in the formulation of Begg and Denny (1969), that the premises should act in a cumulative way; it is assumed that one premise on its own is sufficient to create a specific atmosphere. For example, an E premise is quite sufficient to create a negative atmosphere, and it is no means clear that an O premise will produce additional negativity. However, it must be a cause of concern to proponents of the theory that the results actually go in the wrong direction.

Many people seem somewhat disturbed that such a simple set of principles correctly predicts so many of the responses given to syllogisms. Surely there must be more to complex reasoning than this? Nevertheless, the theory has stood the test of time, and must be regarded as a serious contender. At the very least, alternative theories must provide explanations of why the atmosphere approach accords so well with the data.

On the other hand, atmosphere is clearly not the whole story, since a number of the responses produced are inconsistent with its predictions. We have already seen that 51% of the responses in Dickstein's (1978) study failed to correspond to the predictions of atmosphere theory. Furthermore, evidence of logical processing, which cannot be explained by atmosphere, is frequently found. Revlis (1975a) discovered that the effects of atmosphere were more marked on invalid than valid syllogisms, a finding that can only be explained on the assumption that subjects are making some attempt at reasoning. Finally, the atmosphere theory never predicts that subjects will respond that there is no valid conclusion. However, as inspection of Table 7.2 reveals, this is a very common response. A final comment on atmosphere theory is that, although it predicts the data well, it does not really explain them. None of the atmosphere theorists has ever explained *why* people should respond according to the principles of quality and quantity. Unless plausible explanations of this can be found, this may prove the ultimate downfall of the theory.

Caution

For the sake of completeness, it is necessary to mention the principle of caution, even though this has few supporters nowadays. The principle was put forward by Sells (1936) as an addition to the atmosphere theory. It claims that subjects will tend to err on the side of caution, preferring particular to universal conclusions. There is little evidence to support this claim; there are very few occasions in which atmosphere predicts a universal conclusion but where a particular one is given instead. The main problem, as we have seen, is that people give too few O conclusions—a particular conclusion that caution would lead us to expect!

Matching

The idea that subjects match the quantifier in the conclusion to that used in one of the premises has recently been suggested by Wetherick (1989; Wetherick & Gilhooly 1990). (It should be noted that this is not the same as the matching bias discussed in Chapters 2 and 5 in the context of conditional and disjunctive reasoning.) This matching has its similarities to the atmosphere effect, but in some situations leads to different predictions. It is claimed quite simply that subjects choose conclusions where the quantifier is the same as one of those used in the premises. Where there is a choice of quantifier, subjects have a preference to use the more conservative of the two quantifiers. In effect, this means that subjects will choose the quantifier that commits them to the smallest possible number of positive entities. *No* is clearly the most conservative quantifier, since it commits the speaker to the smallest possible number of positive instances (none), *all* is the least conservative quantifier, while *some* and *some . . . not* are somewhere in between. To illustrate how this principle works, if the syllogism was:

Some A are B
All B are C

then subjects should tend to choose the conclusion "Some A are C", since this uses the more conservative of the two quantifiers *some* and *all*.

Whenever the two quantifiers are the same, atmosphere and matching make exactly the same predictions, as they do in many other situations (e.g. the syllogism just presented). The predictions differ with the premise pairs, IE and OE, where atmosphere predicts an O conclusion, matching an E conclusion. These are known to be premise pairs where atmosphere fares rather poorly, but interestingly matching fares no better. Inspection of the data of Dickstein (1978) reveals that atmosphere correctly predicts the responses to these premise pairs 29% of the time, whereas matching makes the correct prediction 17% of the time.

Another prediction that can be derived from matching theory is that when one of the premises contains *some* and the other *some . . . not*, the preferred response should be *some*. This is not a prediction that the authors themselves make, but it seems to follow from the finding that *some* refers to fewer entities than *some . . . not* (e.g. Newstead et al., 1987). In Dickstein's (1978) data, the average number of I responses on the relevant syllogisms was 10%, while there were 37% O responses. Since there were more O than I conclusions on all eight relevant syllogisms, this result actually goes significantly in the opposite direction to that predicted by Wetherick. It should be noted, however, that atmosphere theory predicts this pattern of results. In addition, Johnson-Laird and Byrne (1989) found that subjects seldom gave conclusions containing the word *only* even when both premises used this quantifier. Hence we can conclude with some confidence that matching does not constitute a significant improvement over atmosphere theory.

Preference for Propositional Conclusions

A well-established finding in the literature is that people do better on the valid syllogisms than they do on the invalid ones (Revlis, 1975b). The explanation offered by Revlis for this is that people do not like to say that "nothing follows" and so they try to give one of the other, propositional conclusions (Revlis, 1975b). Since the correct conclusion for invalid syllogisms is always that there is no valid conclusion, this response bias can readily explain the poor performance on these. Similarly, in tasks where subjects have to produce their own conclusions, they seem to strive to give a conclusion whenever they can, often producing sentences containing modals such as "may" of "might" in order to do so. This can be readily explained in terms of the preference for propositional conclusions, though it should be noted that other explanations are also possible [see, e.g. Johnson-Laird et al. (1989), who suggest that modals are used to describe a conclusion which is consistent with just one of the possible mental models].

Probabilistic Inference

Chapman and Chapman (1959) proposed that two mechanisms could explain syllogistic reasoning behaviour: conversion (which we have already discussed) and probabilistic inference. This latter refers to the assumption that entities which share common properties are likely to be similar in some way. To give a simple example, if the syllogism is of the kind:

Some A are B
Some C are B

then both A and C share the property of being Bs and hence they will be assumed to be linked in some way. This will produce the conclusion "Some A are C", which is a common error on this problem.

Stated simply, probabilistic inference claims that whenever the two end-terms share the middle term in common, they will be assumed to be related to each other, while otherwise they will be assumed not to be related. In other words, if the end-terms are related positively then a positive conclusion will be drawn, while if they are related negatively then a negative conclusion will be drawn. The astute reader may have already detected that this is virtually a restatement of the atmosphere principle of quality. The only difference is that the atmosphere principles are more precise; they indicate quite clearly which response should occur with which premise pairs, while probabilistic inference does not indicate which positive response (*all* or *some*) or which negative response (*no* or *some . . . not*) should occur. Any superior predictive power of the theory of probabilistic inference seems entirely attributable to its greater vagueness (e.g. Begg & Denny, 1969).

There are other arguments which go against the idea of probabilistic inference. As Dickstein (1981) has pointed out, Chapman and Chapman (1959) present no reasons as to why it should occur. They claim that such inferences are common in everyday life, but present no evidence to back this up, and it is far from clear that it is at all prevalent. In addition, one of the predictions can be contested. In the situation where neither of the two end-terms is related to the middle term, Chapman and Chapman (1959) predict that subjects will assume that the sets are unrelated. However, as Dickstein (1981) points out, one could just as well predict that the sets are related, since they share in common the property of not being related to the middle term! In defence of probabilistic inference, one might point out that the idea could have a firm basis in conversational conventions. It would be taken as a deliberate attempt to mislead if, during the course of a conversation, someone stated that "Some students are socialists and some socialists are revolutionaries", and intended the hearer *not* to draw the inference that some students are revolutionaries!

Despite his dissatisfaction with probabilistic inference, Dickstein (1981) puts forward an idea of his own which shares many features in common. He argues that people fail to fully grasp the significance of what is meant by logical necessity, and sometimes give conclusions that are possibly true rather than necessarily true. In syllogisms of the type just presented, the end-terms could be related, even though no relationship is necessarily present. Hence subjects incorrectly say that the conclusion (some A are C) is true. Dickstein found some evidence that instructions stressing the meaning of necessity led to improved performance, but only for invalid conclusions. This is an important, though somewhat neglected finding, since it suggests that an important source of error on syllogisms is failure to understand exactly what the task demands are. Since many studies of syllogistic reasoning do not give details of the instructions used, it is difficult to assess how widespread this problem is. We will return to the idea of misinterpreted necessity in the next chapter.

OVERVIEW OF THEORIES OF SYLLOGISTIC REASONING

As will have emerged from the previous discussion, there exists a mass of research on syllogistic reasoning, and there is no shortage of theories which attempt to explain the findings. However, in the course of the discussion, it has been possible to reject some of the approaches, and we are now in a position to take stock of all the competing theories. First, it would appear that at least one of the interpretational theories, conversion, plays a significant role in syllogistic reasoning. In addition, Gricean errors of interpretation certainly occur, but the evidence that they are a major source of reasoning errors is not conclusive.

Second, we can discount some theories put forward to explain how the two premises are combined. There was little empirical support for the suggestion by Erickson and by Sternberg that mental representations equivalent to Euler circles are used; nor was there firm evidence for the involvement of Venn diagrams or of formal rules. On the other hand, there was good support for the claim that there exist differences in the difficulty of the four syllogistic figures, which seems to suggest that subjects prefer to work through their mental representations in a forward direction. Further, there is a growing body of evidence which is consistent with the mental models theory, though this has largely investigated just one main prediction which may not clearly differentiate mental models theory from other contenders. In the next chapter, we consider research on belief bias effects which enables other predictions of the mental models approach to be tested.

Third, as regards response bias approaches, we can probably discount the claims that caution and probabilistic inference have a role to play. There is good evidence that some kind of response matching occurs, though this seems more likely to be matching the overall mood created by the two premises (i.e. atmosphere) than matching one of the quantifiers used in the premises. However, this approach lacks theoretical underpinning.

What, if any, conclusions can we draw from these findings? There appears to be only one theory that can even come close to explaining all these effects and that is the mental models theory. Conversion can readily be incorporated into the theory by allowing for the fact that subjects might on occasion overlook tokens that have been encoded into the representation but are in fact optional. As we have already seen, the model for the premise "All A are B" is as follows:

[a] b
[a] b
 . . .

In this model, the fact that there could be additional b's that are not a's is indicated by the absence of brackets around the b's. If, however, subjects forgot or failed to represent this fact, then conversion errors would appear (Johnson-Laird & Byrne, 1991). Figural effects can be accounted for in terms of the way in which the premises are integrated and the middle terms brought together. This is, in fact, one of the central assumptions of the theory, since it was devised, at least in part, to explain the directionality effects obtained in tasks where subjects are asked to generate their own conclusions (e.g. Johnson-Laird & Steedman, 1978). Atmosphere is a little more problematic, but can still be encompassed. As Johnson-Laird and Byrne (1991) point out, the predictions of the mental models theory are frequently the same as those made by atmosphere. The underlying mechanisms are very different, in one case being a response bias and in the other being an outcome of the way the premises are represented, but the end result can be very similar. It should perhaps be pointed out here that the predictions of the atmosphere theory are more precise than those of mental models theory. Atmosphere always predicts just one response for any pair of premises, whereas mental models has the power to explain any one of several responses. Part of the attraction of the mental models approach is that it can explain a variety of responses, but this is at the price of not always making specific predictions about the precise conclusion that will be produced.

The success of the mental models approach in explaining the findings should not blind us to the fact that it has problems of its own. It has generated one main prediction which has been widely supported, but investigation of a broader range of predictions is desirable. Nor should it be assumed that it is necessarily the case that a single theory will be able to explain all the findings. It is far from implausible to suggest that the final explanation will encompass elements of conversion theory, elements of atmosphere theory and elements drawn from elsewhere.

There is in fact considerable evidence that there exist individual differences in the way people solve syllogisms. As has already been seen, Galotti et al. (1986) found that "expert" reasoners developed short-cut strategies that less skilful reasoners failed to develop. Widespread individual differences in the tendency to make conversion errors have also been reported (Newstead & Griggs, 1983a; Newstead, 1989). Wetherick and Gilhooly (1990) report two different kinds of subjects in their experiment—those who matched and those who were logical. Matsuno (1987) has reported differences in accuracy in solving syllogisms between people with different representational strategies and different cognitive styles. A similar finding emerged in Guyote and Sternberg's (1981) study, since they found that reasoning ability correlated with performance on a psychometric test of spatial ability. Furthermore, the information-processing models of Erickson (1974) and Guyote and Sternberg (1981) assume individual differences at all levels of processing, whether this be interpretation of the premises, premise combination or response generation. Similarly, Johnson-Laird and Byrne (1991) acknowledge that there may well be individual differences in the mental models constructed and in the search for counterexamples.

Any comprehensive theory of syllogistic reasoning will need to encompass these individual differences. It may be the case that a number of the theories we have discussed are correct, but for different subjects and in different situations. Alternatively, it may prove possible to explain all these findings within a single, all-embracing theory such as that of mental models. Parsimony dictates the latter, but only further empirical research will finally resolve this issue.

Although this is the end of our main discussion of the theories of syllogistic reasoning, we return to these in the next chapter. Some of the theories we have discussed here have been tested not just on syllogisms but on other types of problems as well, for example those involving multiple quantifiers or multiple premises. We will also consider in the next chapter the use of syllogisms in studies of the effects of belief on reasoning.

8 Reasoning with Quantifiers: Beyond Syllogisms

In the previous chapter, we considered syllogistic reasoning and the many theories that have been put forward to explain the responses that subjects typically give. In the present chapter, we consider a wide range of other studies involving quantifiers. The first section looks at belief bias; this research has typically used categorical syllogisms, not with the aim of understanding the processes involved in syllogistic reasoning but as a way of studying the effects of non-logical factors on reasoning in general. The second section looks at research on extended syllogisms, or sorites; these involve more than two premises and produce an unusual and still unexplained pattern of results. The final section examines studies of multiple quantifiers, an area which has only recently attracted research interest.

BELIEF BIAS

The term "belief bias" has a rather strange and restricted usage. Belief bias occurs whenever a person gives a response which is determined by the believability of the conclusion rather than by logical validity. Such effects can be studied using any type of reasoning behaviour, but it seems that this is referred to as belief bias only when syllogisms are used. Indeed, the phenomenon is so closely tied to syllogistic reasoning, that when it occurs in other areas such as Wason's selection task (see Chapter 5) or the THOG problem (see Chapter 6), it tends to be called by a different name such as memory cueing or the effects of content.

The reason for the identification of belief bias with syllogisms seems to be largely historical. Certainly, it has been known right from the beginning of psychological research on syllogisms that the type of material used can affect the responses produced (Wilkins, 1928). It has often been found that people are more ready to accept conclusions that they believe to be true than they are to accept conclusions they believe to be false. For example, subjects would be more likely to accept as valid a syllogism leading to the conclusion "All dogs are animals" than they would one leading to the conclusion "All dogs are rabbits", even if the underlying logic to the two syllogisms was identical. This result has been extensively documented in the literature, some of the best known early studies being those of Gordon (1953), Feather (1964), Henle and Michael (1956), Janis and Frick (1943) Kaufman and Goldstein (1967) and Morgan and Morton (1944). Some of these studies are methodologically flawed, but the basic effect remains even when these flaws are removed (Evans, Barston & Pollard, 1983).

The effect can perhaps best be illustrated with an example from one of the earlier studies. Henle and Michael (1956) gave subjects syllogisms including the following:

All Russians are Bolsheviks
Some Bolsheviks regiment people

There is no valid conclusion to this syllogism, but those subjects with an anti-Russian attitude might be inclined to endorse the invalid conclusion that "All Russians regiment people". There was a slight effect of this kind in Henle and Michael's study, though this was a much smaller effect than had been found previously by Morgan and Morton (1944) using not dissimilar syllogisms. One of the reasons for this discrepancy may be that Henle and Michael, working in the Cold War climate of the 1950s, were unable to obtain "a pro-Russian group large enough for statistical treatment" (1956, p. 122). Hence their comparison was made between an anti-Russian group and a neutral one. Henle and Michael's study is the exception; the great majority of these early studies reported significant effects of belief bias, with subjects being much more likely to endorse believable than non-believable conclusions irrespective of their logical validity.

An interesting finding which has emerged recently in the belief bias literature is that of an interaction between logic and belief. The basic finding is that the effects of belief are stronger on invalid syllogisms than on valid ones (or, looked at from a different perspective, that the effects of logical validity are stronger on syllogisms leading to unbelievable conclusions). The pattern of results obtained by Evans et al. (1983) is shown in Table 8.1. It can be seen that the effects of belief are much stronger on invalid syllogisms than on valid ones; the difference between acceptance of believable and unbelievable conclusions is 61% with invalid syllogisms, but only 33% with valid ones. It should also be noted that this

TABLE 8.1
Overall Percentage of Acceptance of Conclusions as a Function of Logical Validity and Believability in the Study of Evans et al. (1983)

	Believable	*Unbelievable*	*Mean*
Valid	89	56	*72*
Invalid	71	10	*40*
Mean	80	33	

study provides an excellent illustration of the basic belief bias effect; subjects are much more likely to accept believable conclusions (80% acceptance overall) than unbelievable ones (33% acceptance), irrespective of logical validity.

Interestingly, many of the demonstrations of the effects of belief bias occurred in the context of social psychology, and focused on the social processes underlying the effect rather than attempting to model the cognitive processes. There are, however, many important questions that arise; for example, does the belief bias effect stem from a misinterpretation of the premises, from faulty reasoning or from a response bias? Perhaps the most prevalent view has been that the effect derives from a response bias, but other sources have been proposed and have received empirical support. In the following review of theories of belief bias, we consider four main approaches: conversion theory; selective scrutiny; misinterpreted necessity; and mental models. Before considering these, it may be useful to reiterate the basic findings that any theory must explain:

- Believable conclusions are more readily accepted than unbelievable ones.
- Logically valid conclusions are more readily accepted than invalid ones.
- There is an interaction between logical validity and believability such that the effects of believability are more marked on invalid conclusions.

As we shall see, the various theories tend to explain quite well one or two of these findings, but seldom provide a complete account of all the findings.

Conversion Theory

Recent interest in belief bias effects can be traced back to Revlin's work (Revlin & Leirer, 1978; Revlin, Leirer, Yopp & Yopp, 1980). In these studies, the authors claimed that belief bias effects were primarily attributable to conversion blocking. Revlin, it will be remembered from Chapter 7, is one of the main champions of conversion theory, who claims that, conversion aside, subjects will tend to reason logically. Belief bias provides evidence of illogical reasoning, and hence it is important for Revlin to be able to provide some explanation for it. This he does by arguing that believability can affect the interpretation of the premises and that subjects reason logically from such interpretations. Revlin et al. give the following example:

All Russians are Bolsheviks
Some Bolsheviks are undemocratic people

There is in fact no valid conclusion linking undemocratic people and Russians, but if subjects convert the first premise, believing "All Bolsheviks are Russians" to be true, then the conclusion "Some undemocratic people are Russian" follows logically. This is precisely the kind of believable conclusion that subjects have been found to endorse. Note, however, that in Revlin's explanation, the effect arises solely from the interpretation of the premises, and has nothing to do with the believability of the conclusion as such.

The actual syllogisms studied by Revlin et al. (1980) were of the following kind:

No black people in Newton are residents of Sea Side
All black people in Newton are welfare recipients

They argued that subjects would convert the second premise, since they would find the statement "all welfare recipients are black" readily believable. This would lead to predictable errors, and Revlin et al. confirmed that such errors occurred. Similarly, Agnoli (1978) found that reasoning performance improved when conversion was blocked by using realistic material. However, these studies have been roundly criticised on a number of occasions (Evans et al., 1983; Oakhill, Johnson-Laird & Garnham, 1989). In particular, it has been found that strong belief bias effects occur on syllogisms where conversion makes no difference—a finding which also emerged in one of the experiments reported by Revlin et al. (1980). In addition, conversion theory has never attempted to explain the interaction between logic and belief, and it is difficult to envisage how any such explanation could be constructed. At best, conversion blocking is only a fairly small part of the explanation of belief bias.

Selective Scrutiny

The traditional, though often implicit, explanation of belief bias has been that it is a response bias; in other words, it is assumed that subjects effectively ignore the logic of the problem and respond purely on the basis of the believability of the conclusion. This account is almost certainly wrong, since it does not allow for the effects of logical validity or for the interaction between logic and belief. However, a more recent and more sophisticated version of this approach, the selective scrutiny theory, merits more serious consideration.

The term was first used by Barston (1986; see also Evans, 1989), but the idea was first proposed by Evans et al. (1983). These authors claimed that subjects focus on the conclusion to the syllogism and, if this is believable, accept it without looking any further. This means, of course, that subjects do not even look at the premises of such believable syllogisms. Their main evidence in favour of this rather surprising suggestion was derived from verbal protocols taken from subjects thinking out loud as they carried out the logical task. Note that most of these verbalisations were concurrent, and hence are more likely to be accurate than would be retrospective reports (Ericsson & Simon, 1980). The protocols revealed three main types of strategy: "conclusion only", where subjects referred only to the conclusion and not to the premise(s); "conclusion to premises", where subjects referred first to the conclusion and only subsequently to the premise(s); and "premises to conclusion", where subjects mentioned the premise(s) before the conclusion. Each of these strategies was adopted by approximately one-third of the subjects. Subjects were more likely to respond according to the believability of the conclusion if they were classified as using one of the first two strategies, i.e. those in which the conclusion is scanned first. This suggests that these subjects were basing their decision primarily on the conclusion, without considering the premises to any great extent. It is worth noting, however, that even these subjects were influenced by the logic of the syllogisms, and hence cannot have ignored the premises completely.

According to the selective scrutiny account, when subjects encounter an unbelievable conclusion, they then carry out an analysis of the logic of the problem (though the theory is silent as to how this logical processing is carried out). The full selective scrutiny is presented diagrammatically in Fig. 8.1. As can be seen from this decision tree, subjects are assumed to look initially at the conclusion; if this is believable they accept it without further ado, but if it is unbelievable they carry out a logical analysis to determine whether they should accept it.

This account readily explains the interaction between logic and belief, since logical analysis occurs only for unbelievable conclusions. It does not, however, explain why there are effects of logic on believable conclusions. As can be seen in Table 8.1, although the effect of logical validity is lower for believable conclusions, it is still present. Additionally, as Oakhill and Johnson-Laird (1985) have found, belief bias effects still occur when subjects generate their own conclusions and hence where there is no given conclusion to selectively scrutinise. Indeed, Markovits and Nantel (1989) found that the effects of belief were more marked when subjects generated

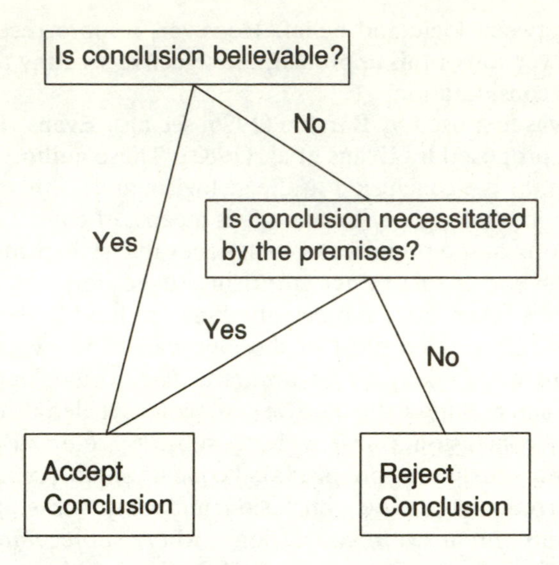

FIG. 8.1 The selective scrutiny model of belief bias.

their own conclusions. The theory also has difficulty in explaining the finding, discussed in the next section, that the interaction between belief and logic disappears with certain types of syllogisms; this theory has to predict that the interaction will be present irrespective of the logical status of the syllogism, since believability is ascertained before any logical processing occurs. However, the theory does predict, for exactly the same reasons, the finding of Evans and Pollard (1990) that there was no interaction between the size of the belief bias effect and the complexity of the problem. The theory can be modified to account for some of the findings it does not currently explain, but it would appear that this theory, despite considerable evidence in its favour, does not provide a fully comprehensive account of all the findings.

Misinterpreted Necessity

This account was proposed by Barston (1986; see also Evans et al., 1983; Evans, 1989) and is based on the ideas of Dickstein (1981). Dickstein claimed that subjects often misinterpret what is meant by logical necessity. In reasoning experiments, subjects are asked to indicate that a conclusion does not follow when it is not necessitated by the premises. For example, given the syllogism:

All A are B
All C are B

subjects must reject the conclusion "All A are C". This is despite the fact that this conclusion could possibly be true; there are situations (e.g. when the three sets are identical) in which this is a valid conclusion, but since there are also situations (e.g. when one of the sets is a subset of the other) where it is an invalid conclusion, it must be rejected. The misinterpreted necessity account claims that, in a situation where a conclusion is possible but not necessary, subjects respond on the basis of the believability of the conclusion. If the above indeterminate syllogism had been:

All trout are fish
All cod are fish

subjects would reject the conclusion that "All trout are cod" on the basis of its unbelievability. But if a believable conclusion had been produced (such as "All trout are animals"), they would accept it. However, the effects of believability would not be present if the syllogism had been determinately invalid. For example, the syllogism:

All A are B
All B are C
Therefore,
No A are C

is clearly invalid, and there is no way of construing the premises in which this conclusion would be valid. Hence this is a determinately invalid syllogism, and no effects of belief bias would be expected on these.

The misinterpreted necessity model can once again be envisaged as a decision tree, as presented in Fig. 8.2. Subjects first of all decide whether

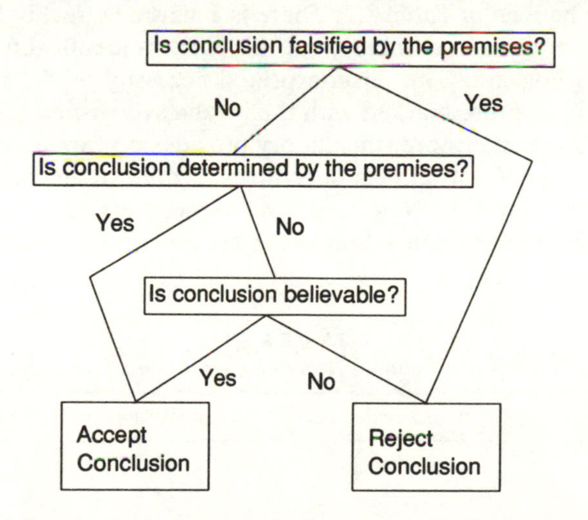

FIG. 8.2 The misinterpreted necessity model of belief bias.

the conclusion is falsified (i.e. rendered logically invalid) by the premises, and if it is they reject it. However, if the conclusion is not falsified, subjects ascertain whether the conclusion is determined by the premises. If it is—in other words, if the conclusion is logically valid—then it is accepted. On the other hand, if the conclusion is not determined by the premises (i.e. if it is indeterminate), then it is responded to on the basis of its believabiilty.

This model readily explains the belief by logic interaction, since belief operates only on invalid syllogisms. The model also explains why the interaction between logic and belief disappears if determinately invalid syllogisms are used (Newstead, Pollard, Evans & Allen, 1992). (As can be seen in Fig. 8.2, it is only on indeterminate syllogisms that believability has an effect.) However, the theory does make a very specific prediction about the belief bias effect itself; that it will occur primarily, or at least more markedly, with syllogisms leading to indeterminately invalid conclusions. Recent evidence has called this into question (Newstead et al., 1992). Consider, for example, the following syllogism:

All fish are phylones
All phylones are trout
Therefore,
All fish are trout

This is a determinately valid syllogism. If, however, the conclusion had been reversed to "All trout are fish", it would have been indeterminately invalid (i.e. it would not logically follow that there are situations in which it could be true). One would expect there to be particularly dramatic belief bias effects on this latter syllogism. The results, however, show no such thing, as can be seen in Table 8.2. There is a marked effect of believability (about which more in a moment), but this effect is identical for both valid and invalid syllogisms. The misinterpreted necessity model predicts that the effects will be more marked with the invalid syllogisms, since these are indeterminate. Furthermore, this theory provides no explanation as to the occurrence of belief bias effects on syllogisms other than those which are indeterminately invalid. Newstead and co-workers' study, like many others, has provided evidence that belief has an effect on valid syllogisms,

TABLE 8.2
Effects of Validity and Belief in Newstead and Co-workers' Experiment 3

	Believable	*Unbelievable*	*Mean*
Valid	92	68	80
Invalid	62	38	50
Mean	77	53	

and the misinterpreted necessity model has to make additional assumptions to explain these effects. Hence it has to be concluded that this theory, too, is inadequate as an explanation of belief bias effects.

Mental Models

There are a number of different strands to the mental models explanation of belief bias. The basic idea is that believability determines how far subjects will go in constructing alternative models to try to falsify the preliminary conclusion they have reached. It is assumed that subjects construct an initial mental model of the premises (see Chapter 7 for a discussion of how this is done) and then generate a conclusion compatible with this model. If this conclusion is believable, then no further processing will take place and the conclusion will be accepted. If, however, the initial conclusion is unbelievable, subjects will be motivated to search for alternative models which will falsify the conclusion (Oakhill & Johnson-Laird, 1985).

This leads to a number of specific and testable predictions. First, there should be no effects of believability on single-model syllogisms, since believability only has its effects on the construction of alternative models where these exist, i.e. on multiple-model syllogisms. This prediction was tested, and found to be wrong, by Oakhill et al. (1989), who found strong belief bias effects on single-model syllogisms. They suggested that the mental models theory be modified to include the concept of "conclusion filtering". This involves subjects rejecting conclusions that they have reached on the grounds that they are unbelievable and either substituting a believable conclusion or saying that no conclusion follows. While this saves the theory, it is clearly something of an *ad hoc* device.

It may be possible to explain why believability has an effect on single-model syllogisms without resorting to conclusion filtering. It may be that when subjects generate an unbelievable conclusion from a single-model syllogism, they try to construct a falsifying model, even though none exists. If this search is error-prone (e.g. if subjects erroneously generate a second model), this can explain the occurrence of errors.

A diagrammatic representation of the mental models theory as it might operate in a conclusion evaluation task is presented in Fig. 8.3. It is assumed that subjects construct a model of the premises and then ascertain if the given conclusion is consistent with this model. If it is not, then the conclusion can be immediately rejected. If the conclusion is consistent with the model, then the believability of the conclusion is examined, and if it is found to be believable it is accepted. If it is unbelievable, subjects attempt to generate alternative models which can falsify it. If there are no such alternative models which invalidate the conclusion it is accepted, but

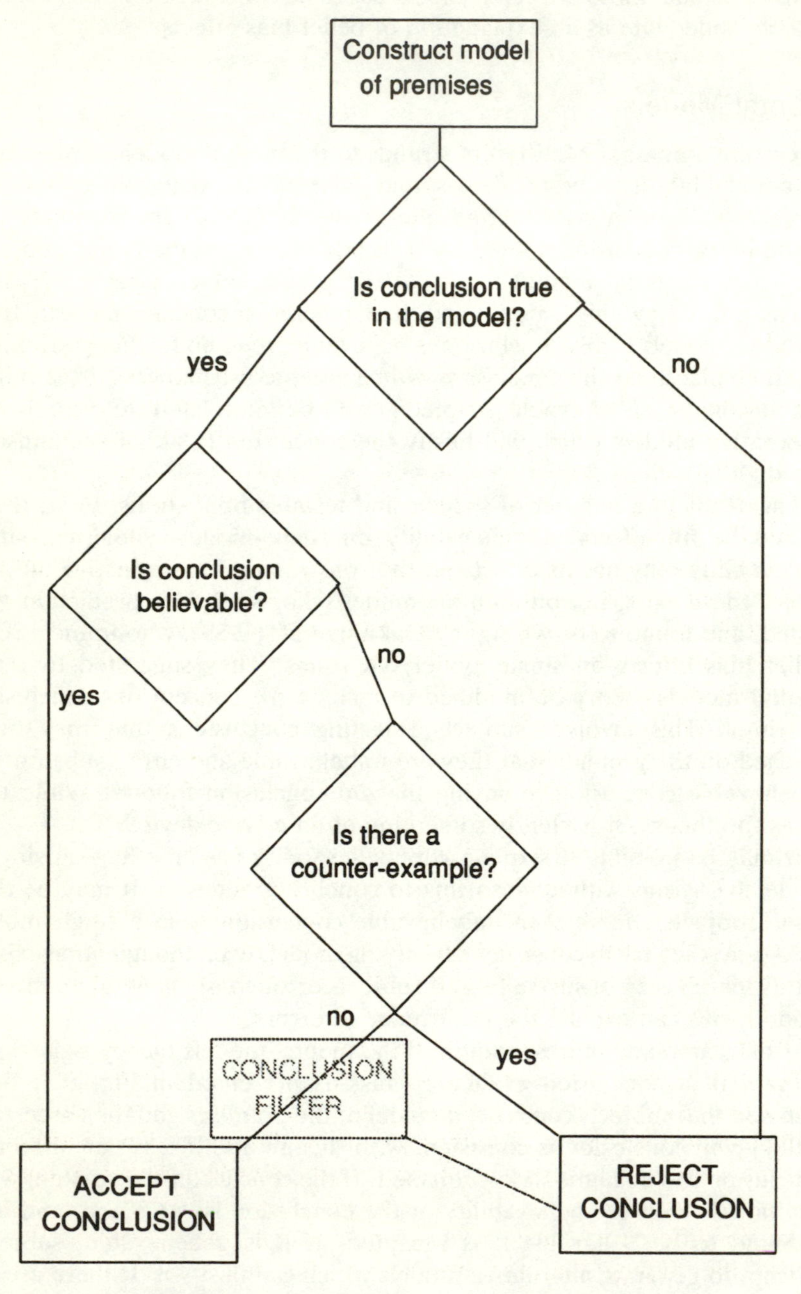

FIG. 8.3 The mental models account of belief bias.

if there are it is rejected. Conclusion filtering, if it occurs, presumably happens following the failure to find an alternative model, and is depicted at this stage in Fig. 8.3. The alternative approach mentioned in the previous paragraph would maintain that errors occur in the attempt to construct counterexamples following the finding of an unbelievable conclusion.

This theory is rather involved, but it generates further testable predictions. Oakhill et al. (1989) investigated whether the believability of "suggested" conclusions influenced the acceptance of conclusions. For example, one of the syllogisms they used was the following:

Some of the houseowners are married
None of the houseowners is a bachelor

It is valid to draw the conclusion that "Some of the married people are not bachelors", but there are other believable conclusions that are "suggested" in the sense that they are compatible with at least one of the models that can be constructed for this syllogism, for example "None of the married people is a bachelor" or "Some of the bachelors are not married". Since these alternative suggested conclusions are believable, they might well be erroneously accepted. The mental models theory predicts that subjects would be more likely to make errors when there are highly believable suggested conclusions (as in the example just given) than in the situation where the alternative conclusions are less believable. This prediction was confirmed by Oakhill et al., but only for invalid syllogisms; with valid syllogisms, such as that just presented, there was no effect of the believability of the suggested conclusion.

This finding is not easily explained by the mental models theory. It suggests that subjects somehow know whether a conclusion is valid before analysing its believability, and yet validity can only be determined after a full examination of the potential falsifying models. This does not fit well with the theory, since as can be seen in Fig. 8.3, believability is assumed to have its effect prior to the construction of falsifying models.This suggests the need for yet further modifications to the original mental models explanation.

Other predictions of the theory were put to the test by Newstead et al. (1992), with generally positive results. In a series of experiments, they found that the interaction between logic and belief occurred only with multiple-model syllogisms. The theory explains this interaction by assuming that the search for falsifying solutions is curtailed when the initial conclusion is believable (see Fig. 8.3). For single-model syllogisms, this should make no difference, since there are no falsifying models to be found. Hence the finding that the interaction (but not the main effect of believability) disappears for single-model syllogisms clearly confirms one of the predictions of the theory. A further experiment by Newstead et al. (1992) confirmed another prediction of the theory, that instructions stressing the importance of logical analysis (and hence presumably the importance of constructing alternative models) also reduced the interaction.

There is thus a growing body of evidence to support the mental models approach. However, the theory is not without problems. The concept of filtering, if it is retained as part of the theory, is something of an *ad hoc* device for explaining an unpredicted finding. In addition, the just-mentioned finding that instructions stressing the importance of logical processing reduce the magnitude of the interaction has not proved easy to replicate (Evans, Allen, Newstead & Pollard, 1993). Furthermore, it may be necessary to modify the theory to accommodate the difference between valid and invalid syllogisms found by Oakhill et al. (1989). The theory has considerable promise, but it cannot at the moment be claimed to explain all the findings.

Overview of Theories

This recent research on belief bias confirms once again that the effect does exist. On occasions, a small number of syllogisms have not produced the effect, but for the great majority it has been found time after time. As regards the locus of the effect, we suspect that interpretational factors (in the guise of conversion theory) do not play a major role. It is true that conversion blocking may play a minor part, but there is ample evidence that belief bias exists in a seemingly undiminished form even when conversion is completely controlled for. Both the selective scrutiny and the misinterpreted necessity models have sound evidence in their favour, but they also make predictions which are not confirmed by the data. Mental models theory has a number of findings supporting its predictions and no findings which directly contradict it. However, this latter is partly due to the fact that the theory is being constantly developed and modified, and has the flexibility to adapt to new findings. This is both a strength and a weakness of the theory: it is a strength in that it can explain a wide range of phenomena, a weakness in that it is not always possible to devise ways of testing to destruction its predictions.

Although the mental models and selective scrutiny theories are seemingly quite disparate, it may be possible to bring them together. One possibility, for example, is that they each explain the behaviour of some subjects. We have seen in the work of Evans et al. (1983) that verbal protocols reveal rather different approaches to the task; and those subjects who focus primarily on the conclusion may well be found to give results best explained by the selective scrutiny theory, while those who scan the premises first may be mental modellers. The main difference between the two theories is that mental models theory assumes that some processing occurs before the effects of belief come into operation, while the selective scrutiny account allows for believability having an influence in the complete absence of any attempt at logical processing. It seems possible that both may occur in different people and in different situations. If this is so, then a challenge that remains in this area is to develop an integrated theory which allows for this.

EXTENDED SYLLOGISMS

Extended syllogisms are referred to technically as sorites, and are usually called set inclusions in the psychological literature. They contain more than the two premises found in classical syllogisms. They permit a valid conclusion only when the quantifier *all* is used. The following is a schematic representation of an extended syllogism:

All A are B
All B are C
All C are D

In the majority of studies that have been conducted, concrete terms have been used. For some reason, that is not particularly clear, the following problem has been widely used:

All the Fundalas of Central Ugala are outcasts
All the outcasts of Central Ugala are hill people
All the hill people of Central Ugala are farmers
All the farmers of Central Ugala are pacifists

From this it is valid to conclude that all the Fundalas are farmers, or that they are all pacifists, or that all the outcasts are farmers, and so on. It is not valid to conclude that the pacifists are hill people, that the farmers are Fundalas, and so on. In other words, any forward inference is valid but any backward inference is invalid.

In a typical task, subjects are presented with the premises and then asked to indicate whether a series of statements are true or false. Returning to the schematic representation of the problem, subjects would be given all possible statements ("All A are B", "All A are C", "All A are D", "All B are C", "All B are D" and "All C are D") and the converses of these ("All B are A", etc.). As mentioned above, it is valid to make all forward inferences but people are not very good at doing so. Furthermore, they become progressively worse over inferential distance (Griggs, 1976). Thus subjects are accurate with adjacent items (i.e. items which correspond to the original premises, e.g. "All A are B"), less good

TABLE 8.3
The Truth by Distance Interaction

Inferential Distance	*True (i.e. Forward Statements)*	*False (i.e. Backward Statements)*
0	0.76 (0.82)	0.47 (0.82)
1	0.67 (0.86)	0.59 (0.84)
2	0.65 (0.88)	0.61 (0.87)

The data present the proportion of correct responses. Figures in parentheses are for linear orderings. *Source*: Griggs (1976).

with inferential items at a distance of 1 (e.g. "All A are C") and even worse on items at a distance of 2 ("All A are D"). (Performance continues to decline over inferential distances of greater than 2 if these are used.)

Under the instructions normally used on these tasks, subjects should say that reverse items such as "All B are A" are false, since *all* statements do not imply the truth of their converses. However, subjects have a tendency to call these statements true, a tendency which increases over inferential distance. In other words, accuracy on forward, or true, items decreases over inferential distance while that on backward, or false, items increases. This pattern of results is referred to as the truth by distance interaction and is presented in Table 8.3. The pattern of results is very easy to replicate, but less easy to explain.

Part of the fascination of these results is that they are in such sharp contrast to what is found with linear orderings (see Chapter 6). These latter involve relationships such as "A is bigger than B, B is bigger than C, C is bigger than D". Exactly the same conclusions are valid as with set inclusions, since all forward inferences are true and all backward inferences are false. The overall level of accuracy is much higher with linear orderings, in general around 90% for all inferences (see the figures in parentheses in Table 8.3). What is more, accuracy on all items tends actually to increase over inferential distance. The question that arises, then, is that of why performance should be so much worse, and so radically different, in the set inclusion task. The explanations that have been proferred include conversion theory, misinterpretation of *all*, schema cueing and response bias.

Conversion Theory

Clearly, the tendency to say that *all* statements imply their converses (i.e. to endorse backward inferences) is our old friend the conversion error, and it is not surprising that this has been a popular explanation of this response (e.g. Griggs, 1976; 1978). One slight problem with this approach is the sheer number of errors made. As can be seen in Table 8.3, subjects endorse the converse of *all* statements 47% of the time, whereas most estimates of the frequency of conversion errors suggest that this is around 30% (e.g. Newstead & Griggs, 1983a). However, there is good empirical evidence for the claim that conversion errors are involved. Newstead and Griggs (1983a) found that conversion errors as determined in an immediate inference task (see Chapter 7) correlated significantly with conversion errors on extended syllogisms.

However, this does not constitute a complete explanation of the truth by distance interaction. It does not explain, for example, why conversion errors should decline over distance, nor why subjects should fail to draw the permitted transitive inferences. Conversion may be part—but it is only part—of the explanation of the errors.

Misinterpretation of *All*

Conversion involves one type of misinterpretation of *all*, but others have been suggested. One proposal is that *all* is interpreted fuzzily; in other words, it is taken to mean *almost all* rather than being interpreted strictly. If subjects do interpret *all* fuzzily, then they might be disinclined to draw transitive inferences, since transitivity does not hold for a sequence of premises involving *almost all* rather than *all*.

This possibility was investigated by Newstead and Griggs (1984), but their study produced ambiguous results. Subjects were assessed as to their interpretations of *all* by asking them to indicate how good this quantifier was as a description of certain situations. In the critical case, the subjects were asked to indicate how good *all* was as a descriptor of the situation in which there was just one exception out of several hundred instances. Those subjects who indicated that it was a moderately good descriptor were assessed as adopting fuzzy interpretations, and they did indeed make more errors on the set inclusion task. However, these errors were predominantly conversion errors, not the transitivity errors the authors had predicted. Hence this theory, too, is of dubious value in explaining the truth by distance interaction.

Schema Cueing

Mynatt and Smith (1979) proposed that the errors might be due to inappropriate schema cueing. They suggested that subjects incorrectly interpret the statements as describing property relationships; thus the statement "All A are B" is taken to mean something like "All As have property B". They claim that the Fundalas passage that has been so often used reads like a set of statements about the attributes of Fundalas. Such a list would not possess the properties of transitivity, and hence such inferences would not be drawn. In other words, subjects are cued into the wrong schema and simply fail to see that the relationship involved is one of set inclusion.

Mynatt and Smith (1979) found that performance could be significantly improved if the appropriate schema was cued in by making it clear that the relationship was one of inclusion. They achieved this by using topographical inclusions ("A is in B") rather than the more typical kind of material. Griggs and Warner (1982) also found evidence to support this claim. In their study, they were able to elicit the appropriate schema by putting the premises in bald syllogistic format, which presumably led subjects to interpret them in a more strictly logical way. However, performance was still far from accurate, and so this theory, too, fails to provide a full account of performance on set inclusions.

Response Bias

The failure of other theories prompted Newstead, Pollard and Griggs (1986) to suggest that there might be a response bias to assume that any relationship is reversible and decreasingly transitive. There were some grounds for proposing this in the work of Tsal (1977). He found that subjects given an unknown relationship (it was depicted by a straight line) assumed that the relationship was both transitive and reversible, though he did not check whether transitivity declined over inferential distance.

Newstead et al. investigated this tendency in two ways. They gave subjects set inclusions in which the relationship was not specified but was indicated by a line or by an asterisk. The results were very similar to those obtained in standard set inclusion tasks, lending support to the response bias theory. However, a second prediction, that similar results would be obtained regardless of the quantifier used, was not confirmed. Response bias could well be a contributory factor in explaining set inclusions, but it is not the only factor.

Overview of Work on Extended Syllogisms

It should be clear that there is no satisfactory explanation of performance on extended syllogisms. There is good evidence that conversion errors occur and are part of the explanation, but neither conversion nor any other theory can adequately explain why transitive inferences decline over inferential distance. The most promising explanation seems to be in terms of schema cueing, but thus far this has only limited evidence in its favour. Hence we are still some way from knowing the precise source of difficulty on this task. Sadly, it has produced little research and no new ideas over the last few years, and hence an early solution to this puzzling pattern of responding is unlikely to be forthcoming.

MULTIPLE QUANTIFIERS

Research on multiple quantifiers is still very much in its infancy, with just a handful of studies having been conducted, and all of these within the last few years. One reason for the lack of research in this area may well be the sheer complexity of the problems. Consider, for example, the following pair of premises, used by Johnson-Laird et al. (1989):

> None of the Princeton letters is in the same place as any of the Cambridge letters
> All of the Cambridge letters are in the same place as some of the Dublin letters

Unlike classical syllogisms, there are now two quantifiers in each premise (*none* and *any* in the first, *all* and *some* in the second). It is valid to conclude from these premises that "None of the Princeton letters is in the same place as some of the Dublin letters" (or equivalently, "Some of the Dublin letters are not in the same place as any of the Princeton letters"). Perhaps not surprisingly, subjects found these problems difficult, with an overall average success rate of around 40%. As we shall see shortly, there were also interesting differences between problems, and in fact the problem given above proved to be among the most difficult (about 25% correct).

Despite their difficulty, multiply-quantified problems can shed considerable light on some of the theoretical issues surrounding reasoning with quantifiers. One of their advantages is that they have been so little studied in the past. This means that they can provide a test bed for theories of quantificational reasoning in an area that has not been previously tried. We have already seen in Chapter 7 that most of the theories that have been proposed fare reasonably well in explaining performance on syllogistic reasoning tasks. Most of them were proposed specifically to explain the pattern of errors that has been found, and so it would be surprising if they did not have some success in doing so. Hence there is a strong case to be made for testing such theories, not on the syllogisms they were designed to explain but on related inferences. Hence multiply-quantified problems provide a novel way of testing these theories. Any theory which does not explain the obtained results would not thereby be disproved but it would be weakened; conversely, any theory which accurately predicts the results will be strengthened.

The principal finding that has emerged from experiments on multiply-quantified sentences is that some problems are consistently harder than others. The problem described above is one of the more difficult ones, but the following, superficially similar, problem is considerably easier:

> None of the Princeton letters is in the same place as any of the Cambridge letters
> All of the Cambridge letters are in the same place as all of the Dublin letters

These premises support the conclusion that "None of the Princeton letters is in the same place as any of the Dublin letters". Accuracy on such problems was typically in excess of 60%.

It is fruitful to explore how the various theories of syllogistic reasoning fare in explaining these findings (see Chapter 7). The various approaches will be considered in turn, but not in the same order as in Chapter 7. The obvious place to start is with mental models theory, since this is the theory that inspired Johnson-Laird and co-workers' (1989) research and which they claim is strongly supported by their data. We will then consider other processing theories of syllogistic reasoning, then interpretational theories and finally response generation approaches.

Mental Models

Johnson-Laird et al. (1989) point out that the problems found to be easiest are single-model ones, while the more complex ones are multiple-model problems. If we take the problem just presented, the first premise can be represented using the following model:

| p p p | c c c |

where *p* represents a Princeton letter, *c* a Cambridge letter, and the vertical barrier means that the items are in different spatial locations. The second premise can be added quite straightforwardly to this model:

| p p p | c c c d d d |

This supports the conclusion that "None of the Princeton letters is in the same place as any of the Dublin letters", and what is more there is no other way of construing the premises which falsify this putative conclusion. Hence this is a valid, single-model syllogism. This is in contrast to the first problem given at the beginning of this section for which there are three quite distinct models which support different conclusions. One such model is that given immediately above, another is the following:

| p p p | c c c d d d | p o d

The last section of this model allows for the possibility that there may be Dublin letters in the same place as Princeton letters, a model which falsifies the conclusion "None of the Princeton letters is in the same place as any of the Dublin letters".

Johnson-Laird and co-workers' (1989) data lent strong support to the prediction that multiple-model problems would be harder than single-model ones. A particularly important finding is that the single-model problem:

None of the X are related to any of the Y
Some of the Y are related to all of the X

is significantly harder than the problem:

None of the X are related to any of the Y
All of the Y are related to some of the Z

This finding is important because the two problems use exactly the same quantifiers, the only difference being in the order in which they occur in the second premise. However, the problems lead to different numbers of mental models, and hence mental models theory can explain the finding that they are very different in their level of difficulty; alternative explanations, for example in terms of differences in the quantifiers used, are effectively ruled out.

Other Processing Theories

Theories involving Euler circles or Venn diagrams have difficulty with multiply-quantified sentences, since there is no way of representing the information contained in such sentences using such techniques (see Johnson-Laird & Byrne, 1991). It is possible that subjects try to do so and fail, but it is not easy to draw specific predictions based on such theories. It seems, however, intrinsically unlikely that subjects are using such representations with multiply-quantified problems given the lack of evidence that such representations are used in syllogistic reasoning (see Chapter 7).

Formal rules can be applied to multiply-quantified sentences, though no complete account has yet been offered. Johnson-Laird et al. (1989) put forward their own version of a formal rules theory, but the predictions made by this were directly contradicted by the data.

Interpretational Approaches

It is not easy to see how conversion theory would explain the data from studies of multiple quantifiers. However, one prediction that might be made is that subjects would treat the premise "Some of the Y are related to all of the X" as synonymous with the premise "All of the X are related to some of the Y". That they do not is clearly indicated by the previously mentioned finding that problems with these two sentences as their second premise but which were otherwise identical led to very different levels of difficulty.

According to Gricean theory, one reason for the difficulty of syllogisms is that subjects interpret *some* in its conversational sense (meaning *some but not all*) rather than its logical sense (*at least one and possibly all*). This cannot really explain why certain problems are more difficult than others, since there are no problems which lead to different conclusions depending on whether Gricean or non-Gricean interpretations are adopted. However, the ambiguity of *some* is an important component of a theory which does seem to explain at least some of the data. Greene (1992) has pointed out that all the valid multiple-model syllogisms in Johnson-Laird and co-workers' (1989) studies led to *none–some* conclusions such as "None of the X are in the same place as some of the Y". Greene claimed that such sentences are both unusual and ambiguous and that this might explain why they are so difficult. He showed experimentally that such sentences were rarely produced as descriptors of an appropriate state of affairs, and that subjects rarely gave such sentences the reading that Johnson-Laird et al. claimed was the preferred one, that there is at least one Y which is not in the same place as any X. In fact, the preferred reading appeared to be one in which *none–some* meant the same thing as *none–any*. Johnson-Laird, Byrne and Tabossi (1992b) concede that this may be the case but believe that mental models can quite readily encompass this finding. Nevertheless, Greene has sounded a useful note of caution. Neither linguists nor psychologists have yet developed a full understanding of the determinants of the scope of quantifiers (see Moxey & Sanford, in press, for a recent review), and until they do it may prove difficult to disentangle such effects in studies of multiply-quantified sentences.

Response Generation Theories

In Chapter 7, it was concluded that atmosphere theory provided a reasonable though incomplete description of the data from syllogistic reasoning tasks, although it did not really explain them. Atmosphere does not provide an adequate account of performance on multiply-quantified problems. Very few of the responses given in Johnson-Laird and co-workers' (1989) study could be accounted for by atmosphere. To give just one example, the two problems mentioned earlier which varied only in that the two quantifiers in the second premise were interchanged, both presumably produced the same atmosphere but yet, as we have seen, they produced quite different responses.

Overview of Theories

The hope expressed at the outset of this section that some light would be shed on theories of syllogistic reasoning has been only partially fulfilled. Theories involving Euler circles, Venn diagrams, formal rules, conversion or atmosphere have difficulty in explaining the findings. The mental models approach, on the other hand, is able to explain the data, and is therefore strengthened. However, there are unfortunately interpretational difficulties with the multiply-quantified sentences used in this research which make the results a little difficult to evaluate fully. Research on these problems is still in its infancy, and a final evaluation will have to await future studies.

CONCLUDING COMMENTS

This chapter has reviewed a number of different areas involving reasoning with quantifiers. The research has been inspired by differing theoretical perspectives, and no one theory is unequivocally supported. Nevertheless, this chapter has provided a good indication of the sheer variety of phenomena that any comprehensive theory must encompass. Aristotle would undoubtedly be amazed at the enormous range of research that has been inspired, either directly or indirectly, by his seemingly innocuous invention of the syllogism.

9 Overview and Conclusions

We have now completed our review of the major findings in the psychology of deductive reasoning. Since this has been organised in terms of the different paradigms used—such as the selection task, or syllogistic reasoning—the function of this final chapter is to draw together the various findings and seek conclusions which apply to the field as a whole. First, we consider the phenomena established by experimentation. We will attempt to summarise and discuss these in an atheoretical manner and focus on what the research has told us about the nature of human reasoning. As in all fields of scientific enquiry, however, the data must be explained and interpreted. In the following section, we therefore summarise the state of theory in the area of human deduction. Finally, we take a brief look at reasoning research in the context of the continuing debate about human rationality.

THE PHENOMENA OF DEDUCTIVE REASONING

In the course of this book, we have referred to the findings of hundreds of experiments which have provided a wide range of phenomena for theorists to explain. Taking these findings as a whole, what can we conclude about the nature of deductive reasoning in human beings? We consider first the issue of the extent of deductive competence and try to identify the main performance factors which constrain it. We then take a closer look at the nature of errors on reasoning, including some specific claims of "biases". Finally, we discuss the ways in which prior knowledge influences reasoning.

We will not attempt here to summarise the large numbers of experimental studies reviewed in the main part of the book. We will instead indicate those findings which are characteristic of the research review and especially those features which generalise across the different paradigms. For purposes of illustration, we will recall some particular examples of the phenomena reviewed.

Deductive Competence and Performance Factors

Most authors—of varying theoretical persuasions—are agreed that the ability to reason deductively is of fundamental importance in human intelligence. Hence, a question which has always been of interest in the psychology of reasoning is the extent to which people manifest deductive competence. The term "competence" is, however, open to more than one interpretation. We could, for example, define deductive competence as the extent of subjects' ability on average to solve logical problems. By this definition, and with textbook logic as a criterion for correctness, we would be forced to the conclusion that competence is poor in most of the paradigms studied. However, we could instead choose to define competence as the ability of subjects to reason logically under ideal conditions.

In his classic work on generative grammars, Chomsky (e.g. 1957; 1965) proposed an important distinction between linguistic competence and linguistic performance. For example, the fact that people produce many ill-formed and ungrammatical utterances in spontaneous speech does not reveal their true level of grammatical competence. This is because the same individual, presented with a transcript of her speech, would often identify the errors and be capable of correcting them in a considered, written form. Hence, true competence is being disguised by *performance* factors. An example of a performance factor in speech might be working memory limitations. A long sentence may end ungrammatically because the speaker has forgotten the construction that was used at the outset.

The competence/performance distinction can also be applied in the study of human reasoning. Indeed, it is essential to theorists such as proponents of mental models or proposers of formal inference rules, who contend that humans have mechanisms for reasoning which provide deductive competence. How else can such theories be maintained except on the assumption that competence is disguised by performance factors? The phenomena themselves also compel us to make use of this distinction. This is because *observed* competence in the use or understanding of a given logical principle varies so widely depending upon the manner in which problems are devised and presented. We will show in this section that there are two major classes of performance factors which constrain competence. Reasoners are limited (1) by the *amount* of processing that they are required to carry out and (2) by the *nature* of the processing. The second factor will be elaborated in our following discussion of the nature of errors in reasoning tasks.

To illustrate the practical difficulties involved in assessing deductive competence, we focus on an arbitrarily chosen example. Consider the question of whether or not people have the competence to perform a Modus Tollens inference of the form *If p then q*, *not-q*, *therefore not-p*. One might think, naïvely, that the matter could be settled in quite a simple manner. All one would have to do is to give human subjects a problem requiring the Modus Tollens (MT) inference for its solution and see whether or not they could solve it. We reviewed a number of such studies in Chapter 2. We found (Table 2.4) that over a range of studies, subjects drew this inference around 60% of the time. This shows that while people can make the inference, they are less consistently able to do so than in the case of Modus Ponens (97% overall). We also noticed that the MT rate varied quite considerably across studies.

When other factors are introduced into the experiments, the story becomes more complicated. Hence, a Modus Tollens argument is much less often endorsed when the antecedent is negative, e.g. *If not p then q*, *not-q*, *therefore p*. We can hardly argue that understanding of the principle Modus Tollens comes and goes with presence of a negative component. (Similarly, we saw in Chapter 5 that inferences drawn from disjunctive statements are markedly affected by the presence of negative components.) It seems more plausible to identify a performance factor, such as a bias to prefer negative conclusions. Similarly, when a range of thematic contents are used, in place of abstract ones, MT rates vary considerably depending upon the content. The MT inference is particularly interesting in this regard, since its fluctuation cannot be accounted for in terms of the implication/equivalence ambiguity of conditionals. If subjects reason in a truth-functional manner, the MT inference would be made under either interpretation.

Matters become more complex still when we look for consistency in the understanding of logical principles form one paradigm to another. Psychologists and philosophers new to the field, for example, sometimes assume that the classic failure to select the *not-q* or FC (False Consequent) card in the abstract Wason selection task (Chapter 4) indicates a failure in Modus Tollens reasoning. Since a *not-q* on one side of the card entails a *not-p* on the other, they argue, any subject who understood MT should select the card. However, the FC selection rate in abstract selection task studies using similar materials to abstract conditional inference tasks is typically much lower than the 60% average MT rate.

Both Modus Tollens reasoning and selection of FC on the Wason selection task can be related to understanding that a conditional is always false when a true antecedent is accompanied by a false consequent. If we look at truth table tasks, however, we find that subjects show very high competence in understanding that TF falsifies the conditional. For example, the studies discussed in Chapter 2 showed that nearly all subjects judged the TF case to falsify the rule. So why do subjects who understand this often fail to make Modus Tollens, and rarely mange to choose FC on the selection task?

This example is typical of research on deductive reasoning, and of human reasoning in general. It illustrates the point that logical performance is not simply a function of the logical principle involved in tasks, but of the *nature* of the processing required of the subject. To draw an example form a different domain—statistical judgement—a question of interest has been whether or not people understand the law of large numbers (LLN), i.e. that samples of a sufficient size are needed to give accurate estimates of population statistics. In a review of work in this field, Evans (1989, ch. 2) noted enormous variation across studies according to the wording and context of the problems presented. Kahneman and Tversky (1972) had originally proposed that subjects ignore sample size altogether when making statistical judgements and had presented several studies in which this was the case. However, later studies were able to show significant or even universal attention to sample size in different kinds of problems.

In a revised view of this field of work, Kahneman and Tversky (1982) introduced a distinction related to that of competence and performance. They suggested that there are *errors of understanding*, in which a principle is not appreciated, and *errors of application*, in which a principle is understood but not applied. They suggested that research on the law of large numbers revealed errors of application. Similarly, we might look, say, at research on the abstract selection task and argue that subjects understand the principle that a true antecedent cannot be paired with a false consequent, but fail to apply this principle in order to select the FC card.

Interest in competence, as opposed to performance, is something which divides authors in the psychology of reasoning. Hence, the extraordinarily poor *performance* on the Wason selection task has made the task of little interest to most inference rule theorists such as Rips (e.g. 1989), who are not concerned with accounting for errors in reasoning. Such authors regard the task as a "cognitive illusion" or an experimental artifact (see Cohen, 1981) and therefore of limited interest. On the other hand, it is precisely because this apparently simple task is so very difficult to solve in its standard form that it has attracted more research study than any other single paradigm in the recent literature. To many authors, it is the performance factors which prevent subjects exhibiting competence which provide the richest source of psychological data.

We have dwelt at some length on the complications associated with describing or inferring competence from the results of reasoning experiments. Bearing these in mind, let us now consider briefly the evidence contained in this book about what people can and cannot do, and the conditions under which they are more or less likely to reason successfully. Perhaps the easiest problems reviewed are those involving transitive inference (see Chapter 6). The evidence seems good that people understand the principle of transitivity, or linear ordering, e.g. that whenever A is above B on a transitive scale and B is above C, then A must be above C. However, even in this case, a number of performance factors become readily apparent. For example, in the study of Clark (1969a), subjects were given two-term series problems such as:

John is shorter than Bill
Who is tallest?

whereas others were given three-term series problems such as:

John is shorter than Bill
Fred is taller than John
Who is tallest?

Performance with two-term problems is almost universally correct, but with three-term series significant numbers of errors creep in. This is indicative of one of the most general performance factors in reasoning, that of limited working memory capacity. Generally speaking, the more information the reasoner has to process, the more errors will be made. It is not quite as simple as this, though, for as we saw in Chapter 6, performance with five-term problems is no more difficult than with three-term problems (Byrne & Johnson-Laird, 1989). This shows the importance of the nature of the processing as well as its amount. Three- and five-term series problems require premise integration, which places an extra load on working memory, so that they are more difficult than two-term series problems.

All else being equal, giving subjects more information to reason about will cause more errors. A clear example is provided by Evans and Pollard (1990, experiment 2; see Chapter 8) in which subjects were asked to reason with problems containing either two or four premises. Although the larger problems required no additional logical principles to solve, associated logical performance dropped drastically. The notion of limited working memory capacity has also been used by mental models theorists to make a theoretical argument that problems requiring more models in their mental representations will be more difficult to solve (e.g. Johnson-Laird & Bara, 1984). However, because the amount of information to be processed interacts with the nature of the processing demands, providing more information can sometimes facilitate inferences (see, e.g. Byrne, 1989a; discussed in Chapter 2).

If we take a weak definition of competence as that which subjects can sometimes exhibit under favourable circumstances, then we can say that subjects exhibit competence in most of the logical principles underlying the various tasks reviewed in this book. Even this weak conclusion is important, because it means that people *can* reason deductively and hence that theoretical accounts must be provided for how this is achieved. It would, however, be a misrepresentation of the field to suggest that this is the main finding for which theories must account. The great majority of studies have been concerned with the many factors which influence performance. We look more closely at these in addressing the issues of errors and of content effects.

The Nature of Reasoning Errors

The observation that subjects frequently fail to achieve logical competence in their reasoning performance raises the question of what they do instead. One possibility—and this occurs to some extent—is that subjects make "random" errors, meaning responses that we cannot account for. Deviations from logical principles are, however, often *systematic*. Such systematic errors are often referred to as "biases". Some regard this term as theory-laden, implying either the use of heuristics or else intrinsic irrationality on the part of the subjects. We use the term in a descriptive sense only, where it is the conventional label for a particular phenomenon.

We have encountered a number of phenomena throughout this review which have been described as biases, including negative conclusion bias in conditional reasoning, matching bias in conditional truth table and selection tasks and atmosphere, figural and belief bias in syllogistic reasoning. We have also encountered a number of factors which systematically influence the ease of solving problems but are not normally labelled as "biases". For example, we noted that conditional inference rates differ significantly between *if then* and *only if* rules (Chapter 2). Of the biases mentioned, belief bias is associated with prior knowledge and hence will be discussed in the following section.

One question that can be raised is whether the variously claimed biases have any generality across paradigms. Negative conclusion bias, for example, has been mostly investigated with just conditional inference tasks, although a related claim that subjects prefer negative conclusions was made in the context of syllogistic reasoning by Sells (1936). Of the main phenomena identified above, matching bias has some claim to generality, having been observed on three conditional reasoning tasks: truth table construction, truth table evaluation and the Wason selection task. The bias is *not*, however, manifest with thematic materials unless these are highly arbitrary (e.g. Manktelow & Evans, 1979) and nor is it observed even with abstract materials when disjunctive statements are used (see Chapter 5). For an argument that matching is part of a yet more general bias towards processing positive rather than negative information, also implicated in explanations of a range of other cognitive tasks, the reader is referred to Evans (1989).

Another possibly general influence on error rates is that of directional processing. For example, De Soto et al. (1965) proposed that on transitive inference problems subjects like to build mental arrays from top to bottom, where "top" is associated with the lexically unmarked comparative. This interpretation of the data is, however, disputed by linguistic theorists as we saw in Chapter 6. The explanation of figural bias in syllogistic reasoning offered by Johnson-Laird and Bara (1984; see also Johnson-Laird & Steedman, 1978), however, involves a similar notion of directional working in the construction and processing of mental models. In addition, we have noted directionality effects associated with *if then* and *only if* rules (see Chapter 2).

We have already indicated that the *amount* of processing required will constrain performance on deductive reasoning tasks. While this factor can explain the presence of error in general, it cannot account for particular biases. This is because working memory constraints, in themselves, need not produce *systematic* errors. Working memory limitations might, however, be seen as creating the conditions necessary for biases to occur. In considering the *nature* of the processing required, we should note that linguistic structure has a major effect. All the biases we have mentioned—except for belief bias—are in fact associated with linguistic manipulations such as the presence of negative components, or the order of premises presented in a syllogism.

Transitive inference research again provides a good illustration of the influence of linguistic complexity. For example, both two- and three-term series problems become much more difficult—as measured by latency and error rates—when negative-equative premises are used, such as:

John is not as tall as Bill

Much of the research reviewed in this book has shown how the linguistic forms used to convey logical information can affect the ease of solution of problems. For example, we have considered logically equivalent propositional forms such as *if then*, *only if* and *either or* as well as a variety of quantified forms (Chapters 7 and 8) which are associated with often quite varied patterns of reasoning. In general, therefore, we can conclude that choosing alternative linguistic structures to convey logical information not only affects the ease of drawing the inferences, but may be the cause of systematic biases in how information is processed. We now turn to the influence of prior knowledge in reasoning.

The Role of Prior Knowledge

Many of the reasoning experiments reviewed in this book have used abstract—or semantically impoverished—problem materials, by which we mean materials that are unlikely to evoke relevant prior knowledge. When thematic—or semantially rich—materials are used instead, we have noted time and again that subjects appear to reason quite differently. In studies of the Wason selection task, for example, a number of studies using within-subject designs have found not only that subjects give quite different responses to thematic versions of the task, but also that there is no transfer to structurally identical abstract versions presented afterwards. This is powerful evidence that our subjects do not think simply about the structure of the task but are highly influenced by the meaning of the materials.

Since we also have evidence that a number of the biases which characterise reasoning with abstract materials disappear when thematic content is introduced, we might wonder what the value of studying abstract reasoning tasks is at all. There are three main reasons why it is done, the first of which is historical. Just as research on human memory has a history of studying memory processes in the abstract, by using of lists of nonsense syllables or more recently unrelated words, so reasoning research has a tradition of using arbitrary problem content. In both fields, this dates to a period when psychologists believed that cognitive processes were largely content-independent and that use of realistic materials would only confuse the search for underlying processes. The second reason is theoretical. The oldest theory of deductive competence is that of mental logic or general purpose inference rules. If there is an abstract logic in the mind, then subjects ought to be able to demonstrate their competence with abstract problem material. Finally, there is a practical justification. While we normally reason in familiar domains, we do sometimes need to work out the consequences of arbitrary rules and regulations. We need to know how well people can do this, and what factors are likely to bias them.

Despite these defences for the use of abstract problem content, it is perfectly obvious that the psychological study of human reasoning has been greatly enriched by the trend towards investigation of content and context effects in recent years. These experiments have also yielded a rich crop of new phenomena for the theorists to explain. As we shall see, in the discussion of reasoning theory which follows, the ability to account for the interconnection of knowledge and inference is vital to theoretical success in this area.

Traditionally, problem content has been seen to have either a facilitatory or inhibitory effect on reasoning. The inhibitory argument is that subjects' judgements of the validity of arguments are prejudiced by their belief in the plausibility of the conclusions (belief bias). Related to this are the findings that subjects reason pragmatically by drawing fallacious inferences in conditional reasoning tasks which follow from prior belief rather than the information presented (see Chapter 2). The contrary, facilitatory argument is that people are confused by abstract problem content and are more able to cope with logical problems when presented in familiar terms. Both arguments arise from the same original paper of Wilkins (1928). Belief bias has largely been studied in the context of syllogistic inference (Chapter 8) and the thematic facilitation effect has mostly been investigated using the Wason selection task (Chapter 4). We will briefly recall the major findings in each area of enquiry.

First, we consider the belief bias effect. Leaving aside the detailed theoretical arguments proposed to explain the effect, the basic facts of the phenomenon are quite striking. Intelligent adult subjects, clearly instructed to make deductive inferences on the basis of the information given, are apparently unable to comply. Although their judgements of validity are significantly influenced by the logic of the syllogisms given, most studies have found a considerable influence of prior belief, especially when the premises are indeterminate (see Chapter 8). The degree of influence which this logically irrelevant feature of the task exerts on adult subjects is quite striking.

As we saw in Chapter 8, the effect is quite robust with regard to procedural variations. Belief bias is observed on a variety of syllogistic forms, on conclusion production as well as evaluation tasks and despite strong instructional manipulations intended to enhance subjects' understanding of the logical properties of the task. Whether we should take this as evidence of irrationality is highly moot, since it can be argued that belief bias reflects a method of reasoning that might be adaptive in the real world (see Evans, 1993b; Evans et al., 1992). What we should note here, however, is that subjects appear to be unable to suspend the influence of their prior knowledge and beliefs when performing a laboratory reasoning task.

Superficially, it might appear that work on *facilitating* effects of thematic material—such as the contexts which greatly improve logical performance on the Wason selection task—stand in contradiction to the belief bias effect. On careful reflection, however, we will see that this is not the case. For example, one of the striking effects reported in the literature discussed in Chapter 4 is the lack of transfer from facilitating contexts to the abstract selection task. Although subjects are presented in close succession with structurally identical problems which vary only in their content, they appear to regard them as completely separate and unconnected. We also found that quite small amounts of contextual information presented prior to the selection task itself can have a major influence on the reasoning observed. Nor is it the case that content effects, when they are observed on the selection task, are always associated with an increase in correct choices of True Antecedent and False Consequent. For example, we saw that some materials induce subjects to pick the combination of False Antecedent and True Consequent—a pattern hardly ever observed on the abstract selection task.

In addition to belief bias, there is another way in which prior knowledge may lead to logical errors. With abstract as well as concrete content, there is a general tendency for people to infer *too much* from the information presented. This is well illustrated, for example, by the findings in studies of syllogistic reasoning (Chapter 7) that subjects frequently endorse as valid the conclusions of indeterminate syllogisms. Similarly, with studies of propositional reasoning with conditionals and disjunctives, we have seen that so-called fallacious inferences, such as Denial of the Antecedent and Affirmation of the Consequent, are frequently endorsed, especially when placed in most real-world contexts in which conditionals may be used (see Chapter 2). However, we must remember that what constitutes an error in reasoning may be a matter of interpretation. For example, many authors, following Henle (1962), would see the endorsement of fallacies not as evidence of illogical reasoning but as an indication of personalised representations.

In fact, the most plausible account of why people make more inferences than the premises justify is because they are expanding the information given with related prior knowledge. The more you assume, the more you can infer. Thus endorsement of the conditional fallacies is particularly marked when the conditional rules take the form of threats, promises or causal statements. While technically illogical, these inferences seem justified, given the context in which the utterances are heard. Even when conditionals are used with abstract content, however, the rate of fallacies is quite high. This may be due to a carryover of habitual methods of reasoning in the real world, since in so many contexts these inferences do appear to follow. Once again, this generalisation has many exceptions when the specific nature of the reasoning task is considered in detail. Hence we saw also in Chapter 2 that prior knowledge can lead to the suppression of inferences.

In summary, then, research on the influence of content and context in deductive reasoning has shown that our reasoning processes are highly influenced by the meaning of the problem materials. This is one of the most important and fundamental findings in the field, and clearly one which should be addressed by all theories of human reasoning.

THEORIES OF DEDUCTIVE REASONING

Throughout this book, we have considered evidence for the four major classes of theory introduced in Chapter 1, namely those based upon the use of formal rules, mental models, heuristics and domain-sensitive rules of schemas. We do not feel that it is appropriate to include an evaluation of the adequacy of each of these accounts in a text of this kind.

One recent attempt to compare and evaluate the four theories was made by Evans (1991a), who assessed their ability to explain the three key empirical issues—as he saw them—of the evidence for competence, bias and influence of knowledge. His main criterion for assessment was therefore completeness of explanation, although he also suggested others such as coherence, parsimony and falsifiability. Evans is, of course, associated with one of the positions—heuristic theory—although his review if anything favoured the mental models account. Other recent reviews of the theories in the field also have in general been written by authors of a particular persuasion. The reader may care to compare the reviews of Johnson-Laird and Byrne (1991) who are, of course, proponents of mental models with those of Rips (1990a), a mental logician, and most recently Holyoak and Spellman (1993), who advocate the theory of pragmatic reasoning schemas. Perhaps significantly, the comparative review of the four approaches offered by Oaksford and Chater (1993), who are not associated with any particular position, finds all four to be seriously deficient! These authors appear to prefer a solution based upon connectionist modelling, although we are not aware of any serious attempt to account for sequential thinking and reasoning tasks by neural networks (see Rumelhart, Smolensky, McClelland & Hinton, 1986, for a speculative discussion).

In this section, we will simply attempt to summarise the current state of theory in deductive reasoning, and restrict our comments mostly to the scope of the theories, i.e. the range of phenomena and issues to which they have been applied. As explained in Chapter 1, the theory of reasoning by formal inference rules—often known by the arguably misleading term "mental logic" theories—is the oldest theory in the field. Although this theory has fallen somewhat from fashion in recent years, it still has a number of distinguished and enthusiastic advocates such as Rips, Braine and O'Brien, whose work has been discussed at various stages in this volume. In particular, we identified the major details of this theory in Chapter 3, in the context of propositional reasoning to which it has most usually been applied.

Specific arguments for and against the inference rule theory of propositional reasoning were reviewed in some detail in Chapter 3 and will not be repeated here. Now that we have the context of the book as a whole, we will only add the comment that the theory has as yet been little applied to the other paradigms reviewed, such as relational and quantified reasoning. Also, while the theory has been applied to the explanation of competence and some error patterns in propositional reasoning, its proponents have been comparatively silent on the subject of the kinds of biases described in our section on reasoning errors as well as on the role of knowledge in reasoning. However, one recent theorist of this persuasion, O'Brien (1993), has taken up the challenge and defended the formal rule account in the light of a variety of research findings including studies of both abstract and thematic versions of the Wason selection task.

Because the phrase "heuristics and biases" has been so commonly used to describe the approach of Kahneman, Tversky and others to statistical judgement (see Kahneman et al., 1982), there is some confusion as to the distinction between a heuristic and a bias. A bias, as we have used the term, is an empirical observation, normally constituting systematic attention to logically irrelevant information or neglect of logically relevant information. By contrast, a heuristic is a theoretical construct—a proposed means of reasoning which may lead to a quick solution but also to error.

In some ways, the heuristic approach has complementary strengths and weaknesses to those identified for the theory of formal inference rules: the theory explains biases but has little to say about competence in reasoning. However, heuristic theories have also provided accounts of some of the content effects observed in reasoning. For example, Pollard (1982), applying the notion of the *availability heuristic* (Tversky & Kahneman, 1973) to deductive reasoning, included discussion of content effects in the selection task and of belief bias, in addition to proposing accounts of non-content related biases. Evans (1984a; 1989), who replaces availability with relevance, has also applied his heuristic-analytic theory to the explanation of a number of biases and content effects. These include matching bias and belief bias effects (see Chapters 2, 4 and 8 for discussion of relevant research).

Following publication of Johnson-Laird's (1983) general theory of mental models in both language and thinking, the particular application to deduction has caused considerable interest. By the time of Johnson-Laird and Byrne's (1991) subsequent book, a considerable amount of both theoretical and empirical work had been conducted in support of the theory. This is reflected, of course, in the numerous references to the theory made throughout our review of research on deductive reasoning. The theory has been applied to all the main paradigms reviewed in this book—propositional, relational and syllogistic reasoning—and has proposed explanations not only for deductive competence, but for a number of biases and content effects as well.

We have referred to the theory of *formal* inference rules in order to convey the notion that reasoning occurs by application of highly abstract and general purpose rules—hence the idea of a "mental logic". However, the theory of reasoning by domain-sensitive rules or schemas has been popular in recent years, and in fact has lead to a vigorous debate between two theories of this type: those which propose the use of pragmatic reasoning schemas and those which propose Darwinian algorithms for social contracts (see Chapter 4).

The obvious limitation of pragmatic schema theory and other proposals of domain-sensitive reasoning mechanisms, is that they cannot account for either the deductive competence or the systematic errors which are biases associated with abstract problem content. A further limitation is that the theories have been almost exclusively investigated with regard to work on the Wason selection task and have not yet been applied to the explanation of content effects observed on other reasoning paradigms, such as the belief bias effect in syllogistic reasoning.

Before leaving the subject of reasoning theories, we will comment briefly on the relation between the different theories and attempts to integrate them. The only theory which really claims to account for the full range of data at present is that of mental models. Others are self-evidently incomplete, as in Evans' unspecified analytic component to account for deductive competence and the selective application of schema theory to reasoning which is influenced by knowledge.

Recently, a number of authors in the mental logic tradition have accepted that formal rules are not sufficient to account for all the phenomena and are willing to agree that other reasoning mechanisms, including schemas, heuristics and mental models, may be needed (e.g. Braine, 1993; O'Brien, 1993; Rips, 1990a). For example, O'Brien says that he agrees with schema theorists that content effects in reasoning cannot be accounted for by formal rules alone, and that he agrees with Evans that there are both logical and non-logical influences on reasoning, although he sees a different balance of the two.

In recent times, there have also been indications of a possible reconciliation between the heuristic-analytic theory and that of mental models. This involves an equation of the notion of relevance with that of explicit representation in a mental model. The potential merging of the theories might provide some complementary advantages: mental models theory obviously provides the account of deductive competence that Evans (1991a) has suggested might replace his unspecified analytic stage. At the same time, the work done on the nature of representational heuristics helps to answer questions concerning which particular models are constructed and in what order. This is illustrated by the development of the mental models account of matching bias by Johnson-Laird and Byrne (1991).

The state of theory in deductive reasoning research is generally healthy, in that psychologists are giving serious thought to alternative explanations and providing detailed analyses of the phenomena. Many of the particular applications of the theories are now well specified via computational modelling. In general, there are at least two rival accounts for every phenomenon, but this of course acts as a spur to the conduct of well-designed experimentation aimed at distinguishing the rival accounts.

Our final task is to consider deductive reasoning research in the context of the debate about human rationality.

REASONING AND RATIONALITY

We have tried throughout this book to stick to our declared resolve of being descriptive rather than evaluative. That is, we have considered what it is that people actually do on reasoning tasks and have assessed the various theoretical accounts in terms of their ability to explain these findings. We have not judged the reasoning concerned as right and wrong or as rational and irrational. When we have used terms such as "logical error" or "bias", these have been descriptive of the behaviour, usually with reference to the accepted normative system of logic for the paradigms in question. However, it would be wrong to end this book without at least some brief consideration of the debate about rationality and its implications for research on human reasoning.

Although arguments about rationality have been implicit in the reasoning area for many years, the debate became clearly articulated following publication of a paper by the philosopher L. Jonathan Cohen (1981), together with a number of peer group commentaries. Cohen's purpose was to argue that human irrationality could not be demonstrated by psychological experimentation. He was concerned particularly by two fields of research: the study of heuristics and biases in probability judgement, led by Tversky and Kahneman, and the study of deductive reasoning. Subsequent papers on the rationality issue have tended to be focused more on judgement than reasoning research (e.g. Berkeley & Humphreys, 1982; Christensen-Szalanksi & Beach, 1984; Funder, 1987; Lopes, 1991; Phillips, 1987), although the issues they raise apply equally to the study of deductive reasoning. In addition, a recent volume dedicated to the rationality issue and edited by Manktelow and Over (1993) includes several contributions specifically concerned with reasoning research.

A feature of this literature is the criticisms of experimental reports of bias and error and the interpretations which authors have made of such findings. Rationalist critics assert that "bias researchers" have provided a misleading picture of human irrationality by claiming far too much generality for their findings. In addition, many specific claims of error and bias are disputed in detail. It has also been suggested that bias researchers are themselves biased! As an example, Christensen-Szalanski and Beach

(1984) claimed evidence for a citation bias in the literature such that papers reporting poor reasoning are cited far more often than those reporting good reasoning. One possible explanation for this (Evans, 1984b) is that researchers can learn more about the cognitive processes when subjects make mistakes. In memory research, for example, it is customary to give subjects longer lists of words than they can remember accurately in order to investigate variables affecting ease of recall.

Naturally enough, reasoning researchers have been moved to defend their work, or at least to clarify their own views on rationality. We will consider briefly here some of the points made by experimental researchers in the deductive reasoning field. Evans (1993b) has argued that much of the argument is due to a confusion between two different notions of rationality: *rationality of purpose*, in which people are assumed to strive to achieve goals; and *rationality of process*, in which it is assumed that people reason logically. Evans argues that people are rational in the first sense—within cognitive constraints—but not in the second. He argues that logic may often provide a poor criterion for assessing the rationality of reasoning. For example, the belief bias effect in reasoning may arise because people habitually accept conclusions they agree with and check the evidence for statements they do not agree with. In the laboratory, this leads to logical errors, but in the real world it is adaptive. We need to sustain large and coherent belief systems, he argues, and do not have enough time and energy to keep checking the evidence for that which we already believe in.

In contrast, a number of authors in the reasoning field clearly believe that deductive competence is the key to rationality. For example, Johnson-Laird (1993, p. 2) states that "At the heart of rationality is the capacity to make valid deductions". This assumption is central to the theory of reasoning by mental models, as is clearly illustrated by Johnson-Laird and Byrne's (1993c) discussion of the relation of the theory to rationality. Not surprisingly, mental logicians also tend to defend a concept of rationality based on logicality (e.g. O'Brien, 1993). However, others prefer the purposive notion of rationality. Hence, Over and Manktelow (1993), in their discussion of deontic reasoning, state that "On evolutionary grounds, it is . . . hard to see how this reasoning directed towards satisfying our basic needs and desires could tend to be anything other than fairly rational". Gigerenzer and Hug (1992) appear to support a similar position when they state: ". . . what counts as human rationality: reasoning processes that embody content-independent formal rules, such as propositional logic, or reasoning processes that are well designed for solving important adaptive problems, such as social contracts or social regulations?" (p. 129).

Rationalist criticisms of interpretations of the reasoning literature have tended to fall into one of three main categories (see Evans, 1993b). First, some authors suggest that subjects are using arbitrary or inappropriate normative theories by which to classify the subjects' responses as right or wrong (e.g. Cohen, 1981). The second argument is that we cannot judge whether or not someone is reasoning logically unless we know their interpretation of the premises (Henle, 1962; Smedslund, 1970; 1990). Finally, many critics of bias research have claimed that authors extrapolate too freely from arguably artificial experiments to the real world (e.g. Cohen, 1981; Funder, 1987; Lopes, 1991). In other words, they assert that reasoning experiments have poor external validity.

A common argument of reasoning researchers is that while subjects do their best to solve the problems set, their rationality is "bounded" by cognitive constraints of various kinds, such as selective attention, working memory constraints or linguistic presuppositions. Hence, the purpose of reasoning research is to explore these bounds and thus understand the underlying cognitive processes. The notion of "bounded rationality" has been around for a long time in cognitive science, and was central to the theory of problem solving proposed by Newell and Simon (1972). Despite the many attacks by rationalist critics on the work of Tversky and Kahneman, they themselves see their work within the context of the bounded rationality tradition of Bruner and Simon (see Kahneman et al., 1982, preface). The idea of bounded rationality has, however, recently been used to criticise rather than support the proposals of reasoning theorists. Oaksford and Chater (1992; 1993) have linked the idea of bounded rationality with an external validity criticism. They argue that *none* of the currently proposed mechanisms for deductive competence (e.g. rules, models) are capable of accounting for real-world reasoning, because they place far too great a demand on the limited information-processing capability of human beings.

Johnson-Laird and Byrne (1991; 1993c) have indicated the relevance of a debate in anthropology between relativists and rationalists. The relativist argument is that rationality is relative to a culture, whereas the rationalists argue for a universal standard in which, for example, a Modus Ponens inference would always be valid. Johnson-Laird and Byrne argue themselves for a form of universal rationality, but one based upon semantics rather than rules. For example:

> In our view there is a central core of rationality, which appears to be common to all human societies. It is the semantic principle of validity: an argument is valid only if there is no way in which the premises could be true and its conclusion false. A corollary of this principle is that certain *forms* of argument are valid, and that these forms can be specified by formal rules of inference. It is a gross mistake, however, to suppose that these rules are *per se* cognitive universals (Johnson-Laird & Byrne, 1991, p. 209).

Johnson-Laird and Byrne (1993c) go on to argue that people are rational in principle but fallible in practice. This is because the mental models theory of reasoning provides a method for ensuring deductive competence which often fails to translate into logically accurate performance because of cognitive constraints such as limited working memory capacity. This is a form of the bounded rationality argument which the mental models theory offered as the central explanation of both the rationality and the bounds. A response to the line of criticism offered by Oaksford and Chater is given by Johnson-Laird and Byrne (1993b).

It is clear from this brief discussion that there are several unresolved threads to the rationality argument so far as reasoning research is concerned. First, there is clear disagreement between researchers as to whether rationality should be defined in terms of achievement of goals or in terms of deductive competence. While there appears to be general agreement among reasoning researchers in the idea of bounded rationality and the importance of studying cognitive constraints, there is profound disagreement on the process by which this is achieved. It is equally clear that authors' views about rationality are closely tied with the kind of theoretical approach that they hold (see previous section).

In conclusion, the debate about rationality has impinged significantly upon reasoning researchers, and most of the leading workers in the area have now clarified their views on the subject. Philosophers clearly have an important role to play in this area also, since it is by no means clear that some of the issues debated by psychologists will be resolvable on empirical grounds.

CONCLUSIONS

The psychological study of deductive reasoning has advanced considerably since the last major review of the field by Evans (1982). In terms of experimental studies, the single most popular paradigm has been that of the Wason selection task (Chapter 4), which has been a particular focus for research on the role of pragmatic influences in reasoning. However, we have seen significant advances in experimental findings in all of the main paradigms reviewed in this book over the past decade. We have, as a result, a more accurate picture of the factors which influence and restrain competence in deduction across a wide range of tasks.

The most striking advances in the past decade or so, however, have been on the theoretical front. At the time of the previous review, there was the traditional mental logic theory, but even this lacked the sophistication of the formal rule theories that developed during the 1980s. Mental logic was contrasted by Evans (1982) largely with a school of thought engendered by Peter Wason which focused on error and bias in reasoning, and which was associated at the time with particular accounts of individual phenomena. This school is still alive and active, but has also developed more integrated theoretical accounts of a range of phenomena. Two of the major classes of theory currently dominant in the field, however, have developed almost from scratch during the past decade. We refer, of course, to the theory of reasoning by mental models on the one hand, and by pragmatic reasoning schemas on the other. As Johnson-Laird and Byrne (1991) have argued, reasoning research has become a test-bed for cognitive science in which well-defined and computationally modelled theories are being pitted against one another.

There is an argument that the current state of reasoning theory is highly fragmented (Evans, 1991a). However, given the very short time period in which the bulk of current theory has developed, this is only to be expected. Our hope is that the next decade will move us towards greater integration of theoretical accounts. We have already indicated in this chapter several ways in which this might happen, and indeed is beginning to happen in some cases. We are happy to end this review with the observation that the study of human deduction is in an excellent state of health. The field is currently attracting more interest, empirical study and theoretical effort than at any time in its history.

References

Agnoli, F. (1978). Content and structure in syllogistic reasoning. *Italian Journal of Psychology*, 5, 245–259.

Andrews, A.D. (1993). Review of Deduction. *The Behavioral and Brain Sciences*, *16*.

Bach, K. (1993). Getting down to cases. *The Behavioral and Brain Sciences*, *16*.

Baddeley, A. (1990). *Human memory: Theory and practice*. Hove, UK: Lawrence Erlbaum Associates Ltd.

Baddeley, A., & Hitch, G. (1974). Working memory. In G.A. Bower (Ed.), *The psychology of learning and motivation*, Vol. 8. New York: Academic Press.

Bara, B.G. (1993). For a developmental theory of mental models. *The Behavioral and Brain Sciences*, *16*.

Barclay, J.R. (1973). The role of comprehension in remembering sentences. *Cognitive Psychology*, *4*, 229–254.

Baron, J. (1993). Deduction as an example of thinking. *The Behavioral and Brain Sciences*, *16*.

Barston. J.L. (1986). *An investigation into belief biases in reasoning*. Unpublished PhD thesis, University of Plymouth.

Bartlett, F.C. (1932). *Remembering*. Cambridge: Cambridge University Press.

Barwise, J. (1989). *The situation in logic*. Stanford, CA: Center for the Study of Language and Information.

Barwise, J. (1993). Everyday reasoning and logical inference. *The Behavioral and Brain Sciences*, *16*.

Beattie, J., & Baron, J. (1988). Confirmation and matching biases in hypothesis testing. *Quarterly Journal of Experimental Psychology*, *40A*, 269–297.

Begg, I. (1987). Some. *Canadian Journal of Psychology*, *41*, 62–73.

Begg, I., & Denny, J.P. (1969). Empirical reconciliation of atmosphere and conversion interpretations of syllogistic reasoning errors. *Journal of Experimental Psychology*, *81*, 351–354.

Begg, I., & Harris, G. (1982). On the interpretation of syllogisms. *Journal of Verbal Learning and Verbal Behavior*, *21*, 595–620.

Berkeley, D., & Humphreys, P. (1982). Structuring decision problems and the bias heuristic. *Acta Psychologica*, *50*, 201–252.

Berry, D.C. (1983). Metacognitive experience and transfer of logical reasoning. *Quarterly Journal of Experimental Psychology*, *35A*, 39–49.

Boole, G. (1847/1948). *The mathematical analysis of logic, being an essay towards a calculus of deductive reasoning*. Oxford: Basil Blackwell.

Bracewell, R.J., & Hidi, S.E. (1974). The solution of an inferential problem as a function of the stimulus materials. *Quarterly Journal of Experimental Psychology*, *26*, 480–488.

Braine, M.D.S. (1978). On the relation between the natural logic of reasoning and standard logic. *Psychological Review*, *85*, 1–21.

Braine, M.D.S. (1993). Mental models cannot exclude mental logic, and make little sense without it. *The Behavioral and Brain Sciences*, *16*.

Braine, M.D.S., & O'Brien, D.P. (1991). A theory of If: A lexical entry, reasoning program, and pragmatic principles. *Psychological Review*, *98*, 182–203.

Braine, M.D.S., Reiser, B.J., & Rumain, B. (1984). Some empirical justification for a theory of natural propositional logic. In G.H. Bower (Ed.), *The psychology of learning and motivation*, Vol. 18. New York: Academic Press.

Braine, M.D.S., & Rumain, B. (1981). Development of comprehension of "or". *Journal of Experimental Child Psychology*, *31*, 46–70.

Braine, M.D.S., & Rumain, B. (1983). Logical reasoning. In J.H. Flavell & E.M. Markman (Eds), *Carmichael's handbook of child psychology, Vol. 3: Cognitive development*. New York: John Wiley.

Brooks, L.R. (1967). The suppression of visualisation by reading. *Quarterly Journal of Experimental Psychology*, *19*, 289–299.

Brooks, P.G. (1984). *Visual and verbal processing in reasoning*. Unpublished PhD thesis, University of Plymouth.

Brown, C., Keats, J.A., Keats, D.M., & Seggie, I. (1980). Reasoning about implication: A comparison of Malaysian and Australian subjects. *Journal of Cross-Cultural Psychology, 11*, 395–410.

Bruner, J.S., Goodnow, J.J., & Austin, G.A. (1956). *A study of thinking*. New York: John Wiley.

Bundy, A. (1983). *The computer modelling of mathematical reasoning*. London: Academic Press.

Bundy, A. (1993). 'Semantic procedure' is an oxymoron. *The Behavioral and Brain Sciences, 16*.

Byrne, R.M.J. (1989a). Everyday reasoning with conditional sequences. *Quarterly Journal of Experimental Psychology, 41A*, 141–166.

Byrne, R.M.J. (1989b). Suppressing valid inferences with conditionals. *Cognition, 31*, 61–83.

Byrne, R.M.J. (1989c). Human deductive reasoning. Special issue on Cognitive Science, *Irish Journal of Psychology, 10*, 216–231.

Byrne, R.M.J. (1991a). Can valid inferences be suppressed? *Cognition, 39*, 71–78.

Byrne, R.M.J. (1991b). The construction of explanations. In M. McTear & N. Creaney (Eds), *AI and Cognitive Science '90*. London: Springer-Verlag.

Byrne, R.M.J. (1992). The model theory of deduction. In Y. Rogers, A. Rutherford, & P. Bibby (Eds), *Models in the mind: Theory, perspective, and applications*, pp. 11–28. London: Academic Press.

Byrne, R.M.J., & Handley, S.J. (1992). Reasoning strategies. *Irish Journal of Psychology: Trinity 400 Special Issue, 13*, 111–124.

Byrne, R.M.J., & Handley, S.J. (1993). *Cognitive processes in meta-deductive reasoning*. Unpublished manuscript, Trinity College, Dublin.

Byrne, R.M.J., & Handley, S.J. (in press). The nature and development of meta-deductive reasoning strategies. In K. Ryan (Ed.), *AI and Cognitive Science '92*. London: Springer-Verlag.

Byrne, R.M.J., & Johnson-Laird, P.N. (1989). Spatial reasoning. *Journal of Memory and Language, 28*, 564–575.

Byrne, R.M.J. & Johnson-Laird, P.N. (1990a). Remembering conclusions we have inferred: What biases reveal. In J.-P. Caverni, J.-M. Fabre, & M. Gonzalez (Eds), *Cognitive biases*. Advances in Psychology Vol. 68. Amsterdam: North-Holland.

Byrne, R.M.J., & Johnson-Laird, P.N. (1990b). Models and deductive reasoning. In K.J. Gilhooly, M.T.G. Keane, R.H. Logie, & G. Erdos (Eds), *Lines of thinking: Reflections on the psychology of thought. Vol. 1. London: John Wiley.*

Byrne, R.M.J., & Johnson-Laird, P.N. (1992). The spontaneous use of propositional connectives. *Quarterly Journal of Experimental Psychology, 44A*, 89–110.

Byrne, R.M.J., Handley, S.J., & Johnson-Laird, P.N. (1992). Advances in the psychology of reasoning: Meta-deduction. In M.T. Keane & K. Gilhooly (Eds), *Advances in the psychology of thinking*, Vol. 1. London: Harvester Wheatsheaf.

Byrne, R.M.J., Johnson-Laird, P.N., & Handley, S.J. (in press). Who's telling the truth . . . Cognitive processes in meta-deductions. In H. Sorenson (Ed.), *AI and Cognitive Science '91*. London: Springer-Verlag.

Ceraso, J., & Provitera, A. (1971). Sources of error in syllogistic reasoning. *Cognitive Psychology, 2*, 400–410.

Chapman, L.J., & Chapman, J.P. (1959). Atmosphere effect re-examined. *Journal of Experimental Psychology, 58*, 220–226.

Chater, N. (1993). Mental models and non-monotonic reasoning. *The Behavioral and Brain Sciences, 16*.

Chater, N., & Oaksford, M. (1990). Autonomy, implementation and cognitive architecture: A reply to Fodor and Pylyshyn. *Cognition, 34*, 93–107.

Cheng, P.W., & Holyoak, K.J. (1985). Pragmatic reasoning schemas. *Cognitive Psychology, 17*, 391–416.

Cheng, P.W., & Holyoak, K.J. (1989). On the natural selection of reasoning theories. *Cognition, 33*, 285–314.

Cheng, P.W., Holyoak, K.J., Nisbett, R.E., & Oliver, L.M. (1986). Pragmatic versus syntactic approaches to training deductive reasoning. *Cognitive Psychology, 18*, 293–328.

Chomsky, N. (1957). *Syntactic structures*. The Hague: Mouton.

Chomsky, N. (1965). *Aspects of the theory of syntax*. Cambridge, MA: MIT Press.

Christensen-Szalanski, J.J.J., & Beach, L.R. (1984). The citation bias: Fad and fashion in the judgment and decision literature. *American Psychologist, 39*, 75–78.

Chrostowski, J.J., & Griggs, R.A. (1985). The effects of problem content, instructions and verbalisation procedure on Wason's selection task. *Current Psychological Research and Reviews, 4*, 99–107.

Clark, H.H. (1969a). Linguistic processes in deductive reasoning. *Psychological Review, 76*, 387–404.

Clark, H.H. (1969b). Influence of language on solving three term series problems. *Journal of Experimental Psychology, 82*, 205–215.

Clark, H.H. (1971). More about adjectives, comparatives, and syllogisms: A reply to Huttenlocher and Higgins. *Psychological Review*, 78, 505–514.

Clark, H.H. (1972). On the evidence concerning J. Huttenlocher and E.T. Higgins' theory of reasoning: A second reply. *Psychological Review, 79*, 428–432.

Cohen, L.J. (1981). Can human irrationality be experimentally demonstrated? *The Behavioral and Brain Sciences, 4*, 317–370.

Cohen, L.J. (1993). Some difficulties about deduction. *The Behavioral and Brain Sciences, 16*.

Cohen, M. R., & Nagel, E. (1934). *An introduction to logic and scientific method*. New York: Harcourt, Brace & Co.

Copi, I.M. (1981). *An introduction to logic*. 6th edn. New York: Macmillian.
Cosmides, L. (1989). The logic of social exchange: Has natural selection shaped how humans reason? Studies with the Wason selection task. *Cognition, 31*, 187–276.
Costello, F., & Keane, M.T. (1992). Conceptual combination: A theoretical review. *Irish Journal of Psychology, 13*, 125–140.
Cox, J.R., & Griggs, R.A. (1982). The effects of experience on performance in Wason's selection task. *Memory and Cognition, 10*, 496–502.
Crawford, J.M. (1993). Tractability considerations in deduction. *The Behavioral and Brain Sciences, 16*.
Cummins, D.D., Lubart, T., Alksnis, O., & Rist, R. (1991). Conditional reasoning and causation. *Memory and Cognition, 19*, 274–282.
Davis, H. (1993). Deduction by children and animals: Does it follow the Johnson-Laird and Byrne model? *The Behavioral and Brain Sciences, 16*.
Denis, M., & Cocude, M. (1989). Scanning visual images generated from verbal descriptions. *European Journal of Cognitive Psychology, 1*, 293–307.
De Soto, C.B., London, M., & Handel, S. (1965). Social reasoning and spatial paralogic. *Journal of Personality and Social Psychology, 2*, 513–521.
Dickstein, L.S. (1975). Effects of instructions and premise order on errors in syllogistic reasoning. *Journal of Experimental Psychology: Human Learning and Memory, 104*, 376–384.
Dickstein, L.S. (1976). Differential difficulty of categorical syllogisms. *Bulletin of the Psychonomic Society, 8*, 330–332.
Dickstein, L.S. (1978). The effect of figure on syllogistic reasoning. *Memory and Cognition, 6*, 76–83.
Dickstein, L.S. (1981). Conversion and possibility in syllogistic reasoning. *Bulletin of the Psychonomic Society, 18*, 229–232.
Dugan, C.M., & Revlin, R. (1990). Response options and presentation format as contributors to conditional reasoning. *Quarterly Journal of Experimental Psychology, 42A*, 829–848.
Egan, D.E., & Grimes-Farrow, D.D. (1982). Differences in mental representations spontaneously adopted for reasoning. *Memory and Cognition, 10*, 297–307.
Ehrlich, K., & Johnson-Laird, P.N. (1982). Spatial descriptions and referential continuity. *Journal of Verbal Learning and Verbal Behavior, 21*, 296–306.
Ellis, M.C. (1991). *Linguistic and semantic factors in conditional reasoning*. Unpublished PhD thesis, University of Plymouth.
Erickson, J.R. (1974). A set analysis theory of behavior in formal syllogistic reasoning tasks. In R.L. Solso (Ed.), *Theories of cognitive psychology: The Loyola Symposium*. Hillsdale, NJ: Lawrence Erlbaum Associates Inc.
Erickson, J.R. (1978). Research on syllogistic reasoning. In R. Revlin & R.E. Mayer (Eds), *Human reasoning*. Washington, DC: Winston.
Ericsson, K.A., & Simon, H.A. (1980). Verbal reports as data. *Psychological Review, 87*, 215–251.
Evans, J.St.B.T. (1972). Interpretation and matching bias in a reasoning task. *British Journal of Psychology, 24*, 193–199.
Evans, J.St.B.T. (1975). On interpreting reasoning data: A reply to Van Duyne. *Cognition, 3*, 387–390.
Evans, J.St.B.T. (1977a). Linguistic factors in reasoning. *Quarterly Journal of Experimental Psychology, 29*, 297–306.
Evans, J.St.B.T. (1977b). Toward a statistical theory of reasoning. *Quarterly Journal of Experimental Psychology, 29*, 621–635.
Evans, J.St.B.T. (1982). *The psychology of deductive reasoning*. London: Routledge and Kegan Paul.
Evans, J.St.B.T. (1983). Linguistic determinants of bias in conditional reasoning. *Quarterly Journal of Experimental Psychology, 35A*, 635–644.

Evans, J.St.B.T. (1984a). Heuristic and analytic processes in reasoning. *British Journal of Psychology, 75*, 451–468.

Evans, J.St.B.T. (1984b). In defense of the citation bias in the judgment literature. *American Psychologist, 39*, 1500–1501.

Evans, J.St.B.T. (1987). Reasoning. In H. Beloff & A.M. Coleman (Eds), *Psychology Survey 6*. Leicester: British Psychological Society.

Evans, J.St.B.T. (1989). *Bias in human reasoning: Causes and consequences*. Hove, UK: Lawrence Erlbaum Associates Ltd.

Evans, J.St.B.T. (1990a). Deductive reasoning in human information processing. In K.A. Mohyeldin Said, W.H. Newton Smith, R. Viale, & K.V. Wilkes (Eds), *Modelling the mind*. Oxford: Oxford University Press.

Evans, J.St.B.T. (1990b). Reasoning with knights and knaves: A discussion of Rips. *Cognition, 36*, 85–91.

Evans, J.St.B.T. (1991a). Theories of human reasoning: The fragmented state of the art. *Theory and Psychology, 1*, 83–105.

Evans, J.St.B.T. (1991b). Review of 'Deduction'. *Quarterly Journal of Experimental Psychology, 43A*, 916–919.

Evans, J.St.B.T. (1992a). *Reasoning and relevance in the selection task*. Unpublished manuscript, University of Plymouth.

Evans, J.St.B.T. (1992b). Reasoning with bounded rationality. *Theory and Psychology, 2*, 237–242.

Evans, J.St.B.T. (1993a). On rules, models and understanding. *The Behavioral and Brain Sciences, 16*.

Evans, J.St.B.T. (1993b). Bias and rationality. In K.I. Manktelow & D.E. Over (Eds), *Rationality*. London: Routledge.

Evans, J.St.B.T. (in press). The mental model theory of conditional reasoning: Critical appraisal and revision. *Cognition*.

Evans, J.St.B.T., Allen, J.L., Newstead, S.E., & Pollard, P. (1993). *Logical necessity and belief bias in reasoning: The effect of instructions*. Unpublished manuscript, Department of Psychology, University of Plymouth.

Evans, J.St.B.T., Ball, L.J., & Brooks, P.G. (1987). Attentional bias and decision order in a reasoning task. *British Journal of Psychology, 78*, 385–394.

Evans, J.St.B.T., Barston, J.L., & Pollard, P. (1983). On the conflict between logic and belief in syllogistic reasoning. *Memory and Cognition, 11*, 295–306.

Evans, J.St.B.T., & Beck, M.A. (1981). Directionality and temporal factors in conditional reasoning. *Current Psychological Research, 1*, 111–120.

Evans, J.St.B.T., & Brooks, P.G. (1981). Competing with reasoning: A test of the working memory hypothesis. *Current Psychological Research, 1*, 139–147.

Evans, J.St.B.T., & Lynch, J.S. (1973). Matching bias in the selection task. *British Journal of Psychology, 64*, 391–397.

Evans, J.St.B.T., & Newstead, S.E. (1977). Language and reasoning: A study of temporal factors. *Cognition, 8*, 265–283.

Evans, J.St.B.T., & Newstead, S.E. (1980). A study of disjunctive reasoning. *Psychological Research, 41*, 373–388.

Evans, J.St.B.T., Over, D.E., & Manktelow, K.I. (in press). Reasoning, decision making and rationality. *Cognition*.

Evans, J.St.B.T., & Pollard, P. (1990). Belief bias and problem complexity in deductive reasoning. In J.P. Caverni, J.M. Fabre, & M. Gonzales (Eds), *Cognitive biases*. Amsterdam: North-Holland.

Evans, J.St.B.T., & Wason, P.C. (1976). Rationalisation in a reasoning task. *British Journal of Psychology, 63*, 205–212.

Eysenck, M.W., & Keane, M.T. (1990). *Cognitive psychology: A student's handbook*. Hove, UK: Lawrence Erlbaum Associates Ltd.

Falmagne, R.J. (1993). On modes of explanation. *The Behavioral and Brain Sciences, 16.*

Feather, N.T. (1964). Acceptance and rejection of arguments in relation to attitude strength, critical ability and intolerance of inconsistency. *Journal of Abnormal and Social Psychology, 69*, 127–136.

Fetzer, J.H. (1993). The argument for mental models is unsound. *The Behavioral and Brain Sciences, 16.*

Fillenbaum, S. (1974a). Or: Some uses. *Journal of Experimental Psychology, 103*, 913–921.

Fillenbaum, S. (1974b). Pragmatic normalization: Further results for some conjunctive and disjunctive sentences. *Journal of Experimental Psychology, 102*, 574–578.

Fillenbaum, S. (1975). If: Some uses. *Psychological Research, 37*, 245–260.

Fillenbaum, S. (1976). Inducements: On phrasing and logic of conditional promises, threats and warnings. *Psychological Research, 38*, 231–250.

Fillenbaum, S. (1978). How to do some things with IF. In J.W. Cotton & R.L. Klatzky (Eds), *Semantic factors in cognition*. Hillsdale, NJ: Lawrence Erlbaum Associates Inc.

Fillenbaum, S. (1993). Deductive reasoning: What are taken to be the premises and how are they interpreted? *The Behavioral and Brain Sciences, 16.*

Fisher, A. (1993). Mental models and informal logic. *The Behavioral and Brain Sciences, 16.*

Fong, G.T., Krantz, D.H., & Nisbett, R.E. (1986). The effects of statistical training on thinking about everyday problems. *Cognitive Psychology, 18*, 253–292.

Foos, P.W., Smith, K.H., Sabol, M.A., & Mynatt, B.T. (1976). Constructive processes in simple linear order problems. *Journal of Experimental Psychology: Human Learning and Memory, 2*, 759–766.

Ford, M. (1985). Review of 'Mental models'. *Language, 61*, 897–903.

Frase, L.T. (1968). Effects of semantic incompatibility upon deductive reasoning. *Psychonomic Science, 12*, 64.

Funder, D.C. (1987). Errors and mistakes: Evaluating the accuracy of social judgements. *Psychological Bulletin, 101*, 75–90.

Galotti, K.M., Baron, J., & Sabini, J.P. (1986). Individual differences in syllogistic reasoning: Deduction rules or mental models? *Journal of Experimental Psychology: General, 115*, 16–25.

Galotti, K.M., & Komatsu, L.K. (1993). Why study deduction? *The Behavioral and Brain Sciences, 16.*

Gazdar, G. (1979). *Pragmatics: Implications, presupposition and logical form.* New York: Academic Press.

Geis, M.C., & Zwicky, A.M. (1971). On invited inferences. *Linguistic Inquiry, 2*, 561–566.

George, C. (1991). Facilitation in Wason's selection task with a consequent referring to an unsatisfactory outcome. *British Journal of Psychology, 82*, 463–472.

Gigerenzer, G., & Hug, K. (1992). Domain-specific reasoning: Social contracts, cheating and perspective change. *Cognition, 43*, 127–171.

Gilhooly, K.J., & Falconer, W.A. (1974). Concrete and abstract terms and relations in testing a rule. *Quarterly Journal of Experimental Psychology, 26*, 355–359.

Girotto, V. (1989). Children's performance in the selection task: Plausibility and familiarity. *British Journal of Psychology, 80*, 79–95

Girotto, V. (1991). Deontic reasoning: The pragmatic reasoning schemas approach. (G. Politzer, Ed.). *Inellectica. Special Issue, 11*, 15–52.

Girotto, V., Gilly, M., Blaye, A., & Light, P. (1989). Children's performance on the selection task: Plausibility and familiarity. *European Bulletin of Cognitive Psychology, 9*, 227–231.

Girotto, V., & Legrenzi, P. (1989). Mental representation and hypothetico-deductive reasoning: The case of the THOG problem. *Psychological Research, 51*, 129–135

Girotto, V., & Legrenzi, P. (1992). The parents of THOG are called SARS: Mental representation and reasoning. Paper presented to the *Second International Conference on Thinking*, Plymouth, UK.

Girotto, V., Light, P., & Colbourn, C. (1988). Pragmatic schemas and conditional reasoning in children. *Quarterly Journal of Experimental Psychology, 40A*, 469–482.

Girotto, V. Mazzacco, A., & Cherubini, P. (1992). Judgements of deontic relevance in reasoning: A reply to Jackson and Griggs. *Quarterly Journal of Experimental Psychology, 45A*, 547–574.

Golding, E. (1981). The effect of past experience on problem solving. Paper presented to the *British Psychological Society Conference*, Surrey University, Guildford, UK.

Goldman, A.I. (1986). *Epistemology and cognition*. Cambridge, MA: Harvard University Press.

Goodwin, R.Q., & Wason, P.C. (1972). Degrees of insight. *British Journal of Psychology, 63*, 205–212.

Gordon, R. (1953). The effect of attitude toward Russia on logical reasoning. *Journal of Social Psychology, 37*, 103–111.

Grandy, R.E. (1993). Rule systems are not dead: Existential quantifiers are harder. *The Behavioral and Brain Sciences, 16*.

Green, D.W. (1992). *Mental models, counter-examples and the selection task*. Unpublished manuscript, Department of Psychology, University College London.

Green, D.W. (1993). Mental models: Rationality, representation and process. *The Behavioral and Brain Sciences, 16*.

Greene, S.B. (1992). Multiple explanations for multiply quantified sentences: Are multiple models necessary? *Psychological Review, 99*, 184–187.

Grice, P. (1975). Logic and conversation. In P. Cole & J.L. Morgan (Eds), *Studies in syntax, Vol. 3: Speech acts*. New York: Academic Press.

Griggs, R.A. (1976). Logical processing of set inclusion relations in meaningful text. *Memory and Cognition, 4*, 730–740.

Griggs, R.A. (1978). Drawing inferences from set inclusion information given in text. In R. Revlin & R.E. Meyer (Eds), *Human reasoning*. Washington, DC: Winston.

Griggs, R.A. (1983). The role of problem content in the selection task and in the THOG problem. In J.St.B.T. Evans (Ed.), *Thinking and reasoning: Psychological approaches*. London: Routledge.

Griggs, R.A. (1984). Memory cueing and instructional effects on Wason's selection task. *Current Psychological Research and Reviews, 3*, 3–10.

Griggs, R.A. (1989). To 'see' or not to 'see': That is the selection task. *Quarterly Journal of Experimental Psychology, 41A*, 517–530.

Griggs, R.A., & Cox, J.R. (1982). The elusive thematic materials effect in the Wason selection task. *British Journal of Psychology, 73*, 407–420.

Griggs, R.A., & Cox, J.R. (1983). The effects of problem content and negation on Wason's selection task. *Quarterly Journal of Experimental Psychology, 35A*, 519–533.

Griggs, R.A., & Cox, J.R. (1992). *Permission schemas and the selection task*. Unpublished manuscript, University of Florida.

Griggs, R.A., & Jackson, S.L. (1990). Instructional effects in Wason's selection task. *British Journal of Psychology, 81*, 197–204.

Griggs, R.A., & Newstead, S.E. (1982). The role of problem structure in a deductive reasoning task. *Journal of Experimental Psychology, 8*, 297–307.

Griggs, R.A. & Newstead, S.E. (1983). The source of intuitive errors in Wason's THOG problem. *British Journal of Psychology, 74*, 451–459.

Griggs, R.A., & Ransdell, S.E. (1986). Scientists and the selection task. *Social Studies of Science, 16*, 319–30.

Griggs, R.A., & Warner, S.A. (1982). Processing artificial set inclusion relations: Educing the appropriate schema. *Journal of Experimental Psychology: Learning, Memory and Cognition, 7*, 51–65.

Guyote, M.J., & Sternberg, R.J. (1981). A transitive chain theory of syllogistic reasoning. *Cognitive Psychology, 13*, 461–525.

Hagert, G. (1984). Modeling mental models: Experiments in cognitive modeling of spatial reasoning. In T. O'Shea (Ed.), *Advances in artificial intelligence*, pp. 389–398. Amsterdam: North-Holland.

Handel, S., De Soto, C.B., & London, M. (1968). Reasoning and spatial representations. *Journal of Verbal Learning and Verbal Behavior, 7*, 351–357.

Hayes-Roth, B., & Hayes-Roth, F. (1975). Plasticity in memorial networks. *Journal of Verbal Learning and Verbal Behaviour, 14*, 506–522.

Henle, M. (1962). On the relation between logic and thinking. *Psychological Review, 69*, 366–378.

Henle, M. (1978). Foreword. In M. Revlin & R.E. Mayer (Eds). *Human reasoning*. Washington, DC: Winston.

Henle, M., & Michael, M. (1956). The influence of attitudes on syllogistic reasoning. *Journal of Social Psychology, 44*, 115–127.

Higgins, E.T. (1976). Effects of presupposition on deductive reasoning. *Journal of Verbal Learning and Verbal Behavior, 15*, 419–430.

Hitch, G.J., & Baddeley, A.D. (1976). Verbal reasoning and working memory. *Quarterly Journal of Experimental Psychology, 28*, 603–622.

Hoch, S.J., & Tschirgi, J.E. (1983). Cue redundancy and extra logical inferences in a deductive reasoning task. *Memory and Cognition, 11*, 200–209.

Hoch, S.J., & Tschirgi, J.E. (1985). Logical knowledge and cue redundancy in deductive reasoning. *Memory and Cognition, 13*, 453–462.

Hofstadter, D., & Dennett, D. (1981). *The mind's I: Fantasies and reflections on self and soul*. London: Harvester.

Holyoak, K.J., & Koh, K. (1987). Surface and structural similarity in analogical transfer. *Memory and Cognition, 15*, 332–340.

Holyoak, K.J., & Spellman, B.A. (1993). Thinking. *Annual Review of Psychology, 44*, 265–315.

Humphreys, M.S. (1975). The derivation of endpoint and distance effects in linear orderings from frequency information. *Journal of Verbal Learning and Verbal Behavior, 14*, 496–505.

Hunter, I.M.L. (1957). The solving of three term series problems. *British Journal of Psychology, 48*, 286–298.

Hurford, J.R. (1974). Exclusive or inclusive disjunction. *Foundations of Language, 11*, 409–411.

Huttenlocher, J. (1968). Constructing spatial images: A strategy in reasoning. *Psychological Review, 75*, 550–560.

Huttenlocher, J., & Higgins, E.T. (1971). Adjectives, comparatives, and syllogisms. *Psychological Review, 6*, 487–504.

Huttenlocher, J., & Higgins, E.T. (1972). On reasoning, congruence, and other matters. *Psychological Review, 79*, 420–427.

Huttenlocher, J., Higgins, E.T., Milligan, C., & Kauffman, B. (1970). The mystery of the 'negative equative' construction. *Journal of Verbal Learning and Verbal Behavior, 9*, 334–341.

Inder, R. (1987). *Computer simulation of syllogism solving using restricted mental models*. PhD thesis, Cognitive Studies, Edinburgh University.

Inder, R. (1993). Architecture and algorithms: Power sharing for mental models. *The Behavioral and Brain Sciences, 16*.

Inhelder, B., & Piaget, J. (1958). *The growth of logical thinking*. New York: Basic Books.

Jackson, F. (1982). Two modes of syllogistic reasoning. *Communication Monographs, 49*, 205–213.

Jackson, S.L., & Griggs, R.A. (1988). Education and the selection task. *Bulletin of the Psychonomic Society, 26*, 327–330.

Jackson, S.L., & Griggs, R.A. (1990). The elusive pragmatic reasoning schemas effect. *Quarterly Journal of Experimental Psychology, 42A*, 353–374.

Janis, I., & Frick, F. (1943). The relationship between attitudes toward conclusions and errors in judging logical validity of syllogisms. *Journal of Experimental Psychology, 33*, 73–77.

Johnson-Laird, P.N. (1972). The three term series problem. *Cognition, 1*, 58–82.

Johnson-Laird, P.N. (1975). Models of deduction. In R.J. Falmagne (Ed.), *Reasoning: Representation and process in children and adults*. Hillsdale, NJ: Lawrence Erlbaum Associates Inc.

Johnson-Laird, P.N. (1983). *Mental models*. Cambridge: Cambridge University Press.

Johnson-Laird, P.N. (1993). *Human and machine thinking*. Hillsdale, NJ: Lawrence Erlbaum Associates Inc.

Johnson-Laird, P.N., & Bara, B.G. (1984). Syllogistic inference. *Cognition, 16*, 1–62.

Johnson-Laird, P.N., & Byrne, R.M.J. (1989). Only reasoning. *Journal of Memory and Language, 28*, 313–330.

Johnson-Laird, P.N., & Byrne, R.M.J. (1990). Meta-logical reasoning: Knights, knaves and Rips. *Cognition, 36*, 69–84.

Johnson-Laird, P.N., & Byrne, R.M.J. (1991). *Deduction*. Hove, UK: Lawrence Erlbaum Associates Ltd.

Johnson-Laird, P.N., & Byrne, R.J.M. (1992). Modal reasoning, models and Manktelow & Over. *Cognition, 43*, 173–182.

Johnson-Laird, P.N., & Byrne, R.M.J. (1993a). Precis of 'Deduction'. *The Behavioral and Brain Sciences, 16*.

Johnson-Laird, P.N., & Byrne, R.M J. (1993b). Rules or models? *The Behavioral and Brain Sciences, 16*.

Johnson-Laird, P.N., & Byrne, R.M.J. (1993c). Models and deductive rationality. In K. Manktelow & D. Over (Eds), *Models of Rationality*. London: Routledge.

Johnson-Laird, P.N., Byrne, R.M.J. & Schaeken, W. (1992a). Propositional reasoning by model. *Psychological Review, 99*, 418–439.

Johnson-Laird, P.N., Byrne, R.M.J. & Tabossi, P. (1989). Reasoning by model: The case of multiple quantification. *Psychological Review, 96*, 658–673.

Johnson-Laird, P.N., Byrne, R.M.J. & Tabossi, P. (1992b). In defence of reasoning: A reply to Greene. *Psychological Review, 99*, 188–190.

Johnson-Laird, P.N., Legrenzi, P., & Legrenzi, M.S. (1972). Reasoning and a sense of reality. *British Journal of Psychology, 63*, 395–400.

Johnson-Laird, P.N. & Steedman, M.J. (1978). The psychology of syllogisms. *Cognitive Psychology, 10*, 64–99.

Johnson-Laird, P.N., & Tagart, J. (1969). How implication is understood. *American Journal of Psychology, 2*, 367–373.

Johnson-Laird, P.N., & Tridgell, J. M. (1972). When negation is easier than affirmation. *Quarterly Journal of Experimental Psychology, 24*, 87–91.

Johnson-Laird, P.N., & Wason, P.C. (1970). A theoretical analysis of insight into a reasoning task. *Cognitive Psychology, 1*, 134–148.

Jones, S. (1970). Visual and verbal processes in problem solving. *Cognitive Psychology, 1*, 210–214.

Kahneman, D., Slovic, P., & Tversky, A. (1982). *Judgment under uncertainty: Heuristics and biases*. Cambridge: Cambridge University Press.

Kahneman, D., & Tversky, A. (1972). Subjective probability: A judgment of representativeness. *Cognitive Psychology, 3*, 430–454.

Kahneman, D., & Tversky, A. (1982). On the study of statistical intuition. *Cognition, 12*, 325–326.

Kaufman, H., & Goldstein, S. (1967). The effects of emotional value of conclusions upon distortions in syllogistic reasoning. *Psychonomic Science, 7*, 367–368.

Keane, M.T. (1987). On retrieving analogues when solving problems. *Quarterly Journal of Experimental Psychology, 39A*, 29–41.

Keane, M.T. (1988). *Analogical problem solving*. Chichester: Horwood.

Keane, M.T., Byrne, R.M.J., & Johnson-Laird, P.N. (1993). *The generation of arguments*. Unpublished manuscript, Trinity College, Dublin.

Keane, M.T., Ledgeway, T., & Duff, S. (1991). Similarity and ordering constraints on analogical mapping. In *Proceedings of the 13th Annual Conference of the Cognitive Science Society*. Hillsdale, NJ: Lawrence Erlbaum Associates Inc.

Keeney, T.J., & Gaudino, D.L. (1973). Solution of comparative and negative-equative three-term series problems. *Journal of Experimental Psychology*, 101, 193–196.

Kern, L.H., Mirels, H.L., & Hinshaw, V.G. (1983). Scientists' understanding of propositional logic: An experimental investigation. *Social Studies of Science, 13*, 131–146.

Klaczynski, P.A., Gelfand, H., & Reese, H.W. (1989). Transfer of conditional reasoning: Effects of explanations and initial problem types. *Memory and Cognition, 17*, 208–220.

Klayman, J., & Ha, Y.-W. (1987). Confirmation, disconfirmation and information in hypothesis testing. *Psychological Review, 94*, 211–228.

Kodroff, J.K., & Roberge, J.J. (1975). Developmental analysis of the conditional reasoning abilities of primary grade children. *Developmental Psychology, 13*, 342–353.

Krauth, J. (1982). Formulation and experimental verification of models in propositional reasoning. *Quarterly Journal of Experimental Psychology, 34A*, 285–298.

Krauth, J., & Berchtold-Neumann, M. (1988). A model for disjunctive reasoning. *Z. Psychol., 196*, 361–370.

Kroger, J.K., Cheng, P.W., & Holyoak, K.J. (in press). Evoking the permission schema: The impact of explicit negation and a violation-checking context. *Quarterly Journal of Experimental Psychology, A*.

Kuhn, D. (1977). Conditional reasoning in children. *Developmental Psychology, 13*, 342–353.

Lakoff, R. (1971). If's, and's and but's about conjunction. In C.J. Filmore & D.T. Langendoen (Eds), *Studies in linguistic semantics*. New York: Holt, Rinehart and Winston.

Lawson, R. (1977). Representation of individual sentences and holistic ideas. *Journal of Experimental Psychology: Human Learning and Memory, 3*, 1–9.

Lee, G., & Oakhill. J. (1984). The effects of externalisation on syllogistic reasoning. *Quarterly Journal of Experimental Psychology, 36A*, 519–530.

Legrenzi, P., & Sonino, M. (1993). The content of mental models. *The Behavioral and Brain Sciences, 16*.

Lemmon, E.J. (1965). *Beginning logic*. London: Nelson.

Levesque, H.J. (1986). Making believers out of computers. *Artificial Intelligence, 30*, 81–108.

Light, P.H., Blaye, A., Gilly, M., & Girotto, V. (1990). Pragmatic schemas and logical reasoning in six to eight year olds. *Cognitive Development, 4*, 49–64.

Lopes, L.L. (1991). The rhetoric of irrationality. *Theory and Psychology, 1*, 65–82.

Luchins, A.S., & Luchins, E.H. (1993). Gestalt theory, formal models and mathematical modeling. *The Behavioral and Brain Sciences, 16*.

MacLennan, B. (1993). Visualising the possibilities. *The Behavioral and Brain Sciences, 16*.

Macnamara, J. (1986). *A border dispute: The place of logic in psychology*. Cambridge, MA: Bradford Books/MIT press.

Maki, R. (1981). Categorisation and distance effects with spatial linear orders. *Journal of Experimental Psychology: Learning, Memory and Cognition, 7*, 15–32.

Mani, K., & Johnson-Laird, P.N. (1982). The mental representation of spatial descriptions. *Memory and Cognition, 10*, 181–187.

Manktelow, K.I., & Evans, J.St.B.T. (1979). Facilitation of reasoning by realism: Effect or non-effect? *British Journal of Psychology, 70*, 477–488.

Manktelow, K.I., & Over D.E.(1991). Social roles and utilities in reasoning with deontic conditionals. *Cognition, 39*, 85–105.

Manktelow, K.I., & Over D.E. (1992). Utility and deontic reasoning: Some comments on Johnson-Laird & Byrne. *Cognition, 43*, 183–186.

Manktelow, K.I., & Over, D.E. (Eds). (1993). *Rationality*. London: Routledge.

Marcus, S.L. (1982). Recall of logical argument lines. *Journal of Verbal Learning and Verbal Behavior, 21*, 549–562.

Marcus, S.L., & Rips, L.J. (1979). Conditional reasoning. *Journal of Verbal Learning and Verbal Behavior, 18*, 199–233.

Margolis, L. (1987). *Patterns, thinking and cognition: A theory of judgement*. Chicago, IL: University of Chicago Press.

Markovits, H. (1984). Awareness of the 'possible' as a mediator of formal thinking in conditional reasoning problems. *British Journal of Psychology, 75*, 367–376.

Markovits, H. (1985). Incorrect conditional reasoning among adults: Competence or performance? *British Journal of Psychology, 76*, 241–247.

Markovits, H. (1988). Conditional reasoning, representation, empirical evidence on a concrete task. *Quarterly Journal of Experimental Psychology, 40A*, 483–495.

Markovits, H., & Nantel, G. (1989). The belief bias effect in the production and evaluation of logical conclusions. *Memory and Cognition, 17*, 11–17.

Markovits, H., & Savary, F. (1992). Pragmatic schemas and the selection task: To reason or not to reason. *Quarterly Journal of Experimental Psychology, 45A*, 133–148.

Markovits, H., & Vachon, R. (1990). Conditional reasoning: Representation and level of abstraction. *Developmental Psychology, 26*, 342–351.

Marr, D. (1982). *Vision: A computational investigation into the human representation and processing of visual information*. San Francisco, CA: W.H. Freeman.

Matsuno, T (1987). Cognitive style and representational strategies in categorical syllogistic reasoning. *Tohoku Psychologica Folia, 46*, 97–102

Maybery, M.T. (1990). Sternberg's mixed model applied to indeterminate linear syllogisms: A mismatch. *British Journal of Psychology, 81*, 271–283.

Maybery, M.T., Bain, J.D., & Halford, G.S. (1986). Information-processing demands of transitive inference. *Journal of Experimental Psychology: Learning, Memory and Cognition, 12*, 600–613.

Mayer, R.E. (1978). Qualitatively different storage and processing strategies used for linear reasoning tasks due to the meaningfulness of premises. *Journal of Experimental Psychology: Human Learning and Memory, 4*, 5–18.

Mayer, R.E. (1979). Qualitatively different encoding strategies for linear reasoning premises: Evidence for single association and distance theories. *Journal of Experimental Psychology: Human Learning and Memory, 5*, 1–10.

Moeser, S.D., & Tarrant, B.L. (1977). Learning a network of comparisons. *Journal of Experimental Psychology: Human Learning and Memory, 3*, 643–659.

Morgan, J.J.B., & Morton, J.T. (1944). The distortion of syllogistic reasoning produced by personal convictions. *Journal of Social Psychology, 20*, 39–59.

Moxey, L.M., & Sanford, A.J. (in press). *Communicating quantities: A psychological perspective*. Hove, UK: Lawrence Erlbaum Associates Ltd.

Moyer, R.S., & Beyer, R.H. Mental comparison and the symbolic distance effect. *Cognitive Psychology, 8*, 228–246.

Mynatt, B.T. & Smith, K.H. (1977). Constructive processes in linear ordering problems revealed by sentence study times. *Journal of Experimental Psychology: Human Learning and Memory, 3*, 357–374.

Mynatt, B.T., & Smith, K.H. (1979). Processing of text containing artificial inclusion relations. *Memory and Cognition, 7*, 390–400.

Neimark, E.D., & Chapman, R.A. (1975). Development of the comprehension of logical quantifiers. In R.J. Falmagne (Ed.), *Reasoning: Representation and process*. New York: John Wiley.

Newell, A. (1981). Reasoning, problem solving and decision processes: The problem space as a fundamental category. In R. Nickerson (Ed.), *Attention and performance*, Vol. 8. Hillsdale, NJ: Lawrence Erlbaum Associates, Inc.

Newell, A. (1990). *Unified theory of cognition*. Cambridge, MA: Harvard University Press

Newell, A., & Simon, H.A. (1972). *Human problem solving*. Englewood Cliffs, NJ: Prentice-Hall.

Newstead, S.E. (1989). Interpretational errors in syllogistic reasoning. *Journal of Memory and Language, 28*, 78–91.

Newstead, S.E. (1990). Conversion in syllogistic reasoning. In K. Gilhooly, M.T.G. Keane, R. Logie, & G. Erdos (Eds), *Lines of thought: Reflections on the psychology of thinking*, Vol. 1. London: John Wiley.

Newstead, S.E. (1993). *Conversational implicatures as an explanation of syllogistic reasoning performance*. Unpublished manuscript, Department of Psychology, University of Plymouth.

Newstead, S.E., & Evans, J.St.B.T. (1993). Mental models as an explanation of belief bias effects in syllogistic reasoning. *Cognition, 46*, 93–97.

Newstead, S.E., & Griggs, R.A. (1983a). Drawing inferences from quantified statements: A study of the square of opposition. *Journal of Verbal Learning and Verbal Behavior, 22*, 535–546.

Newstead, S.E., & Griggs, R. A. (1983b). The language and thought of disjunction. In J.St.B.T. Evans (Ed.), *Thinking and reasoning: Psychological approaches*. London: Routledge and Kegan Paul.

Newstead, S.E., & Griggs, R.A. (1984). Fuzzy quantifiers as an explanation of set inclusion performance. *Psychological Research, 46*, 377–388.

Newstead, S.E., & Griggs, R.A. (1992). Thinking about THOG: Sources of error in a deductive reasoning task. *Psychological Research, 54*, 299–305.

Newstead, S.E., Griggs, R.A., & Chrostowski, J.J. (1984). Reasoning with realistic disjunctives. *Quarterly Journal of Experimental Psychology, 36A*, 611–627.

Newstead, S.E., Griggs, R.A., & Warner, S.A. (1982). The effects of realism on Wason's THOG problem. *Psychological Research, 44*, 85–96.

Newstead, S.E., Manktelow, K.I., & Evans, J.St.B.T. (1982). The role of imagery in the representation of linear orderings. *Current Psychological Research, 2*, 21–32.

Newstead, S.E., Pollard, P., Evans, J.St.B.T., & Allen, J. (1992). The source of belief bias in syllogistic reasoning. *Cognition, 45*, 257–284.

Newstead, S.E., Pollard, P., & Griggs, R. A. (1986). Response bias in relational reasoning. *Bulletin of the Psychonomic Society, 2*, 95–98.

Newstead, S.E., Pollard, P., & Riezebos, D. (1987). The effect of set size on the interpretation of quantifiers used in rating scales. *Applied Ergonomics, 18*, 178–182.

Oakhill, J. (1991). Review of J.St.B.T. Evans: 'Bias in human reasoning'. *Quarterly Journal of Experimental Psychology, 43A*, 306–307.

Oakhill, J., & Johnson-Laird, P.N. (1985). The effect of belief on the spontaneous production of syllogistic conclusions. *Quarterly Journal of Experimental Psychology, 37A*, 553–570.

Oakhill, J., Johnson-Laird, P.N., & Garnham, A. (1989). Believability and syllogistic reasoning. *Cognition, 31*, 117–140.

Oaksford, M. (1993). Mental models and the tractability of everyday reasoning. *The Behavioral and Brain Sciences, 16*.

Oaksford, M., & Chater, N. (1992). Bounded rationality in taking risks and drawing inferences. *Theory and Psychology 2*, 225–230.

Oaksford, M. & Chater, N. (1993). Reasoning theories and bounded rationality. In K.I. Manktelow & D.E. Over (Eds), *Rationality*. London: Routledge.

Oaksford, M., & Stenning, K. (1992). Reasoning with conditionals containing negated constituents. *Journal of Experimental Psychology: Learning, Memory and Cognition, 18*, 835–854.

O'Brien, D.P. (1993). Mental logic and irrationality: We can put a man on the moon, so why can't we solve those logical reasoning problems. In K.I. Manktelow & D.E. Over (Eds), *Rationality*. London: Routledge.

O'Brien, D.P., Braine, M.D.S., Connell, J., Noveck, I., Fisch, S.M., & Fun, E. (1989). Reasoning about conditional sentences: Development of understanding of cues to quantification. *Journal of Experimental Child Psychology, 48*, 90–113.

O'Brien, D.P., Noveck, I.A., Davidson, G.M., Fisch, S.M., Lea, R.B., & Freitag, J. (1990). Sources of difficulty in deductive reasoning. *Quarterly Journal of Experimental Psychology, 42A*, 329–352.

O'Brien, D.P., & Overton, W.F. (1980). Conditional reasoning following contradictory evidence: A developmental analysis. *Journal of Experimental Child Psychology, 30*, 44–61.

O'Brien, D.P., & Overton, W.F. (1982). Conditional reasoning and the competence–performance issue: A developmental analysis of a training task. *Journal of Experimental Child Psychology, 34*, 274–290.

Oden, G.C. (1987). Concept knowledge and thought. *Annual Review of Psychology, 38*, 203–227.

Ohlsson, S. (1984). Induced strategy shifts in spatial reasoning. *Acta Psychologica, 57*, 47–67.

Ormrod, J.E. (1979). Cognitive processes in the solution of three-term series problems. *American Journal of Psychology, 92*, 235–255.

Osherson, D. (1974–1976). *Logical ability in children*, Vols. 1–4. Hillsdale, NJ: Lawrence Erlbaum Associates Inc.

Osherson, D. (1975). Logic and models of logical thinking. In R.J. Falmagne (Ed.), *Reasoning: Representation and process in children and adults*. Hillsdale, NJ: Lawrence Erlbaum Associates Inc.

Over, D. (1993). Deduction and degrees of belief. *The Behavioral and Brain Sciences, 16*.

Over, D.E., & Manktelow, K.I. (1993). Rationality, utility and deontic reasoning. In K.I. Manktelow & D.E. Over (Eds), *Rationality*. London: Routledge.

Overton, W.F., Byrnes, J.P., & O'Brien, D.P. (1985). Development and individual differences in conditional reasoning: The role of contradiction and cognitive style. *Developmental Psychology, 21*, 692–701.

Overton, W.F., Ward, S.L., Noveck, I., Black, J., & O'Brien, D.P. (1987). Form and content in the development of deductive reasoning. *Developmental Psychology, 23*, 22–30.

Paris, S.G. (1973). Comprehension of language connectives and propositional logical relationships. *Journal of Experimental Child Psychology, 16*, 278–291.

Pelletier, F.J. (1977). 'Or'. *Theoretical Linguistics, 4*, 61–74.

Phillips, L.D. (1987). On the adequacy of judgemental forecasts. In G. Wright & P. Ayton (Eds), *Judgemental forecasting*. Chichester: John Wiley.

Platt, R.D., & Griggs, R.A. (in press a). Facilitation in the abstract selection task: The effects of attentional and instructional factors. *Quarterly Journal of Experimental Psychology*.

Platt, R.D., & Griggs, R.A. (in press b). Darwinian algorithms and the Wason selection task: A factorial analysis of social contract selection task problems. *Cognition*.

Polich, J.M., & Potts, G.R. (1977). Retrieval strategies for linearly ordered information. *Journal of Experimental Psychology: Human Learning and Memory, 3*, 10–17.

Politzer, G. (1986). Laws of language use and formal logic. *Journal of Psycholinguistic Research, 15*, 47–92.

Politzer, G. (1990). Non-logical solving of categorical syllogisms. In J.-P. Caverni, J.-M. Fabre, & M. Gonzalez (Eds), *Cognitive biases. Advances in Psychology* Vol. 68. Amsterdam: North-Holland.

Politzer, G., & Braine, M.D.S. (1991). Responses to inconsistent premisses cannot count as suppression of valid inferences. *Cognition, 38*, 103–108.

Politzer, G., & Nguyen-Xuan, A. (1992). Reasoning about conditional promises and warnings: Darwinian algorithms, mental models, relevance judgements or pragmatic schemas? *Quarterly Journal of Experimental Psychology, 44*, 401–412.

Polk, T. (1993). Mental models, more or less. *The Behavioral and Brain Sciences, 16*.

Polk, T.A., & Newell, A. (1988). Modelling human syllogistic reasoning in SOAR. In *Proceedings of the Tenth Annual Conference of the Cognitive Science Society*, pp. 181–187. Hillsdale, NJ: Lawrence Erlbaum Associates Inc.

Pollard, P. (1981). The effect of thematic content on the Wason selection task. *Current Psychological Research, 1*, 21–30.

Pollard, P. (1982). Human reasoning: Some possible effects of availability. *Cognition, 12*, 65–96.

Pollard, P. (1990). Natural selection for the selection task: Limits to social exchange theory. *Cognition, 36*, 195–204.

Pollard, P. (1993). There is no need for (even fully fleshed out) mental models to map onto formal logic. *The Behavioral and Brain Sciences, 16*.

Pollard, P., & Evans, J.St.B.T. (1980). The influence of logic on conditional reasoning performance. *Quarterly Journal of Experimental Psychology, 32*, 605–624.

Pollard, P., & Evans, J.St.B.T. (1981). The effect of prior beliefs in reasoning: An associational interpretation. *British Journal of Psychology, 72*, 73–82.

Pollard, P., & Evans, J.St.B.T. (1983). The effect of experimentally contrived experience on reasoning performance. *Psychological Research, 45*, 287–301.

Pollard, P., & Evans, J.St.B.T. (1987). On the relationship between content and context effects in reasoning. *American Journal of Psychology, 100*, 41–60.

Pollock, J. (1989). *How to build a person: A prolegomenon*. Cambridge, MA: Bradford Books/MIT Press.

Potts, G.R. (1972). Information processing strategies used in the encoding of linear orderings. *Journal of Verbal Learning and Verbal Behavior, 11*, 727–740.

Potts, G.R. (1974). Storing and retrieving information about order relationships. *Journal of Experimental Psychology, 103*, 431–439.

Potts, G.R. (1976). Artificial logical relations and their relevance to semantic memory. *Journal of Experimental Psychology: Human Learning and Memory, 6*, 746–758.

Potts, G.R. (1977). Integrating new and old information. *Journal of Verbal Learning and Verbal Behavior, 16*, 305–320.

Potts, G.R. (1978). The role of inference in memory for real and artificial information. In R. Revlin & R.E. Mayer, (Eds), *Human reasoning*. New York: John Wiley.

Potts, G.R., & Scholz, K.W. (1975). The internal representation of a three-term series problem. *Journal of Verbal Learning and Verbal Behavior, 14*, 439–452.

Quinton, G., & Fellows, B.J. (1975). 'Perceptual' strategies in the solving of three-term series problems. *British Journal of Psychology, 66*, 69–78.

Ray, J.L., Reynolds, R.A., & Carranza, E. (1989). Understanding choice utterances. *Quarterly Journal of Experimental Psychology, 41A*, 829–848.

Reich, S.S., & Ruth, P. (1982). Wason's selection task: Verification, falsification and matching. *British Journal of Psychology, 73*, 395–405.

Revlin, R., & Leirer, V.O. (1978). The effects of personal biases on syllogistic reasoning: Rational decisions from personalised representations. In R. Revlin & R.E. Mayer (Eds), *Human reasoning*. New York: John Wiley.

Revlin, R., Leirer, V., Yopp, H., & Yopp, R. (1980). The belief bias effect in formal reasoning: The influence of knowledge on logic. *Memory and Cognition, 8*, 584–592.

Revlis, R. (1975a). Syllogistic reasoning: Logical decisions from a complex data base. In R.J. Falmagne (Ed.), *Reasoning: Representation and process*. New York: John Wiley.

Revlis, R. (1975b). Two models of syllogistic inference: Feature selection and conversion. *Journal of Verbal Learning and Verbal Behavior, 14*, 180–195.

Richardson, J.T.E. (1987). The role of mental imagery in models of transitive inference. *British Journal of Psychology, 78*, 189–203.

Rips, L.J. (1983). Cognitive processes in propositional reasoning. *Psychological Review, 90*, 38–71.

Rips, L.J. (1986). Mental muddles. In M. Brand & R.M. Harnish (Eds), *The representation of knowledge and belief*, pp. 258–286. Tucson: University of Arizona Press.

Rips, L.J. (1989). The psychology of knights and knaves. *Cognition, 31*, 85–116.

Rips, L.J. (1990a). Reasoning. *Annual Review of Psychology, 41*, 85–116.

Rips, L.J. (1990b). Paralogical reasoning: Evans, Johnson-Laird and Byrne on liar and truth-teller puzzles. *Cognition, 36*, 291–314.

Rips, L.J., & Conrad, F.J. (1983). Individual differences in deduction. *Cognition and Brain Theory, 6*, 259–289.

Rips, L.J., & Marcus, S.L. (1977). Suppositions and the analysis of conditional sentences. In M.A. Just & P.A. Carpenter (Eds), *Cognitive processes in comprehension*. New York: John Wiley.

Roberge, J.J. (1970). A study of children's ability to reason with basic principles of deductive reasoning. *American Educational Research Journal, 7*, 583–596.

Roberge, J.J. (1971). Some effects of negation on adults' conditional reasoning abilities. *Psychological Reports, 29*, 839–844.

Roberge, J.J. (1974). Effects of negation on adults' comprehension of fallacious conditional and disjunctive arguments. *Journal of General Psychology, 91*, 287–293.

Roberge, J.J. (1976a). The effect of negation on adults' disjunctive reasoning abilities. *Journal of General Psychology, 91*, 23–28.

Roberge, J.J. (1976b). Reasoning with exclusive disjunctive arguments. *Quarterly Journal of Experimental Psychology, 28*, 419–427.

Roberge, J.J. (1977). Effects of content on inclusive disjunction reasoning. *Quarterly Journal of Experimental Psychology, 29*, 669–676.

Roberge, J.J. (1978). Linguistic and psychometric factors in propositional reasoning. *Quarterly Journal of Experimental Psychology, 30*, 705–716.

Roberge, J.J., & Antonak, R. P. (1979). Effects of familiarity with content on propositional reasoning. *Journal of General Psychology, 100*, 35–41.

Roberts, M. (in press). Human reasoning: Deduction rules or mental models or both? *Quarterly Journal of Experimental Psychology*.

Rodrigo, M.J., de Vega, M., & Casteñeda, J. (1992). Updating mental models in predictive reasoning. *European Journal of Cognitive Psychology, 4*, 141–157.

Roth, E.M. (1979). Facilitating insight into a reasoning task. *British Journal of Psychology, 70*, 265–72.

Rumain, B., Connell, J., & Braine, M.D.S. (1983). Conversational comprehension processes are responsible for reasoning fallacies in children as well as adults. *Developmental Psychology, 19*, 471–481.

Rumelhart, D.E. (1980). Schemata: The building blocks of cognition. In R.J. Spiro, B.C. Bruce, & W.F. Brewer (Eds), *Theoretical issues in reading comprehension*. Hillsdale, NJ: Lawrence Erlbaum Associates Inc.

Rumelhart, D., Smolensky, P., McClelland, J.L., & Hinton, G.E. (1986). Schemata and sequential thought processes in PDP Models. In J.M. McClelland & D. Rumelhart (Eds), *Parallel distributed processing: Explorations in microstructure*, Vol. 2. Cambridge, MA: MIT Press.

Savion, L. (1993). Review of Deduction. *The Behavioral and Brain Sciences, 16*.

Scholz, K.W., & Potts, G.R. (1974). Cognitive processing of linear orderings. *Journal of Experimental Psychology, 102*, 323–326.

Sells, S.B. (1936). The atmosphere effect: An experimental study of reasoning. *Archives of Psychology, No. 200*.

Shaver, P., Pieron, L., & Lang, S. (1975). Converting evidence for the functional significance of imagery in problem solving. *Cognition, 3*, 359–375.

Simpson, M.E., & Johnson, D.M. (1966). Atmosphere and conversion errors in syllogistic reasoning. *Journal of Experimental Psychology, 72*, 197–200.

Smalley, N.S. (1974). Evaluating a rule against possible instances. *British Journal of Psychology, 65*, 293–304.

Smedslund, J. (1970). On the circular relation between logic and understanding. *Scandinavian Journal of Psychology, 11*, 217–219.

Smedslund, J. (1990). A critique of Tversky and Kahneman's distinction between fallacy and misunderstanding. *Scandinavian Journal of Psychology, 31*, 110–120.

Smith, E.E., Langston, C., & Nisbett, R. (1992). The case for rules in reasoning. *Cognitive Science, 16*, 1–40.

Smith, K.H., & Foos, P.W. (1975). Effect of presentation order on the construction of linear orders. *Memory and Cognition, 3*, 614–618.

Smyth, M.M., & Clark, S. E. (1986). My half-sister is a THOG: Strategic processes in a reasoning task. *British Journal of Psychology, 77*, 275–287.

Sperber, D., & Wilson, D. (1986). *Relevance*. Oxford: Basil Blackwell.

Staudenmayer, H. (1975). Understanding conditional reasoning with meaningful propositions. In R.J. Falmagne (Ed.), *Reasoning: Representation and process*. New York: John Wiley.

Staudenmayer, H., & Bourne, L.E. (1978). The nature of denied propositions in the conditional sentence reasoning task. In R. Revlin & R.E. Mayer (Eds), *Human reasoning*. New York: John Wiley.

Stenning, K., & Oberlander, J. (1993). Non-sentential representation and non-formality. *The Behavioral and Brain Sciences, 16*.

Sternberg, R.J. (1979). Developmental patterns in the encoding and comprehension of logical connectives. *Journal of Experimental Child Psychology, 28*, 469–498.

Sternberg, R.J. (1980). Representation and process in linear syllogistic reasoning. *Journal of Experimental Psychology: General, 109*, 119–159.

Sternberg, R.J. (1981). Reasoning with determinate and indeterminate linear syllogisms. *British Journal of Psychology, 72*, 407–420.

Sternberg, R.J. (1990). Mayday for Maybery: A reply to an invalid critique of the mixed model of linear-syllogistic reasoning. *British Journal of Psychology, 81*, 285–286.

Sternberg, R.J., & Turner, M.E. (1981). Components of syllogistic reasoning. *Acta Psychologica, 47*, 245–265.

Stevenson, R. (1993). Models, rules, and expertise. *The Behavioral and Brain Sciences, 16*.

Taplin, J.E. (1971). Reasoning with conditional sentences. *Journal of Verbal Learning and Verbal Behavior, 10*, 219–225.

Taplin, J.E., & Staudenmayer, H. (1973). Interpretation of abstract conditional sentences in deductive reasoning. *Journal of Verbal Learning and Verbal Behavior, 12*, 530–542.

Tarski, A. (1956). The concept of truth in formalized languages. In *A. Tarski. Logic, semantics, and metamathematics: Papers from 1923–1928*. Oxford: Oxford University Press.

ter Meulen, A.G.B. (1993). Situation theory and mental models. *The Behavioral and Brain Sciences, 16*.

Trabasso, T., Riley, C.A., & Wilson, E.G. (1975). The representation of linear order and spatial strategies in reasoning: A developmental study. In R.J. Falmagne, (Ed.), *Reasoning: Representation and process*. New York: John Wiley.

Traugott, E.C., ter Meulen, A.G.B., Reilly, J.S., & Ferguson, C.A. (1986). *On conditionals*. Cambridge: Cambridge University Press.

Tsal, Y. (1977). Symmetry and transitivity assumptions about a non-specified logical relation. *Quarterly Journal of Experimental Psychology, 29*, 677–684.

Tversky, A., & Kahneman, D. (1973). Availability: A heuristic for judging frequency and probability. *Cognitive Psychology, 5*, 207–232.

Tversky, A., & Kahneman, D. (1983). Extensional *vs* intuitive reasoning: The conjunction fallacy in probability judgment. *Psychological Review, 90*, 293–315.

Tweney, R.D. (1993). Scientific thinking and mental models. *The Behavioral and Brain Sciences, 16*.

Tweney, R.D., Doherty, M.E., Warner, W.J., Pliske, D.B., Mynatt, C.R., Gross, K.A., & Arkkezin, D.L. (1980). Strategies of rule discovery in an inference task. *Quarterly Journal of Experimental Psychology, 32*, 109–124.

Valentine, E.R. (1975). Performance on two reasoning tasks in relation to intelligence, divergence and interference proneness. *British Journal of Educational Psychology, 45*, 198–205

Valentine, E.R. (1985). The effect of instructions on performance in the Wason selection task. *Current Psychological Research and Reviews, 4*, 214–223.

Van Duyne, P. C. (1974). Realism and linguistic complexity in reasoning. *British Journal of Psychology, 65*, 59–67.

Van Duyne, P.C. (1976). Necessity and contingency in reasoning. *Acta Psychologica, 40*, 85–101.

Von Domarus, E. (1944). The specific laws of logic in schizophrenia. In J.S. Kasinin (Ed.), *Language and thought in schizophrenia*. Berkeley, CA: University of California Press.

Ward, S.L., & Overton, W.F. (1990). Semantic familiarity, relevance and the development of deductive reasoning. *Developmental Psychology, 26*, 488–493.

Wason, P.C. (1960). On the failure to eliminate hypotheses in a conceptual task. *Quarterly Journal of Experimental Psychology, 12*, 129–140.

Wason, P.C. (1964). The effect of self-contradiction on fallacious reasoning. *Quarterly Journal of Experimental Psychology, 20*, 273–281.

Wason, P.C. (1966). Reasoning. In B.M. Foss (Ed.), *New horizons in psychology*, Vol. I. Harmondsworth: Penguin.

Wason, P.C. (1968). Reasoning about a rule. *Quarterly Journal of Experimental Psychology, 20*, 273–281.

Wason, P.C. (1969). Regression in reasoning? *British Journal of Psychology, 60*, 471–480.

Wason, P.C. (1970). Psychological aspects of inference. In G.B. Flores d'Arcais & W.J.M. Levelt (Eds), *Advances in psycholinguistics*. Amsterdam: North-Holland.

Wason, P.C., & Brooks, P.G. (1979). THOG: The anatomy of a problem. *Psychological Research, 41*, 79–90.

Wason, P.C., & Evans, J.St.B.T. (1975). Dual processes in reasoning? *Cognition, 3*, 141–154.

Wason, P.C., & Golding, E. (1974). The language of inconsistency. *British Journal of Psychology, 65*, 537–546.

Wason, P.C., & Green, D. (1984). Reasoning and mental representation. *Quarterly Journal of Experimental Psychology, 36A*, 597–610.

Wason, P.C., & Johnson-Laird, P.N. (1969) Proving a disjunctive rule. *Quarterly Journal of Experimental Psychology, 21*, 14–20.

Wason, P.C., & Johnson-Laird, P.N. (1970). A conflict between selecting and evaluating information in an inferential task. *British Journal of Psychology, 61*, 509–515.

Wason, P.C., & Johnson-Laird, P.N. (1972). *Psychology of reasoning: Structure and content*. London: Batsford.

Wason, P.C., & Shapiro, D. (1971). Natural and contrived experience in a reasoning problem. *Quarterly Journal of Experimental Psychology, 23*, 63–71.

Wetherick, N.E. (1989). Psychology and syllogistic reasoning. *Philosophical Psychology, 2*, 111–124.

Wetherick, N.E. (1993). Review of Deduction. *The Behavioral and Brain Sciences, 16.*

Wetherick, N.E., & Gilhooly, K. (1990). Syllogistic reasoning: Effects of premise order. In K. Gilhooly, M.T.G. Keane, R. Logie, & G. Erdos (Eds), *Lines of thought: Reflections on the psychology of thinking*, Vol. 1. London: John Wiley.

Wildman, T.M., & Fletcher, H.J. (1977). Developmental increases and decreases in solutions of conditional syllogism problems. *Developmental Psychology, 13*, 630–636.

Wilkins, M.C. (1928). The effect of changed material on the ability to do formal syllogistic reasoning. *Archives of Psychology, No. 102.*

Wood, D., Shotter, J., & Godden, D. (1974). An investigation of the relationships between problem solving strategies, representation and memory. *Quarterly Journal of Experimental Psychology, 26*, 252–257.

Woodworth, R.S., & Sells, S.B. (1935). An atmosphere effect in syllogistic reasoning. *Journal of Experimental Psychology, 18*, 451–460.

Yachanin, S.A. (1983). *Cognitive short-circuit strategies: The path of least resistance in inferential reasoning*. Unpublished PhD thesis, Bowling Green State University, Ohio.

Yachanin, S.A. (1986). Facilitation in Wason's selection task: Contents and instructions. *Current Psychological Research and Reviews, 5*, 20–29.

Yachanin, S.A., & Tweney, R.D. (1982). The effect of thematic content on cognitive strategies in the four-card selection task. *Bulletin of the Psychonomic Society, 19*, 87–90.

Author Index

Subject Index